Harvest of Violence

Harvest of Violence

The Maya Indians and the Guatemalan Crisis

Edited by Robert M. Carmack

University of Oklahoma Press : Norman and London

BY ROBERT M. CARMACK

Quichean Civilization: The Ethnohistoric, Ethnographic, and Archaeological Sources (Berkeley, Calif., 1973)
La Formación del Reino Quiché segun la arqueología y etnologia (with John Fox and Russell Stewart) (Guatemala City, 1975)
Archaeology and Ethnohistory of the Central Quiché (editor, with D. T. Wallace) (Albany, N.Y., 1977)
Historia social de los Quichés (Guatemala City, 1979)
The Quiché Mayas of Utatlán: The Evolution of a Highland Guatemala Kingdom (Norman, 1981)

Library of Congress Cataloging-in-Publication Data

Harvest of violence.

Bibliography: p. 295
Includes index.
1. Mayas—Government relations. 2. Indians of Central America—Guatemala—Government relations. 3. Guatemala—History—1945– . I. Carmack, Robert S., 1947– . II. Title.
F1435.3.P7H37 1988   972.81′052   87–40550
ISBN 0–8061–2132–7 (alk. paper)

The paper in this book meets the guidelines for permanence and durability of the Committee On Production Guidelines for Book Longevity of the Council on Library Resources, Inc.

Contents

Maps

Editor's Preface

Most North American attention to Central America concentrates on El Salvador and Nicaragua, yet Guatemala may be the most strategic country. It has by far the largest population (more than eight million), the only important oil reserves, the heaviest United States business investment, and a long, porous border with Mexico. It has always taken a leadership role in Central American affairs, from colonial times, when the Spanish court was situated in Guatemala, through the nineteenth century, when its Liberal reformer and dictator, Justo Rufino Barrios, made virtual puppets of other Central American republics. When a democratically elected president, Jacobo Arbenz Guzmán, attempted to chart a course independent of the United States in the early 1950s, Washington was so alarmed that it used the Central Intelligence Agency to overthrow him. Subsequently the United States provided extensive military and economic aid to turn Guatemala into its Central American showplace.

Unfortunately, despite encouraging signs in the years immediately following the 1954 coup, things have not gone well in Guatemala. One corrupt military government after another has left the country in chaos. Against this military-dominated order, armed dissidents initiated civil war in 1962. Although the fighting shifted from eastern to western Guatemala in the 1970s, it continues today. Economically the country is in a shambles, deeply in debt and plagued with high inflation and unemployment. Wealth and land are more concentrated in a few national and foreign hands in Guatemala than in any other Central American country. The indices of health, education, and standard of living are abysmal. Three to four million Maya Indians have been the object of continuous and massive discrimination. To top it off, Guatemala has one of the worst human rights records in the Americas. Reliable estimates place the death toll from political repression at more than 100,000 since the 1954 coup, while persons "disappeared" for political reasons number in the tens of thousands. A civilian, Vinicio Cerezo, was finally elected president in 1986, but the economic crisis, civil war, forced patrols, and human rights violations continue much as before.

Obviously, something is seriously wrong in Guatemala as well as the rest of Central America. The U.S. government's explanation of the problem has not changed fundamentally since the 1950s and, in summary, is as follows: (1) the root cause of the crisis is Communist subversion, directed by the Kremlin and implemented through its Cuban and Nicaraguan satellites; (2) the Guatemalan military is justified in suppressing the radical opposition, for the alternative is totalitarian communism; (3) violations of human rights are regrettable but inevitable in such mortal struggles—they are caused equally by both sides; (4) nevertheless, the situation is improving under U.S. tutelage, as shown by the democratic elections of 1986.

Besides the fact that policies based on this analysis have consistently failed to bring reform and stability, as scholars have pointed out, it is simplistic. Framing the region's complicated events in East-West terms fails to come to grips with the complex and particular dynamics of Guatemalan society and thus misinterprets what is happening there. An alternative explanation, grounded in the particular characteristics of the region, reads more or less as follows: (1) the Guatemalan crisis is caused by historically based internal inequalities and injustices, as well as by pervasive U.S. meddling to protect its economic and political interests; (2) rather than suppress the opposition, the Guatemalan government must find ways to accommodate it or face inevitable revolution; (3) the violation of human rights is part of a long-term systematic program to suppress advocacy of change—it is not an unavoidable consequence of the conflict; (4) the situation in Guatemala has progressively worsened, with each cosmetic change (military coups, oppositionless elections) resulting only in more violence. Even the election in 1986 of a civilian president does not substantially alter these conclusions. Unfortunately, mounting evidence indicates that the armed forces continue to violate human rights unchecked by the Cerezo administration.

These polar explanations of Guatemala's problems and what must be done to solve them provide the basis for debate in the U.S. Congress over Central American policy. Similar opposed positions underlie the debate over aid to the Nicaraguan contras and support for the Salvadoran military. We are not dealing with idle semantic games, for the answers Americans give to these questions weigh heavily on the lives of millions of Central Americans. The answers will also shape the relationships between the United States and Central America and other parts of the world for years to come.

This is where the anthropologists who have written *Harvest of Violence* come into the picture. We too were thrust into the debate, since many of the native peoples we had worked with through the years were killed, forced out of their communities, or adversely affected in other ways. We raised the same questions to ourselves and sought answers in the way anthropologists have traditionally sought answers to their questions: through prolonged, direct contact with the people concerned. Some modifications had to be made in our modus operandi, such as expanding horizons to take into account extralocal forces and focusing on topics like violence and killing heretofore little studied. It became readily apparent that, in general, our findings were in sharp conflict with the U.S. government's explanation of the Guatemalan crisis though in general agreement with that of many other scholars.

A particularly important example of such scholarly work is a comprehensive study of recent violence in Guatemala by Shelton H. Davis and Julie Hodson, *Witnesses to Political Violence in Guatemala*, based on the personal testimony of 115 North American missionaries, development workers, and researchers with long experience in the country. The authors concluded, among other things, that "the army . . . killed thousands of innocent people" whereas "there is no indication that the guerrillas terrorize and massacre civilian populations as is frequently claimed by the Guatemalan government." A similar conclusion was reached by Jim Handy in his scholarly synthesis of recent Guatemalan history, *Gift of the Devil: A History of Guatemala.* He found that, while "not all the murders in the villages could be laid at the feet of the military, . . . the vast majority of the killings was the work of the military or right-wing death squads acting in conjunction with the government."

The chorus of condemnation of the Guatemalan government and its paramilitary associates by scholars, human rights groups, and other independent observers has fallen on deaf ears in the Reagan adminis- tration. Spokespersons for the U.S. State Department have repeatedly denied reported massacres of Guatemalan Indians and categorically rejected the claim that genocide had been perpetrated by the Guate- malan military against native populations. As the reader will discover, we document many instances of both. Further, the State Department has consistently argued that the worst of the violence came from the guerrilla forces, the Guatemalan government only reacting to that vio- lence. We found instead that most of the violence came from the Gua- temalan army and its collaborators, that it was part of an integrated program of terror designed to crush any possible movement of native peoples into the guerrilla camp and to gain total control over the In- dian populations. State Department officials also claim that the Indi- ans were accidental victims of the violence, caught in the middle when Marxist guerrillas chose the Indian region as their base of operations. We found, in contrast, that much of the violence was specifically di- rected against the Indians and that they became active participants in the military struggle itself, thus pushing it in the direction of a "peas- ant war." Finally, the U.S. government tells us that the recently estab- lished civil patrols are a voluntary system that protects the Indians from the guerrillas. We found the system to be a coercive means of military control over the Indians and a new form of forced labor.

As anthropologists entering the debate over the crisis in Guatemala and Central America, have we any more grounds for our position than the U.S. government has for its position? Testimony offered in 1985 before an immigration court by the senior political officer of the American embassy in Guatemala clarifies how the State Department goes about gathering much of its information on Guatemala. The tes- timony reveals that there is heavy reliance on tracking with computers. Many of the data come from newspapers and the Guatemalan govern- ment. When embassy officials do visit rural zones to determine what is happening, they frequently travel by helicopter and are usually accom- panied by Guatemalan military officials. In fact, military personnel stationed in the rural areas were said by this embassy official to be the main source of information during such visits. Any interviews with

Indians are conducted in Spanish rather than in the native languages. Overall the visits last only a few hours.

The use of advanced technology such as computers and helicopters to gather information has its place, but it cannot substitute for the direct and personal contact required to understand what is going on in culturally distant places like Guatemala. Can officials who fly into isolated rural areas in helicopters accompanied by army officers really expect the Indians to tell them the truth about repression by the same army? How reliable is information about complicated events that is obtained in a few hours by foreigners who do not speak the native language or know the local customs and power structure? This embassy official argued that on-site military personnel are better informants than Indians, though, he said, the word of resident missionaries and development workers is also taken seriously.

Even the guerrillas take precedence over the Indians as sources of information, which leads us to suspect that the problem is not merely one of language and communication. It goes deeper than that, apparently, to the widely held assumption that Indians are primitive. That is to say, we are dealing with a problem of racism, with the same superiority complex that moves U.S. policymakers to reject indigenous ideas about what is needed throughout Central America. State Department officials simply assume that Indians are incapable of knowing what really happened to them over the past few years.

The contrast between how the U.S. government has gone about getting its information on the Guatemalan crisis and how the anthropologists who write here have done so could not be more dramatic. Above all we have listened to the Indians, obviously the best source since they are the main victims of the recent violence. Having resided in the communities, in many cases for years, we can draw on relations of confidence with the natives. Testimony can be taken in the appropriate language and interpreted in the context of local custom and political conflict. Who is a reliable informant and who is not can be learned, as can the antecedent conditions, which provide an all important comparative perspective for interpreting unfolding events. Furthermore, crude neoevolutionist doctrine has not guided the thinking of these anthropologists about Indians. While our individual theories of culture vary in detail, we share a deep appreciation for the relative merits of different cultures, the complexity of continuously evolving cultures, and the dynamic transformations that such cultures are experiencing under the influence of worldwide economic, political, and cultural forces.

Of course, the methods by which the anthropologists writing *Harvest of Violence* obtained their understanding about Guatemala are subject to criticism and no doubt could be improved. Nevertheless, by any criteria they easily surpass the information-gathering techniques of the U.S. government on this subject. Therefore, they should yield explanations much closer to the reality which Guatemalan Indians have faced over the past few years.

Lars Schoultz, a political scientist and expert on Central America, points out that U.S. policymakers need social scientists to recognize "when changing circumstances have made familiar formulas obsolete." Schoultz is surely correct when he writes:

The process of mobilization has gone beyond a critical point in Guatemala, and that country will enjoy neither peace nor stability until the basic needs of the people are met by a fundamental restructuring of privilege. That is the new reality US policymakers must accept as the fundamental premise of an effective policy toward Guatemala and, indeed, toward all of Central America. There is no alternative. [From Martin Diskin, ed., *Trouble in Our Backyard.*]

Harvest of Violence was written out of the desire to help define the "new reality" to which Schoultz refers and to demonstrate why U.S. policy toward Guatemala must be shifted along lines that will allow the Indians and their ladino (non-Indian) compatriots to achieve the "basic needs" being denied them.

We seek to reach out, then, to U.S. citizens and their government to explain what has been going on in the rural areas of Guatemala. We employ information gathered according to anthropological methods to demonstrate that much of the interpretation of events provided by policymakers has been grossly misleading and fails to reflect the realities confronting the Maya Indians of that small country. It is our hope that once the American public realizes the true nature of the Guatemalan crisis it will pressure its government to alter U.S. policy in the direction called for by Schoultz. In the hope of reaching a broad public, we have dispensed with the usual scientific canons of writing style, citation, and formal language. Much of the information about what has happened in the Indian communities is presented in narrative form, and wherever possible important points are made through concrete examples. Despite this informal style the accounts are based on fact, and the accepted methods of social science were employed in their gathering. Those readers who prefer more formal treatment of the subject are referred to the chapter notes on sources and the selected bibliography on Guatemala at the end of the book, where many important published sources are listed.

This book is an outgrowth of three conferences held in conjunction with the annual meetings of the American Anthropological Association (AAA) in Washington, D.C. (1982), Chicago (1983), and Denver (1984). At the conferences organized by the AAA's Advisory Panel on Guatemala, papers were presented that analyzed the ongoing crisis there. Among those presenting papers were eight of the authors whose essays appear in this book.

Benjamin Paul and William Demarest's dramatic paper at the Denver meetings on the rise and fall of a death squad in the Lake community of San Pedro la Laguna seemed to be a particularly apt model for one kind of contribution anthropologists can make to a broader understanding of the Guatemalan crisis. These two anthropologists had carried out research in the community over many years; they attempted to link local events with the wider revolutionary conflict engulfing the country as a whole; and they used narration and example to humanize the unfolding tragedy. Since accounts with these features have been generally lacking in publications on the Guatemalan situation, it was felt that a series of such accounts prepared by anthropologists and other scholars with wide experience in Guatemala might lead to a better understanding of the events unfolding in that beleaguered country. The result is *Harvest of Violence,* in which ten anthropologists, a geographer, and a political scientist share their understanding of what has been happening in specific Indian communities during the past few years of counterinsurgency war.

Each chapter tells the story of a particular community and should not be seen as a microcosm of the whole Guatemalan picture. Together, however, the chapters illustrate the different levels of violence inflicted on Indian communities. We now know that these different levels correspond to the Guatemalan army's overall counterinsurgency strategy: Indian communities were classified by the army according to their supposed guerrilla sympathies and were labeled on maps with green, red, pink, and yellow pins. The "green" communities, those thought to be free of subversion, were watched but generally left alone. "Red" communities were supposedly in enemy hands. In these communities the army made no essential distinction between the resident

Indians and the guerrillas; in some instances whole villages were wiped out. The "pink" and "yellow" communities, in which guerrilla influence was thought to be more ambiguous, were punished with selective violence. As one observer put it, in these communities "terror and threats were used to force guerrilla sympathizers into submission, exposing and isolating the 'hard core' revolutionary cadre, who could be picked off clinically."

The chapters that follow are organized according to the level of counterinsurgency violence experienced by the Indian communities that they describe. The communities described by me, Beatriz Manz, and David Stoll were "red" communities, those that experienced generalized violence. It is not coincidental that all of them are in El Quiché Department, where the Guerrilla Army of the Poor (EGP) has consistently operated. The chapters by Benjamin D. Paul and William J. Demarest, Sheldon Annis, and Roland H. Ebel describe events in "pink" or "yellow" communities, where selective violence characterized their counterinsurgency experience. These three communities fell within the operating zone of the guerrilla group known as the Revolutionary Organization of People in Arms (ORPA). The chapters by Robert E. Hinshaw and Carol A. Smith describe "green" communities in which indirect violence, especially in the form of drastic economic hardship, was experienced. These two communities are geographically close to one another, along a line that falls roughly between the two revolutionary organizations operating in the western highlands. Both communities are deeply involved in commercial activities, much more so than their agriculturally oriented neighbors. The chapters by Ricardo Falla and Duncan M. Earle describe the refugees of violence, exiles driven from red communities, for the most part. They have struggled to survive in new, difficult settings. The "internal" refugees of whom Falla writes continue to be threatened by the violence that drove them from their home communities, while the "external" refugees described by Earle face new problems in Mexico.

Shelton H. Davis's introduction provides a historical and cultural backdrop for the accounts that follow and also offers a concrete example from northwestern Huehuetenango of the generalized violence described thereafter for other red communities. Richard N. Adams carefully compares and contrasts the accounts from each community in the the last chapter. He lays out for us the main lines and dimensions of the violence and assesses its impact on the Indians now and in the future. He reminds us that, despite the horrible tragedy that has befallen the Indians of Guatemala, a longer view of their historic struggle suggests that they will survive and will be heard from again, the next time with a new political awareness. To help the reader become oriented to the recent history of Guatemala, a chronology is provided at the end of the book.

On behalf of my fellow authors, I would like to express gratitude to the University of Oklahoma Press and its editor-in-chief, John Drayton, for publishing a book like *Harvest of Violence,* which some will consider controversial. I also give my heartfelt thanks to the other authors of the book who willingly wrote the essays and suffered through the editing, such as eliminating footnotes. They did so without expecting the financial and academic rewards that usually accompany their professional writing. This generosity, I know, springs from their love and respect for Guatemala and its indigenous peoples. All of us have gained much as scholars and human beings from our contact with that country, and we hope that what we give of ourselves in this book will someday redound to the benefit of its vibrant people.

Albany, New York   ROBERT M. CARMACK

Harvest of Violence

CHAPTER 1

Introduction: Sowing the Seeds of Violence

By Shelton H. Davis

One of the greatest riches of Guatemala and one which gives her a special face in the concert of nations is the plurality of indigenous cultures evident in the different ethnic groups which populate Guatemala. Descended from the immortal Mayas, our Indian population merits every respect and admiration. Unfortunately, they have not received it over several centuries since the time of the Conquest. Rather, the entire Guatemalan socioeconomic structure has rested upon the foundation of a subjugated and impoverished Indian people. It cannot be forgotten that the Indians form the majority of the Guatemalan people, and that they have inalienable rights. The new constitutional legislation, recognizing the great values of our indigenous cultures, should make very clear the legal foundations for a respect and fostering of cultural patterns of our ethnic groups. There should be an absolute avoidance of every form of racial discrimination practice, which persists even now, and the rights of our Indian people to their own languages, traditions, and life-styles should be taken into account.

—*To Build a Peace: A Collective Pastoral Letter by the Guatemalan Bishops Conference* (Guatemala, June 1984)

Guatemala, in contrast to the other countries of Central America, is rich in cultural and linguistic diversity. In a population of nearly eight million people, at least half speak at least one of more than twenty native Indian languages. Descendants of the great Maya peoples who created the magnificent pyramids and ceremonial centers of the Mexican and Central American lowlands, the contemporary Indians of Guatemala live in hundreds of small rural communities scattered throughout the majestic western and central highlands. They are es-

La Esperanza

Playa Grande

The Ixcán

Rubelquiché

Cobán

San Cristobal
Verapaz

Uspantán

o Chixoy

Rabinal

Río Motagua

San Martín Jilotepeque

himaltenango

Guatemala City

Antigua

San Antonio
Aguas Calientes

△△△ Refugee Camps in Chiapas, Mexico

      Volcanoes

━ ━ ━ Pan-American Highway

─ ─ ─ All-weather roads

0   10   20   30   40   MILES

Map 1. The western highlands of Guatemala.

sentially subsistence farmers who live on Indian maize, beans, and squash. For more than a century they have been integrated into the national and international economies as consumers of Western commercial goods and seasonal workers on the large coffee and cotton plantations of the Guatemalan Pacific Coast.

In the late 1970s the social tensions always present in agrarian, multiethnic Guatemala exploded into a full-scale civil war that has had a permanent effect on the country's large indigenous population. Although the Indian communities have been undergoing important social and cultural changes for more than a century, it was not until the 1980s that they became a source of mobilization and support for the country's several guerrilla organizations and hence a perceived threat to the country's powerful economic and military elites.

In 1980, after Nicaragua had experienced a social revolution that had taken more than 40,000 lives and when a guerrilla victory in El Salvador appeared imminent, Guatemala erupted into what many observers have described as the "dirtiest war" in Central America. For a brief period, it seemed that the Maya Indians of Guatemala might be turning to the revolutionary cause, as more and more areas of the western and central highlands came under guerrilla control. The guerrilla mobilization and victories of the early 1980s proved short-lived, however, and, in late 1981 the Guatemalan army—one of the largest and best-trained armies in Central America—began its infamous counterinsurgency campaign, which culminated in the extensive massacres, scorched-earth programs, and population displacements of the summer of 1982. By the end of that year the Guatemalan army, under the stewardship of a born-again Christian general named Efraín Ríos Montt, could claim victory in its war against subversion and begin the long and arduous process of bringing its rebellious Indian population back into the fold.

Throughout this period of political violence and civil strife, numerous humanitarian and religious organizations documented serious human rights violations against Guatemala's Indians. In September 1982, for example, the prestigious Inter-American Commission on Human Rights of the Organization of American States (OAS) conducted an on-site investigation in Guatemala that included discussions with church officials who worked in Indian areas, the bishop of the predominantly Indian Department of Alta Verapaz, Indian members of the newly formed council of state, and local Indian leaders and farmers. The Inter-American Commission also visited several highland Indian villages where massacres were alleged to have occurred, and it sent two staff members to Chiapas, Mexico, to interview and obtain testimony from Indian refugees who had escaped the violence in their native villages.

In its report of 1983, *The Situation of Human Rights in the Republic of Guatemala,* the Inter-American Commission on Human Rights noted that violations of the "right to life" dominated the entire question of human rights. Since the military coup of March 1982, violence in urban areas had decreased, but rural violence had reached unprecedented levels. Although the Inter-American Commission found it difficult to assess all the accusations of army massacres against Indians made by such nongovernment human rights organizations as Amnesty International, it did review fifteen incidents of violence in rural Indian communities and concluded that there was strong evidence to substantiate the contention that the Guatemalan army's counterinsurgency campaign was "directly responsible" for massive violations of the right to life in rural areas. The commission also noted that there was evidence of "serious and reproachable" acts of violence against the civilian Indian population by the guerrilla movement but that these were not on the same level as those committed by the army.

In its 1983 report the Inter-American Commission expressed concern for three other problems that were directly related to the human rights situation of the rural Indians. The first problem concerned the social and cultural effects of the army's newly instituted rural social programs. Specifically, the commission described the serious human rights implications of the Guatemalan government's highly publicized "guns and beans" program, which had organized large sections of the rural Indian population into local civilian defense patrols, and the "model village" program, which had resettled thousands of people displaced by the violence into new government-controlled hamlets, where they were provided with housing, food, and work.

Second, the Inter-American Commission, in its discussion of the right to freedom of religion and conscience, expressed concern about threats to the integrity of the Roman Catholic church in rural areas of Guatemala, especially given the previous human rights violations against church personnel and the espoused Protestant fundamentalism of the then president of Guatemala. Although the commission noted that there were no new reports of priests being assassinated, kid-

EL

MEXICO

HUEHUETENANGO

Nebaj
•

EL QUICHÉ

ALTA

Cobán

Huehuetenango
•

Rabinal
•

BAJA
VERAPAZ

SAN MARCOS

TOTONI-
CAPAN

San Marcos
•

Totonicapán
•

QUEZALTENANGO

Quezaltenango
•

SOLOLA

Sololá
•

CHIMALTENANGO

GUATEMALA

Guatemala
City
•

RETALHULEU

SUCHITE-
PÉQUEZ

SACAPTE-
PÉQUEZ

ESCUINTLA

SANTA
ROSA

O   20   40   60   80   100 MILES

Map 2.   The departments of Guatemala.

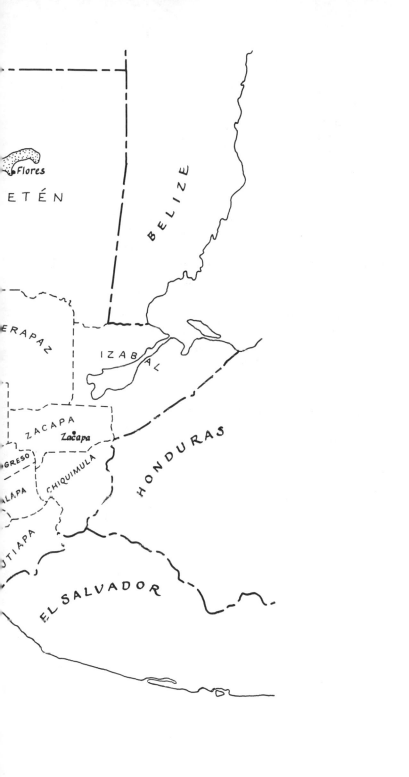

napped, or tortured, as had occurred with great regularity during the previous regime of Gen. Romeo Lucas García, it did describe how an Indian catechist was murdered during the visit of Pope John Paul II to Guatemala in March 1983. It also described how Roman Catholic clergy feared reopening more than seventy social-action centers that had been closed during the previous regime, how religious polarization had increased since Gen. Ríos Montt had assumed power, and how Catholic lay leaders were being harassed by local military commanders.

Finally, in its discussion of the right to freedom of movement and residence, the Inter-American Commission described how the recent violence had forced many Guatemalan Indians to flee into Mexico and how, by the end of 1982, 32,800 people were living in twenty-eight refugee camps or zones along the Mexico frontier. The Inter-American Commission also described the serious situation of displaced persons inside Guatemala, who, according to church sources, were estimated to number between 250,000 and 1 million people. The commission noted that the army's "model village" program was separating the Indians from their native lands and making them more dependent on the government for food and work.

Although there were dramatic changes in the political situation in Guatemala after the Inter-American Commission's site visit of September 1982 (e.g., the coming to power of Gen. Oscar Mejía Victores in August 1983; the nomination of a constituent assembly and the writing of a new constitution in 1984 and 1985; and the election of a new Christian Democrat civilian president, Marco Vinicio Cerezo Arévalo, in December 1985), it is only recently, with the reestablishment of government control in rural areas, that the full nature, scope, and consequences of human rights violations against the Indians have come to public light.

In March 1984, for example, a North American rural assistance group called Programa de Ayuda a los Vecinos del Altiplano (PAVA) conducted a survey of the social consequences of political violence in rural areas of Guatemala. This survey, which was based on interviews with local municipal officials, found that in four areas of northern Guatemala alone—Huehuetenango, El Quiché, western Petén, and Playa Grande—there were at least 150,000 people who had fled and were in Mexico and another 250,000 people (representing 50,000 families) who were internally displaced and/or in need of food, medical assistance, and economic support. A survey of fifty-one townships and thirty-one individual villages made by PAVA personnel discovered a significantly high incidence of population displacement, widows with orphans, and persons without subsistence and medical support as a result of the violence of prior years.

These patterns of population destruction, uprooting, and displacement were confirmed by an official census of widows and orphans conducted by the judicial branch of the Guatemalan government in September 1984. A preliminary tabulation of the census found that in three of the country's twenty-two departments—Chimaltenango, El Quiché, and San Marcos—there were 51,144 orphans. It is estimated that this figure represents at least 25,000 adults who had been killed in those three departments alone during the height of the political violence. In January 1985, Guatemalan newspapers reported that 116,000 orphans had been tabulated by the judicial branch census throughout the country, the vast majority of them in the Indian townships of the western and central highlands.

What is the meaning of all the deaths, suffering, and social upheaval for the indigenous peoples who experienced this period of political violence, terror, and civil strife? This book attempts to answer the question by presenting anthropological studies of Indian and refugee communities that have been affected or created by the political violence that gripped Guatemala in the early 1980s. These studies present before-and-after pictures of what the Guatemalan political crisis has meant socially and culturally for the country's Indians.

Although there has been a great deal of commentary about the role played by the Indians in the rise of the modern guerrilla movement in Guatemala and the human rights violations committed by the Guatemalan army in its counterinsurgency and pacification campaigns, to date there has been no systematic assessment by anthropologists of the effects that this tragic period in Guatemalan history has had on the social relations and culture of the country's indigenous communities. In the introductory comments that follow, I examine some of the special social and cultural effects of the violence in highland Mayan communities. To do so, I draw on the experience of one of Guatemala's indigenous ethnolinguistic groups, the Kanjobal-speaking Maya Indians of northern Huehuetenango. They number more than 120,000 in six townships, San Juan Ixcoy, San Pedro Soloma, San Miguel Acatán, San Rafael la Independencia, Santa Eulalia, and Santa Cruz Barillas,

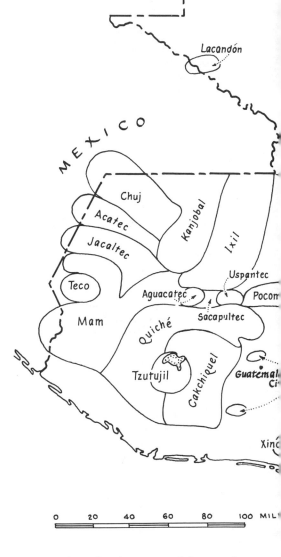

Map 3.   The Indian languages of Guatemala.

in the far-northern part of the western highlands near the Mexican frontier.

In the mid-1960s, I began conducting anthropological and historical studies of the Kanjobal-speaking people of Huehuetenango. Since 1981, I have also been interviewing Kanjobal refugees who, displaced by the violence, now live in Los Angeles, California; Arizona; southern Florida; and other parts of the United States.

In May 1985, as part of the work I have been doing among the Kanjobal refugees, I revisited several of the indigenous communities in northern Huehuetenango that I knew from my previous anthropological studies. In the following pages I describe the findings of that trip and highlight some of the broader themes underlying the several studies presented in this book.

The Precrisis Situation in the Highlands

The indigenous peoples of Guatemala are the poorest, most exploited, and most discriminated against sector of the Guatemalan population. Although Indians make up a majority of the population, they have always been treated as a "sociological minority"—a "special caste," as numerous anthropologists described them in their writings of the 1930s and 1940s—by the dominant ladino, or non-Indian, sector of the population. For more than a century successive Guatemalan governments have tried to break down the castelike structure of the country by passing laws intended to integrate Indians into the national society and culture. With the exception of the agrarian reform program instituted by the government of Jacobo Arbenz Guzmán between 1952 and 1954, however, no regime has attacked the agrarian roots of racial and cultural discrimination in Guatemala. Thus well into the present century Maya Indian communities have remained localized and highly exploited ethnic enclaves within the larger social structure of the country.

During the period from about 1950 until 1975, however, two phenomena occurred that had a major effect on the political role of Indians in the wider society of Guatemala. The first phenomenon, stimulated by increasing population growth and a relatively unchanging pattern of land distribution and concentration, was an intensification of the agrarian crisis in local indigenous communities. Between 1950 and 1970 the number of farm families—most of them Indian—possessing parcels of land too small to provide subsistence increased from 308,070 to 421,000. During this same period, the average size of farms in Guatemala dropped from 8.1 hectares (20 acres) to 5.6 hectares (14 acres), and the number of landless peasants increased to about one-fourth of the rural work force. In the western and central highlands, where most of the Indians live, land problems were particularly severe; the average size of farm units in this area, for example, decreased from 1.3 hectares (3.2 acres) per person in 1950 to less than 0.85 hectare (2 acres) per person in 1975.

An important outcome of this agrarian crisis was an accelerated seasonal migration of Indians to Guatemala's large coastal plantations in search of work. Between 1960 and 1974 an economic boom took place in the agroexport sector of the Guatemalan economy. During this period the export value of Guatemalan coffee increased from $75 million to $173 million; that of cotton, from $6 million to $71 million; that of sugar, from $0.1 million to $50 million; and that of meat, from $0.2 million to $22 million. Overall, the value of Guatemala's five major agricultural exports increased from $105 million to $368 million, making it one of the top agricultural-export performers in Latin America.

Indians began to migrate at the rate of more than 300,000 a year to the coastal plantations, where they worked from two to six months out of the year. A study of working conditions on the plantations conducted in 1970 by the International Labor Office for the Guatemalan government found that the plantations were characterized by, among other things, inappropriate labor recruiting systems; low salaries out of proportion to the sacrifices that the workers and their families had to endure; subhuman conditions of transport between their homes and the coast; working and lodging conditions totally unacceptable in terms of health, education, and morality; widespread contagious diseases; poor health and hygiene conditions; situations of penury and peonage; and lack of schooling among the workers' children, who had to leave their home communities and accompany them to the farms, thus interrupting their schooling in the communities and plantations. One study of migrant labor and debt peonage in Guatemala stated, "So oppressive are the conditions under which [the Indians] must work in the coastal belt that, despite the conditions in the hills, no peasant having an annual income of more than 100 U.S. dollars migrates voluntarily to the coast."

The other phenomenon that occurred during this period, one that is well documented in the anthropological literature, was a widespread "sociological awakening" of the Guatemalan Indian population. The roots of this sociological mobilization can be traced to the political changes, e.g., the formation of political parties, trade unions, and peasant leagues, that took place in Guatemala in the period of popular democracy and social reformism from 1945 to 1954. This mobilization gained force from the more traditionally based Catholic Action movement, which was established in Guatemala in 1948 and began to grow significantly after the military coup of June 1954.

Originally the Catholic Action movement was an attempt by the conservative church hierarchy to stem the tide of Protestant fundamentalism and radical peasant politics that were gaining popularity among the Indians in the countryside. As the religious movement grew, however, it became the basis of a fairly strong ethnic revitalization and rural modernization movement. By the late 1960s, Catholic Action was intricately associated with a budding rural cooperative movement in Guatemala, a movement that, in the early 1970s, received large inputs of technical assistance and funds from the Peace Corps and the U.S. Agency for International Development (AID) and became one of the fastest growing movements of its kind in Central America.

In the early 1970s opposition political parties, especially the Christian Democratic (CD) party, also began to organize and to gain influence in the Guatemalan countryside. Although the military denied the CDs an electoral victory in the 1974 presidential contest, the CDs and other opposition parties were successful in municipal elections that year. In the largely Indian Department of Chimaltenango, for example, the CDs and the Revolutionary party (PR) won 70 percent of the presidential vote, compared to only 30 percent for the right-wing, official MLN-PID coalition. Similarly, Indian candidates ran in eleven of the sixteen mayoral races in Chimaltenango and were victorious in eight. In Patzicía, an Indian town that had staged a rebellion against its small ladino population in 1944, the Indians gained control of the municipal government for the first time in history. In San Martín Jilotepeque an Indian mayoral candidate won election, but his victory was not recognized by the official electoral registry.

I was able to witness a similarly charged political environment during a visit to Huehuetenango in the summer of 1973. During that period, the first of what was to become a series of major strikes was called by the National Teachers Union. Although the strike began in Guatemala City, it soon spread to the countryside and began to mobilize other sectors of the population, including factory, agricultural, and public sector employees. To my surprise, events in the national capital were followed closely by people in the relatively isolated and traditional highland Indian towns of northern Huehuetenango. In fact, a branch of the National Teachers Union was formed in the provincial capital of Huehuetenango and began reaching out to both Indian and ladino schoolteachers in the surrounding hill towns. The representatives of opposition political parties were also traveling to these towns, soliciting the support of Indian political bosses and passing out electoral propaganda posters to be pasted on houses and public buildings.

Following the earthquake in Guatemala in February 1976, a surge of activity took place in the urban trade-union movement that also had an important impact on the rural Indian population. Although the trade-union movement never acquired the degree of unity and organization it had experienced under the Arbenz regime, it did begin to reach out to newly industrialized sectors of the urban population as well as to farm workers and peasants in the countryside. Perhaps the major event in the revitalization of the Guatemala labor movement was the formation in April 1976 of the National Committee for Trade Union Unity (CNUS) by a number of independent trade unions and worker organizations. From its inception CNUS maintained close links with peasant and rural worker organizations, while at the same time guarding its independence from radical political parties and a nascent guerrilla movement.

In 1978, CNUS, along with a number of other religious, labor, and popular organizations, began protesting the increasing militarization that was taking place in rural areas. The key event in mobilizing this broad-based protest movement was the massacre that took place in Panzós, in Alta Verapaz, in May 1978. Despite counterclaims by large landowners, for several months the Kekchí-speaking Indian peasants of Panzós—with the assistance of attorneys of the labor movement— had been soliciting the National Institute of Agrarian Transformation (INTA) for titles to their lands. At one point the government actually

Map 4. *The regions of Guatemala.*

Lake Petén

Flores

WLANDS

BELIZE

Panzós

Zacapa

HONDURAS

STERN

OTHILLS

EL SALVADOR

did promise to issue the titles, but the Indians were met by heavily armed soldiers when they marched on the town hall to obtain them. The soldiers opened fire, and in the ensuing encounter more than one hundred Kekchí peasants were killed.

In the months before the Panzós massacre, the Committee of Peasant Unity (CUC) was formed to link the urban and rural labor movements with the country's large indigenous peasant population. CUC was the first Indian-led labor organization in the history of Guatemala and the first to bring together highland Indian peasants with poor ladino farm workers. Although it was forced to function in secrecy, it was reported to have the support of thousands of seasonal and permanent farm workers. Perhaps its major success, before its affiliation with the guerrilla movement and involvement in clandestine activities, was the organization in February 1980 of a strike of 70,000 canecutters and 40,000 cotton pickers, an action that, along with another CUC-initiated strike of coffee pickers in September 1980, forced the government to raise the minimum wage of farm workers from $1.12 to $3.20 a day.

In summary, by the end of the 1970s the first steps of a generalized social and political mobilization had taken place in the Guatemalan indigenous population. Although the degree of mobilization varied among regions and ethnolinguistic groups and within individual Indian communities, there is little doubt that the Indians' social and economic aspirations had been expanded by the activities of foreign missionaries, rural development workers, opposition political parties, and the urban trade-union movement. Under different socioeconomic conditions (i.e., those more conducive to political democracy and social reform), this mobilization would have naturally evolved into Indian participation in all aspects of Guatemalan society. The Guatemalan military and the wealthy agrarian and commercial elites who controlled the economy of the country, however, were not prepared to allow Indians to participate as independent actors in national politics. Nor were the recently reorganized revolutionary movements, which by the late 1970s were organized into four distinct guerrilla groups, ready to accept a nonviolent path to change in Guatemala. The region was in political turmoil, and after two decades of right-wing death squads and left-wing guerrilla movements it was not surprising that the country fell into widespread violence, chaos, and civil war.

Social and Cultural Consequences of the Violence

Many anthropologists see the violence that gripped Guatemala in the early 1980s as causing a demographic, social, and cultural "holocaust" in Maya communities similar to that experienced by the ancestors of these people in the aftermath of the Spanish invasion and conquest of the sixteenth century. In fact, a case can be made that the full scope of this social and cultural upheaval will not be known until several decades from now when another generation of anthropologists possesses the historical distance needed to trace out the full structural implications of the violence.

This book should be seen as a first step in the process of systematically investigating the sociological and cultural consequences of contemporary political violence for the Maya people of Guatemala. Here I would like to focus on some of the more important social and cultural consequences of the violence, such as the undermining of the rural cooperative movement, the dislocation and uprooting of indigenous communities during the height of the counterinsurgency campaign, and the creation of a "culture of fear" in rural Guatemala.

In June 1982, I was the coauthor of a report for the hunger-relief agency Oxfam America. The report, entitled *Witnesses to Political Violence in Guatemala: The Suppression of a Rural Development Movement*, was based on a questionnaire survey of nearly 250 North American relief, development, and religious workers with experience in Guatemala. The results demonstrated that much of the violence against civilians in rural areas carried out by the Guatemalan army and security forces during the regime of Gen. Romeo Lucas García was intended to suppress the rural development movement that had arisen in the years just before and after the earthquake of 1976.

A study carried out for U.S. AID in March, 1976, just a month after the earthquake, revealed that there were 510 rural cooperatives in Guatemala organized into eight large federations with a combined membership of more than 132,000. Fifty-seven percent of the cooperatives were in the Indian highlands, where, according to reports written at the time, they were having a major impact on the Indians' political attitudes, marketing strategies, and agricultural techniques.

Fearing a threat to security from the guerrilla movement in the aftermath of the earthquake, the Guatemalan army carried out counterinsurgency operations in the northern part of the country, where the rural cooperative movement was particularly strong. Three Ixil-speaking communities, Nebaj, Chajul, and Cotzal, forming the so-called Ixil Triangle in the far-northern part of the Department of El Quiché, suffered greatly at that time. In the months after the earthquake the Guatemalan army made selective attacks on residents of those towns, killing several people, including the head of a local Catholic Action committee, five sacristans in local Catholic churches, and four bilingual schoolteachers. Members of the cooperative movement felt the brunt of these early army actions in the Ixil Triangle; between February 1976 and the end of 1977, for example, 68 cooperative members were killed in the Ixcán region of El Quiché, 40 in Chajul, 28 in Cotzal, and 32 in Nebaj.

When Lucas García assumed the presidency in 1978, the army began a frontal attack on the cooperative movement and its Indian leaders. After initially courting the cooperatives with promises of government support for a peasant colonization program in the northern lowlands, Lucas García reversed his position and turned much of the army's counterinsurgency apparatus against the leaders, the national support structure, and the local members of the cooperative movement.

In October 1981, when the president's brother, Benedicto Lucas García, took command of the counterinsurgency campaign in the highlands, the president of the National Institute of Cooperatives (INACOOP), a government agency created with U.S. funds, declared 250 cooperatives illegal because of their supposed "Marxist inspiration." One U.S. AID worker who was interviewed in the Oxfam America study in 1982 described how INACOOP had become a "front for collecting names of the most active (and dedicated) people in the community—people who would later be eliminated."

Before the INACOOP action right-wing death squads and government security forces closed several cooperative training schools and murdered dozens of staff members of national cooperative federations. A North American priest described how this process took place in an isolated northern province where he worked during the early years of the violence:

Between 1975 and 1977, 47 project leaders were assassinated or disappeared. One returned. He suffered torture and witnessed the murder of some 30 members of his community. . . . In March, 1981, 15 members of our co-op were dragged from their homes and murdered by the military. In December 1981, assassins in army uniforms and with government trucks entered a remote village and assassinated several co-op leaders. Five others were found later, crucified with sharp sticks to the ground and tortured to death.

Another respondent in the Oxfam America study, a Peace Corps volunteer, described the following situation in the Indian town where she worked:

I was working in one town which was trying to organize a bread-baking and shirt-making co-op to raise funds for community projects such as a pharmacy. Several of the members were murdered in an attack by uniformed government soldiers. I did not witness this, but I saw the effects on the project and the source was truthful beyond any doubt. I later read an account in a U.S. publication that said that these "terrorists" (bread makers) had been roasted alive in the schoolyard in front of their friends and families.

Still another respondent described the general situation of the rural cooperatives during the last years of the Lucas García regime:

Any campesino involved in the organization of other campesinos was notified of his inclusion on the death list and subsequently either ceased his activities or was kidnapped and presumed dead. . . . In one area, where we conducted soybean agricultural extension classes, through an existing network of *extensionistas*, we have heard that most of them have been killed or have fled.

One of the major findings of the Oxfam America study was that Indians began joining with the guerrilla organizations not because of a deep ideological understanding of or commitment to their cause but rather as a means of individual and community defense against the selective killings and acts of terror by the army and the death squads. In response to the Indian mobilization, however, the army stepped up its counterinsurgency efforts in the highlands. This new stage of offensive army actions began in the fall of 1981 and continued after the March 1982 military coup. During this period thousands of troops swept across the western and central highlands and throughout the northern lowlands, killing suspected community leaders, burning houses and fields, and attempting to drive a wedge between the indigenous population and the guerrilla organizations.

In this second stage of the counterinsurgency effort, the army organized local "civilian militias" as a front line of attack against the guerrilla movement and as a test of the allegiance of the Indian population. It was also during this stage that thousands of people left their native communities and sought refuge with the guerrillas in the hills, in the slums of Guatemala City, or in primitive refugee camps on the Mexican side of the frontier.

One of the areas most severely hit during this period was the Ixcán region of northern El Quiché and Huehuetenango. In the weeks just before and after the March 1982 military coup, more than two thousand soldiers stationed at the Playa Grande Army Base began carrying out counterinsurgency operations, with helicopter support, against almost all of the pioneer settler cooperatives in the Ixcán region. One of the worst incidents occurred in 1982 at the La Unión Cooperative, where, according to survivor reports, the army killed three hundred people, including all of the directors of the cooperative. Eighty children were orphaned in this attack.

By May 1982 more than three thousand people from that area alone had escaped into a cluster of hastily constructed refugee camps in Mexico. Journalists who interviewed the survivors of the Ixcán massacres in the spring and summer of 1982 found them traumatized by the scope and brutality of the army's counterinsurgency campaign. As one survivor told an inquiring journalist, "I guess the government does not want any more Indian race." The journalist's report, which appeared in the May 5, 1982, edition of the *San Diego Union*, was appropriately headlined "Guatemalan Refugees: They Talk of Death."

Most observers are in agreement that the purpose of the Guatemalan army's counterinsurgency campaign was as much to teach the Indian population a psychological lesson as to wipe out a guerrilla movement that, at its height, had probably no more than 3,500 trained people in arms. In essence, the purpose of the campaign was to generate an attitude of terror and fear—what we might term a "culture of fear"—in the Indian population, to ensure that never again would it support or ally itself with a Marxist guerrilla movement.

On my trip to Guatemala in May 1985, I was able to learn firsthand just how complex and pervasive was this sense of fear among the Indians. The incident that provided the most insight into this psychocultural phenomenon was an encounter I had with a Kanjobal man, a carpenter whose family I had known when I lived in the area many years before. Actually, I had seen the brother of this man on the day I arrived in his township, and he had invited me to his village for lunch the following day. When I arrived at the village, we exchanged jokes and other pleasantries, and then my carpenter friend, whom I shall call Pascual, began telling me about the violence and the fear experienced by him and other people in the area.

Pascual began his description by showing me an old, weathered Montgomery Ward catalog that a North American priest had given him in 1966 so that he could find designs for the chairs, tables, beds, and other furniture that he produced. In the early 1980s, when the army began to enter the area, Pascual decided to bury his catalog. He opened up one of the dirt-covered pages of the catalog and showed me a section containing advertisements of hunting rifles and men in green camouflage pants and red hunting jackets. Pascual had feared that if the army saw these pages he would be accused of cooperating with the guerrillas. So he had buried the catalog because he was afraid of being associated in any way with the army's perception of the guerrilla movement and had dug it up again only a few weeks before my visit.

According to Pascual, when the army first went looking for the guerrillas in that area, every Indian was suspect. In his village things were not so bad because the township of which it formed a part did not have a reputation for being held by guerrillas. Nevertheless, people were frightened, and they buried anything that might associate them with the guerrillas in the eyes of the army: their prayer books, because the army had accused the Catholic priests in the area of being Communists; their metal hoes, because the army had accused the peasants of using their hoes to help the guerrillas dig up and destroy the only road leading into the area from the provincial capital; and even their *huipiles* (long white embroidered smocks worn by the Indian women) and *capixchays* (black, sheep's wool, sleeveless jackets worn by the Indian men) because the army felt—at least in the final months of the Lucas García regime—that all the Kanjobal Indians had cooperated with the guerrillas and therefore should be castigated or killed.

Pascual's fears extended beyond the violence of the army, for, he told me, the guerrillas also used terror and instilled fear in the indigenous population. In early 1980 the Guerrilla Army of the Poor (Ejército Guerrillero de los Pobres, or EGP), one of the four guerrilla organizations in Guatemala, became active in northern Huehuetenango, stopping buses and other vehicles along the road, holding armed propaganda meetings in the town squares, and trying to mobilize Indian youths for the revolutionary cause. Pascual did not have much to say about the EGP, its ideology, or its membership. But he pointed to a cluster of houses across the valley from where we were sitting and said: "You see those houses. One day, the guerrillas passed through that area, and they entered those houses and forced the people to give them food. They told them that they now controlled this area and, if the people did not give them food, they would kill them."

Pascual, like many other people in the Kanjobal region with whom I talked, said that the violence in their villages from early 1980 through late 1982 had placed them "between two thorns"—the guerrilla movement, represented by the EGP, and the national army, represented by the troops stationed at the army bases in the provincial capital and surrounding towns. Although there is little doubt that the scope of army violence against civilians was greater than that of the guerrillas, the local population views both institutions as creating a situation of generalized violence and making it impossible for them to carry on their traditional ways of life.

Many of the people to whom I talked asked whether the same sort of violence that had occurred in Guatemala in the early 1980s had also occurred in the United States and other parts of the world. They have a sense of having been individually and collectively castigated for this period of violence; when they speak about it, they often use an impersonal idiom referring to it as *la cosa* ("the thing") or *el problema* ("the problem") and noting that it is only *por la gracia de Dios* ("by the grace of God") that they have survived.

Almost everyone I talked to had some personal incident to tell about family tragedy or loss. My carpenter friend Pascual's brother-in-law, for example, had moved to the agriculturally rich Ixcán region in the mid-1970s as a member of a church-sponsored colonization project. In the summer of 1982, when the army began its scorched-earth campaign in the region, Pascual's brother-in-law escaped with his family into the refugee camps in southern Mexico. For more than two years Pascual heard nothing from his brother-in-law, and his wife's family thought for certain that he had been killed.

On the afternoon I visited with Pascual, I told him and his wife that a North American priest whom we all knew had recently traveled to Mexico and had seen his brother-in-law in a refugee camp in Campeche. He and his wife were overjoyed to hear the news, and they immediately sent one of their sons to inform their grandfather in a neighboring village.

Up to this time Pascual and his wife's family—like thousands of other people in Guatemala—did not know the whereabouts of their family members or whether their loved ones were alive or dead. People live constantly with the memories of past horrors, as well as with anxieties about the location of refugees, displaced persons, and the "disappeared." Because these memories are all-pervasive in modern-day Guatemala, it is legitimate to refer to them as part of a more encompassing "culture of fear." From an anthropological perspective it is one of the major cultural consequence of the terror and violence that have gripped Guatemala in recent years.

The Civil Patrol System in Northern Huehuetenango

The civil patrol system, which the Guatemalan army established as the cornerstone of its rural counterinsurgency program in the early 1980s, stands out as the dominant institutional legacy of the period of violence in rural Guatemala. Although much has been written about the civil patrol system from human rights and journalistic perspectives, very little is known about its functions in the contemporary social structure of Guatemalan Indian communities. For this reason, during my May 1985 visit to Guatemala I focused a great amount of attention on the civil patrol system, trying to unravel what it meant for Indian people who participated in it and for Indian culture, values, and ways of life.

On the surface the civil patrol system, which in 1985 was said to include more than 900,000 men, is a relatively simple institution. Under the direction of the army, all able-bodied men between the ages of eighteen and sixty years are expected to spend one day every eight to fifteen days protecting roads and inhabitants of their villages from guerrilla intrusions. The army claims that patrol duty, or *la patrulla*, as it is called by local people, is voluntary, and it is supposed to be a means of maintaining local peace and security by ensuring that "subversives" do not gain a foothold in the countryside.

In the "areas of conflict" defined by the army, it was easy to observe the presence of the civil patrol system. Traveling the road north and eastward out of Huehuetenango into the Indian hill country, for example, we encountered more than fifteen checkpoints between the provincial capital and the frontier town Santa Cruz Barillas. Each of these checkpoints was manned by a half-dozen or so members of the local civil patrol unit, armed with old rifles, shotguns, and pistols supplied by the army. There was a roadblock at each checkpoint where the civil patrol members stopped all passing vehicles, checked travelers' papers, and inquired about the purposes of their trips.

In all the hill towns were small military bases built by the army at the height of the counterinsurgency campaign. In some towns there were also small resident army units, who maintained radio and helicopter communication with the regional army base in the provincial capital and helped the civil patrols monitor human activities and movements in the area.

From interviews it is clear that most of the Indians who participated in them had mixed opinions of the civil patrols. On the one hand, many people said that the civil patrol system was a good thing because it provided the local population with some degree of security and tranquillity after a period of chaos and violence. On the other hand, the same people also claimed that participation in the civil patrols was a heavy burden that took time from their agricultural and other productive activities and weighed heavily on them during a period when economic conditions were worsening in the countryside. In many of the Indian towns people wondered how long they would need to maintain the civil patrol system, especially when it was clear that the guerrillas were no longer the threat that they had been in the past.

Particularly striking, at least in the Kanjobal region, was the degree of guilt and shame that people had internalized as a result of their participation in the civil patrol system. Apparently people had such guilt because the army entered the region like an angry father, accusing the Indians of being rebellious children who were responsible for the civil damage and strife created by the guerrilla movement. In its early stages the army presented the formation of the civil patrols to the Indians as a way of extricating themselves from any association with the guerrillas. During this period when the civil patrols were being formed, the army forced Indians to go on *rastreos* (hunts for guerrillas) and sometimes to stone or machete to death fellow villagers who were suspected or accused of being "subversives." Many of those who refused to participate in these acts or who tried to escape from civil patrol duty were punished by local authorities or sent to the regional army base for punishment.

The civil patrol system was also being used to settle personal or interfamily rivalries and was a source of great abuse of authority and power in local Indian communities. In fact, one of the most striking features of the civil patrol system was the way it replaced the national judicial system as an institution for resolving local conflicts and disputes. In the past people would go before the local mayor, who served as a judge of first instance, or to a higher-level judge in the provincial capital to settle differences or denounce personal damage or a crime. Land disputes, for example, have been litigated before municipal and national courts for several decades and are a major cause of political factionalism and strife throughout the western and central highlands.

Although the national judicial system always discriminated against Indians and was based on bribery and other forms of corruption, it did provide some degree of control over interpersonal, familial, communal, and interethnic violence. In 1985 there was virtually no judicial system in the rural Indian communities, and most disputes were settled through arbitrary acts of violence by local civil patrol commanders, members of rival civil patrol units, or, in the final instance, local or regional army commanders.

Brief mention needs to be made of the large amount of time that Indian people were required to spend on civil patrol duty, road-building projects, and other activities relating to the army's counterinsurgency and rural development programs. In most highland towns each Indian man must spend one day of every eight fulfilling his civil patrol duty. Although it was possible to pay for a replacement, on the average each able-bodied Indian man must devote approximately forty-five to fifty days of labor each year to participation in his local civil patrol unit. If we assume that an Indian male could earn 2.25 quetzales (earlier $1 Guatemalan quetzal was equivalent to one U.S.; since 1983 it has decreased drastically in value) a day by selling his labor, each man was contributing, through his participation in the civil patrols, approximately 101.25 to 112.50 quetzales a year to the state in the form of an indirect "labor tax." With the per family monetary income in rural Guatemala somewhere between 300 and 500 quetzales a year, this "labor tax" represented an enormous financial drain on the peasant household economy, as well as on the amount of cash flow in the local, regional, and national economies. In other words, the civil patrol system, along with other factors of a more purely economic nature (e.g., inflation and devaluation), was contributing to the undermining of Guatemala's rural peasant economy.

The civil patrol system, to state the case more simply, was serving different functions from those claimed by the Guatemalan army,

which praised the institution as the cornerstone of its successful counterinsurgency campaign. Although the civil patrol system may have
been initiated by the army as a means of suppressing the rural guerrilla
movement, by 1985 it had become a means of controlling the indigenous population. In those areas where it was strongest, such as northern El Quiché and Huehuetenango, the civil patrol system was being
used as a means of surveillance to check the papers of local residents,
monitor their movements, and ensure their allegiance to the "new order" created by the army. Relative order and tranquillity had been
restored in most of the highland Indian towns, but at the price of the
establishment of a new institution that oversaw and controlled nearly
every aspect of Indian community life. As we shall see, the new civilian
government has remained ambiguous about the civil patrol system,
claiming that it is now voluntary but not taking any formal legal steps
to dismantle it in all Indian villages or towns.

Indian Rights and the Democratic "Opening"

Numerous observers have considered the recent return to civilian rule,
especially the drafting of a new constitution and the election of the
president, as indicative of a positive political trend in Guatemala. After thirty years of almost uninterrupted military rule and one of the
worst human rights records in the hemisphere, Guatemala is seen as
one of many Latin American states now on the road to democracy and
hence, from the perspective of North American policymakers, worthy
of renewed economic and military aid.

What, though, is the meaning of these political trends for the country's large indigenous population? This question, I believe, is an important one for much of the discussion of contemporary Guatemalan
politics has assumed the perspective of Guatemala's urban political
parties and elites. Few people in positions of power understand what
is going on in rural areas of the country, nor is there much comprehen-
sion of what Guatemala's indigenous people want from a return to
constitutional government and civilian rule.

Indian people in the isolated hill towns far from the national capital
clearly have not been untouched by national political events of the past
several decades; they have lived through a traumatic period of political
violence and civil strife during which thousands of their relatives and

neighbors were killed, uprooted, or forced into exile. Today many towns and villages are occupied by a "foreign" army that forces them, often against their wishes, to participate in local civil defense activities against an enemy that at one time may have been in the ascendancy but is now contained and has limited immediate political relevance. Hence, for these people, the true measure of the current "democratic opening" is the degree to which the army retreats from their communities, providing them with the social, psychological, cultural, and spiritual space they needed to reestablish their indigenous community cultures and ways of life.

A similar perspective on the current "democratic opening" has been made by other contemporary observers of Guatemalan political and civil society. For example, in June 1984, just a month before the elections were held for the members of a new constituent assembly, the Guatemalan Bishops Conference, led by Archbishop Próspero Penados del Barrio, released a pastoral letter entitled "To Build a Peace." The letter outlined the historical and structural roots of political violence in Guatemala and called on the new members of the constituent assembly to draft a constitution that would recognize the human rights of the country's indigenous peoples and create the social, economic, and political reforms necessary for a lasting and enduring peace in Guatemala.

One of the most important aspects of the pastoral letter was its criticism of the civil patrol system. Although the bishops did not presume to have the expertise to judge the tactical or strategic value of the system, they believed that it posed serious issues of an ethical and human nature. According to the bishops, the "forced service" in the civil patrols placed an "added weight" on the "weakest and most needy sector of our nation." These "unpaid services," the bishops' document continued, represented "new sacrifices" for the peasants and Indian communities, encouraged actions against innocent persons and the development of "a more warlike spirit," and severely limited the freedom of movement and association of the rural population. "The law of the land," the bishops' pastoral letter pleaded,

should state very clearly that no one may be obliged by authority to give un remunerated services nor made to do so by force; that the defense of Guatemala's territory is the task of the army; and that it cannot oblige anyone to become a patrol member against his will except in extreme cases specified by law. Moreover, vigilance corresponds to the police, and civilians cannot be obliged, to the detriment of their work, family, religious, and educational responsibilities, to organize vigilance.

Similar concerns were voiced by the Inter-American Commission on Human Rights in its *Annual Report to the General Assembly of the Organization of American States* of 1984–85. In May 1985 the Inter-American Commission conducted a second on-site investigation in Guatemala to assess the human rights situation since the government of Gen. Mejía Victores assumed power in 1983. Like other international observers, the Inter-American Commission praised the Mejía Victores government for complying with its promise to reestablish conditions for a return to civilian rule in Guatemala. At the same time it raised serious questions about the government's failure to deal with the problem of the "disappeared" and the human rights implications of the army's social programs in rural areas of the country.

In its discussion of the latter programs the Inter-American Commission noted that what had begun as a military response to a situation of emergency in rural areas had become a permanent administrative and military structure. By the time of the commission's visit in May 1985, the army had already grouped several of the "model villages" for displaced persons and returned refugees into a more integrated system of regional "poles of development," created a national system of "interinstitutional coordinators" to coordinate and monitor all public sector and nongovernmental activities in rural areas, and organized nearly a million persons into the local civilian defense patrol. According to the commission's analysis, these three institutions—the poles of development, inter-institutional coordinators, and local civilian defense patrols—constituted the basis of a "military administrative pyramid" directed, coordinated, controlled, and executed by a chief of staff of national defense.

Even more important, the commission noted that these new institutions have serious human rights implications for the indigenous population. Among other things, information obtained by the commission during its site visit revealed that abuses of power associated with the establishment of these three institutions, especially the local civilian defense patrols, led to serious violations of rural and indigenous people's rights to life, integrity, and personal liberty; movement and residence; freedom of reunion and association; due process and judicial guarantees; and the rights of children and the family.

Finally, the commission charged that the right to equality before the law, protected by article 24 of the American Convention on Human Rights, was being abrogated in Guatemala. According to information received by the commission, the majority of the population, comprised of Indians and ladinos living in rural zones, was not receiving the protection, guarantees, and rights accorded to persons residing in urban zones, especially in Guatemala City. The commission observed:

The Guatemalan Indian population, according to some of their leaders, has historically demanded recognition of their identity that is essentially different from the Spanish culture that shaped the Republic of Guatemala. They assert that there has always existed, and in fact still exists a linguistic, racial, social, and cultural difference that, because it has not been taken into consideration, constitutes a problem hampering the process of integration in the country and in practice causing the discriminatory treatment complained of by the Indians.

Although Guatemalan law, and especially the new constitution, does not contain any provisions that are explicitly discriminatory, it is clear from the reports of both the Guatemalan Bishops Conference and the Inter-American Commission on Human Rights, as well as from numerous other human rights reports, that severe de facto racial and cultural discrimination exists in Guatemala. This situation, which is a historic one and is shared by other Central American nations, has been intensified by the new military and social programs established by the Guatemalan army in rural areas. Only a progressive dismantling of these programs (i.e., a demilitarization of rural areas) can set the institutional groundwork for a return to political democracy and civilian rule in the countryside and thereby provide Guatemalan Indians with the human rights protections to organize around their own social interests and to ensure their survival as distinct ethnic groups.

Soon after his landslide victory in the runoff presidential elections of December 1985, a jubilant Vinicio Cerezo went to Washington, D.C., where he held a press conference on the future policies of his newly elected government. Although most of the questions at the press conference had to do with his personal views of political relations with the Guatemalan military and other Central American countries, two questions focused on his future government's policies toward the country's indigenous peoples and the Maya Indian refugees in southern Mexico. The eyes of the young president widened with interest when he heard these questions, and he declared to the press that a measure of the success of his government would be its receptivity to the needs of the country's many indigenous ethnic groups and its response to the problem of Guatemalan refugees in Mexico. The Indians, Cerezo said, had suffered more than any other sector of the Guatemalan population during the years of violence and civil strife, but they would be shown new respect by his government and given an opportunity to "genuinely participate" in the benefits of national society and development. Those who had been uprooted by the violence, who were living in the army's "model villages," or who had sought refuge in camps in Mexico would be provided with secure conditions—free from fear and harassment—to return to their native villages and homes. In fact, he and his advisers were about to travel to Mexico, where, even before his inauguration, he would discuss with the Mexican authorities and the UN high commissioner for refugees the establishment of a commission to facilitate the voluntary repatriation of the refugees.

As a political democrat, Vinicio Cerezo is undoubtedly personally concerned about the fate of his country's Indian population. In his inaugural address of January 14, 1986, for instance, he chose as one of his central themes the rights of all citizens, including the Indians, to be respected in their human rights and participate equally in the nation's new experiment in democracy. At the end of his speech he chose a theme from Maya mythology—the idea that the ancestors of the Mayas received their strength because they were fashioned by their gods out of corn—to highlight the courage and strength that would be needed by his government. "Guatemala," Cerezo concluded his inaugural address,

land of the Men of Corn, of poor hands but courageous hearts. We know that the greatness of civilization, as one of our countrymen has said, is measured not only by its material output, but by the courage and stoicism with which its men face adversity. Guatemalans: we have suffered so much. We have more than adequately proven that we can overcome adversity. Let us seize this opportunity to go forward together, united in a common effort like the corn which the gods put in our veins.

Despite these rhetorical pleas, the Christian Democratic government of Cerezo has been characterized more by its political pragmatism and ambiguity than by a strong response to social injustices and human rights violations. Speaking before the United Nations General Assembly in September 1986, for instance, Cerezo said:

We breathed violence, we could feel it in the atmosphere, it conditioned our response. Despite this, probably, because of our magical and utopian culture, by virtue of our ancestral humanism, because of our religious formation, instead of this becoming a generalized form of life, it was a reason for our systematically and permanently rejecting authoritarian governments and violence as political instruments.

Despite this condemnation of political violence and celebration of democracy, Cerezo delayed setting up an official government commission to investigate past crimes by the military against civilian populations, including many well-documented massacres in Indian villages. Nor has he responded adequately, at least in the eyes of numerous human rights organizations, to the pleas and protests of the Mutual Support Group (GAM), a group of Guatemalans seeking information about their missing relatives, for an official investigation of the thousands of people who "disappeared" at the height of the Guatemalan violence.

Similar ambiguities between public statements and actual policies exist in relation to the Cerezo government's response to the military's rural civilian defense and social programs. To its credit, the Cerezo government has disbanded the system of interinstitutional coordinators, which was severely criticized for its surveillance functions by the Inter-American Commission on Human Rights and other human rights bodies. The government has also taken steps to bring all publicly funded rural development programs under civilian control. However, the twenty-eight "model villages" set up by the military before Cerezo became president to resettle displaced rural populations are still in place, and the military's counterinsurgency and pacification program—including the civil patrol system—still exists in many Indian villages and towns.

In large measure the continuing presence of the military in the countryside and the refusal of the Cerezo government to investigate past human rights violations by the military against the civilian Indian population explain why the estimated 46,000 Indians still living in refugee camps in Mexico refuse to return to Guatemala. The Cerezo government on several occasions has tried to persuade the refugees to return voluntarily, while realizing that it lacks the power to ensure their safety. Besides these security considerations, many refugees also fear that the lands on which they worked before the violence are now occupied by promilitary factions in their villages and that they will have no legal protection from a government that has taken no position on the vital issue of land reform.

In conclusion, the recent democratic opening in Guatemala, which for very legitimate reasons has raised hopes within the country and received much international acclaim, must be understood within the framework of the historical and current militarization of the Guatemalan countryside. This book, in the best humanitarian traditions of anthropology, provides insight into the social, cultural, and existential conditions of the majority indigenous population of Guatemala. The story it tells is a tragic one, but it is a story that should be read by every policymaker and citizen who is genuinely interested in seeing Guatemala transcend its dark winter of violence and again become proud of its reputation as the Land of Eternal Spring.

PART ONE
Generalized Violence

CHAPTER 2

The Story of Santa Cruz Quiché

By Robert M. Carmack

I lived in Guatemala for two and a half years as a young man during the 1950s and became fascinated with the ancient Maya cultures, many of whose remains I saw. Later, when I entered graduate studies in anthropology, it was quite natural that I should choose the Maya cultures of Guatemala as the object of my specialized research. Specifically, I focused on the ancient Quiché Maya kingdom that flourished in the highlands of western Guatemala when the Spaniards reached the region. At first I concentrated on the native documents that have come down to us, including the famous "bible of the Quichés," *Popol Vuh*. Later I returned to the western highlands to carry out fieldwork among the living Quiché Indians in an isolated, traditional community. Learning the Quiché language and studying Quiché customs firsthand whetted my appetite to learn more about that remarkable culture. After all, the Quichés were the most powerful of the Maya kingdoms encountered by the Spanish conquistadors.

A logical next step was to work at the ancient capital of the Quiché kingdom, which I had visited only briefly before 1970. The old capital, now a community named Santa Cruz del Quiché (Saint Cross of the Quichés), had become a departmental center and the residence of more than thirty thousand Quiché-speaking Indians. About two miles outside town the ruins of the ancient site are witness to the past grandeur of these Indians. In neighboring Chichicastenango, the Quiché Indians burn incense in front of the church and participate in markets bursting with native crafts. Santa Cruz is greatly overshadowed by Chichicastenango, and its present-day Indian culture and ancient ruins are virtually unstudied. Thus it is scarcely possible to exaggerate the excitement my colleagues and I in the State University of New York at Albany (SUNYA) felt as we initiated a long-term project to study the Quichés of Santa Cruz. For the next ten years (1970–80) we investigated their language, customs, history, and archaeological remains.

When we came onto the scene early in the 1970s, Santa Cruz had long ceased to be a sleepy village. The department governor and other bureaucrats lived there, as did the officers and soldiers of an important military base. Spanish priests who administered the affairs of the Catholic church in the region had their headquarters in Santa Cruz. The town was also a market and transportation center for the entire region. Its many general-merchandise stores provided manufactured goods for the region, and its large bus terminal was crowded with buses coming and going at all hours of the day.

Santa Cruz of the 1970s was in the middle of a population boom; in thirty years its population had more than doubled. As compared with other townships of the region, the town center had become unusually large, with about eight thousand persons (about 23 percent of the total population) residing there. More than half of the townspeople were ladinos, who owned stores and buses or provided services for the departmental government, the army, the church, and various commercial establishments. Some Indians lived in town and performed administrative and commercial tasks, although most were simple wage earners. The rural people, 77 percent of the population and almost all Indian, scratched out an existence on lands that were capable of supporting only about one-third of the population. Large numbers of them migrated to the coast a few months each year to work on plantations. Others manufactured hats by weaving together palm fronds, the major cottage industry of Santa Cruz.

Social life in Santa Cruz was boiling over with division and conflict. The struggling factions divided Indians against ladinos, Catholics against Protestants, town against country, rich against poor. In town Protestant sects competed with one another and with the Catholics for "souls," and these religious lines tended to overlap with competing political parties. In the countryside the Catholics had launched a large-scale catechist movement, known as Catholic Action. It split the Indian peasants into traditional and modern (catechist) factions. And because the modern faction gravitated toward the Christian Democratic party, political and religious lines were intertwined in the rural area. Rural development programs followed similar cleavages, the cooperatives, water projects, and agricultural programs tending to favor the progressive catechists. By far the deepest split in Santa Cruz, however, was that between Indians and ladinos. The town ladinos controlled the most lucrative stores and bus lines, dominated the government posts, and found ways to exploit the labor and goods of the rural Indians. Widespread mutual mistrust and hostility prevailed between the ladinos and Indians, though the hostility was submerged, and social life seemed peaceful.

Very little of the old Quiché culture remained at Santa Cruz. Town rituals having been "purified," the saint processions were largely devoid of native symbols. No council of elders oversaw the protection of ancient ways. The one native town official, the "Indian alcalde" (mayor), was subject to the municipal alcalde. Those aspects of traditional culture that persisted in the rural area were no longer associated with traditional clans and hamlets that had once existed. Practicing shamans could be found, the Quiché language was widely spoken, and the old altars, including the ancient ruins, were used sporadically for burning incense to the ancestors. Nevertheless, the traditional way of life, although still an option in rural Santa Cruz, was marginal.

As we learned to our disappointment, Santa Cruz residents showed little interest in the ancient Quiché culture. The old capital site lay ruined and neglected, its glorious past forgotten by all, even those most directly descended from its ancient occupants. The growing numbers of modernizing Indians, whether in town or in country, were leaving the Quiché culture behind. The ladinos viewed it either as a source of profit—through tourism or the looting of mounds—or as a symbol of their domination of the Indians. The shamans and marginal peasants still found meaning in the ancient ways, but even for them the traditions represented only a "culture of refuge," a means that the most conservative of them used to retain a semblance of community identity in the face of modernizing forces. It was a struggle of attrition; each year more ancient patterns were being rejected by new recruits of change.

This was the Santa Cruz we found in the early 1970s. We knew that research there would be difficult—just how difficult we could not have predicted—but the opportunity to study one of the great Indian civilizations of the Americas seemed to us worth the challenge.

It soon became clear that the schism between ladinos and Indians would be a source of recurrent problems for us. The rural Indians, deeply suspicious after years of exploitation by ladinos, extended their suspicions to us. One elderly Indian woman would not allow us to excavate the large archaeological mounds on her property; an Indian man in a nearby town stuck a pistol in my face when I tried to gain access to his lands to examine mounds there. To make matters worse, the Spanish priests did not trust us, and they communicated this distrust to the catechists throughout the countryside.

Our problems with the town ladinos, much more serious, were never resolved. Many "middle class" ladinos, however, were friendly. Among these was the alcalde, a local storekeeper who as a young man had traveled widely throughout Mexico and had even worked as a bracero in the United States. But the ladino elites saw us as a definite threat to their domination of the rural Indians and the community as a whole. Broadcasts on the local Radio Quiché began accusing us of coming to rob Santa Cruz of the riches buried in its ancient sites. Gossip ran rampant through the town, and committees of concerned citizens began to obstruct our work. We traced the broadcasts to a sergeant at the local military base, but conversations with him made it apparent that he was only the agent of powerful ladinos in town.

The Indian merchants living in town saw us less as a threat than as an opportunity for exploitation. Some of them who owned lands on which ruins stood began demanding exorbitant fees from us in exchange for permission to excavate their lands. It was clear that they were digging for artifacts to be sold on the black market; a few had purchased the lands specifically to "farm" them for artifacts. Our appeals to their Indian identity were in vain; they were interested only in the money that could be earned from their property. Many of the rural Indians, by contrast, became genuinely interested in our studies and what could be learned about the ancient Quiché culture. A few town Indians, more "middle class" than the merchants, also took a genuine interest in our work and the Quiché culture. Some of them had organized a study club, and we were invited to speak at their meetings from time to time.

Attacks from elite ladinos were relentless throughout the years. Evidence suggested that the leader of the ladino opposition was a wealthy lawyer who controlled important businesses in town. A congressman of the Conservative party, he eventually rose to national leadership. I visited him several times, but he would never admit that he was working against us. He was a tall, handsome man with reactionary ideas. Because he shared the deep-seated ladino prejudices against the Indians, they hated him. He had other enemies as well. Consequently he kept a small cadre of bodyguards outside his office and a pistol on his table. Toward the end of our studies in Santa Cruz, when we discovered some spectacular gold pieces in the ruins, he informed the president of Guatemala that we were robbing the "national patrimony." His accusations against us and our university reached the nation's leading newspapers. At that time we turned to the other congressman from Santa Cruz, a Christian Democrat who placed the best interests of Santa Cruz above his own. I was struck by his Anglo name, Hamilton Noriega, and by his kind, understanding consideration of our problem. The contrast between the two congressmen symbolized well the contradictions that so badly fragmented the community.

One reason we did not retreat in the face of so many problems was that the ladino alcalde stayed by our side. In Guatemala, however, alcaldes cannot succeed themselves. A new alcalde was elected in 1978, the same year in which Gen. Lucas García became president of Guatemala. The results of the election filled us with renewed hope. The new alcalde, Andrés Avelino Zapeta y Zapeta, was the first Indian elected in Santa Cruz for perhaps two hundred years. Furthermore, he seemed to represent a link between town and country, ladinos and Indians. He worked as a carpenter in a hamlet on the outskirts of town and was a leader in the catechist movement. He was a kind, gentle man, neither cynical about the future (like some peasants) nor indifferent to Quiché culture (like many town Indians). He was proud of his Indian heritage, and he offered to help us learn about the ancient ways, which, he said, were "the true history of Guatemala." With Alcalde Zapeta at the helm, things were looking up for us and for Santa Cruz.

A Personal Tragedy

By 1979, however, when we tried to expand our work at Santa Cruz, all was not well in Guatemala. It had been widely reported in both Guatemalan and foreign newspapers that the army had massacred more than one hundred Kekchí Indians at Panzós in May 1978. Guerrillas were known to be operating among the Ixil Indians living in the mountainous northern part of El Quiché Department.

I was personally quite conscious of the escalation of violence after the 1978 election of General Lucas García. I wrote in my diary that year: "Revolution is at the door; people are so tired of problems that none will defend the government. Only the army defends, and it has become a privileged elite, selfish and unpopular." Still I considered the violence simply a part of the conflict that had long characterized Guatemalan social life. Not wanting to believe that the situation was as serious as it really was, I allowed myself to be persuaded by voices of moderation. The director of the U.S. AID mission in Guatemala, a man I admired, spoke of U.S. efforts to support the poor. The governor of Quiché, an army officer, claimed that the guerrillas were restricted to the northern area and were not succeeding. A Protestant minister from Santa Cruz who traveled extensively throughout the Quiché region told me that the guerrillas had failed to win over the Indians, although they did have a few supporters in the northern mountainous zone.

In 1980 we won another grant to continue work at Santa Cruz. But, growing nervous for the safety of my colleagues and me at Santa Cruz, I determined to discover whether or not guerrilla activity actually existed in the community. I was shown leaflets containing death threats against persons in Santa Cruz. The leaflets, I was told, had been delivered by masked men armed with machine guns. Other death threats had been painted on walls. The townspeople claimed that the latter threats had been painted by army soldiers early one morning. The consensus seemed to be that there were a few guerrillas in the area but that the real action was in the north.

The situation at Santa Cruz continued to deteriorate. Soon it became obvious that it was dangerous for us to work there any longer. Indian friends of ours living near the ancient ruins—actual descendants of the Quiché kings—told us about the murder of an Indian, a cooperative leader, that they had witnessed directly in front of the ruins. Our friends said that the army appeared to have done the killing. Alcalde Zapeta also admitted that murders were occurring in Santa Cruz, although he believed that the guerrillas were committing atrocities as bad as those of the army.

In June 1980, the guerrillas ordered all Americans to leave the Quiché Department. Some archaeologists from our project who were overseeing the preservation of artifacts recovered during excavations beat a hasty retreat.

In July, after one priest had been assassinated and his own life threatened, the Spanish bishop ordered his priests to abandon the diocese. In September I decided to return to Santa Cruz for one last visit, mainly to bid farewell to Alcalde Zapeta, our good friend and supporter. I found a very tense town. Several friends came up to me and whispered that it was dangerous for me to be there, that I should leave at once. I stayed long enough to have a final interview with the alcalde. What I learned in that meeting and afterward I recorded in my diary when I had returned to the safety of my hotel in Guatemala City:

September 24, 1980.
I write at this moment because I want to capture the heartache and the outrage that I feel. I just learned that yesterday the mayor of Santa Cruz Quiché, a rural town in the mountains of Guatemala, was assassinated by a band of gunmen. Perhaps his death is nothing special, for several thousand Guatemalans have been assassinated for political reasons in the past few years. But I knew this man, even more, I had a long and warm conversation with him the very morning before his tragic death. I want his people to know who he was, and why he died, because I do not want his death to be in vain. Perhaps his story can help us understand what is happening in this tiny Central American country, and what might be done someday to change the course of events there. . . .

The ladinos considered Zapeta incompetent for the post [of mayor], and, indeed, he was not prepared for the exquisite machinations that characterize town politics even in an obscure, small town such as Santa Cruz. It was obvious to the observer that Spanish was not Zapeta's native language, a fatal flaw in a culture that places great stock in oratory agility. His rural background had not prepared him for the kinds of problems he would have to confront in town: finding sufficient sources of potable water, constructing paved roads in and around town, striking a balance between serving the ladinos and helping the Indians, dealing with "development" agents from the City, dampening the quarrels between members of his own town council, and many others.

The characteristic that probably represented Zapeta's greatest liability was his deep religious convictions. Despite the fact that Guatemala is a Catholic country, and most people in Santa Cruz hold religious beliefs (agnosticism is virtually unthinkable), political life is highly secular. Zapeta's simple beliefs ill-prepared him for the elaborate struggles for power and wealth that give form to politics in towns like Santa Cruz.

But I found in Zapeta much to admire, and I loved him. He reminded me of my own father in some basic way. He was refreshingly open—innocent—about the centuries-long conflict between Indians and ladinos. Even in that last conversation he repeated again the story of how his mother and father had warned him about the ladinos, and how they would try to keep the Indians from progressing. This was said in the presence of my ladino companion, a government official from the City, a gesture of courage very rarely exhibited in this country.

Zapeta was proud to be an Indian, and said so openly. Most Indians of

Santa Cruz try to hide the fact, hoping thereby to avoid in some small way the scornful discrimination heaped on them by a ladino-dominated society. Zapeta was like a child who had discovered a new world in school; he had determined that his native culture was, after all, one of dignity and worth. Each time I saw him he would recall the beliefs and practices of his parents and forefathers, and would moralize about how the old ways should not be lost as the Indians take on new ways. I always felt certain that these lectures were exactly the ones he gave to his own family and to the many peasant Indians who visited his mayor's office to seek advice and counsel.

Zapeta was a carpenter and farmer. He worked with his sons in a humble shop attached to his house. I can imagine that his skills, and even his tools, were not too different from those applied by Jesus of Nazareth. Zapeta's economic conditions seemed to have led him to deep religious convictions. He was attracted to a progressive Catholic movement sweeping Guatemala in the 1950s and 1960s, which in many ways stood in relation to traditional Catholicism as did the Puritan reforms of 16th- and 17th-century Europe. Under the direction of European priests, the movement had some social and political goals—land reform, free elections, honesty in government—but in Santa Cruz it mainly consisted of simplifying the Church sacraments, and living a good life. Zapeta became a catechist and leader in the movement, but as best as I could tell, he never assimilated the secular goals.

It would require a long and complicated account to describe the political conditions that brought Zapeta into office, and that have risen like a dark storm since then. To put it as succinctly as possible, forces have been unleashed in Guatemala from both the extreme right and left that have destroyed all middle positions. Even a town as isolated and economically insignificant as Santa Cruz had fallen prey to those forces. That very day, yesterday as I write this, Zapeta had told me in plain and simple language what was happening in his town. In one hamlet the Catholics had been harassed and several of them killed by government soldiers, and some had now taken up arms. They had attacked an army patrol on maneuvers nearby, and apparently had joined with guerrilla bands operating in the area. Zapeta was totally opposed to this, and had told them so. "Where in the Bible does it say we should kill?" he had asked them.

That morning when we visited Zapeta, his melancholy was apparent, but he was happy because he was about to take two weeks' leave from his mayor's job to work at his home. I thought, as I left him, of the sacrifice it was for Zapeta to serve as mayor. To be devoid of political ambitions, and worse, political understanding, and yet to suffer the recriminations from former brothers and the hated ladinos alike. This was too heavy a sacrifice to make. His love of church, family, Indian culture, work, and virture seemed so out of place in the world in which Guatemala was now living.

The radio report was simple: "Avelino Zapeta, mayor of Santa Cruz Quiché, was ambushed and assassinated by an armed band as he walked to his fields to hoe his maize plants. The identity of the assassins is unknown."

Alcalde Zapeta's assassination was a deep personal tragedy to me. Something dies in us with the cruel death of someone as good as the alcalde. But truth can also be born of such tragedy, and I experienced an abrupt awakening. Deep inside I knew that the alcalde had been innocent, and no amount of rationalizing could justify his death. I knew also, finally, that many, perhaps most, of the other Indians and ladinos being killed in Guatemala were also innocent. The situation in Santa Cruz took on an entirely different light for me, and I vowed to determine what was really happening in the community and the specific causes of the alcalde's death.

Making Guerrillas at La Estancia

The key to a much better understanding both of Alcalde Zapeta's death and of the political situation in Santa Cruz was provided by Indians from the so-called guerrilla hamlet described to me by the alcalde during our last interview. The hamlet, La Estancia, is on a large plateau adjacent to the ruins. Archaeologists from our project surveyed ruins there, and in the 1960s and 1970s I interviewed Indian leaders from the hamlet regarding their history and customs. Then, in 1982, I had the good fortune to interview José Efraín, one of the hamlet's most important leaders, now a refugee in Nicaragua. This humble, sincere man and other Indians from La Estancia have spoken out clearly and forcefully, and their testimony greatly clarifies the events that occurred in La Estancia and the facts surrounding the death of Alcalde Zapeta.

Our attention must be on very recent history, but it is worth mentioning that even during the previous century La Estancia was a place of conflict. Around 1830, a reform-minded Guatemalan government attempted to settle outside Indians in the southern section of the hamlet. The La Estancia natives resisted and, under the leadership of a chief descended from a princely line of the ancient Quiché kingdom, fought a battle against the government forces. The government forces prevailed, although later the territory once more became part of La Estancia jurisdiction. The site of the battle was known as Xualchoj (The Fight), the name now used for the southern section of the hamlet.

The first half of the twentieth century, a period of slow change for Santa Cruz, must have been slow for La Estancia too. Even the reforms introduced by the revolutionary government between 1945 and 1954 had little impact on the traditional peasant culture at La Estancia. The Indians were largely turned inward, their loyalties given to the families and clans that organized daily life. Integration at the hamlet level was provided mainly by the elders who oversaw traditional ritual. The Indians made their living in traditional fashion, growing corn, beans, and a little wheat and weaving skirts. Both agriculture and weaving were based on ancient techniques. Because the Indians of La Estancia were poor, many had to take out loans and work on the hated coastal plantations. The situation is described by Cristina, a woman from La Estancia who remembers those times:

> I was born in La Estancia, a village in the Department of El Quiché. I am the oldest of four children. My parents, brothers and sisters, and I are poor Indian peasants. When I was three, I began going with my parents to the south coast plantations for the cotton and coffee harvests. The first child in my family to be killed, died there because of the poison sprayed on the coffee plants. After my brother died, my mother, who was picking coffee, kept him on her back the whole day. She waited until she had weighed the coffee before she put him down, and we buried him in a hole we dug behind the shelter where we slept with the rest of the workers from our village. None of them reported my brother's death, because the boss would have fired all of us on the next day. I never went to school because, being the oldest, I had to help my father plant and tend the corn. I learned all about farming the same as a man. At sixteen I went to church and learned my catechism. There I taught myself how to read.

La Estancia's situation had begun to change by the time I first visited the hamlet in 1967. The Indians there were known to be "progressive," and I found little evidence of traditional Quiché culture. Most of the inhabitants belonged to Catholic Action, the reformed catechist movement sweeping western Guatemala. Young catechists seemed to have replaced the traditional elders as hamlet leaders, and the public shamans had disappeared at the same time. New techniques to improve agriculture had been introduced, notably the use of fertilizers. Hat making involving the use of sewing machines was going strong, as were savings and loan cooperatives. It was no longer necessary for the La Estancia Indians to work on the coastal plantations, a change for which they were most grateful. What was bringing about these dramatic changes at La Estancia?

Beginning in the 1960s, La Estancia began to feel the impact of extremely powerful modernization forces, the most powerful of which came from the church, specifically from Spanish priests who were assigned jurisdiction over Quiché by Guatemala's conservative military government. At first the Spanish priests encountered stiff resistance from the Santa Cruz Indians. One of the priests reported:

What we found was like a closed circle with two faces: there was one face of total defense of their identity, of their traditions, of their ways. The Indian world appeared to be hermetically sealed. It seemed to have a wall of defense which no one could penetrate. They defended their world through their religious organization. It was as if they had cloaked their internal organization with a religious mantle to defend their ways.

To break those defenses, the priests concentrated on isolated hamlets such as La Estancia. A chapel was built there, one of thirty-three chapels in various Santa Cruz hamlets. The dramatic breakthrough at La Estancia and elsewhere came when the priests finally realized that traditional religion had permeated all aspects of community life:

There was no distinction between meeting in a chapel, in the schoolroom, or speaking to the mayor. . . . We gradually began to realize that the dynamic element in the Indians' life and social organization was religion. The chapel became the center around which everything evolved.

Responding to their discovery, the Spanish priests integrated the secular with the sacred. Father Luis Gurriarán, who had gone to Canada to learn about savings and loan cooperatives, soon introduced them to La Estancia and other hamlets of Quiché; more than one thousand members were recruited in Santa Cruz in less than a year. Later, consumer cooperatives were also founded at La Estancia and other hamlets. Classes on social welfare and political consciousness were part of the program that became known as Catholic Action. Some of the excitement created by Catholic Action at La Estancia during those times is captured in testimony given by Cristina:

Because of my outgoing personality, I joined the Catholic Action group when I was very young. I was the only woman who went to meetings. Some of the women would talk about me, saying I liked to be with the men, but I didn't care because I knew I wasn't doing anything wrong, and I had my parents' permission to be involved. So I learned more things. I learned why there are rich people and poor people, why we have to struggle, why we women can be involved, and that we have the same rights as men. I heard all these lectures in town, and when I'd go back to my village, I would seek out my women neighbors and relatives and teach them in the Quiché language what I had learned. In those days a priest began to come to the village with some Indian and Ladino youths. They taught us how to read and write and how to fertilize the earth for planting; they spoke to us of civic–mindedness, human rights, and other things. With these talks many of us in my village began to "open our eyes and our ears."

Catholic Action at La Estancia and elsewhere in rural Santa Cruz began to take off once it had replaced the traditional community organization. This was the Alliance for Progress period, and the Indians in Catholic Action became the primary beneficiaries of the many "development" projects introduced to Santa Cruz. At La Estancia and other hamlets new schools were opened, building materials supplied, water and electricity installed, and fertilizer purchased. The secular side of the movement began to overrun the sacred side. The priests responded by helping link up the Catholic Action organization with the National Federation of Peasants and the Christian Democratic party. Thus, while religion still permeated and dominated all aspects of social life at La Estancia, its leaders now were young catechists rather than elders, and its goals were modern, not traditional.

The dramatic changes at La Estancia and other hamlets of Santa Cruz did not come about without opposition, opposition that would grow with time and eventually radicalize the Indians. The most powerful and dangerous opposition came from the Santa Cruz ladinos. The progressive development of hamlets like La Estancia was opposed by virtually all ladinos: the governor, the military commander, the alcalde, the plantation owners, and even some Spanish priests. The ladinos feared that the Indians would unite and violently overthrow their ladino superiors. They labeled Indians such as those from La Estancia "Communists" and began to infiltrate their organization with spies. José Efraín, who became president of Catholic Action for all Santa Cruz, describes the growing repression by the ladinos:

> In 1972, spies began to infiltrate the existing organizations and to accuse and slander our leaders to the authorities. There was a case in 1973. I was a leader in my community. I was called before the governor of my town, who threatened to send me to jail if I continued talking about injustice, freedom, exploitation, poverty. He quoted from the Bible: "Blessed are the poor, because theirs is the kingdom of heaven;" and he also told me, "If the poor did not exist, the rich would not eat."

The very gains that the new Catholics had achieved began to work against them as they came up against the power of the Santa Cruz ladinos. By the elections of 1974, a certain desperation had begun to set in at La Estancia:

> We looked and looked. The co-ops didn't work; schools were no good; none of our projects had helped. What were we going to do? We thought the Christian Democratic party would be our salvation. We would win the mayor's seat. We would take over the local government and run things our way.

In fact, the Christian Democratic candidates for both mayor of Santa Cruz and for president of Guatemala did win. But the presidential candidate, General Ríos Montt, was denied office by the army, and driven in exile in Spain, and the new Santa Cruz mayor, the ladino who had befriended us during our fieldwork at Santa Cruz, largely turned his back on the Indian sector of Santa Cruz. The election results further frustrated the Indians and led to increased repression.

This was a critical point in La Estancia's history. Blocked in their attempts to raise themselves through legitimate institutionalized means— the church, economic development, political elections—the leaders of La Estancia joined other frustrated highland Indians in a politically effective organization. Called the Committee for Peasant Unity (CUC), it was more ideological than any previous Indian organization had been. To ideas about the church and local social conditions were added ideas about the shared economic condition of Indians as a whole and even of poor ladinos. As one of its organizers at La Estancia explains:

> When CUC was formed, we no longer talked about religion, but about exploitation, about the struggle for equality, freedom for workers, better wages. People from all the groups could relate to that.

José Efraín tells us that planning for CUC began in 1974, when Catholic Action leaders began meeting secretly with Indian leaders from the wider Quiché area. Among the visiting leaders was Pablo Ceto, an Ixil Indian who attended secondary school at Santa Cruz. He belonged to the study club of middle-class town Indians at which we had been invited to speak. Ceto later became a national CUC leader, and eventually he helped found a small guerrilla organization.

After two years, the entire La Estancia Catholic Action group declared itself in favor of CUC. Cristina, then president of female Catholics, says simply that the people in Catholic Action "shifted . . . membership to the CUC." Young men and women were the most enthusiastic joiners, and even children were admitted. Committees for propaganda, self-defense, intelligence, and the like were set up at La Estancia, and a regional network tied together the various hamlets of Santa Cruz. At that time CUC had no armaments at La Estancia or at any other hamlet, nor was it connected with any guerrilla organization. Opposition to CUC in La Estancia came mostly from merchants living in the southern Xualchoj section of the hamlet. José Efraín told us that the bishop knew about CUC and opposed it but that the CUC members were able to convince the other priests that they were not Communists.

From 1976 onward, external repression and internal radicalization intensified at La Estancia. The CUC led the community to participate in political events that were shaking Guatemala at the time. In 1976, when the devastating earthquake struck the area, CUC members were "the first to rush to the rescue." According to José Efraín, the Indians of Santa Cruz "didn't have this before when everyone went their own way, when everybody was involved in their own work." In 1977, when miners from the northwest went on strike and marched 270 miles to the capital, they were joined by CUC Indians from La Estancia and elsewhere, swelling the ranks of marchers to more than 100,000 persons. Again, in 1978, when CUC first appeared publicly at the May Day parade in Guatemala City, the La Estancia Indians participated. The spectacle of thousands of Indians marching together in their distinctive native dress frightened the ladinos of the city but inspired the Indian participants.

La Estancia began to receive Indian refugees from the violent struggle between the guerrillas and the army in the northern region of the department. Among those who came to live at La Estancia was Vicente Menchú, a Quiché-speaking Indian who had been a Catholic Action leader for his hamlet in the northern zone. He had been cast into prison on different occasions for attempting to defend his community against the loss of lands. His fourteen-year-old son, along with more than twenty other young Indians, had been taken by the army, tortured (his fingernails were pulled out, his tongue cut off, the soles of his feet mutilated, and his skin burned), and finally burned to death in front of his family. Vicente left the north with the express purpose of educating the Quiché Indians about what the army was doing to their people. His impact on the inhabitants of La Estancia was profound, as we learn from a woman from there:

> The period when more people from La Estancia joined CUC was when Don Vicente Menchú and one of his sons sought refuge with us. . . . They told us that it was no longer possible to live in northern Quiché because of the repression. When the army of the rich arrived in the hamlets and villages, it killed everyone. They told us how the soldiers stole everything and raped the women. They said this was war, and the war would not end until everyone became organized and began to struggle for their rights.

In January 1980, Vicente and a few other Indians from Santa Cruz joined the delegation of protesters who, after being rebuffed at the American embassy, attempted to peacefully occupy the Spanish embassy in Guatemala City. Vicente died there with twenty-two Indian companions when the embassy was fire-bombed by Guatemalan security police. He has since become a martyr of the revolutionary cause.

The violent repression heaped on the Indians of the north soon came to bear on Santa Cruz. With the election of General Lucas García in 1978 and the fall of Anastasio Somoza in Nicaragua in 1979, the government appears to have made a decision to prevent the revolutionary forces from prevailing in Guatemala (as they had in Nicaragua), no matter what the cost. The Indians of Santa Cruz and elsewhere, now organized into Catholic and peasant groups, were seen as the main source of support for the guerrillas. In 1979, as we nervously continued our fieldwork at Santa Cruz, the army was already setting in motion plans to terrorize the Indians. In May of that year, paramilitary forces locked 250 Indians from La Estancia inside the chapel, "terrorizing them and threatening them that if they continued talking about injustices they would be assassinated by the army."

The killings started in 1980. The Indian murdered in front of the ruins in April, reported to us by our friends living nearby, was Fabián, a cooperative leader from La Estancia. José Efraín, who was Fabián's cousin, happened to be pedaling by on his bicycle just after the killing took place. He saw one of the murderers, a man wearing a black mask, who appeared to be a ladino. Baltasar Toj Medrano, the Indian director of Radio Quiché, was kidnapped in May and found the next day with his hands tied and his skull crushed. Other Indian leaders in Santa Cruz began to disappear or to be killed as part of a selective terror campaign that was prelude to what was to come.

In September the "death squad" came to La Estancia. Thirty to fifty masked men who, witnesses claim, were ladinos from eastern Guatemala, arrived at 5:00 A.M. in jeeps, using the road that passes alongside the ruins. I paraphrase José Efraín's account of what transpired:

> The heavily armed men systematically went from house to house and, using name lists, tracked down the Catholic, CUC, and cooperative leaders of the hamlet. By the time they were finished, fifteen people had been assassinated. The victims included several adolescents. My brother, leader of the CUC, was crucified between two trees. After being stabbed in his side, he was strangled.

This must have been the "clash" between the La Estancia "guerrillas" (read Catholics) and the "army" that Alcalde Zapeta had told me about during our last talk. José Efraín emphatically denies, however, that the Indians had arms or that they were tied in any direct way to the guerrillas. The only weapons they possessed were the traditional ones: machetes, slings, and stones. In fact, they realized that they were defenseless. They also realized that there were spies at La Estancia who had provided names for the lists, and they suspected certain merchants from Xualchoj, the southern section of the hamlet. While the paramilitary assassins were eastern ladinos, the Indians were quite certain that the local instigator of the death squad was the same ladino congressman who had given us such a difficult time during our stay in Santa Cruz.

Alcalde Zapeta was assassinated nineteen days later. His family witnessed the cruel deed, saw two masked men spray his body with machine-gun bullets and then speed away in an army jeep. The alcalde's death appears to have been carried out by members of the same death squad that had murdered the cooperative leader in front of the ruins and massacred the men, women, and children of La Estancia. His death was part of the army's terror campaign against the Santa Cruz Indians. The alcalde was not, however, involved in peasant organizations, as were the La Estancia leaders; in fact, he actively opposed their growing activism. Why, then, was he killed? If, as the La Estancia Indians suspected, the local congressman was involved in death-squad activity, this powerful man, who shared the town ladinos' hatred for Indians who sought equality, was probably responsible for his death. The order to kill my friend, I believe, had a local origin.

Like the debacle at the Spanish embassy a few months earlier, the deaths of leaders like Alcalde Zapeta galvanized the Santa Cruz Indians against the ladino-dominated government. In some hamlets, including two near La Estancia, Indians began to organize guerrilla forces. The same might have happened at La Estancia had not the violent repression overrun it first. In November the army arrived at La Estancia in force. Again I paraphrase José Efraín:

> About 150 soldiers armed with machine guns and Galil rifles came before 6:00 A.M. This time they used the road from the south, though they sent a jeep as decoy along the road that passes by the ruins. One of the officers was a black man; the soldiers were Indians (from other areas) and ladinos. They started from the southern section (Xualchoj), and we could hear the machine-gun blasts from our section. They searched house by house for weapons. Entire families were killed in cold blood, riddled with bullets as they cowered in their beds and houses. When it was finally over, 50 people had been killed, many of them women and children. A seventy-year-old man was also killed.

I have the names and some biographical information and details about the deaths of all the victims. In this massacre, Cristina states, she lost her sisters, her brother-in-law, and other relatives. Miraculously, her two-month-old nephew was saved when the corpse of his mother shielded him from the soldiers' bullets.

From José Efraín we learn the conclusion of the La Estancia massacre. The dazed Indians buried their dead in a huge hole dug for that purpose. Bringing coffins from town and holding proper burials would have been branded subversion. It was impossible even to report the killings. When the community identified the informer, a group of women was authorized to execute him. At a market in a nearby town, they beat the suspected spy to death while other women concealed the action from market officials. Next a band of forty young Indian men and women left La Estancia for the north to join the guerrillas. Finally, the inhabitants of La Estancia, almost one thousand strong, broke up into individual families and, as rain poured down on them, silently abandoned their homes. Although they were not guerrilla recruits like the band of young men and women who had left for the north, these dispersed inhabitants of La Estancia—to a man, woman, and child—had become guerrilla sympathizers and opponents of the government.

War Comes to Santa Cruz

The Guatemalan government, through its army and paramilitary squadrons, had declared war on the Indians of Santa Cruz. In 1981 and 1982, attacks similar to those launched against La Estancia in 1980 were launched against almost all the hamlets of Santa Cruz and neighboring communities. Even after the Evangelical General Ríos Montt replaced Lucas García as Guatemala's leader in March 1982, the attacks continued. In fact, only one day after the coup that brought Ríos Montt to power, José Efraín learned from relatives of the massacre of thirty-five Indians, including six cousins, in a neighboring community. He was secretly visiting La Estancia at the time to see if he could salvage anything from the abandoned settlement. He hurried to his relatives' hamlet, where he saw the charred remains of seventeen people, including a seventeen-hour-old baby, who had been burned to death. José Efraín told of finding fragments of an Indian woman's huipil stuck to pieces of flesh that had withstood the burning. He further testified that the other eighteen victims were beheaded. Similar

atrocities reported in the Santa Cruz area during 1981 and 1982 substantiate José Efraín's account of the techniques used by the army
against the Indians.

After 1980, the Indians in Santa Cruz began to fight back. José Efraín estimated that more than one thousand Indians from Santa Cruz
alone joined the guerrillas. These and many others recruited from surrounding communities were organized, trained, and armed by the
Guerrilla Army of the Poor (EGP), the guerrilla organization that for
ten years had been operating in the northern part of the Quiché Department. José Efraín claims that the leaders are both Indians and ladinos, that no Cubans or Nicaraguans are in the organization, at least
not in the Santa Cruz groups. Indians from Santa Cruz have their own
unit, the "Ho Chi Minh," and those from Chichicastenango have another, "Augusto Sandino." Still another in the area is called "Vicente
Menchú," named for the man who once resided at La Estancia and
later died in the Spanish embassy. In July 1981 the Ho Chi Minh unit
was responsible for blowing the tower off the building where the governor adminsters departmental affairs. This structure, the largest in
Santa Cruz, is strategically located near the central park, the cathedral,
the military garrison, and the main stores. The explosion damaged
buildings and residences and killed two passersby. At the same time
other guerrilla units stopped traffic and dynamited roads leading into
and out of Santa Cruz.

Our information on the war in the Santa Cruz area is fragmentary.
I have found reference, mostly in Guatemalan newspapers, to approximately thirty-five hamlets of Santa Cruz in which the army allegedly
killed Indians during 1981 and 1982. The number of deaths attributed
to different army actions varied from 1 to 1,000 per hamlet. The actions included selective killings and massacres similar to those in La
Estancia in 1980, and often they involved the killing or theft of cattle,
pigs, and chickens, and the burning of houses and crops. The reported
deaths for the Santa Cruz area for the two years totaled 4,077; the
official count of "unnatural" deaths at the Santa Cruz morgue was
2,020. Both figures are probably too low; if the La Estancia massacre
is any indication, many deaths were never reported, and large numbers
of bodies were never taken to the morgue. One Indian from a community adjacent to Santa Cruz claims that 800 people were killed in
his hamlet alone, though none of these deaths was ever reported.

In Chichicastenango well over one thousand women were widowed
as a result of the violence; the number of men and children killed in

that community alone must have totaled more than four thousand. Perhaps someday we will know the true extent of the mass killings in the Santa Cruz area, but our fragmentary information persuades me that Santa Cruz and adjacent communities lost at least 10 percent of their Indian population. Nor should we forget the tens of thousands who left their settlements and became part of the estimated one million displaced persons fleeing from the army in Guatemala.

The figures alone do not tell of the personal tragedies suffered by the Quiché Indians as a result of such "military actions." José Efraín witnessed one massacre. After abandoning La Estancia, he became an internal refugee, moving from one highland community to another. In 1982, while he was living with CUC friends in the Xesic hamlet of Santa Cruz, he awoke one morning to find the hamlet entirely surrounded by army troops. As the soldiers closed in, the people fled in panic, only to have helicopters drop grenades on them. Seventy-five men, women, and children were killed. José Efraín again escaped, but this time he left Guatemala for good. He went on foot with his family to Nicaragua.

Similar testimonies of the "counterinsurgency" techniques used by the army against the Quiché Indians have been given by Indians of the area. For example, a woman who escaped a massacre of more than one thousand people living in and around the Chichicastenango hamlet of Chupol told a reporter what had happened in her village toward the end of 1981. A guerrilla leader, who had learned firsthand about such military "actions" while he was a prisoner at the Santa Cruz base, said that junior and senior military officers had participated in the Chupol massacre. In fact, he claimed that Gen. Benedicto Lucas García, the army chief of staff and brother of the president, had directed the action from his blue-and-white helicopter.

Army officers stationed at Santa Cruz freely admitted to visitors that the army was waging a terror campaign against the Indians, and General Ríos Montt's press secretary as much as publicly admitted it:

> The guerrillas won over many Indian collaborators. Therefore, the Indians were subversives. And how do you fight subversion? Clearly you had to kill Indians because they were collaborating with subversion. And then it would be said that you were killing innocent people. But they weren't innocent; they had sold out to subversion.

We have few details on the military actions of the Santa Cruz Indian guerrillas. José Efraín claims that they operated out of camps set up in woods around Santa Cruz. He mentions that there were guerrillas in a hamlet near La Estancia and that La Estancia itself became a source of food for the guerrillas, who entered it at night to harvest the maize crops. Patzité, a community just south of La Estancia, was another important guerrilla center. Perhaps most of the hamlets in the isolated mountainous zones of Santa Cruz and Chichicastenango harbored guerrillas. The number of guerrillas in the camps during 1981 and 1982 was said to be large; they were trained in military tactics by the experienced cadre of the Guerrilla Army of the Poor. According to a young Indian from La Estancia who served with the guerrillas for a time, they were often short of food, and lack of water for hygienic needs was an especially acute problem. José Efraín reports that they had few weapons; many of them used hunting rifles, some of which were antiques.

Indian guerrillas in the Santa Cruz area appear to have retaliated against local ladinos responsible for violence against the Indians. In the community of San Pedro Jocopilas, near Santa Cruz, a wealthy ladino was shot by Indians using old rifles. They also fired on the hated military commissioners, local men who forcibly recruited Indians for the army. Guerrilla action of this type may have occurred at Santa Cruz as well, but it must have been quite limited.

The Quiché guerrillas attempted to gain control of the highways leading into and out of Santa Cruz. They planted mines in the roads, one of which blew up a bus, killing twelve Indian occupants. They stopped traffic of all kinds, and they sabotaged official vehicles. They ambushed army patrols, as often as three or four times a day, on the Quiché roads. Toward the end of 1981 the guerrillas virtually controlled the roads around Santa Cruz, in some places trenching them to stop the flow of traffic. The guerrillas painted the words "Viva EGP" ("Long live the Guerrilla Army of the Poor") at regular intervals along the paved highways. By 1982, however, the army had bolstered its troop levels, moved in armed vehicles, and regained control of the roads around Santa Cruz. Trees and houses along the roadside were leveled to prevent ambushes.

The guerrillas mounted their major offensives during the second half of 1981 and early 1982. The dynamiting of the government building took place at that time, as did attacks on police outposts in Chichicastenango and Santa Cruz. Four policemen died during the Chichicastenango attack. In December 1981 a guerrilla force of five hundred attacked the army base at Santa Cruz, though the results are unclear. In January 1982, Santa Cruz's electrical transmission tower was blown up, and as a result the entire Quiché Department was blacked out for four hours. Two technicians were killed during the attack on the station. After the blackout, most guerrilla actions became smaller in scale, consisting of attempts to mine roads, ambush small patrols, and track the police in the rural area. The army had gained the upper hand, at least within the main population centers and along the most important roads.

The guerrillas' strongholds were in the rural zones surrounding their camps. They visited the Indians living in hamlets, attempting to elicit their support. An aged Indian from Chichicastenango told a U.S. reporter that the guerrillas would arrive at the hamlet centers, call the population together, and state their case. According to the Indian, if the people listened and said nothing, they had no problems. "But if you object to something, then they will come to your house at night and kill you." His daughter, he said, the mother of nine children, spoke out and was killed by the guerrillas.

Hamlets that fell under guerrilla control were organized for defensive purposes. The people were instructed in the placement of sentries to guard entries into the hamlets, and escape routes to the canyons and forests were planned. The people lacked arms, but along the boundaries of at least some hamlets they dug holes and placed wooden stakes in them to serve as traps against the army. The guerrillas came to the people's aid during army attacks on hamlets in the Santa Cruz area. When Chupol was attacked in March 1982, the guerrillas fired at the helicopters as they flew by. Eight soldiers were said to have fallen into guerrilla-laid traps during the attack. Later, according to an Indian woman from Chupol, "a group of young people who belonged to the guerrillas helped us organize the departure and calmed us down and told us to trust them, that they would help us." Indians from Santa Cruz Quiché were among the guerrillas trying to aid the Chupol vistims.

The guerrillas' presence among the rural Indians of the Santa Cruz area was used by the army as justification for the mass killings. Most survivors of the massacres, however, have identified the army as the guilty party. The confusion about the killings is well illustrated by two massacres at hamlets of Chichicastenango and Santa Cruz in 1982, shortly after General Ríos Montt came to power. The army blamed both massacres on the guerrillas. The first resulted in the deaths of twenty-five children, fifteen women (three of whom were pregnant), and three men, all of whom were mutilated. A U.S. reporter who visited the site a few days after the killings found only an elderly Indian woman who could not speak Spanish. The reporter noted that the ground was littered with cartridges from the Israeli-type Galil rifles used by the army. The second massacre took place several days later at a hamlet close to the first one; in it fifteen people were killed, some of whose throats were slit. This time a U.S. reporter arrived on the scene only a few hours after the killing. He found three Indians nearby and asked them what had happened:

> They said that at about 6:00 A.M. some 60 soldiers had surrounded the village, shouting for everyone to come out so they could search the place. Then they took some villagers, struck them down with machetes and shot them as they lay on the ground.

The reporter next asked the Indians whether the attackers were guerrillas or soldiers. They replied:

> They were soldiers from Chajul [in the northern militarized zone of the Quiché department]—I know because I have seen them there—they only changed their hats.

Such evidence as we have suggests that the guerrillas operating in the rural zones did commit acts of terror and did kill people but that they were highly selective. Most of their victims were combat soldiers or suspected spies. The army, by contrast, killed and mutilated masses of rural Indians. The guerrilla operations in town and along the roads caused relatively few casualties. Our evidence suggests that the army killed at least one hundred times as many people as the guerrillas—and made refugees of thousands more.

Some Indians killed by the army were guerrillas. More significant from the army viewpoint, however, is that the scorched-earth tactics denied the guerrillas their main support base. After 1982 the Quiché guerrillas withdrew to safer locations, admitting that they had lost the battle though not the war. In an official publicaction they stated as much:

> In the 1981–1982 offensives the civilian population suffered divisive blows as a result of which the popular movements [guerrillas] partially lost initiative. In many places, counterinsurgency offensives dealt severe blows to popular organizations. Many of their leaders have fallen.

Leaders of CUC, the peasant union turned revolutionary, said that only three or four of the original forty founders survived the army's 1981–82 campaign of terror. One of the survivors, Emeterio Toj Medrano, was an announcer for Radio Quiché who had kindly allowed us to make announcements over the air during our research project at Santa Cruz. He was kidnapped in 1981 and tortured in several military centers, including the Santa Cruz base, and his and his family's lives were threatened. Under these pressures Toj publicly denounced his role as a revolutionary leader. Later he escaped and went underground, presumably rejoining the guerrillas. He has since provided valuable information on counterinsurgency techniques used by the army in the Santa Cruz area.

Military Occupation of Santa Cruz

War in the Santa Cruz area led to a military buildup that would have been almost impossible to imagine during the 1970s, when we did research there. We knew that headquarters for a military zone had been situated in Santa Cruz since the past century, but it was a small contingent of about four hundred soldiers and seemed relatively inactive during the 1970s. The base commander and other officials were friendly, even lending special support to our research efforts from time to time. But the military establishment was not as harmless as it seemed. As early as 1976 counterinsurgence intelligence activities were being carried out at the base. Indians suspected of collaborating with the EGP guerrillas in the northern part of Quiché Department were regularly sent there, where they were interrogated, tortured, and sometimes executed.

Reporters visiting Santa Cruz after 1980 have frequently mentioned the conspicuous presence of the military. By 1982 there were fifteen to twenty thousand soldiers in the Quiché Department as a whole, and three thousand soldiers were based in Santa Cruz Quiché itself. The soldiers were well equipped with new Israeli weapons, and the town and the main roads were jammed with jeeps, trucks, and armed personnel carriers. Santa Cruz became a major army air base for helicopters and other aircraft. As early as 1976 the army had attempted to gain shared rights to the municipal airport on the southern outskirts of town. The ladino mayor at that time had strongly opposed the army's initiative as being harmful to the community. Later, after Alcalde Zapeta was assassinated and the government began appointing mayors, the army confiscated the facilities. The airstrip was enlarged, a tower and lights were installed, and auxiliary buildings were erected. One reporter described the base this way:

> The army has set up an impressive field headquarters unlike anything in El Salvador. Neatly painted signs mark the motor pool areas, latrines, mess hall and dispensary. Sand bags protect the large black rubber bladders that hold fuel for Israeli-made troop transport planes.

This contrasts dramatically with the "cow pasture" we saw in the 1970s, which was used mainly by small planes carrying food to Ixcan colonizers in the north.

The army also took over most of the Catholic church buildings after the priests left in 1980. Army barracks were set up in several of them, though not at Santa Cruz. Late in 1982 the pope named a priest to occupy the bishop's residence next to the cathedral. The priest, a member of an elite Santa Cruz family, has been much more cooperative with the army than were the Spanish priests. The church is under continual surveillance by the army, as shown by a reporter's visit to Santa Cruz in 1983. The reporter, on assignment for a Catholic news magazine, attended a late-afternoon mass at the cathedral. The next day she was taken into custody by two plainclothesmen, who interrogated her at the military base. It turned out that they had been watching her every move. Not only the two plainclothesmen but also other people participating in the mass had been spying on her. The frightened reporter was set free only after an army captain arrived and examined her credentials.

Military control of the municipal government and church has given the army a vise grip over the Santa Cruz town. Every aspect of social life is permeated by the army. At a recent celebration of the "Day of the Natives," pretty Indian girls dressed in full native costume danced before the base commander and the bishop. Despite such displays of power, the army realizes that control over the town, where the ladinos already dominated the Indians, is the easy part. Much more difficult is control of the Indian hamlets. The army has attempted to militarize the rural Indians through the civil patrol system.

The army began organizing the Indians of Santa Cruz into civil patrols in 1981 as an extension of the war being waged against them. All adult men of the hamlets were to take direct orders from the army, ostensibly to guard their people against the guerrillas. The real objective, however, was for the patrols to inform on guerrilla sympathizers in the community. The program was expanded in 1982 under General Ríos Montt, who called it "beans and bullets." Civil guards were given a few guns and were called on to serve as shock troops during army raids against the guerrillas. In exchange for these services, the hamlets were to receive food and other social services. In fact, however, the Santa Cruz Indians have received very little food or social service from the army or other government agencies. Almost all the aid in the area has been directed to the town and within the town to the ladino sector in the form of road repair, water and electricity, and building construction. Rather than a social program, the civil patrol system in Santa Cruz has been a coercive means of military control.

The army has claimed repeatedly that the civil guards have been attacked and sometimes killed by the guerrillas in the Santa Cruz area. But the testimony of the Indians is very different. Consider for example, what happened with the civil patrol at Cruz Che, an isolated hamlet that we studied in the 1970s. The guards were given the task of "finishing off" five people suspected of being "subversives," a term that those rural, Quiché-speaking Indians could hardly have understood. According to the Cruz Che Indians' own testimony,

the civil patrol members who received these orders did not know what to do. When they arrived at their village they told the people what the army had ordered them to do. After many hours of reflection and community prayer, those who had been condemned by the army made a decision: "If we escape, the army will come and kill everyone. They have done this in other villages. It is better that you kill us." Then everyone went to the cemetery where they dug the graves. The executions were carried out amid the weeping and prayers of the community.

Similar "executions" have taken place in virtually all the hamlets. Another such incident in a hamlet near the town of Chichicastenango was investigated by a foreign diplomat in Guatemala. He learned that

patrols from six small villages went to the town of Chijtinamit in July and August of 1983 and confronted the local patrol with a list of villagers whom they suspected of being subversive. The visiting patrols threatened to attack the town if the local patrol did not execute the reputed leftists, so the patrol complied by killing 25 of their own men.

Two months later in the same hamlet fourteen civil guards were executed by fellow guardsmen when they failed to show up for patrol duty.

The army has not denied that the civil patrols perform such "security" functions. One officer from Santa Cruz has used the metaphor of taking the water away from fish; the guards separate the guerrillas from their people. What is questionable is whether those being killed are guerrillas. Also questionable is the army's claim that the civil patrols are voluntary organizations. This is contradicted by virtually every visitor to Santa Cruz who has been able to speak with the Indians living there. Of special importance is the testimony of a knowledgeable Santa Cruz Indian, formerly associated with our project, who secretly gave us this account:

> All men, sometimes as young as ten years of age, must join the Patrulla de Autodefensa Civil [Civil Patrol]. They call it "self-defense." It's very ironic. If a man refuses to join, then the army shoots him and says he is a subversive. We have to go out once a week for twenty-four hours. We receive no pay, which is a hardship for us because we are now in bad times. In our group there are six. Three of us are given guns. We walk around the countryside of our hamlet in pairs. If we see anybody walking around, even people we know, we have to bring them to the army base for interrogation. After 6:00 P.M. we have to shoot anyone we see.

It is clear from such accounts that the civil guards themselves are terrified of what the army might do to them. They in turn terrorize each other and the people of their hamlets. Any action that might remotely suggest connection with the guerrillas—leaving town, collaborating too closely with the church, hiding relatives—is reported to the army. The civil patrols of Santa Cruz are directly tied to the so-called G-2, or intelligence, agents of the military base. The Indian quoted above described them as follows:

> The men in charge of "disappearing" people have a special name. They are located in the army base, but they don't wear uniforms. We know them because they are from around here. During the day you can recognize them because they wear fine boots. They always wear good clothes. But when they come to get you, they cover their faces, and they don't speak. And when they take you away, they take your possessions as well. I used to have a television set. But the ones they take aren't guerrillas. They are just people.

Another Indian who was turned over to the army by the civil patrol recounted his experience with G-2 at the Santa Cruz base:

They began to hit me and then they told me: "Well, the amnesty period is over. You jerk, you haven't wanted to turn yourself in!"

They're officers. People say they're from G-2. They say it's G-2 because they're dressed as civilians but they're there with the army. They're higher up than the soldiers because they take charge of the interrogations.

There in the Quiché barracks . . . they hit me a lot. And the next day they made me give a confession but before that they tied up my hands and blindfolded me. . . .

They hit me and they gave me electric shock. They gave it to me four times (on the ear). . . . They told me they were going to put it on my testicles. . . . [They said] they had to do it to me. . . . And then they connect it and that's when you get it. You fall on the floor. . . .

Hamlets in the Santa Cruz area where the inhabitants were massacred and driven into flight are guarded by the army rather than by civil patrols. Besides La Estancia, an example is Lemoa, a large hamlet south of town next to a small lake. The very poor, unsophisticated Indians from there had cooperated with our project during the 1970s, but in 1981 more than one thousand of them were killed by the army, and hundreds more fled into hiding. In 1983 a reporter for *Soldier of Fortune* magazine visiting Santa Cruz was taken to Lemoa to observe the Guatemalan army on location. His account, intended to present a positive image of the army's struggle against "communism," reveals instead the army's repressive control of hamlets too dangerous to risk civil patrols. Three Indian peasants were taken into custody for "carrying bundles of foodstuff"—to the guerrillas, according to the army. They were brusquely interrogated, and when their answers to the lieutenant seemed "evasive," they were labeled "Communists" and hauled away.

The reporter, who knew nothing about the language, culture, or history of these people, believed that they owed much to the army. He totally missed the significance of what was going on in Lemoa: this once bustling community of Indians had been reduced by official violence to a state of fear, and was now under total military domination.

By 1983 the militarization of the rural hamlets of Santa Cruz was complete. One could see civilian patrols every few kilometers along the road leading into Santa Cruz. Once again the time had come to paternalize relations between the ladino-ruled army and the Indian masses. The educated new commander at Santa Cruz, Col. Roberto Mata, boasted about "his" Indian civil guards and how they had once been guerrilla supporters. In 1985, at a ceremonial gathering of more than six thousand Indian guards, held in a rural area between Santa Cruz and the neighboring town San Pedro Jocopilas, Colonel Mata addressed both their fears and their hopes. He reminded them of the "bad things" that had happened to them, from which they were "to learn lessons for the future." Then, as the Indian girls selected by the town as candidates for "Miss Patrol" looked on, the civil guards marched in procession swearing allegiance to the Guatemalan flag carried by the colonel himself.

Colonel Mata's message to outsiders seemed designed to disguise the harsh truth of what has taken place at Santa Cruz over the past few years. He won over foreign correspondents by arguing that the army's forces had been successful against the guerrillas because they had not been helped by the Americans. And he spoke of "a war against hunger, a war against the lack of education" that still needed to be fought. Finally, while admitting that not all the Indians might like the new reality, he solemnly declared, "It's a beneficial change."

For those of us who lived at Santa Cruz during the 1970s and experienced firsthand the vitality of a community of Indians on the move upward, Colonel Mata's view of what was taking place at Santa Cruz was difficult to accept. Closer to the mark is the picture painted by a former member of our research team who recently revisited the community and compared what she found with what had once existed there. Her account tells the side of Santa Cruz that Colonel Mata refused to see:

> Life in Santa Cruz today is a modern version of life in the colonial period. Social life has been reduced to household units, whose function is little more than work for survival and compulsory service to the military. There are no social institutions that represent the Indians of Santa Cruz to the nation. Even at a community level, they have no voice, no functioning institutions to deal with local problems such as land disputes, marriages, and family feuds. The established ways have collapsed with the disruption of the old authority system and the imposition of new authorities who have no knowledge of people's problems or of the most reasonable ways to solve them. Indeed, the new authorities—the armed forces—appear to lack all concern for such problems.

The military net has been cast around Santa Cruz, and it is now tightly drawn. But the Indians have experienced such control by outsiders before, and we can be sure that their struggle for freedom and dignity will continue.

Concluding Thoughts

The Santa Cruz story has been difficult for me to accept, steeped as I am in my memories of the community of the 1960s and 1970s. There is so much to react to, and there are so many ways to react. It is impossible to escape personal hurt since so much of Santa Cruz that was good and beautiful has been destroyed. The heinous assassination of that lovely Indian man, Alcalde Zapeta. The torture and killing of our Indian friends at the radio station, who allowed us to state our case to the community. All those thousands of rural Indians from La Estancia and other hamlets who cooperated with us, victims who wanted only a chance to live with decency and hope. The good Christian Democratic congressman, Hamilton, who tried to help us and later lost his life. The thousands of other poor Indians who either have had to flee into a nightmarish life of continual dislocation or have been forced into degrading subjection to military overlords. One understands that Santa Cruz is not really exceptional in the violent context of recent Guatemalan politics, but the personal anguish remains nonetheless.

The repression in Santa Cruz that I have attempted to describe is real in the most primitive sense of the word. It would be possible to analyze that reality, to draw scientific and even moral lessons from it. But I am more struck by the symbolism of what has happened. We went to Santa Cruz originally because it was of historical significance. Reading the ancient accounts of the Quiché kingdom and excavating its ruins transformed Santa Cruz into a place of wonder for me. Practically every hamlet, every ruined mound, every traditional ritual practice, and every Indian family name took on special meaning in the context of our emerging studies. The badly eroded mounds at the main archaeological site outside town were no longer merely mounds: they were the ancient residences and temples of identifiable kings and princely lines whose blood descendants we came to know. The tiny and seemingly insignificant, isolated hamlet of Cruz Che became associated with the first political center of the Tamubs, confederate partners of the ruling Quiché dynasty. And La Estancia, in recent times a hamlet of progressive Catholics, was anciently the strategic western flank where warriors guarded the imposing Quiché capital standing just across the ravine.

There surely is something paradoxical in rediscovering remnant peoples and places of a great civilization after half a millennium of obscurity at virtually the same time that brutal contemporary forces crush and destroy these same peoples and places. It is hard to forget, for example, the arduous work and excitement that eventually brought us to the mountain hamlet of Ximbaxuc, where the founders of the Quiché kingdom had anciently encountered people living in deerskin tents. We restored it to the historical map in 1975, only to have it erased again seven years later. According to an Amnesty International report of 1982: "Armed men entered the village of Ximbaxuc, Chinique, Quiché, robbing, burning, and killing 40 *campesinos*, including men, women, the elderly and children."

I remember too our struggle to gain access to the ruins so that we could excavate and reveal the ancient lifeways at the Quiché capital. Three years after our departure the military commander celebrated the "Day of the Indians" by driving personnel carriers onto the fragile plaster floors of those ruins.

Another symbolic feature of the Santa Cruz story should be marked. More than one observer has called attention to the parallels between the Spanish conquest of the Quichés and the Guatemalan army's current military "counterinsurgency" program. The Spanish conquistadors, after first accepting the Quichés' offer of peace, seized the rulers of the kingdom and assassinated them. They burned the capital and then terrorized the surrounding rural peoples, who by that time had taken up arms. Spanish victory was achieved through superior weaponry (horses and firearms) and ruthlessness (Indians were massacred and chained as slaves). In many ways, the army's recent actions in Quiché duplicate the ancient conquest. Curiously, and perhaps symbolically, the army's initial terrorist act, the murder of Fabián, the La Estancia leader, took place in front of the old capital. Alcalde Zapeta's killing was another significant public execution of an Indian leader. Similarly, the army's rural campaign resembled that of the conquistadors: well-armed soldiers, ruthlessly torturing and killing Indians and burning their homes without real resistance, crushed the guerrilla opposition. In response, the poorly armed Indians dug traps and placed stakes in them—exactly as the ancient Quichés had done against the invading Spaniards.

The use of traps makes it clear that the Indians were aware of the parallels between the ancient Spanish and present-day army conquests: they claim to have learned about the traps by reading Popol Vuh. An Indian shaman from a neighboring community to Santa Cruz announced that Tecum, the martyred Indian hero of the Spanish conquest, had returned to earth. According to the tale, Tecum returned "to bring justice to Guatemala." Significantly, he is said to have brought two million "warriors" (read "guerrillas") with him, though they were allowed to enter the fight only two or three at a time. The tale suggests that the more traditional Indians have, in fact, seen that the Santa Cruz war is analogous to the Spanish conquest. The guerrillas too have taken note of the parallel. One Indian guerrilla, an avowed Catholic, now searches for images in Popol Vuh to help her understand the violence. Because the evil power in that book takes the form of gods who resided in an underworld called Xibalbá, she believes that evil is "when repression came to the Quiché. Since we were all born here, how can those men [the soldiers] do this killing. . . . [And bury them in] clandestine cemeteries! Those men, those soldiers who killed us . . . that is what we call Xibalbá."

A few years ago I wrote that traditional Quiché culture as a way of life had all but disappeared from Santa Cruz. Nevertheless, I felt that "in some new revitalized guise, this dynamic culture will yet inspire the native peoples of Quiché in years to come." Little did I know how quickly forces would reach Santa Cruz that would dramatically create this revitalization process, nor did I suspect the grim form that it would take. That, of course, is only one of the many profound implications of the Santa Cruz story.

CHAPTER 3

The Transformation of La Esperanza, an Ixcán Village

By Beatriz Manz

Over the last decade, Guatemala has experienced the growth of the liberation theology movement (see chapter 4 for more on this movement), cooperatives and colonization; a mass rural movement; landlessness and plantation-wage dependency; army sweeps, massacres, and scorched earth; oil developments; guerrillas; and displacement, refugees, and military development poles. A microcosm of these forces that have so marked Guatemalan society can be found in La Esperanza (throughout this chapter pseudonyms are used for villages and people), a northern Quiché hamlet situated in the municipality of Ixcán and part of the Playa Grande development pole.

I went to Santa Cruz Quiché in 1973 as a graduate student in anthropology. The poverty of the Indians and the discrimination against them shocked me even though I had grown up in a rural area of Chile. The literature I had read had led me to expect the Indians' resignation to these conditions and lack of desire to change, and on the surface Santa Cruz Quiché was quiet and complacent. I soon realized, however, that in reality there was much uneasiness and discontent, especially among Indian youth. I became intrigued by the contrast between the social reality and the political consciousness of the people I met.

The person I came to know best in Santa Cruz Quiché was a young Indian from La Estancia named Francisco Piedra. He worked with the cooperatives and thus was deeply involved in the colonization efforts in remote rain forests north of Quiché, an area then known as Zona Reyna. This colonization was led by Father Lionel, a Spanish priest. Francisco introduced me to Lionel and to others involved in the movement and made it possible for me to visit La Esperanza, the first colonization site in the area.

I flew in with Lionel and Francisco in a small plane. We flew the length of Quiché, over Sacapulas and Nebaj, and finally penetrated the forest area. Along the way we saw Padre Jorge in his plane and made a quick stop at his colonization site in Ixcán, between the Ixcán and Xalbal rivers. From there we continued on, landing on an airstrip at San Miguel. Horses and mules were waiting for us there. We headed north following a narrow trail. We reached the Verde River and, since the water was low, crossed it on horseback. Finally we arrived at La Esperanza.

The spirit and consciousness of the people were the most striking features of the community. Materially they were no better off than those in the highlands and in most respects seemed worse off as a result of the isolation, climate, terrain, health problems, and unusually arduous work. Yet there was a universal sense of hope, confidence, pride, and freedom. Voices sang lively songs of liberation and brotherhood, and Lionel's homilies were less about ancient Palestine and more about modern Guatemala. There was a sense that this was their place and that they were going to shape their future and destiny. Here they could develop and put into practice their emerging vision that it was not right to be exploited and discriminated against and that it was a social sin, not an act of God, to deny people land and the means to sustain life. They were courageous and confident that they could do something about the injustice and dependency that dominated their lives.

In the years after my journey in 1973, I often thought about La Esperanza. At times information trickled out; for example, I received news about army repression and the murder of community leaders in the mid-1970s. There were also reports of the formation of the Guerrilla Army of the Poor (EGP) and a growing Indian base of support for this guerrilla group. I received information concerning oil explorations, the construction of a major road across the northern half of the country, and generals grabbing land in the strip called the Northern Transversal Strip. Much later I learned how the army had massacred and burned entire villages.

Refugees began to stream into Mexico. I went to the Lacandón forest in the Ixcán in 1982 and heard firsthand accounts of the army's violence against villagers. One can hardly imagine the pain these people suffered in leaving behind their lands on which they had labored so hard and having to find their way to refuge. They did so solely because their very lives were at stake. Indians have gone through much in the last 450 years, but perhaps never before have entire communities abandoned their traditional lands. Refugees in Mexico told how their villages had been burned to the ground by the army and how all of them had fled, leaving all their belongings behind. The fate of those who had not reached Mexico and the current condition of their villages were unknown. Since the area is difficult to reach and is still considered a conflict zone, no journalists or anthropologists had ventured in.

I was finally able to return to La Esperanza in 1985. In the early morning of December 8, I arrived at the bridge over the Chixoy River. It was heavily guarded by dozens of soldiers. On the other side of the river was the massive military base of the Playa Grande development pole, where between 2,000 and 3,000 soldiers were reportedly stationed. After questioning us, a soldier entered our car and rode along as we crossed the bridge and passed through the military base, the only available route for vehicles. His Galil automatic rifle pressed against the driver during the ride. In the days that followed, I crossed the bridge a dozen times, sometimes on foot, other times in a pickup truck. A soldier accompanied pedestrians or vehicles traveling this half-mile route in either direction. Two days later, led by a ladino and an Indian who volunteered to be guides, we started on foot down a winding muddy jungle trail. Five hours later, exhausted and dehydrated, we arrived at the site of La Esperanza.

Setting Up a Colony in the Tropical Rain Forest

The idea of colonization began as a result of Father Lionel's efforts to establish cooperatives in Santa Cruz Quiché in the mid-1960s. In all their discussions, the cooperative members realized that their biggest problem was the lack of land. Then they came up with the idea of moving to zones where idle national land, even though isolated, could be used.

A nucleus of people emerged who were interested in colonizing. Typical of the highlands dwellers, these people had no land or too little land to support their families. Most of them were in their mid-twenties. The composition of La Esperanza's original colonizing group is shown in the following table.

No. Families	Family Size	Total No. Persons
9	Single men	9
10	2 (couples without children)	20
10	3	30
23	4	92
13	5	65
20	6	120
16	7	112
10	8	80
1	9	9
3	10	30
Total 115		567

Father Lionel made the initial inquiries of the Institute of Agrarian Transformation (INTA). At first the group thought about moving to El Petén, where colonization projects were already under way. But INTA dissuaded them, pointing to the idle national land in the northern part of El Quiché.

By the end of 1969 the people were determined to establish the colony. They decided who was most in need, and also who was most willing to be a pioneer in what was then an almost impenetrable forest. Self-selection followed, and a group of forty determined volunteers formed. In January 1970 they traveled to Uspantán, and then left the highlands behind them as they began the long journey on foot. The trip took a week. They arrived in San Miguel (which later also was colonized), the last village reachable by trail. They found seven Kekchí families who had settled there at the turn of the century, living almost as nomads. The Kekchís would settle for a few years in a place where there was adequate land and water, clear the jungle, burn the trees and brush, and then cultivate. Such cultivation gives two or three crops, but without proper precautions, the land easily loses its fertility. Consequently, every five or six years these families would simply move somewhere else. The inhabitants were few, and the forest was vast.

The Kekchí families were very hospitable and made the colonization efforts of these Quiché newcomers much easier. As a result of this hospitality the Quiché colonists established their base camp there for the first four months. The Kekchís offered advice on how to proceed and on which sites might be most suitable for colonization. The colonists crossed the Verde River and selected their home site. They spent the next few months opening trails with machetes and axes, and in the fourth month they moved permanently into La Esperanza.

The people cleared the site by planned rotation. The first group of forty colonists stayed five months, after which a steady stream of newcomers began arriving to take the place of those returning to the highlands. The returnees would seek work on the southern coastal plantations for a few months to save money to purchase food and other necessities for the new colony.

The first two years were difficult ones, particularly the first nine months. The colonists often went hungry, and many became sick; they were not accustomed to the environment and had a difficult time adjusting. Nevertheless, they cleared the land and built their *ranchitos,* or huts, from materials they found in the environment. Preparing the land for cultivation was especially difficult. The colonists would cut the trees with axes and then wait for the sun to dry the wood and leaves before burning them. Some branches did not dry, and the fallen trees often had to be split so that the sun could penetrate and dry the wood. Even though the colonists arrived in the summer (i.e., the dry season), about three months passed before they could burn the trees. Once the land was somewhat cleared (only tree trunks remained), the first maize was planted. By August or September of that first year, they had their first harvest. In two years they had produced enough corn for their own needs.

From the very start the colonists set aside some land for experimentation, to determine what could be produced successfully. They tried watermelons, cantaloupes, sweet potatoes, and new types of beans. They also experimented with cash crops, such as vanilla, pepper, coffee, and cardamom. Cardamom seemed to have the most potential. Green chiles also gave good results.

At this stage the cooperative numbered 116 families, or *parcelarios.* Each family received a 1-hectare (2.7- acre) lot, plus a farming parcel of about 30 hectares (81 acres). The community was laid out around a center core. The core was referred to as the "civic center," a large area containing the schools, the cooperative building, the social center, the church, and a large house where the priest and other community leaders lived. Between the cooperative building and the social center was a large area set aside for the Sunday market. There were also a soccer field and, eventually, an airstrip. In the outlying area surrounding the center were the house lots; surrounding the lots were the land parcels for cultivation.

After a few years the Wings of Hope, a Saint Louis, Missouri, charitable organization, donated a plane to the colony; it also provided a volunteer American pilot. The cooperative had a band radio, which enabled the colonists to communicate with Santa Cruz Quiché. There were daily flights between Santa Cruz Quiché and La Esperanza when the weather was good.

The *parcelarios* received further aid from an organization in Madison, Wisconsin, called Amigos del Quiché, and from the Catholic Relief organization CARITAS. Still another organization, the Heiffer Foundation, helped them begin cattle breeding. Each family received one head of cattle, and the collective herd flourished. José, now a refugee in Quintana Roo, claims to have had thirty-five head of cattle at the time the army destroyed the village. The *parcelarios* claim that the colony eventually had about one thousand head of cattle.

Education was a key component of community life. Under the direction of the Catholic church in the highlands, there was already an emphasis on adult literacy and consciousness raising. The colony's educational program, according to the church, focused on "the problems of different subjects so as to create a critical attitude and thinking among the peasants concerning the content of the educational programs themselves and the reality they faced." Subject matter included social and political economy (political history, agrarian problems, political parties, and so on); organization (leadership, communal work, etc.); and processes of decision making and consensus (representation, women's roles, peasant-worker unions, etc.). Other fields covered were agriculture and forestry, administration and management, health, adult literacy, and civil-legal education.

I observed classes and the conduct of regular meetings. There was a general sense of confidence—looking back, some would say overconfidence. The *parcelarios* were informed of their rights and instructed in how to put those rights into practice so that when they had to confront the authorities, whether from oil companies or the government, they were able to defend themselves. One person related an incident in 1979:

A commercial network was created between most of the cooperatives. In reality, the idea, besides obtaining food supplies, was also to have better links among the cooperatives and a stronger organization. The government, through the Institute of Cooperatives, opposed the creation of a Federation of Cooperatives of Ixcán. The cooperative members said they did not need the authorization of the government in order to work well, and they went ahead and created the Association of Cooperatives (ACO-IXCAN). Through this association it became possible to do many tasks and achieve participation in communal projects, especially in education and conciousness raising.

This association made it possible to organize the sale of products such as cardamom and thus obtain higher prices. These experiences enhanced the self-confidence of the cooperative members. The results were obvious and impressive: they received the high price of 500 quetzales (then equivalent to $500 U.S.) per hundredweight for their cardamon. The cooperatives also upheld their rights against oil companies:

In 1980 the Petromaya, an American company, began explorations in cooperative lands, destroying cultivated fields. It threatened the peasants with the army. By then we were well organized and began a claims struggle. It was the first of this type. The demand was that the oil company pay for the damage. What happened then was the lands appeared in the name of the oil company. A suit was filed against the oil company, in the name of the peasants. The oil company was made to pay for the destroyed fields, for five years of production. There were threats.

Life revolved around the cooperatives. Officials were elected for two-year periods, and certain commissions, such as education and commerce, were set up. Family disputes or community problems were brought before the cooperative for resolution. In one case, for example, a man became drunk, beat his wife, and injured a neighbor's horse with a machete. At a special meeting, the wife spoke first, explaining the problem; then the owner of the horse spoke. Finally the accused had his chance to talk. The officials read the cooperative's rules and recommended a sanction. This was discussed and finally accepted by all, including the wrongdoer.

In another case, the cooperative members believed that one of the teachers was remiss in his duties. The education commission took up the case after warning the teacher several times. A meeting was called, and a petition was filed with the ministry of education to dismiss the teacher.

Violence Comes to La Esperanza

The cooperatives in the area believed themselves to be in control of their own social and economic well-being, but the military began to break down that control as early as 1976. The military claims to have gone into the area in 1975 to combat the EGP, which had its first military action in that year. The army's penetration marked the first stage of military repression, consisting of the selective assassinations of community leaders in Ixcán. The first person killed in La Esperanza was Rosa Aguayo, an impressive and dedicated schoolteacher, the director of the grade school. Rosa originally from Guatemala City, belonged to a Christian youth group and had come to the remote site for a visit. Inspired by what she saw, she had asked permission to stay permanently. Soon she was not only teaching in La Esperanza but organizing adult educational programs in other cooperatives. Father Lionel recalls:

Rosa was a committed person. This commitment with the adults made her suspect. The army began to accuse these adults of being *guerrilleros* or of helping the subversives. What the army would do in those days was to look for people with leadership qualities, those that were responsible for educational programs in particular, and it was for that reason that Rosa became a target and was killed.

Rosa was murdered on January 11, 1976, at the age of twenty-seven. She was the first of the nine community leaders, who resided together "as a family of friends," to be killed; only Lionel survived. The community leaders who were killed included the schoolteachers, the health promotores, and the two Quiché Indians who had been sent to the University of Wisconsin to learn about cooperatives and to study English. According to Lionel, "The eight were killed over a period of five years, beginning with Rosa in 1976, and the last to be killed was Mario de León, the health promoter in 1981." Lionel was captured by the army in 1975 at the Santiago Ixcán airstrip. He was questioned, accused of being a Communist, and threatened. At that point he and an American Maryknoll priest, Padre Jorge, who was also helping set up cooperatives in the Ixcán, decided that they should leave. Neither wanted to go because they were very attached to the colonists, and they were also concerned about whether the cooperatives could continue functioning without their presence. Lionel said:

In a paternalistic way we thought that if we left the cooperatives would not continue. That they wouldn't progress. That it was necessary for us to be there. Because of those paternalistic ideas we did not want to leave. But finally sometime between August and September [1976] we decided that we would leave. Padre Jorge said he had too much work yet, so he couldn't leave until December. I left for Nicaragua in September, and Padre Jorge expected to leave in December. He was killed by the army on November 20th.

A further blow to the La Esperanza cooperative came with the assassination in Santa Cruz del Quiché of Francisco Piedra, of La Estancia. He was the crucial link between the colony and the highlands. Working for the cooperative in Santa Cruz del Quiché, he took part in the flights that brought in goods, took out the products, and, when necessary, evacuated the sick. He was also needed to maintain radio communication. With Francisco's death in 1980 the cooperative's umbilical cord was cut, and thereafter it was largely on its own.

The guerrilla forces grew in number of combatants and rapidly extended its civilian base of support. By 1981, 260,000 people were supporting the guerrilla organizations which, according to some estimates, operated in nineteen of the twenty-two departments. The EGP, the largest of the organizations, had expanded throughout the highlands, particularly the Ixil area, Santa Cruz del Quiché, Chimaltenango, Alta Verapaz, and Huehuetenango. It regularly held public meetings in the Ixcán villages. The Mexican weekly *Por Esto* reported the presence of the EGP in La Esperanza in 1981. It described the guerrilla unit as being made up almost totally of Indians of different ethnic groups. The final showdown between the people of La Esperanza and the military came in February 1982. For the first time the army began massacring and burning entire villages, and one of the first was La Esperanza. The people of La Esperanza were apprehensive, waiting to see what would happen. At 4:00 on the afternoon of February 13 they heard the first shots on the trail, about two miles from the village. Soon bombs and grenades exploded. Bullets whistled through the village. Everyone fled into the jungle. At 6:00 P.M. the army entered the village, marking the end of the original community.

The village was deserted when the troops arrived. What they found were silent huts, thousands of domesticated animals, a church, a social center, a large cooperative building packed with merchandise, machinery, tools, 12,000 quetzales in the safe, a building with an electric generator, a small tractor, motors for the river launches, the band radio, and many other items of value. The army spent the night in the village while the villagers hid in the forest nearby. For the next five days the soldiers went from house to house and building to building, taking everthing they wished, exactly as a conquering army would do. There was much to loot in the village—an accumulation of material goods and savings won with eleven years of hard labor. The *parcelarios* could hear their cattle being slaughtered with gunfire as the soldiers feasted each day.

Finally, on February 18, the army finished its looting and began setting fire to the village. The *parcelarios* could see the flames. It took three days to burn everything: the dwellings, schools, clinic, cooperative, priests' house, church. The entire village was reduced to ashes.

That was the beginning of the displacement. For the colonists, much of what followed was chaos. Families became separated; in one family the father and a daughter headed in one direction while the mother and the three other children went in another. In another family, the wife fled one way, and the husband with their two children another. Four years later brothers and sisters, parents and children still do not know each others' fate. They are convinced, however, that if they had not fled they would all be dead. In fact, a soldier later told them that they would have been burned along with their village, as the army had done in other places, if they had not escaped.

Life in the forest was difficult. The people went hungry, got sick, and were emotionally devastated; some were caught by the army and killed. No one knows the exact number of people from La Esperanza who were murdered or died. One former colonist recalled that about thirty people were killed, but he knew nothing of the fate of many with whom he had lost contact—more than two-thirds of the village ended up as refugees in Mexico or remained in the forest. When the amnesty was announced in 1982, about thirty La Esperanza families (including seven widows) decided that they could no longer hide in the jungle because their children were becoming increasingly ill. Constantly fearful of encountering the army, they reluctantly took the risk of turning themselves in. They were taken to the military base in Playa Grande and remained in the hands of the military for a year. During that time at least nine of them were severely tortured during interrogations, and some of them were reportedly killed. After a year the military told them to return to their village. These are the *antiguos* ("old ones"), as they refer to themselves, differentiated from the *nuevos,* or "new ones," who were later brought to La Esperanza by the army.

Most of the *parcelarios,* however, did not turn themselves in to the military. They decided to hold out in the jungle, surviving for a year under precarious conditions. José, a refugee leader from La Esperanza, now living in Quintana Roo, says:

After a year it became clear that the army was not going to leave and our food sources became scarcer; life got more difficult in the jungle. We were always moving. At one point we decided to head toward Mexico and cross the border. That was how some of us arrived in Chajul [a large camp with more than 3,000 refugees in the Lacandón forest] near the Mexican border, and from there we were forced to go to Campeche and Quintana Roo.

I had gone to the Lacandón forest for the first time in November 1982. In August 1984, at the height of the tensions over relocation, I was part of the first human rights delegation allowed to observe the relocation process and talk to the refugees who were refusing to move. Many refugees had crossed the Lacantún River and fled rather than be relocated. At that time, the Mexican military completely burned the Puerto Rico camp, which had housed more than 5,000 refugees. In Chajul, just north up the Lacantún River, I spoke with José who, along with 1,500 other refugees, was resisting the move. They had a large, well-kept camp. They were close to La Esperanza and did not want to move to some distant place. A year later, in 1985, I found José once again, this time facing a new difficult life in a camp in Quintana Roo, far to the east in Mexico.

In addition to those who turned themselves in to the Guatemalan army and those who became refugees in Mexico, a third group remained in the jungle. Today they form part of what some Guatemalans refer to as the "population in resistance."

La Esperanza Today

La Esperanza today is part of Ixcán, a newly created municipality containing 1,174 square kilometers of territory, with 116 villages and about 35,000 inhabitants. I was told in Playa Grande that only 3,238 people from the municipality voted in the 1985 presidential elections; the people of many other communities in Ixcán did not register to vote and thus did not cast ballots.

The *parcelarios* who had turned themselves in to the army were taken back to the site of La Esperanza in early 1983. The military set up an outpost with 60 or 70 soldiers who initially resided there but now check in only intermittently. One elderly man recalled his feelings as he entered the destroyed colony: "There was nothing, nothing. It was totally burned. It looked like an ashtray. To tell the truth one could not hold back the tears." The old man stopped, reflected for a few minutes, and then added: "It took eleven years to build and just three days to destroy." He paused again and then in a positive tone said: "But here we are. We escaped death."

The army immediately organized the civil defense patrol, gave the members obsolete weapons, and had them build lookout posts and moats. Today La Esperanza has 108 patrol members, organized into nine squads of 12 each. Every eight days each man takes a twenty-four-hour shift. If he cannot take his assigned shift, he must pay 6 quetzales for a replacement.

Throughout the Ixcán area there is a general sense of frustration with the civil patrol, even among people who do not serve in it and who are close to the miltary. It is perceived as a great nuisance and waste of time. At one checkpoint near an impassable muddy, hole-filled road, there is a log gate blocking passage. The gate is raised once the patrol determines that the vehicle and passengers can proceed. I asked the driver of our four-wheel drive vehicle, a ladino from eastern Guatemala, the reason for blocking passage in this isolated area. He laughed and said: "That's what we mean about the absurdity of the civil patrols. What do they think, that the subversives have cars, and that they will enter this village through the main road?" He then blamed the Indians for being "too stupid" and used their continued participation in the civil patrols as an example. He said it gave them a sense of power. He resented the fact that he had to respond to even the simple, perfunctory, and polite question about where he was going, particularly given the remoteness of the area. There was only one place he could possibly be going. There are no exits off the road, and one has to come back the same way. With a very bored expression and in a low tone, he mentioned the next village, pointing straight ahead with his finger. Quite often the civil patrols just wait until one approaches and then raise the gate without bothering to ask questions.

Another ladino said: "This doesn't make sense, the military is just making the people waste their time. For whom are they waiting? Waiting for nobody [Esperando a nadie]," he answered his own question, laughing. The civil patrols cannot become totally lax about their duties, however, for one never knows when the system will be tested by the army; e.g., agents (*orejas*) might visit the area to see whether the patrols are doing their duty.

In accordance with the army's rural strategic plans, the village is laid out for maximum military control. Rather than rebuild their homes on the old lots, the colonists must live concentrated in one small area, one home next to the other, in the former civic center. The army said that this layout was designed to protect the villagers from the subversives. But the settlers complain: "We want to go back to our lots. We were better off in our lots. We are now crowded; we can't raise animals. But at the military base they got upset when we asked if we could return to our lots. They threatened us and warned us not to ask again."

During 1983 the army imported people from many different parts of the country, until there were 116 families again working the 116 land parcels. Four languages are now spoken at La Esperanza. The new arrangements were made without consultation with the original inhabitants. New families (the *nuevos*) were given the land of *parcelarios* who had been killed or those who had become refugees in Mexico. One *antiguo* commented, "We would like the refugees in Mexico to come back so we can be a community again."

Ricardo, an *antiguo* who is a ladino, fled in 1981 when he was threatened by the guerrillas, making it as far away as Washington, D.C. He returned upon receiving word that the situation was calm. Claiming to have a friend who is a colonel, he says that he was brought back in a helicopter. He states that everyone coming back is checked very thoroughly, and he explains the strategic importance of the new layout of the colony:

> If we went back to the lots, it would be better; here we are mounted one on top of the other. We can't raise animals. But, in the lots, how can one see who enters a house and who leaves? How does one know then what's going on?

People are guarded in what they say to one another. Even Ricardo, who obviously has nothing to fear from the military, never uses the word "guerrilla." In a long interview I had with him, even though he was very outspoken and articulate, he was vague about why he had left, simply saying, "I was threatened [Estaba amenazado]. Some people gave me the 'flash,' so I escaped." When asked who was threatening him, he answered, "The others because I didn't want to collaborate." I asked him to elaborate: "I used to go out of the village a lot, so they became suspicious . . . that I might be a spy. . . . they would say a spy for the army." Later on, when discussing the future and particularly the colonists' return to their lots, he suggested that much depends on whether the "negative forces" return. Ricardo is not very optimistic. He thinks often about Mexico and the United States. He feels that he is stuck now and complains:

> We have nowhere to turn [No tenemos para donde agarrar]. We are very demoralized. We lost everything. We came back with our arms crossed; we

had nothing. The army offered roofing but hasn't given us any. The economic
situation is terrible. Everything is going up. The prices of necessities have gone
up three times. For example, a grinder that in '82 was 20 quetzales is now 60
or 80 quetzales. Sugar is the only thing that has not gone up. Yet cardamom
is only 75 or 80 quetzales per hundredweight.

Newspapers in Guatemala City have carried a series of articles with
shocking photographs of severely malnourished children in Ixcán. The
new priest in nearby Cantabal told me there are thousands of severely
malnourished children in his parish as well as thousands of orphans.
While the newspapers carry front-page stories about the human tragedy in Ixcán, the government hails its development poles. Licenciado
Ramón Zelada Carrillo, a government public relations spokesman,
says that five thousand families are being benefited in the development
poles. "These poles constitute areas that give better possibilities for
peasant families. They get housing, technology, electricity, potable water, and other resources needed for subsistence" (*Prensa Libre*, December 12, 1985). The *parcelarios* of La Esperanza would recognize the
list above as enumerating those things that they do *not* have. In fact,
many of these items they had acquired as a result of their own efforts,
but they had been destroyed or plundered by the military.

So life goes on with not a little difficulty and despair. One La Esperanza man stated: "We are screwed [*fregados*]. Before, we could make
decisions. Every Monday we had meetings. The whole community
would get together because we were a cooperative and used to discuss
things." Two major changes have taken place, one economic and one
political. First, individuals are using their own resources rather than
pulling together the resources of the community. Given the scarcity of
economic resources, this individual approach clearly limits the potential for economic betterment. Each *parcelario* is on his own. Second,
political decisions are severely limited by military-imposed constraints.

Our conversation turned to the election of Vinicio Cerezo that had
been held just two days before. A number of the men expressed hope
that Cerezo would be able to change things, that the military would
let him bring change. "We can't go on like this, with this dictatorship,
we could not make it another five years. Let's not even think about it.
We have nowhere to go. If it doesn't work now with the new government, then I don't know what we will do. It's the last hope we have."
Another stated, "They could easily turn the tortillas [Nada les cuesta
darle vuelta a la tortilla]" on Cerezo, meaning there could be a coup.

Given the economic situation, the geographic and political isolation, the composition of the village, the fear and distrust, the insecurity, and the total dependence on the army and government agencies, it is difficult for people in these circumstances to alter their condition. They have extraordinary confidence in their abilities since, with hardly any outside help, they had built the community from scratch. But the objective conditions in which they could put their skills and abilities into practice are not present. For that to happen, more than elections are needed. The elections did not change anything in the village or the village's relation to the power structure. While a civilian in the national palace in Guatemala City might have an immediate impact, particularly in the international arena, in the rural areas his presence might hardly be felt. Many of the same individuals who were responsible for past atrocities remain in command and are supposedly the new guarantors of democratic rights. The issue is not one of justice alone but also that an unpunished and uncontrollable military continues to instill fear. Nowhere is this felt more deeply than in villages such as La Esperanza. The survivors cannot pretend that nothing has happened, cannot just forget and forgive. It is not a matter of vengeance: either it was right, and they deserved what was done to them because they were guilty, or it was wrong, and the guilty should be punished. They need to know unequivocally why they were so punished before they can proceed. Unlike other holocausts, neither the nation nor the world has rendered judgment on the violence unleashed against the Guatemalan Indians.

The La Esperanza *parcelarios* dread the continued domination by the military. They are still forced to labor for the military base. Mario, from a nearby colony, explained:

A note came yesterday from the [military] zone stating that everyone must present themselves for work—half of them today, the other half tomorrow. The *jefes* [bosses] are a bit mean; they have a blacklist of whoever doesn't go. We are punished and threatened. So, even if one doesn't feel like going, one is obliged to go.

A group of men listening agreed with what Mario said. They get no pay for this work; in fact, they all laughed at the very question. They joked that it was done on the basis of "custom" (*costumbre*):

The worst is that after you do forced labor then you still have to do your patrol shift the next day. So, you lose a day working for them, then you lose a day on your shift. If they call you again, you have to go, because if you don't show interest, they say you are against them.

When asked why the soldiers at the base do not do the work themselves, one man responded: "It's because they have become accustomed to bothering the civilian population. They are already accustomed to do what they want with the civilian population." Mario then
told about a man from a port city who had recently settled in a colony
close to the Mexican border:

> He told us, and he is right, that this is slavery. The soldiers do nothing. They
> tell you that they saw some [subversive] men somewhere, so you have to go
> look for them, and if you don't do as you are told, they punish you. The
> soldiers do nothing. If there is any trouble, they say the civil patrols should go
> and check it out.

The civil patrols are often ordered on long military sweeps with the
soldiers. They walk in line, one soldier followed by one civilian and
then another soldier. This formation is meant to provide added protection for the soldiers against potential guerrilla ambushes.

During a conversation about the Mutual Support Group (GAM)
and its activities in Guatemala City on behalf of disappeared relatives,
Claudio, a ladino *parcelario,* made the following comment:

> The people in the capital can demand to know the whereabouts of their
> disappeared relatives, but here, who is going to lay claim to the people from
> Trinitaria, Santo Tomás, El Quetzal, and all the other villages that were mas-
> sacred? Who is going to raise his voice? Those souls don't count. Those souls
> were swallowed by the earth. And the military, they are proud of what they
> have done.

La Esperanza has settled into what superficially appears to be a normal routine. The day starts early and ends early. People begin their
daily activities before 6:00 A.M., when the sun's rays have not yet illu-
minated the clearing in the forest. Barefoot women wearing the dress
styles of Joyabaj, Cobán, and other highland *municipios* walk toward
the center of the village carrying on their heads plastic pans full of
soaked corn kernels to be ground. The sound of the only motor in the
village announces the beginning of the day. The women stand silently
in line waiting their turn to have their corn ground. The fog is still low
as it hangs over the village, interwoven with the huts and tall jungle
trees. Inside the huts fires are made on the ground, and smoke filters
out through the thatched roofs; the flag is raised. Soon one hears the
rapid rhythmic sound of tortilla patting. The sun finally appears over
the surrounding forest. The men move out to their milpas and cardamom fields. The patrols sit in the lookout posts and hang around the

center of the village. The women, accompanied by the children, cook, wash the dishes and clothes in the stream, husk and thrash the corn, and care for the infants. Later in the afternoon the children play, running up and down slopes, their laughter and chatter being heard everywhere. The day ends as the sun begins to fade. The patrols congregate for a civil act. The flag is lowered, folded, and put away until dawn. By now it is dark. Here and there a faint candle may be seen in a hut, and a few voices or a baby's cry breaks the silence. Late into the dark night patrols converse in low voices. Finally, the roosters sing, and another day will soon begin.

The La Esperanza people live side by side but not as a community. They distinguish between the *antiguos* and the *nuevos*. The *antiguos* share a long highland background, when they were part of the cooperatives and belonged to other village organizations. They followed the path to Ixcán together, built the community, and shared both the earlier successes and the later repressions. The *nuevos* did not share in the slow development of a philosophy and tradition, the risks and joys of starting a new community, of depending on one another for survival. As a result, they feel like outsiders. The newcomers also bear the special burden of heavy debts which the agricultural bank (BANDESA) forced on them. Little consideration was given to social planning for the village, and there has been an almost haphazard mingling of people, similar to what happens in urban centers. Rural communities need more common ground and cooperation to function well. The more these face-to-face societies are able to share experiences and visions, the more successful they will be as communities. That was certainly true before, and now they complain that "there is no cooperation, there is no trust among us. We don't know each other now [No nos conocemos ahora]."

Why did the military place different Indian groups together? In La Esperanza efficiency in administering social services was obviously not the reason since no services are provided, not even a road. A more likely explanation is social dispersion to prevent the villagers from acting in a strong, unified way. The future of this community depends not on the will of the *parcelarios* (*antiguos, nuevos,* or repatriated refugees) but rather on the wider politics of the country. The *parcelarios* cannot independently pursue initiatives, develop networks, or establish contacts with outside communities or organizations of their own choosing. It is not even clear to them just what the army will or will not allow. It is clear, however, that the army does *not* approve of the old cooperatives and peasant organizations which the *parcelarios* know give positive results. The thing that is clear above all else, though, is that they should not antagonize the army. The army makes its rounds, coming to the village about once a month with about sixty soldiers, who stay for a day or two. In addition, the village's military commissioner and patrol chiefs must inform the military base in Playa Grande of developments in and around the village. As one *parcelario* put it: "We cannot complain. Where? To whom? The most we can do is plead [*suplicar*]. We are at the mercy of the army. There are no other authorities."

What is to happen to the former owners of this land who are now refugees in Mexico? La Esperanza is not a new land settlement; these lands have claimants. The army and now the civilian government maintain that they want the refugees back, yet every effort has been made to deny the refugees their land and thereby prevent the unification of this formerly strong community. Even should the refugees return, there is no guarantee that they could get back their lands. According to INTA, the agrarian reform agency, land that is abandoned for more than one year automatically becomes property of the government. Refugees returning from Mexico to reclaim their property will find that they have no legal right to do so and will be forced to resettle elsewhere.

Indian Transformation

It is not surprising that in Ixcán the EGP has grown so rapidly, attracting a predominantly Indian cadre and base of support. The people in Ixcán wanted to be set free from the heavy "burden of injustice," and many could identify with a struggle to bring about revolutionary change in society. In the beginning the isolation of the jungle provided the EGP with an important advantage in developing its military and political forces in a relatively secure area. They also had the advantage of knowing the terrain better than the army. Over time, the army learned to overcome these handicaps and displayed a willingness to use heretofore unimagined brutal methods of counterinsurgency.

In analyzing the events in La Esperanza, two questions might be asked: What caused the colony's collapse? What are the prospects for its future? The answer to the first question seems clear enough. There

is no disagreement among the colonists about who burned their village, who did the torturing and killings. They understand now that
they had underestimated the army's capacity to use brutal force.

The second question is more difficult to answer. The lives of these
people have been irreversibly changed. The Indians will neither totally
lose their traditional culture nor withdraw completely to isolated communities. Amid the horror, the fear, the despair, and the sadness, there
remain alive the inner strength and affirmation of a generation of Indians who have participated in grass-roots political movements. That
experience cannot be erased. Nor can the military erase the experiences that broke the ideological bonds which had dominated the Indians for centuries. Daniel, an Indian refugee in Mexico, states:

> The head of a civil patrol (often considered an army collaborator) might
> follow the army's orders step by step, but he does not feel he is the Indian of
> ten years ago. No, now he feels he is a transformed Indian, an Indian that
> knows how to express himself, who understands why he is poor, who is in-
> volved in the whole political life of the nation.

In response to the accusation that "Indians don't talk this way" and
that he was perhaps brainwashed by the revolutionary organizations,
Daniel replies: "That's not so. Poverty brainwashed us. Reality and
practical experience in the struggle made us think differently." He goes
on to describe the differences in thinking between his and his parents'
generations:

> What we see is the emergence of youth, in 1965 or 1966, a youth who is
> totally different, a youth who thinks differently, who cares for his people, a
> youth who thinks it's worth combating discrimination, who no longer accepts
> discrimination. Many felt that exploitation did not hurt as much [no pesaba
> tanto] as discrimination. The relation to the city makes one confront discrimi-
> nation much more. This youth became a key support base for the CUC and
> later for the revolutionary organizations. We were born with another vision.
> We saw the possibility of struggle for our rights.

Daniel evaluated the revolutionary organizations within the context
of the Indians' own experiences: "CUC (the national peasant union)
presented alternatives, concrete and clear ones people could relate to.
That explains why the CUC grew so fast." He gives mixed marks to
the revolutionary organizations, recognizing that many mistakes were
made. But he credits them for "the great strides they made possible"
for the Indians, giving them a sense of strength, a vision of a better
society, and "breaking the ideological domination of the Indian and of

his inferiority." He is very positive about the Indian ethnic movements, and considers the "Indian question" one of the most important
issues in Guatemala today. He feels that for the Indians to maintain
their culture there must be an end to exploitation:

Poverty, the high cost of living, exploitation, are what little by little erode
our culture. Those who have been in power in Guatemala since the Spanish
conquest have never appreciated or valued the richness of the Indian cultures.
Instead they show contempt, because that's the only way they can subject us
to exploitation and oppression. In order to dominate a people they have to
say, "That culture is not worth anything, it is inferior." We have to struggle to
end the discrimination we have suffered.

Thus we see that Indians, as a result of consciousness raising in the
past decade, combined with their suffering, have experienced a dramatic awakening. Like Indians throughout Guatemala, the La Esperanza Indians are expressing pride in their culture and are analyzing
their role in Guatemalan society. Now, when Indians come in contact
with other Indians, regardless of language, in the words of a Mam
Indian, "we feel more human warmth, we feel closer, more fraternal."
This broad sense of community is being maintained and enhanced despite the efforts by conservative political forces which violently seek
to deny small-scale fraternity to communities such as La Esperanza.

CHAPTER 4

Evangelicals, Guerrillas, and the Army: The Ixil Triangle Under Ríos Montt

By David Stoll

Guatemalans are the chosen people of the New Testament.
We are the New Israelites of Central America.

—Efraín Ríos Montt, quoted in Wall Street Journal, December 7, 1982

The Evangelicals' prayers for Brother Efraín were not answered. After a sixteen-month march toward the New Jerusalem, the first born-again dictator in history was shunted aside by the same army which had placed him in power. But while General Efraín Ríos Montt occupied the presidential palace in Guatemala, he drew the world's attention to the Protestant evangelical awakening in Central America. According to church growth projections, in 1981 that movement claimed 21 percent of the Guatemalan population, probably a majority of the country's active churchgoers. If 10 percent–plus annual growth rates continue into the 1990s, Guatemala could be the first country in Latin America with a Protestant majority.

Ríos Montt and his supporters hoped to turn this religious movement into a new political order. Traditionally, Protestants have ascribed violence and backwardness in Latin America to Latin Catholic culture, not to foreign dependency or the class structure. What Latin America has lacked, they conclude, is a "biblical" foundation. If poverty and civil strife are fundamentally moral problems, it follows that only a moral reformation can solve them. It was on this premise that, describing himself as God's chosen representative, Ríos Montt announced that he would moralize national life from the top down. To the astonishment of the world, which continued to receive horrifying

reports of the Guatemalan army's behavior, that institution's new com-
mander-in-chief made moral renovation his favorite topic.

Ríos Montt's urgency stemmed from the fulfillment of long-held
fears. As long ago as 1936, a U.S. missionary wrote a novel in which
a Russian Bolshevik leads an uprising of Guatemala's Maya Indians,
only to be foiled by a Maya evangelist wielding God's word. Under
the lawless praetorian regime which preceded Ríos Montt's, Indians
throughout the western Guatemalan highlands joined Marxist guerrilla movements. This revolutionary threat was materializing, moreover, in what the new dictator and his brethren regarded as a particularly insidious guise: a radical interpretation of their own Christian
faith.

We can therefore imagine the hymns of praise which greeted a true
soldier of God. The confrontation between North American fundamentalism and liberation theology made Central America, in the
words of an evangelical missionary, "one of the strategic battlefields in
the spiritual warfare over the allegiance and eternal destiny of the
world's inhabitants." An elder of Ríos Montt's Word church stated
that the fundamentalist Gospel was a "stabilizing factor." It would
transform Guatemala into a "spiritual stronghold," prevent its rich oil
and titanium reserves from falling into Marxist hands, and become a
buffer between the United States and Communist advance. "After
Guatemala," warned Gospel Outreach, Word's budding parent church
in the United States, "only Mexico remains!" But that was not all. For
a Latin America which these ideologues considered to be lost in the
darkness of folk Catholic idolatry, and now stalked by Communist
wolves in the sheep's clothing of liberation theology, Guatemala was
to become a beacon of light. It would serve as a model of biblical
righteousness for other countries threatened by the same satanic
forces: it was to become a theological "New Israel" of the Americas.

This geopolitical faith seemed to confirm the worst fears of the left.
When revolutionaries began singing the praises of Christian consciousness raising and liberation theology, the Guatemalan army responded by crushing church activists and promoting a more amenable
form of worship. Catholic Indians were said to be converting to Protestantism en masse to save their lives. Here was a true alternative,
television evangelist Pat Robertson declared, "between the oppression
of corrupt oligarchies and the tyranny of Russian-backed Communist
totalitarianism." Encouraged by men like Robertson, North American

evangelicals were said to be pledging millions of dollars for Ríos Montt's pacification program.

Relief efforts for the stricken Indians were coordinated by Gospel Outreach, to whose Guatemalan branch, the Word church, Ríos Montt belonged. Helped by several members of the Summer Institute of Linguistics, Word started a much-publicized program in the western highlands. Soon its pronouncements were flouting the findings of human rights organizations, in a campaign to justify Ríos Montt's "bullets and beans" policy of concentrating Indians into resettlement villages and conscripting Indian men into army-supervised civil patrols.

Gospel Outreach

For spiritual guidance Efraín Ríos Montt looked to the elders of the Word church. And for their own spiritual direction, Word's young North American and Guatemalan elders looked to Eureka, California. Situated north of San Francisco along the coast, the town is named for the "Eureka!" (Greek for "I have found it,") which fortunate prospectors shouted during the California gold rush. Now that the logging boom which made Eureka is dead, the area's leading industry is the cultivation of marijuana, introduced by hippies from San Francisco. But early in the 1970s, some of these flower children rediscovered the traditional opiate of the people. A decade later, they were the spiritual advisers of a military dictatorship.

The leader of the new movement in Eureka was a generation older than his followers: alcohol, not hallucinogens, had brought the portly, avuncular Reverend Jim Durkin to ruin. But the same Lord had saved both him and his followers, and now this successful real estate broker and Assemblies of God lay preacher told the long-haired penitents that they had been put on earth to change history. They would evangelize the world.

The new movement acquired the Lighthouse Ranch commune, a nearby social experiment which also was evolving from drugs to Christianity. There Durkin put his followers on a strict regimen. Haircuts were only the beginning. Moral discipline was so severe that members of the opposite sex reputedly could not be alone in the same room together. Originally, the ranch had tried to pattern itself after the primitive communists of the first-century church. Durkin decided to teach his followers how to run a business, and support their ministry too, by starting commercial enterprises in which members could earn their room and board at the ranch. In exchange for a multiple tithe of the profits, businesses were turned over to members to operate as their own. If man is made in the image of God, then the Lord began to look like the confident young graduate of a business school.

Durkin's followers had once been supreme relativists. Hippies just wanted to do their own thing: anything was O.K. as long as it did not hurt anyone else, everything would be beautiful if you just let it happen. But Durkin told them that this tolerant philosophy had not only worn down their sense of right and wrong but also allowed the devil to take over their lives. Now were they to keep the smallest part of their lives from God, that was where the devil would return and drag them down to hell. If something in their lives was not of the Kingdom of God, then it was of the Kingdom of Darkness—otherwise known as "the world."

The main target of Durkin's moral reformation program was what he called the "I–centered" approach to life. Once his egotistical young followers had been brought face to face with their true worthlessness, he showed them how, with God's help, they could take their own special place in an awe-inspiring millennial drama. In fulfillment of biblical prophecy, these reformed representatives of the "me" generation would have an enormous historical impact. The reason is that the world, as Durkin sees it, is clearly headed for disaster, an awful retribution for the sins of mankind which will end with the Second Coming of Christ and his thousand-year reign on earth. One implication of this view is the group's survivalist tendency. Profoundly pessimistic about the future of what he calls "debt capitalism," Durkin advises followers to prepare for the coming financial crash by staying out of debt, diversifying investments, and storing ample food supplies.

Although this prophet believes that the Lord's return will come in his lifetime, he suspects that it will not occur until God's people have multiplied all over the earth. The mission of his church, therefore, is to serve as a base for evangelism, to send out and support the "elders," now in their late thirties and early forties, who have been trained to start churches elsewhere. Hence the group's name, Gospel Outreach. In 1983, four thousand people were said to be attending its services. There were forty congregations in the United States, most of them on the West Coast, and six abroad, in Europe as well as in Guatemala City; Managua, Nicaragua; and Quito, Ecuador.

Guatemala appeared on Gospel Outreach's horizon following the 1976 earthquake. As the group's volunteers helped rebuild low-income neighborhoods around the capital, they blended in with a larger charismatic movement, drawing in members of the upper classes and then spinning them off into a number of churches. Many of the converts often spoke English, had become infatuated with North American business and consumer culture, but needed something more than the amoral pursuit of profits and pleasure as communism menaced outside the gate. They were grateful for the fellowship and moralism of Gospel Outreach's attractive young North Americans. By early 1982, a well-heeled, enthusiastic congregation of five hundred persons was meeting under a circus tent staked a block from the luxury Camino Real Hotel.

Could the Lord Have Something in Store for Brother Efraín?

When the Word elders found themselves in the middle of a military coup on the morning of March 23, 1982, they were not totally unprepared. They already knew that, thanks to the remarkable correspondence between the East-West conflict and the impending millennial showdown, any outbreak around the world would be a step on the march toward Armageddon. Had not Communist victories invariably destroyed the freedom to preach the Gospel? They were aware that, as a defender of religious liberty, the administration of General Romeo Lucas García (1978–82) left something to be desired. Anxious that church and union organizing was fronting for small but growing guerrilla organizations, Lucas unleashed death squads. Coordinated from an annex of the National Palace, the death squads destroyed the country's political center and pushed thousands of survivors into the guerrilla movements.

Evangelical church leaders were not eager to address the disintegration of the country. Their centennial history of Protestantism in Guatemala, published at the height of the violence in 1982, managed to avoid the subject. Corruption, disrespect for authority, communism, and evil were surely on the increase, these men preached, but their Kingdom was not of this world. The Christian church was apolitical. This line of reasoning did not, of course, prevent certain of them from supporting the official party's 1982 presidential campaign, a sure winner, to judge from the army high command's theft of the previous two elections.

A month before the March 7, 1982, balloting, a conference held in Guatemala City of five hundred pastors honoring the one hundredth anniversary of Protestantism in the country was interrupted by helicopters bearing the official presidential candidate, General Anibal Guevara. Prominent pastors in the general's campaign had arranged the appearance, promising free chalk and notebooks to everyone who attended. To the hallelujahs of evangelical supporters, the general shouted, "Praise the Lord!" and, observing standard delicacy before men of God, asked for prayer that the Lord's chosen man would win the election. Guevara's wife mentioned that their daughter-in-law had become an evangelical and, while they themselves had not taken the big step, they were certainly considering it. That noon, the cafeteria buzzed with angry talk about selling one's birthright for a mess of pottage. The church was supposed to be above politics. Guerrillas erupted to distribute pamphlets signed by the Vicente Menchú Revolutionary Christians.

Over at the Word church, meanwhile, the elders were keeping an eye on the retired general in their midst, a man who had run for president eight years before and probably won. Campaigning as a Christian Democrat and reformer, Efraín Ríos Montt had been far ahead on election night 1974 when suddenly television screens across the nation went dead. Broadcasting did not resume until the next morning, by which time the official candidate was the winner by a large margin. Once again, the army clique ruling the country had imposed its own candidate. Four years later, when Ríos Montt began showing up at their religious functions, the Word elders wondered why a big-league politician was coming around to them. He proved himself, they now relate, by cleaning out toilets.

Fortunately, the Word church's 1983 biography of Ríos provides a revealing account of his frustrations and dreams. Conversion to Protestantism, it turns out, grew out of his lifelong, frustrated ambition for the highest office in the land. That his fellow army officers had cheated him out of the presidency, the Word elders discovered, was the deepest wound of his life. When Ríos came home from exile in 1977, it was in the vain hope of winning a second nomination from the Christian Democrats for the next year's election. It was only after this second, seemingly terminal disappointment that the general found his way to the Word church. God had a very special purpose in store for him, elders told Efraín. Charismatic religion became a balm for his wounds, transfigured his ambitions, and offered to realize them in the Lord's way.

Still, the Word elders were of two minds on the privilege of ministering to a major political figure. Yes, he had made a "covenant" with them as a brother in Christ and thus had an important relation of trust among Word members. Yet as the political parties settled on their candidates for the March 1982 national election, the elders were not pleased to pick up their newspapers and read that Brother Efraín was considering a third run for the presidency. Hoping to keep him and their church out of the race, the elders made Efraín's never-quenched presidential ambitions the subject of three days of prayer and fasting, during which various prophecies indicated that running in these elections was not of the Lord. Efraín's time was yet to come. Although they would support him if he chose to run, the Lord was telling them that "another door" would be opened for him. But it was only the collapse of the party coalition that offered him the candidacy—not their three days of advice and prophecy—which settled the matter against running.

When young army officers called Ríos to the national palace on the morning of the takeover, he was at his job administering Word's day school. He seemed to be taken aback. But with his sudden appearance on television that night in battle fatigues, it occurred to more than one Word elder that their brother in Christ had broken covenant with them by planning the coup. The planners had struck on the eighth anniversary of the day that Ríos went into exile in Spain. If certain conspirators are to be believed, Ríos took Word's prophecies so seriously that he helped plan the revolt which brought him to power. In view of the early-1982 ruling-class consensus that the Lucas regime had to go, not to mention Ríos's prominence as a defrauded president-elect eight years before, it would be little short of miraculous for him not to have been involved in some way. Ríos is said to have dealt with both of the two groups who planned the March 23 coup.

The first group was the National Liberation Movement (MLN), placed in power by the U.S. Central Intelligence Agency (CIA) in 1954 and known as "the party of conspiracy" for its reliance on strong-arm tactics, including death squads. Ríos Montt was no MLN enthusiast: its 1982 presidential candidate, Mario Sandoval Alarcón, had supported the theft of Ríos's presidency eight years before. But Ríos's wife, Teresa, was from an important military family, the Sosa Avilas, enmeshed with the party, and worked in Sandoval's MLN campaign. Ríos himself allegedly organized an MLN paramilitary group for the 1982 election.

The source of this last claim is Danilo Roca, an MLN ally at the time. According to Roca, MLN agents inside the government had confirmed that the ruling party was planning to steal the March 7 election. To protest the fraud, according to Roca, the MLN planned to start riots in the capital which would force sympathetic army officers to intervene against the corrupt high command. One of Roca's associates, who asked not to be quoted by name, provided me with a detailed account of nightly planning sessions chaired by Ríos in his home during the month preceding the election. According to the source, at those meetings Ríos said that he was not going to let happen to Mario (Sandoval Alarcón, the MLN candidate) what had happened to him in 1974. The last time he had not been prepared, Ríos is supposed to have said, but this time they would be ready. He also stressed that the unit's provocateurs were under no circumstance to confront the army, which was being brought into the plan by another route. The night of the election, according to Roca and his associate, Ríos aborted the plan.

The second group plotting the March 23 coup was made up of young army officers. Some of them were MLN supporters, others not, but all were disenchanted with a corrupt high command that was losing the country at their expense. According to one of the young officers, from the start of their plan, Ríos had been chosen to head the new junta, owing to his upstanding reputation and because he had been elected president in 1974. But Ríos had not been informed beforehand, the young officer insisted, because if word of the choice had leaked, he would have been killed.

The night of the coup, the MLN was flabbergasted to hear Ríos invoke God to denounce not just the deposed Lucas regime but civilian politicians, including them. It was the Lord who had put him where he was, Ríos declared, closing ranks with fellow army officers and leaving the MLN in the street.

It might seem implausible that a general could end up leading a coup which he had not even planned. But for the Word elders and other evangelicals, Ríos Montt's legitimacy hinged on the claim that he had not taken part in the conspiracy. To them, the most important question was the purity of his motives. Only if his arrival in the palace had been undefiled by the dirty world of politics, they felt, could it be of the Lord. Efraín insisted that he had nothing to do with planning the coup, and the Word elders decided to honor their covenant with the man by believing him. The drama of the moment touched their own sense of destiny (some say megalomania). Had not they received a prophecy that they would counsel heads of state? Through nothing but prayer on their part, they concluded, the Lord had placed his servants at the center of the cosmic struggle between good and evil. With two Guatemalan elders at the presidential palace as Ríos Montt's advisers, and with other elders joining weekly prayer sessions with him, the Word church had become, in fulfillment of its own prophecies, a door for Brother Efraín and a leader of nations.

The International Love Lift

As Guatemala's first evangelical president deactivated government death squads in the capital and pushed back the guerrillas in the countryside, a noteworthy date was approaching in November 1982. It was the one hundredth anniversary of the first Protestant mission in Guatemala. Surely, many evangelicals believed, this convergence of the centennial year of their faith, the nation's first Christian leader, and national deliverance was a sign from the Lord. Like the Word church and Ríos Montt himself, they concluded that he was "God's man" to save Guatemala from communism and lead the nation to Christ. For believers who previously had preferred not to discuss politics, a taboo subject suddenly turned into an act of God.

Many evangelical missionaries did not, to be sure, share the thunderstruck vision of the Word church. There were some North Americans who, while rejecting revolutionary violence, decided that Ríos Montt was using their faith to legitimize continued terror. Another, much larger group of missionaries shared Word's fears as well as the hope that Ríos would succeed in stabilizing Guatemala. But, unlike the hallelujah wing of North American evangelism, these more pragmatic, experienced missionaries supported the new army regime because they regarded it as a lesser evil than communism.

Despite their alleged Rasputin-like influence over the new president, the Word elders' only visible function in the new regime was vouching for its integrity. This, to be sure, was no small or unimportant task. Only by whitewashing the bloodstains on the army's record could the new administration ensure the support from Washington, D.C., which it might need to survive. But in the western highlands the army's strategy, despite the announcement of a new era of morality, was producing unprecedented numbers of Indian refugees. Their needs were not being met, and their stories of army barbarism contradicted Ríos's claims to respect human rights.

In public, the Word elders never faltered. As personal friends of the new president, they knew that he could not be ordering such crimes. They admitted that Ríos could not be held responsible for every act committed by an army of twenty thousand soldiers. But now that he had brought the security forces under control, they could not be committing such crimes. The blessings unleashed by the Holy Spirit on March 23 were so powerful that, according to the Word church, they produced a 180-degree turn in the behavior of soldiers and guerrillas alike. Regrettably, not everyone was willing to recognize this new fact. Soon the Word elders were locked in spiritual warfare with what they regarded as two of the most insidious manifestations of secular humanism in the world today.

The first of these was religious liberals. Not all Christians were rallying around the new president, and in the persistent slanders from certain so-called church groups, the Word elders detected the influence of liberation theology—that Marxist, man-centered plan to replace evangelism with social activism and twist the Gospel into a justification for violent revolution. But Ríos's most deadly enemy was the secular liberal media, with their blatant biases and propaganda. Blinded by the night and fog which shroud the vision of unbelieving men, journalists were not reporting the truth as the Word church so clearly perceived it.

Where could Word find fellow Christians to help it fight these lies? A few years before, the western highlands had been populated by missions, agencies, and centers for the development of this or that, usually financed by foreigners. Then the army had identified these efforts as the Trojan horse of subversion. Their local Indian leaders had been placed on death lists and diligently hunted down. Now, shocked benefactors were wondering how to help survivors of the violence without stimulating further bloodshed. Most decided to wait.

But a few, including a local community health promotor, Dr. Carroll Behrhorst, and certain members of the Summer Institute of Linguistics (SIL), did not wait. Eleven of Behrhorst's forty-seven Maya extension agents had died mysteriously under the Lucas García administration, ending their community development program. As for the Summer Institute, it had collaborated in the regime's literacy program. Although the new literacy drive was administered by the national police, who might be less interested in producing new readers than in gathering intelligence, this had been SIL's chance to pursue its policy of serving God by serving the government. While eager to serve authority, most of SIL's Bible translators had been reluctant to waste time thinking about politics; that got in the way of their mission. Yet as threats and violence mounted, the translators were forced to respond. They did so by pulling out, taking their Maya assistants to the capital to finish their New Testament translations as quickly as possible. These groups would not return to the countryside until it was brought under control, which required bringing the army under control. Could the new president provide that guarantee?

To prove that he could, Ríos Montt appointed a board member of the Behrhorst health organization, Harris Whitbeck, to serve as his personal representative in relief work. A former U.S. Marine sergeant and construction contractor who proved to have influence in Washington, D.C., Whitbeck would serve as liason between the military and private relief efforts. With their own direct line to the president, by July 1982 the three groups—the Word church, the Behrhorst organization, and several Summer Insitute translators—organized the Foundation for Aid to the Indian People (FUNDAPI). Behrhorst personnel and Summer Institute translators would serve as field agents, while the Word church would provide staff in the capital and raise funds in the United States. There had been much talk about how North American evangelicals would come to the aid of Ríos Montt; on one occasion, he tossed out the figure of $1 billion. Late in July, he announced that International Love Lift, the relief arm of Gospel Outreach in California, would coordinate relief efforts from the United States. In Guatemala, the new FUNDAPI officers braced themselves for an avalanche of funds.

Providing food, medicine, clothing, shelter, and tools the Word elders anticipated, would not only meet the needs of the refugees but also win their support for the new government and create openings for evangelism. In private, the elders hoped that a Christian presence would restrain the army from crimes which they knew it was still committing. They also hoped to bolster Ríos Montt's credibility in the

United States. Appeals for funds would lend the names of spiritual leaders such as television evangelist Pat Robertson; Bill Bright, of the Campus Crusade for Christ; and Moral Majority founder Jerry Falwell to the cause of the new Christian president.

Soon FUNDAPI was taking visitors to a place where it could show them firsthand "how it really is," in startling contrast to the picture painted by refugees, the press, human rights groups, and revolutionary sources. However brutal the army had been before Ríos Montt, FUNDAPI told visitors, the guerrillas were the ones who had provoked the violence. Why did the army's critics never mention that the guerrillas used unarmed, unwilling civilians as shields against army firepower? The people had been caught in the middle, FUNDAPI maintained, and now they were fleeing to the army for protection. Other refugees were said to be still held captive by the guerrillas, who killed those who tried to escape. There was simply no proof that Ríos Montt had ordered atrocities, FUNDAPI staffers argued. In many cases, they further insisted, supposed army massacres had turned out to be perpetuated by guerrillas who wanted to discredit Ríos Montt and prevent the United States from resuming military aid to Guatemala. To judge from their own experience, they concluded, press and human rights reports were so one-sided as to lose credibility.

The Ixil Triangle

FUNDAPI gave visitors a "true" picture of the war in its main theater, the Ixil Maya country of northern Quiché, a bitterly contested stronghold of the Guerrilla Army of the Poor (EGP). The road into the Ixil Triangle—the Indian municipalities of Nebaj, Cotzal, and Chajul—switchbacks up the wall of the Cuchumatanes range, wraps around a mountain shoulder and disappears into the clouds. As it drops into a green mountain valley, the mud walls and red roofs of Nebaj in the distance seem as remote as Shangri-La. But that is not the case. Early in the century, the three Ixil towns were occupied by ladino merchants who sold the Indians liquor, trapped them into debt, seized their lands, and forced them to work on the coffee plantations. When in the 1930s the Nebaj Indians finally rose up against forced labor and drove the ladinos out of town, government troops shot nine elders and deported five hundred men to the malarial jungles of Petén, where many are said to have died.

Two decades later, in 1955, a new Catholic order took charge of Quiché Department. The Missionaries of the Sacred Heart arrived the year after the Catholic hierarchy supported the CIA's overthrow of the Arbenz regime. They did not seem like revolutionaries; their job was to defend the population from communism as well as from the evangelical missionaries who were beginning to take up residence there. But as educated Spaniards, the priests were shocked by the way ladino bosses treated Indians. Business methods in the Ixil area were backward even by Guatemalan standards; for example, it was customary for ladino merchants to demand Ixil girls as loan collateral.

Implementing Catholic social doctrine, the Spanish priests launched development projects which upset the equilibrium of oppression in the zone. By offering Maya farmers new alliances against their exploiters, they attracted enthusiastic constituencies. New village committees organized cooperatives and initiated other improvements. Indians bought back land taken from them by ladinos and demanded better wages. The first Ixil professionals graduated from teacher-training schools and universities. Encouraged by the Catholic church, many Indians joined the Christian Democratic party.

One turning point in the Ixil area was the election of March 1974, in which the Christian Democrats—and their presidential candidate Efraín Ríos Montt—swept Quiché. The chagrined official party correctly blamed the Catholic church for its defeat. According to a Protestant missionary living in the area, the first death-squad abductions in Nebaj took place soon after. As Ríos Montt stewed in exile in Spain, his defrauded and persecuted Indian followers were forced to look to other outlets for their political energies.

Another pivotal event in the Ixil area was the Guerrilla Army of the Poor's first execution of a tyrannical plantation owner, in June 1975. The EGP had been started by survivors of an earlier, non-Indian insurgency, living in the jungles along the Mexican border. When they chose northern Quiché as the most promising terrain in the country from which to launch a liberation war, among the factors said to have influenced their decision was the strength of Catholic organizations in the area.

To the disgust of more conservative priests, a few of their colleagues apparently were turning church organizations into organizing vehicles for guerrilla warfare even before government reprisals radicalized much of the clergy. Particularly implicated were a group of itinerant

Jesuits, who were promoting Christian consciousness raising as an educational method to train church extension agents, called catechists, and cooperative leaders. According to the Guatemalan Church in Exile, as these men became disillusioned with the results of development schemes, they directed their message "not to solve economic problems through a new technology or financial organization [but] to free the mind from traditional constraints, the most profound being respect for the authorities." It was a message which subverted the law.

As the army began to crack down, the Catholic organizations helped the people fight back. According to Luis Pellecer, a Jesuit EGP collaborator kidnapped and "turned" by Guatemalan security forces in 1981, the catechist movement provided not just a new form of communication between the masses and Catholic clergy but a new common consciousness among Indians divided by ethnic barriers. It became a bridge into the guerrilla movement.

One priest recalls objecting to catechists getting involved with the EGP in 1979. "Are you afraid of the army?" a colleague taunted him. He was, and with good reason. When guerrilla activity confirmed the fears of ladino bosses and their army backers about Indians, the army went on the rampage against the catechist movement, in the belief that it was finding guerrilla leadership there. From 1975 on, as the EGP staged rallies, ambushed soldiers, and assassinated informers, the army responded with wider and wider reprisals against the Ixil Indians. Its agents kidnapped and murdered virtually every kind of Indian leader, including Protestant pastors, and wiped out entire villages. The Guatemalan Church in Exile claims that from 1976 to 1979—that is, before the worst of the violence—more than 350 leaders were kidnapped from the three Ixil municipalities alone. Among the victims were three Sacred Heart missionaries, none of them political activists, who were methodically hunted down by government killers. In 1980 the bishop of Quiché ordered his clergy into exile, and at least two priests of the diocese went over to the guerrillas along with many of their parishioners. By the end of that year, the three SIL teams assigned to the Ixil region had also pulled out.

The army's violence backfired. Instead of suppressing the guerrillas, it multiplied a small band of outsiders into a liberation army, mostly Indians drawn from local communities. By the end of 1980, government atrocities seemed to have alienated the entire Ixil population. Exuberant over the Sandinista victory in Nicaragua, the EGP rushed into the political vacuum and raced headlong across the highlands. By early 1982, guerrilla armies seemed to control all of Quiché and Hue-huetenango departments except for a few garrison towns. They were on the point of cutting the Pan-American Highway. It was not hard to imagine the Indians of the western highlands marching on the capital half a million strong.

But the guerrillas had few weapons to give their followers. Nor did fear of soldiers necessarily mean solid support for the revolution. Un-like smaller, more cautious revolutionary groups, the EGP organized entire communities into its ranks. Its mass organizing strategy de-stroyed the "neutral" middle ground where many Ixil Indians might have preferred to stay. In the Nebaj township of Salquil, government-controlled refugees told me, EGP militants planted revolutionary flags at night. If the flags remained until the army arrived, the entire neigh-borhood would be suspected of supporting guerrillas. But if neighbors removed the banners, they would identify themselves as government supporters. This kind of polarization tactic, which evangelical mis-sionaries called "provoked repression," eventually turned against the guerrillas. Once a neighborhood was under attack from the army, its EGP defenders could scarcely tolerate neutrality, let alone any sign of support for the government. They too were forced to crush dissent. The people became all too aware that it was EGP organizing which provoked the army's fury and that the guerrillas were not protecting them from the army as they had promised to do.

Early in 1982, just before Ríos Montt replaced Lucas García in the presidential palace, the army turned its full force on what seemed to be the strongest of the guerrilla organizations, the EGP. One of the first areas the army decided to retake was the Ixil Triangle.

Pastor Nicolás

FUNDAPI missionaries attribute the turn of the tide in the Ixil area to a single believer, Pastor Nicolás Toma, of the Pentecostal Church of God in the town of Cotzal. When I met him one night there in Decem-ber 1982, this thoughtful, articulate man seemed haunted by the choice he had made. After an EGP raid on the Cotzal army barracks on July 28, 1980, his own brother and brother-in-law had been among the sixty-four unarmed townsmen butchered by the army in reprisal. But when the guerrillas hit the Cotzal garrison a second time on

January 19, 1982, the pastor helped the army track the retreating insurgents.

"The guerrillas only provoke the army, and then they go," Pastor Nicolás said bitterly. "We are the ones who suffer the consequences." In several hours' discussion, Pastor Nicolás did not cite a single religious or ideological justification for his decision to support the government. Apparently his only reason was survival, for his people as well as for himself. The army had killed "thousands" of unarmed civilians in the municipality of Cotzal alone, the pastor claimed. If he had not helped the soldiers, Nicolás told me, they would have killed him, too.

When a new military commander arrived after the second EGP raid on the barracks, he told Pastor Nicolás and other religious leaders that, at the present rate, the army would have to "finish with" Cotzal. The army apparently had decided that since the entire Cotzal population appeared to support the guerrillas the entire Cotzal population might have to be eliminated. Despite pledges of cooperation, troops and helicopter gunships continued to rampage through the countryside, killing anyone they found. "I can no longer control them," the commander told Nicolás, pointing out that the soldiers were from other garrisons. Later that year, a young government official came out from the capital. He discovered that, of Cotzal's twenty-nine rural neighborhoods on his list, only three were still in existence. During the antiguerrilla offensive, soldiers had burned the others to the ground.

The army had announced that all those who did not move into town would be considered guerrillas; that is, they would be liable to be shot on sight. A number of survivors did surrender to the army, but the town remained paralyzed with fear. To the commander, therefore, Pastor Nicolás offered his own life as a guarantee for the good behavior of the inhabitants. With the aid of informers provided by Pastor Nicolás, then a civil patrol which he had helped to lead, the army was, for the first time, able to strike at EGP combatants, extract information, and dismantle guerrilla infrastructure.

An SIL prayer letter describes what happened next. "We have been spectators, only able to watch from far away, but we are cheering wildly," one of the SIL-Cotzal translators wrote in May 1982. "Beginning in January, the believers, led by Pastor [Nicolás], have taken desperate risks and aligned themselves with the national army. Civil patrols have been organized and given arms. The incredible result has been the eradication of guerrilla revolutionary forces from the Cotzal area!"

Actually, war between the army and the Ixil population had turned into civil war among the Ixils. In December 1982, the head of the Cotzal civil patrol claimed that the local army detachment had not lost a single man since his civil patrol was organized in January but that his 900-man civilian force had lost 76 dead to the guerrillas. Pastor Nicolás found himself on an EGP death list. Still, by December 1982, he thought that the people had "more confidence," that because the army "cares for the people, the people are aware that being on the side of the army is the solution to their problems." Yet the new civil patrols and compulsory public meetings and workdays were taking people away from worship service, Pastor Nicolás complained. His protests only earned the enmity of the local authorities. One Sunday morning in March 1983, a few weeks after a crisis in the civil patrol led to his appointment as its chief, Pastor Nicolás was shot and killed on his way to preach at an outlying church.

Before Nicolás died, according to FUNDAPI missionaries, word of his arrangement with the army spread far and wide through Ixil country. His example in Cotzal is said to have shown Ixil Indians in Nebaj and Chajul that they, too, could survive the holocaust by cooperating with its perpetrators. According to the Guatemalan army, Cotzal provided the model for the civil patrols which, under Ríos Montt, drafted more than three-quarters of a million Indian men—many of them guerrilla sympathizers—into the antiguerrilla cause. The elders of the Word church drew their own conclusions: were they to back up pastors like Nicolás with relief supplies and influence in the capital, they could humanize the army's treatment of civilians and win Indian support for Ríos Montt.

Providing an Alternative

On July 5, 1982, a Summer Institute couple who had spent three decades in Nebaj returned for a visit to evaluate International Love Lift's first project in the area. As four North American dentists pulled nine hundred aching teeth, the Bible translators heard many stories which contradicted Ríos Montt's human rights claims. Converts told them of beatings and death threats from soldiers. If the army commander discovered that the victims had complained, they could expect worse.

Teenage girls feared that they would be dragged to the barracks, to be gang-raped and killed as others had.

The missionary couple was horrified but regarded the army victory as less of an evil than continuing warfare, with its appalling cost for civilians, or guerrilla victory, which they feared would turn Guatemala into a Communist prison camp, destroying freedom to propagate the Gospel. Besides, to them Ríos Montt's leadership seemed to hold out the possibility of a new deal for Indians, a middle way between right-and left-wing oppression. With the army still an oppressor and thousands of refugees still afraid to surrender, the couple decided that the Ixil Indians needed "an *alternative* to the pressures being put upon them by the guerrillas."

They recommended that the army (1) refrain from shooting un-armed civilians just because they were running away or digging holes to hide in; (2) begin remunerating its forced-labor crews, many of whom had no way to feed themselves or their families; (3) provide the refugees it had created with corn and blankets; and (4) provide its compulsory civil patrols with arms, instead of sending them out to fight well-equipped guerrillas with machetes and hunting weapons.

To judge from what I was able to see in Nebaj five months later, the linguists' advice was being followed. Perhaps the best gauge of the North Americans' influence was their success in having the Nebaj army commander—whom a civil patrol leader blamed for the murder of his own father and ninety-six other civilians—transferred to an-other post.

The Summer Institute couple was especially concerned for the safety of evangelicals in Salquil, an EGP-controlled township in the north-west. Few of its inhabitants had surrendered to the army, for reasons which the translators understood all too well. Word that the army was now respecting the lives of the innocent needed to "trickle up to them," one of the SIL members wrote in early July. To this end, he pondered using a light plane with a public-address system or air-dropping packets of Scripture.

Less than a month later, several hundred evangelicals fled from guerrilla control in Salquil under cover of darkness. Their leader, an-other pastor of the Pentecostal Church of God, told the SIL couple that the group had escaped from murderous religious persecution. The guerrillas "insisted that we should oppose the president," the pastor explained. "But we kept remembering that the Bible says that we should obey the president. The Bible tells us that we shouldn't join ourselves to the guerrillas. Here we were in a situation where the guerrillas would kill anyone who refused to do what they said. And they've actually killed some of us."

Like many refugees under government control, the pastor claims that the guerrillas "deceived" his people. EGP combatants had promised that they would feed the people who fed them, provide arms for defense against the army, and win the war by the March 1982 election. When soldiers destroyed their crops and homes, however, the people went hungry. "We no longer had food, and we no longer had houses," said a refugee leader. "We were without clothes, without medicine, and there had been many deaths among us." Because the guerrillas had taken away their government identity papers, they could not even flee to the Pacific Coast to work on the plantations, on which many depended for their livelihood.

Six members of his church had been killed by guerrillas, the Salquil pastor testified. Four had been strangled with ropes in the hamlet of Tu Jolom in June 1982 for filling in stake pits which the EGP had placed near their church. These booby traps would have brought army reprisals and, according to the elders, violated the biblical injunction to love thy neighbor.

But the army had also killed members of the Pentecostal church, twenty-nine of them in the hamlet of Tu Chobuc on May 4, 1982. When helicopters landed, three families gathered to pray. After the troops discovered an empty guerrilla storage pit nearby, they took the men, women, and children there and cut their throats, the pastor told me in the presence of soldiers.

Two days later, according to the pastor, troops destroyed all the houses in Salquil. But over the radio the evangelicals of Salquil could hear the country's new president using their kind of religious language and offering amnesty. Visitors, whom the pastor called "spies," from the town of Nebaj arrived to say that the people there had new confidence in the army; possibly this was a missionary-inspired initiative. On August 3, in any case, the pastor led 237 evangelicals out of Salquil at night by a circuitous route. Escorted by soldiers, another 50 converts escaped in the same direction.

These Protestant refugees, along with many more Salquileños, who may have been rounded up more forcefully, were sent to "Camp New Life," at the Nebaj airstrip. Soldiers were stationed at the highest points, and refugee huts were built down the hillside, while trees were felled in every direction to guard against ambushes. With occasional overflights by machine-gun-mounted helicopters, Camp New Life looked like a strategic hamlet in Vietnam. It was one of the first of a series of carefully controlled resettlement sites, called "model villages" or "development poles," subsidized by the U.S. Agency for International Development.

Even in these government showcases, refugees were often willing to relate how army killings and ultimatums had driven them from their homes. "If we obey," a model villager explained, "they don't kill us anymore." According to a wave of refugees who reached Mexico, troops supported by helicopters assaulted their villages in Chajul from April 1982 into 1983, killing livestock, men, women, and children. But what seemed to keep the Salquil refugees at Camp New Life in late 1982 was not physical coercion but a food-for-work program and the physical security of being on the stronger side. There seemed to be too much freedom of movement for it to be the concentration camp described in guerrilla releases. FUNDAPI missionaries were the fairy godmothers of the Ixil survivors: besides keeping an eye on army administrators, they seemed to be providing most of the available aid—corn, blankets, metal roofing—giving preference to widows. But nothing like the billion dollars in North American evangelical aid promised by Ríos Montt materialized. Whether owing to reports of army atrocities, fund-raising costs, or the many other causes vying for evangelical dollars, money did not pour into the Word church. In 1984, as contributions dried up, FUNDAPI reported having raised only about $200,000.

What does the Ixil case teach us about the evangelical contribution to army counterinsurgency? Until Ríos Montt arrived on the scene, the government had so disgraced itself that revolutionaries dominated the country's moral landscape. Ríos Montt challenged them "morally as well as militarily," providing a rationale for those who wished to support the army but had been stupefied by its behavior. In Cotzal, Pastor Nicolás helped pioneer the amnesty and civil patrols which, under Ríos Montt, offered Indians protection from further large-scale army massacres in exchange for turning against the guerrillas. In Salquil, as violence by the Guatemalan army escalated, evangelical teachings seem to have become a wedge in the split between civilians and their ineffective guerrilla defenders. When Summer Institute translators began to return in July 1982, their moderating influence on the army may have proved instrumental in persuading more refugees to surrender.

But only in the Ixil area did FUNDAPI play such an active role. Another measure of the evangelical component of Ríos Montt's counterinsurgency program is the continued minority status of evangelicals in all but exceptional municipalities. It is true that the more punishment Indians took, the more the evangelical churches seemed to grow. Among the Kekchís of Verapaz, Southern Baptists reported "some loss of complete congregations." But the more Kekchís were killed, the more new churches seemed to spring up. In the three Ixil towns, Protestant churches grew more rapidly during the violence, and spectacularly so in Chajul, where the evangelical count soared from negligible to three substantial churches and as many as 1,000 members. There, however, the break to Protestantism was led by former Catholic charismatics, men accustomed to running their own affairs as well as the town, whom a new parish priest had offended. In Huehuetenango, the Central American Mission reports that its Mam, Kanjobal, and Chuj churches, which account for most of the Maya evangelicals in the department, spurted in growth during the most violent years. Rates have since fallen back to the lower, prewar growth rate, however, generally accounting for around 10 percent of the population.

The testimony of Ixil evangelicals suggests that dictates of survival, rather than their faith or the efforts of missionaries, brought them into the army's hands. This raises the question how revolutionary strategy encouraged the growth of politically conformist, fundamentalist churches. If the EGP made Christian consciousness raising a step in transforming indigenous resistance to the level of armed struggle, the Guatemalan army was not far behind in its use of religion. It turned politically conformist fundamentalism into a "dustpan" into which its repression pushed remnants of the consciousness-raising movements and other Ixil survivors.

As for the EGP, it lost most of the population it had controlled and took refuge in a few remote areas. The devastating setback eventually forced its leaders to recognize a grave error, that of expanding too rapidly to defend the people they were organizing. However much the EGP was responding to the Ixils' own historical struggle, it channeled that resistance so as to make truly staggering demands on the Ixils, demands which many could not meet. As a result, what the EGP called "popular revolutionary war" no longer looked very popular among the Ixils.

Let the Dead Bury the Dead

At the first anniversary of the March 23 coup, Ríos Montt appeared in jungle fatigues surrounded by the departmental commanders of the Guatemalan army. In a sweat, his eyes darting around the palace, and hemmed in by impassive colonels, he seemed like a Caesar awaiting his Brutus. To clear the way for the New Israel, Ríos had cast aside political parties and the high command. But he never threw himself against the steel paunch of the military hierarchy, the colonels in charge of the departmental garrisons. When Ríos donned his camouflage uniform and web gear on March 23, 1983, he ritually made himself one with his like-uniformed subordinates and hailed the supremacy of the army. It had been a week of rumors about another coup, which finally came to pass four and a half months later.

Ríos preached to the nation every Sunday evening, moralizing against subversion and the sorry state of private as well as public life. But he never indicted the single institution which, more than any other, had devastated the country, because it was the institution which had put him in power. Even though trusted brethren confirmed at least a few of the many accusations against the army, in public Ríos issued only denials, punctuated toward the end with a vague plea for forgiveness. "We know and understand that we have sinned, that we have abused power," he confessed after a year in the palace. "What can I do with a second lieutenant who won't accept my order not to kill?"

This pathetic admission suggested what Word elders will now admit, that Ríos Montt had never really controlled the army. A born-again Christian was serving at the pleasure of an institution of which the devil could boast. That is what a pastor from Jacaltenango believed. The army had certainly committed the massacres, he told a visitor, but it was not really to blame, for it was an instrument of Satan. Not a single case was resolved by Ríos's "disappearance office" at the National Police headquarters, nor, apparently, was a single army officer brought to trial under his government. Since the army has never disciplined officers for even the most flagrant violations, Ríos and his advisers chose not to risk airing its laundry in public. Ríos did try to avoid repetition of certain acts by reassigning guilty commanders, and

Word elders got into shouting matches with army officers, which may have contributed to his downfall.

Ríos's supporters appealed to the realities of power, but this did not prevent them from continuing to flail the human rights lobby, to minimize what they were covering up and justify their denial. Since Word's biography of Ríos does admit "some abuses" by the army despite his orders, the two it mentions deserve our attention because they were typical of so many others.

In the first incident, at the Finca San Francisco in Huehuetenango in July 1982, the army wiped out a large village of Chuj men, women, and children. This was not a case of civilians getting caught in a crossfire because there had been no resistance. Gang rape—the Guatemalan army's routine reward for soldiers about to massacre women—torture, execution, and ritual cannibalism were supervised by officers who alighted from a helicopter, indicating the involvement of the department commander or his orderlies. Yet, although the evidence was unusually good—survivors compiled a list of 302 dead, and an experienced neutral observer visited the remains four days later—the Word elders, their FUNDAPI advisers, and the U.S. embassy made jokes about it, saying that it was a prime example of the smear campaign against Ríos Montt. As it turned out, the U.S. embassy's "investigation" consisted of passing over the site in a helicopter, which did not land. When a FUNDAPI adviser finally reached the place in January 1983, he was shaken to discover skeletal remains and confirm the story in the nearest extant village.

The second abuse admitted by Word was the army's February 1983 murder of Patricio Ortiz Maldonado, an Indian professional employed by a U.S. AID–financed bilingual education program. The army claimed that Ortiz and his three campanions had been killed while trying to escape. His supervisors proved that he had been taken to the army garrison at La Democracia, the end of the road for many a disappeared person. According to an army captain who served at that base before seeking asylum in the United States, orders from the colonel to "process" prisoners were actually a code for murdering them. This was nothing new: every year thousands of Guatemalans are taken into official custody and never seen alive again. The authorities deny all knowledge of their whereabouts, in the "night and fog" technique devised by the Nazis. But this time one of the victims was on official business for the U.S. government, in the first of several murders of

Guatemalan U.S. AID employees which continued after Ríos's fall and which demoralized the embassy community.

Denials and counteraccusations have, nonetheless, made the "smear" of Ríos Montt part of evangelical mythology. Convinced that the general had been victimized by a well-coordinated misinformation campaign, even moderate evangelical leaders in the United States lent their weight to rehabilitating his name. In March 1984, Ríos Montt made his North American debut in a tour of evangelical talk shows. He also addressed enthusiastic conventions of the Full Gospel Business Men's Fellowship, the National Religious Broadcasters, and the National Association of Evangelicals. The tours are intended, Gospel Outreach has explained, to break the silence about Ríos Montt since his overthrow, build ties with top Christian leaders, and prepare an international prophetic ministry for him.

The resulting legend apparently appeals to the religious right's wish to perceive Central America as a clean, simple showdown between East and West, freedom and communism, good and evil. When North American evangelicals applaud Ríos Montt, they seem to be buying into the illusion that U.S. military intervention in Central America is a godly struggle against a satanic foe. The level of perception can be astounding. One North American pilgrim returning from a visit to Guatemala assured me that the army's crimes had actually been committed by Cuban infiltrators in government uniform. They were all over the country; he knew this for a fact, he said, because they had almost arrested him.

As for Guatemalan evangelicals, some maintained that Ríos had been forced out of power because the churches had not prayed enough for him. Others muttered that maybe God had put him out of office because of what he had done there. For his supporters, in any case, Ríos Montt became something of a prophet. Like every other prophet, they comforted themselves, his warnings had fallen on many a deaf ear. Some sinners had repented; many others had not; and under a just and wrathful God there probably would be worse days ahead. Since it is God who gives and takes away authority, the Word church reasoned, Ríos Montt had been removed so that he could share the Gospel with the world. Yet he continued to talk and act like a Guatemalan army general, for example, attributing his fall to Russians working through the U.S. State Department. As for North American evangelicals, Ríos said, they needed to send pastors to Guatemala so that they would not have to send Marines. Christians had "paid more attention to [the massacre reports in] the *New York Times* and the *Washington Post* than to the Word of God," he lamented. "That is a sign of the last days because we didn't believe each other."

The toll of pastors and evangelical congregations under Ríos Montt may never be reported because the Indian churches are afraid to report them. Let the dead bury the dead is their attitude; otherwise, you are likely to join them. Yet now that the guerrillas were a distant presence, pushed back to a few departments, the main enemy, even for many businessmen, seemed to be the army high command, for its economic incompetence, looting of the national treasury, and brutality. By 1985, the military hierarchy had reached the point of killing spokesmen for the private sector as well as Ríos Montt's brother-in-law, General Sosa Avila, perhaps for the crime of consulting with young officers about changing the administration.

When the Saints Go Marching in

A man who tries to take the long view is the owner of the Pan-American Hotel in downtown Guatemala City, a Californian in his thirties who served as a platoon leader in Vietnam. At Chuck Smith's Calvary Chapel in southern California, a church catering to the same kinds of young people as Gospel Outreach, John Carrette imbibed the doctrine of the Rapture, the quintessence of evangelical escapism. According to Rapture teaching, as the world enters into the Great Tribulation, Christians will be taken up in the air—or "raptured"—to be with Christ, avoiding all the unpleasantness which the end of the world will mean for the rest of us. In a tourist boom in the late 1970s Carrette's hotel produced profits like a money machine, and his theology seemed to be serving him well. But as Communist guerrillas overran the western highlands, the tourist trade evaporated, and bankruptcy loomed. Carrette felt that the Lord had abandoned him. What was this Joblike tribulation? Now that the world was rushing into the Great Tribulation, where was the Rapture? Why was he not being taken up to meet the Lord in the air?

One night, after having been estranged from the Lord for a good six months, Carrette was looking down on the lights of the capital when he realized that God was speaking to him. Down there is a great army, the Lord told Carrette, but they do not know that they are in a war, that they are a great army, or who the enemy is. Who is the army, Lord? he asked. It is not the guerrillas or the Guatemalan army, the Lord told Carrette. It is the church, whose struggle is not against flesh and blood but against the principalities and powers of evil. His job was to stay, not to be raptured out, Carrette realized. His job was to mobilize the church to pray for the overthrow of the devil's government in Central America.

It should be mentioned that, in Carrette's view, Latin America has been under the domination of Satan since before the Spanish conquest. That is what the Indian nature gods were about: they were Satan's hierarchy (or government) of principalities and powers. True, the warm sunbeams of Christianity began to shine through the overcast with the arrival of the Catholic church. But it was still dim. Now the radiant beams of Christianity were shining stronger, setting off the terrible regional conflict in which the Guatemalans found themselves. The preaching of God's word in Catholic as well as Protestant churches, Carrette believed, was ripping the entire area from the hands of Satan. We were seeing a contest over who would control Central America, God or the devil, Carrette said. It was a spiritual war.

Now the church had taught Christians to pray for each other as the nation went down into the chaos of the Great Tribulation. Our only hope, the church had taught, is the light beyond the grave and God's thousand-year reign on earth—*after* the Tribulation. But, according to the Bible, this place, Guatemala, was the land of milk and honey, Carrette realized. It was necessary to pray for the nation. So it was that, in the darkest days of the Lucas García regime, in the months preceding Ríos Montt's eruption on the scene, Carrette began to urge church leaders to pray for Guatemala. In the name of Jesus, he exhorted them, command Satan to leave this country.

We can only imagine the sense of the miraculous which Carrette and his brethren felt when, on March 23, 1982, the Lord answered their prayers in the form of a palace coup. "What we had done in the Spirit was made visible in the streets," Carrette explained. "Ríos Montt was put in because the church did its job in the spirit. He brought the church together for six to eight months, astounding it into unity and intercession—for a while. Ríos Montt was taken out again because the church didn't do its job of intercession. The church didn't do its job and so the devil was not bound." Now, Carrette felt, the country was going through a time of wrenching, of birth pains. But he was sure that Satan was going to be taken off Guatemala and that Jesus would soon be free to pour out his blessings. Strikes over wages, protests over prices, and corruption in the army high command, Carrette predicted, would set off a civil war among the very military. There were all the makings of a real bloodbath. But along with it would come a mighty revival in Guatemala, a revival which would spread throughout Central America. By the end of 1986, Carrette was convinced, the entire region would be on the mend.

"The body-count concept rules the evangelical church here," Carrette complained:

There's an emphasis on sales, like the commercial chain concept, of putting a McDonald's on every corner. That's the American concept of missions in Latin America. But the Lord is coming back, and he wants more than numbers. The church that is well organized and reports back to Springfield doesn't cut the mustard. He wants us to bind the devil. He wants signs and wonders here in Latin America. Bureaucracies concerned about body counts are not important, spiritual warfare is the thing. We're on the brink of a real transformation. God is going to put his man in. God will heal the economy, the guerrilla situation, the army, everything. The kingdoms of this world have become the kingdoms of Christ. That's Revelation 11:15.

PART TWO
Selective Violence

CHAPTER 5

The Operation of a Death Squad in San Pedro la Laguna

By Benjamin D. Paul and William J. Demarest

In 1941, when one of us (Paul) first worked in peaceful San Pedro la Laguna, there was no sign that the Maya Indians of highland Guatemala were destined to be caught in the toils of a brutal civil war and that the trouble would eventually reach the shores of Lake Atitlán, claiming the lives of informants who had become good friends in the course of a dozen return visits during the ensuing years. San Pedro, an all-Indian town, has proved to be an instructive example of the process of rapid social transformation at the community level. The shift from a predominantly subsistence economy to a mainly market economy has been accompanied by remarkable changes in San Pedro's technology, political system, and religious organization. Gone are the six *cofradías* (religious brotherhoods) and their colorful processions on saints' days. Gone, too, is the monopoly enjoyed by traditional Catholicism; a vigorous Protestant movement has generated fourteen separate fundamentalist churches, embracing nearly 40 percent of the town's six thousand inhabitants.

By the time of our visit to San Pedro in 1979, the massacre of the Kekchí Indians at Panzós had already been condemned in the world press. But Panzós seemed remote from the tranquil Lake Atitlán area, and guerrilla action far to the north and west was scarcely in the news. The purpose of our 1979 trip was to gather information on social change at San Pedro. San Pedro had contributed more migrants to the city than other Indian *municipios* in the area, and we knew that one reason for this was prior experience in Guatemala City of Pedranos who had been volunteering for two-year hitches in the army ever since the late 1930s when Gen. Jorge Ubico Castañeda was president. In 1979 we wanted to find out how many of the current residents had a history of army service. Adolfo (all names of living Pedranos mentioned here are pseudonyms), a man known to us from prior visits, told us that he was a close friend of another Pedrano, Jacinto, who could supply an estimate because, as *comisionado militar* (military commissioner), he was in charge of recruiting soldiers from the village. It was troubling to learn that some young men in San Pedro tried to hide from Jacinto for fear of being captured and forced to enter army service. Military training, once an attractive opportunity for Pedranos, was now considered a harsh experience to be avoided if at all possible.

Our final interview on that 1979 trip was memorable. We conversed with an old friend named Francisco. The father of six children, he was a successful baker, a Protestant pastor, an astute man with an engaging personality. Having heard something about anthropology, he asked whether we really believed that man descended from monkeys. Although we did not quite convince him that evolution and the Bible could be reconciled, we left with a resolve to seek him out on our next trip to San Pedro for an account of his involvement in the cause of evangelical Protestantism. But there would be no next time for Francisco. Jacinto, his friend Adolfo, and the baker Francisco—each would play a role in the deadly drama that began to unfold the year after we left San Pedro in 1979.

In July 1980, a middle-aged woman named Marta wrote author Paul to acknowledge receipt of a check, adding that the price of corn had risen sharply, that her most able-bodied son was out of work, that a local electrical employee had been accidentally electrocuted (*carbonizado*), and that another man had been found dead in a bar, the victim of alcohol. In San Pedro only bad news qualifies as reportable news. Marta concluded her letter by writing, "And recently a group of guerrillas arrived and we were very fearful, but they didn't do anything [to us]." Author Paul has known Marta since 1941, when, at age fifteen, she served as house helper, errand girl, and occasional interpreter (in those days very few women spoke Spanish). She is now a poor widow with eight children. The oldest is Adolfo, friend of Jacinto, the military commissioner.

Late in 1980, Marta again had occasion to acknowledge receipt of money. This time her letter sounded a note of alarm: things were critical in San Pedro. The baker Francisco had been abducted in the middle of the night, and a few weeks later they had carried off another man. Now people were afraid to walk the streets after dark. This was no time, she warned, to visit San Pedro; it was too dangerous.

Far from the scene of action, we could only speculate about the identity of the abductors. Were they guerrillas? Were they army soldiers? Would we indeed be in danger if we went to San Pedro? In an atmosphere of heightened tension, would informants assent to interviews? Would their association with us put them under suspicion?

Eventually we learned that the abductions, which continued during a two-year reign of terror, came to a halt in October 1982. Calm had been restored by the time we paid our next visit to San Pedro in April 1983. We found Pedranos to be as informative as ever. Relatives of the victims and many others supplied a host of details that enabled us to reconstruct the course of recent events.

Four events had followed each other in rapid order during 1980, when General Lucas García was in power. On May 20, an Organización del Pueblo en Armas (ORPA) guerrilla group had addressed the villagers in the central plaza and denounced the injustices of Guatemala's oppressive regime. Some of the younger and better-educated Pedranos cheered the group. Within hours the guerrillas vanished, and to this date none have reappeared in San Pedro. Another event was the establishment of an army post near neighboring Santiago Atitlán. Before that there had been no military encampment anywhere on Lake Atitlán.

Still another event was the expansion of Jacinto's role. He had been empowered by the army to appoint a large number of assistants so that there was now a corpus of military commissioners made up mainly of Pedranos with a history of military service. They were to guard against subversion and had been given arms to protect the town from guerrilla activity. Jacinto was chief military commissioner, with Marta's son Adolfo second-in-command. The fourth event of 1980 shook the town: the abduction of Francisco the baker, the first of about twenty-five abductions and killings.

The Long Black Night

Many Pedranos described what happened on the fateful night of September 29, 1980. At 11:00 P.M., Francisco heard someone knock on the door. He thought it was a harmless drunk. When he opened the door, he was seized by armed men dressed as soldiers and wearing masks. Some surrounded the house, while others rushed in and demanded to know where Francisco hid his pistol. Wildly searching everywhere for a nonexistent weapon, they turned the house into a shambles. Francisco directed his wife to produce a bag with $2,000 in cash he had borrowed only a few days earlier from a development bank to help pay for the construction of a new church for his congregation, El Redentor Alianza Cristiana y Misionera. He offered the money to the hooded intruders in return for setting him free. They made off with the money, as well as Francisco, but not before snatching everything else of value—a new pair of boots, clothes, a record player, baskets of bread, four dozen eggs, and two pounds of meat.

As the men marched off on the road to the neighboring town of San Juan la Laguna, they encountered a truck returning in the night to San Pedro. They halted the vehicle and relieved the driver and his helper of their watches and some items of food. Not until next day did the Pedrano truckers realize that the band had Francisco with them.

As soon as the men left town with their captive, Francisco's wife ran to the municipal building to tell the guards on duty what had happened. The guards were stunned; nothing like this had occurred before. It was thought that Francisco had been dragged off to Santa Clara la Laguna, the town above San Juan la Laguna. A relative of Francisco with army experience and connections went to ask the colonel in command of the military post in Santa Clara to help find the captive. The commander promised that he would make inquiries in the capital and that the man would be released if he was in the custody of the army, but nothing came of it. It was doubtful, the colonel concluded, that Francisco was being held by the army. Nor was the body ever located. For a while there was a vague rumor that it had been abandoned in Nahualá. Francisco's father went to Sololá to inspect a corpse that might have been his son's. It was not.

When asked why Francisco was a target for abduction, Pedrano informants came up with several possible reasons. First, because Francisco had openly objected to the presence of policemen in San Pedro and of soldiers stationed in the vicinity, and because he had cheered the guerrillas when they appeared in San Pedro, secret informers had doubtless turned in his name as a "subversive." In the second place, he was a prominent member of a rural cooperative. In the third place, he was sometimes seen boarding a bus early in the morning to sell his freshly baked bread, and some may have suspected him of secretly provisioning guerrillas in the hills.

The same wrenching scenario—a nighttime knock on the door, a capture, a vain effort to find the victim or his body—was replayed in San Pedro again and again over the next two years. People slept fitfully, fearing the sound of a footfall and finally blessing the arrival of dawn.

At the outset people assumed that the kidnapping was the work of the army, but when the third man was hauled off, it became evident that San Pedro's own military commissioners were responsible, or at least deeply implicated. Disguises and cover of night did not prevent victims' families from overhearing snatches of Tzutujil, the local Maya language, or recognizing the voices of particular Pedranos. As time went on and the commissioners became drunk with power—and with liquor as well—their tongues loosened, divulging details within earshot of other tavern patrons, who channeled the news through the town's gossip circuits. But knowing who were responsible was not enough to dispel the darkness of what became, in one Pedrano's words, an endless noche negra ("black night").

The commissioners played a duplicitous game, doing their dirty work by night, posing as protectors by day. They feigned a guerrilla presence by firing shots and setting off bombs after dark. They painted ORPA and other guerrilla signs on walls, and they scattered guerrilla-type leaflets around. They ordered a six o'clock curfew. When it suited their purposes, they made the town electrician turn off the switch of the central power plant. Their rule was unabridged. One informant overheard a conversation in which the chief of the army reserves assured two of the local commissioners that they wielded maximum authority and could overrule the mayor of San Pedro. They had guns; the mayor did not.

On two occasions the commissioners alerted the army to a supposedly impending guerrilla attack and told people living near the forested mountainside, in the higher part of town, to leave their homes. The army landed troops on the shore beyond San Pedro. In a pincer movement the soldiers converged on the area above town, but there were no guerrillas to be caught. Once an army officer, encountered on the road to Santiago Atitlán, told a Pedrano truck driver that he feared to enter San Pedro because it was reputed to be a hotbed of guerrilla activity and that the army at one point had even considered bombing the town. In fact, however, no guerrilla groups operate in San Pedro territory, which extends up the northern, or lakeside, flank of huge San Pedro Volcano. On the southern or Pacific side of the more distant Atitlán Volcano is where ORPA has its headquarters, under the command of Rodrigo Asturias, son of Miguel Ángel Asturias, winner of the Nobel prize for literature in 1967, according to the *Economist* (September 21, 1985, p. 29).

When the San Pedro commissioners staged what was to be their final abduction late in 1982, they tried to throw villagers off their scent by leaving behind two of their own men tied up with ropes to create the impression that the commissioners had fought with guerrillas during the night and had been beaten before the intruders made off with the victim. Actually the gang had disposed of their captive by tying him to a sandbag and sinking him in the lake.

One of the many victims was a woman living in a nearby town. She was fingered by a commissioner who had asked the woman, a seamstress by trade, to sell him on credit two fine skirts for his daughter's wedding. She delivered the skirts and repeatedly asked for payment. Her payment was death. Wearing clothes typical of the town of Santiago Atitlán, the Pedrano commissioner led soldiers to her house at night. He told her to come out. She tried to escape from a window but was killed by machine-gun fire. The identity of the Pedrano is known because the victim's daughter recognized his voice and his tall, portly figure.

We inquired whether the seamstress, like the baker Francisco, might have been blacklisted as a "subversive." Well, yes, we were told. In her travels about the country to sell her clothes, she reportedly attended a gathering in Quiriguá to celebrate the second anniversary of the Sandinista victory in Nicaragua. Another "error" she made, we were told, was to collaborate with the director of the short-wave radio station set up in Santiago Atitlán by the priests of Misión Católica de Oklahoma (Micatokla) to promote adult education in the local Maya language.

The blacklisting of Pedranos apparently began at Christmastime 1979 when one of the three policemen posted to San Pedro two years earlier shot a man from another town who had come to a holiday fair in San Pedro to operate a a Ferris wheel. The policeman was drunk; he fired his gun wildly and killed the man by accident. The people of San Pedro, long accustomed to policing their own community, had been nursing a grudge against the officers for ordering them off the streets and generally pushing them around. Enraged by the shooting incident, a pack of Pedranos assaulted the trigger-happy policeman and chased his companions out of town. The names of those who led the attack, including the baker Francisco, were turned in to the army by informers on the lookout for individuals who showed disrespect for authority.

A number of the victims, however, were doomed for reasons other than presumed disloyalty. Personal vengeance was a recurrent motive. Adolfo killed his brother-in-law in a tavern. The brother-in-law was celebrating the birth of a baby boy. In the midst of a crowd and emboldened by drink, he incautiously accused Adolfo, who was armed, of involvement in the abduction of the baker. In a heated argument, Adolfo drew his pistol and shot the man point-blank in the chest. Adolfo's ire was fueled by more than alcohol and momentary taunts. The son of a poor widow, propertyless Adolfo had long been envious of the advantages his brother-in-law enjoyed as the scion of an intact family of moderate means. It rankled him that his father-in-law, for instance, would pay the son's bar bill but not the son-in-law's.

Adolfo argued that he did not kill his brother-in-law. He claimed, implausibly in the opinion of numerous witnesses, that in a scuffle for possession of Adolfo's revolver the other man had accidentally shot himself. The slain man's father refused to press charges, not because he held Adolfo to be innocent but because, as he told us, Adolfo was armed and because he heeded the counsel of the resident nuns, who advised him to pray and let God do the judging. In any case, Adolfo's commissioner status put him beyond reach of punishment. His chief, Jacinto, had only to assure his army superiors that the murdered man was a subversive.

On another occasion, Adolfo was angry when he learned that one of his younger brothers had been mauled by a muscular Pedrano in a bar fight. The injured brother brought charges against his assailant in the local courthouse, and the defendant was ordered to pay for the medical treatment the brother needed. But Adolfo was not satisfied, vowing that the attacker would have to pay more dearly. He did. He was captured by soldiers and became one of the "disappeared" of San Pedro.

By no means was Adolfo the only commissioner to use his office to settle personal scores. One abduction, for example, was explained as a commissioner's retaliation against a man who had married a woman who was formerly the commissioner's wife. Personal animosity was often a compounding factor, not the only cause. Thus one of the commissioners thought to have participated in Francisco's abduction is said to have had personal reasons for vengeance, as though the baker's outspoken stance, along with the reasons already listed, were not enough to spell his doom.

There seems to be little doubt that the army authorities kept a blacklist and that they were responsible for kidnappings in San Pedro. But they could not have acted alone. Insiders had to show soldiers where the targets resided in a large, crowded town with no named streets. And insiders, whether local commissioners or other Pedrano informers, had to supply the names of "subversives" for blacklisting. There can be no doubt that the commissioners collaborated with the army. The army expected them to do so.

Often however, the commissioners acted entirely on their own. In fact, more than one of our informants speculated that the baker was captured not by soldiers but by commissioners disguised as soldiers, that they were not really searching for Francisco's pistol but for his cash, and that their success created a taste for easy money. One of the two ringleaders of this first kidnapping was said to be the same commissioner who later led soldiers to the home of the seamstress who had sold him skirts on credit. That commissioner, the oldest of the group, was characterized by some as the most villainous (*el más pícaro*) of the lot. It was even suspected that he, and possibly other Pedranos, had a hand in the slaying on July 28, 1981, of Father Stanley Rother, the American priest in charge of the Catholic mission in Santiago Atitlán.

If a commissioner developed misgivings, he could not easily withdraw from the gang. One of our most trustworthy informants recalled that Adolfo had come to him at about the halfway point in the reign of terror. He was obviously worried about something. The two of them, both Protestants, prayed together, and they talked, but Adolfo said only that he was anxious to renounce his commission. He had gone to army headquarters in Huehuetenango and Chichicastenango asking for permission to resign, but had been refused. He said that he had also told his confederates of his wish but had been warned that they could not be responsible for him if he resigned. Unable to extricate himself from the mire, Adolfo sank deeper into it.

Another commissioner, who, unlike Adolfo, continued to run with the pack, ran afoul of his companions and paid for his lapse with his life. He was a butcher who failed to turn over to his cronies the money received from Pedrano housewives for the meat of a steer the gang had commandeered, claiming he had lost the money. But he became a marked man for an additional, more compelling reason. His companions learned that the butcher was tipping off intended victims to stay on guard and was beginning to leak incriminating information. In gangland fashion, he was taken for a "ride," or rather a walk on the beach near the pier at night with two of the commissioners. One shot him twice at point-blank range (the 22-caliber bullet wounds were less than one inch apart in the area of the right kidney), while the other fired shots into the air with a carbine to support their claim that they had seen a tall, blonde guerrilla jump from behind the pier and shout, "Hands up!" before killing the butcher.

A Pedrano who had just returned from military duty as a paratrooper told people that he had heard soldiers gossiping that local commissioners were to blame for the epidemic of abductions in San Pedro. By carelessly repeating what he had heard in the army, the former soldier forfeited his life. Disrespect for the commissioners' authority could be fatal. One man repeatedly defied the commissioner's curfew by drinking and walking the streets at night. He disappeared.

The appetite for easy money was readily satisfied by resort to extortion. Typically, a commissioner would approach a family man, informing him that his son's name appeared on a blacklist and offering to save the son's life if the father could produce a few hundred dollars. The money ostensibly would be used to persuade the army personnel—the commissioner had connections—to eliminate the name from the list. Alternatively, the commissioners would simply demand money from someone, under the threat of denouncing him as a subversive if he balked. Protests of innocence were unavailing. Defiance could be fatal.

Nor did payment always ensure survival. One of the wealthier citizens delivered nine hundred dollars to keep from losing a son who had openly expressed his opposition to the military commissioners. The son continued to oppose the clique and lost his life. The commissioners sank him in the lake and, as already indicated, tied up two of their own men to make it appear that guerrillas had been at work. The aggrieved father later compiled a list of forty-four Pedranos who had paid extortion money totaling tens of thousands of dollars.

Money was not the only thing the gangsters appropriated. They got a fair haul when they called late one night at the home of a Pedrano living in the coastal settlement San Pedro Cutzán. They roused the man out of bed, demanded the keys to his pickup, and drove away with it, as well as with the owner clad only in his underwear. They sold the vehicle; some claimed that it was later seen in Quezaltenango. The kidnapped man was never seen again.

The commissioners roamed widely in search of loot, picking up a goat in Santa Clara la Laguna, two hogs in Panyevar (a distant hamlet of San Juan la Laguna), and other booty elsewhere. They reached out around the lake as far as Tzununá (a hamlet of Santa Cruz la Laguna) to extort goods. They also stole cameras and other valuables at gunpoint from foreign tourists who rented dollar-a-night rooms on San Pedro's lakefront. According to one inn owner, Jacinto, the chief military commissioner, once wanted him to give his daughter on loan for a month to a friend of the commissioner living in Guatemala City. The girl was the town's beauty queen that year. Her father promptly sent her off to Mexico. Of course, only a limited number of Pedranos had the means and the connections to send threatened family members to distant places. Some of those families did just that, for it was generally the richer Pedranos who had the most to fear from the predatory commissioners.

The gang was able to live high off the hogs they commandeered. They held lavish saturnalias on the beach, feasting and drinking and enjoying sex with women they invited or coerced. Some of the revelers had two women, one informant told us, and squandered most of the money they collected on alcohol. Their chief, Jacinto, drank so continuously toward the end of his reign that he was unable to do any work. Rape was no rare event. The commissioners molested female *jípis* ("hippies") staying in lakeside inns. They stripped one Pedrano woman and made her appear naked in the streets. Another woman was gang-raped by a dozen men.

Because of the army's perception—manipulated by the commissioners—that San Pedro was a dangerous place, a military officer came to town in May 1981 to announce that the number of commissioners would have to be expanded. A leading citizen, the more respected of the town's two *güizaches* (paralegal aides), then spoke up. He requested that all the commissioners be replaced. The visiting officer replied that that would not be done, that if the town had problems with the existing group, that was a matter to be taken up with the local justice of the peace.

Accordingly, the *güizache* and the mayor (who doubles as the justice of the peace in San Pedro) drew up a document requesting the change. Although challenging the corrupt commissioners was a dangerous thing to do, twenty-seven citizens bravely signed the petition. (It may be no coincidence that two of the *güizache's* sons later vanished, one never to reappear, the other to return with a gunshot wound sustained in an attempt to escape.) Copies of the petition were sent to the governor, the minister of defense in the capital, and President Lucas García. The appeal was ignored, and the crime wave rolled on.

For their part, the commissioners, only some of whom had weapons—a few old pistols and shotguns—moved to strengthen their grip by appealing for more weapons. On February 27, 1982, they drew up a petition in which their leader, Jacinto, asked the defense minister, General Anibal Guevara, to supply arms to all the commissioners listed in the petition. Jacinto's list ran to twenty-six names. Several months later the petitioners received carbines.

From the beginning, the exact number of commissioners operating in San Pedro could only be surmised. There were covert as well as overt members, and the numbers increased over time. Apparently Jacinto was given a free hand to select his assistants. Some members of the group were coerced into joining, we were told, by the threat that they would be denounced as subversives if they failed to cooperate. Some of the Pedranos who scorned the threat disappeared.

On March 23, 1982, shortly after Jacinto submitted his request for more arms, a coup brought Ríos Montt to power. The new president publicly promised to eliminate unnecessary violence and clean up corruption in the army. He invited citizens to report abuses. Pedranos, encouraged, redoubled their efforts to expel the evil commissioners. Individuals and delegations protested and appealed in all directions. A document signed by a multitude of townsmen and endorsed by the mayor was taken to Guatemala City by Antonio, a singularly civic-minded individual. As former mayor, he had formed a political relationship with someone working as secretary to Ríos Montt. The secretary took the petition, saying that he would have the president consider it. Antonio was advised to return in ten days. He did and was informed that the petition was being studied by the minister of government. Ten days later Antonio again traveled to the city and was told by the secretary that arrest of the commissioners was unlikely; Ríos Montt reportedly had said that the country needed men with the strength to kill. Antonio then tried to deliver a copy of the petition to the commander of Military Zone 14 (Department of Sololá) where it was rejected on the grounds that it had already been considered by the president. A similar petition by the town's permanent force, a group of about one hundred Pedranos with military-service experience, was no more successful.

It was a policy of the Ríos Montt regime to rotate military commanders periodically and replace municipal officeholders. Accordingly, the mayor of San Pedro was ordered out of office on June 15, 1982. He had been elected by popular vote, he was well regarded, and his term was not yet up. The town wanted to keep him on or at least be allowed to select his successor but had to accept Jorge, favored by the clique of commissioners and designated mayor from above. Jorge took office June 16, 1982.

Jorge had gone to Guatemala City in 1956 as a youth to sign up for military training and had stayed on to make a career of army service. He was an honor guard, then a president's guard, then a driver and doorkeeper at the presidential residence, and finally a cook at the residence of the defense minister. Periodically he would visit San Pedro, where he married and maintained a family. He inherited land in San Pedro and after many years of service in the military establishment decided to return to his hometown. When the opportunity came to be mayor, he obtained a recommendation from the minister whom he had loyally served, and this in turn secured him the backing of the military commander in Sololá, whose approval of Jorge's appointment was decisive. People realized that Jorge, unlike the mayor he replaced, would be more hindrance than help in their campaign to end the violence. They were convinced that he sided with the evildoers who had initiated or supported his appointment. But they did not give up their fight to rid the town of criminals.

At a meeting in August 1982, members of the permanent force demanded of the visiting colonel, who chaired the assembly, that the present commissioners be replaced because, among other things, some of them did not even have army training. The colonel was not swayed by their argument, saying that he was interested in expansion, not replacement. Among the former soldiers demanding a change was the young man who was later seized and dropped into the lake tied to a bag of sand. When the victim's father went to the mayor's office to report the abduction, Jorge told him that his son had been taken away by guerrillas. The father retorted that it was not so: "Things are really bad when we kill our own kind. You should repent."

Jorge was the target of other accusations during his tenure in office, which lasted more than a year. Fernando, one of several potential candidates for mayor at the time Jorge gained the post, added the latter to the list of individuals he denounced as criminals and collaborators in a stream of telegrams he sent to higher authorities. The mayor and several commissioners in turn accused Fernando of indulging in character assassination. They denounced him to the commander of the military post in Santiago Atitlán, who ordered Fernando to appear for judgment. Not knowing what fate had in store for him, Fernando gave his wife the text of a telegram to be dispatched to Ríos Montt in case he failed to return home that evening. Fernando had been active in the Christian Democrat party when it supported Ríos Montt's unsuccessful bid for the presidency in 1974.

An official document (the minutes of the meeting signed by all the participants) dated October 25, 1982, summarizes what happened that day in Santiago Atitlán. Fernando was charged with the crime of disseminating false accusations against the six Pedranos confronting him. Four of the plaintiffs were commissioners: Jacinto, Adolfo, and two others. Jorge, the mayor, was another plaintiff. Still another was Mario, a litigious *güizache* with an unsavory reputation in San Pedro. Exhibited as evidence were copies of numerous documents that Fernando had presented to "the highest authorities of the nation." There was no witness for the defense. Testimony by the plaintiffs, said the minutes, proved Fernando's accusations to be false, without foundation, and the product of acrimony stemming from the defendant's frustrated desire to be named mayor of San Pedro without popular support. For having committed calumny and false testimony the commander of the army post ordered that Fernando be detained at the military base until he could be transferred to the appropriate prison. When Fernando failed to return that evening, his wife sent the prepared telegram to Ríos Montt. A few days later seven of San Pedro's military commissioners were arrested, and Fernando was released.

Sudden Daylight

The long *noche negra* ended as suddenly as it had begun twenty-five months earlier when Francisco the baker was kidnapped. On October 28, 1982, a company of military men crossed the lake in two launches and arrested Jacinto, Adolfo, and five other commissioners. This swift operation put a sudden stop to kidnappings, threats, and demands for money, as well as signs of purported guerrilla activity: shots in the night, slogans on walls, provocative leaflets. To be sure, only some of the evil commissioners were hauled away while other members of the gang remained at liberty, but that was enough to restore peace to San Pedro—for just over two years.

Why the military command decided to crack down when it did, turning against the same two top-level commissioners it had found innocent of Fernando's charges only three days earlier, or why the military struck at all, given its record of repeatedly ignoring complaints, remains a matter of conjecture. At what level was the decision to strike made? Was there a change of heart or of military commanders?

One woman in San Pedro attributed the crackdown to information she supplied. She was a seamstress who traveled to different places to sell her goods, like the seamstress who was killed in a neighboring town. Jacinto and Adolfo had told her that she was suspected of taking food to the guerrillas and was on a blacklist but that a payment of three hundred dollars plus sexual favors would save her life. With great difficulty she raised the money but decided that before handing it over she would make inquiries directly at the army post. She did this on the advice and with the help of an intermediary in Santiago Atitlán. When she asked a major at the post to whom she should give the money to get her name off the list, he said that she was on no list and asked her to name the Pedrano commissioners who were demanding payment. She did. She thinks, as do some others in town, that what she revealed at the base played a significant part in getting the military to make the arrests.

Many believed that the decision to strike was made at a higher level. Five or six months had elapsed since Antonio made three trips to the city in what seemed at the time to be a vain effort to persuade Ríos Montt to act on the community's request for intervention. In retrospect, however, it was thought that the president was only biding his time until he could rotate or rein in his field officers and that the crackdown on the commissioners was his delayed response to the petition Antonio had delivered or perhaps to the demand submitted by the permanent force. Others thought that the president was moved to act by the telegrams he received from Fernando, his one-time political supporter.

Still others had reason to believe that the decision to end the town's suffering was made at a yet higher level. The bereaved father who admonished Jorge, the mayor, to repent, told us that after his son's abduction he and the pastor of his church, the Assembly of God, prayed day and night for one month until, finally, the commissioners were arrested.

In point of fact, there were two military posts across the lake, the army post outside Santiago Atitlán, and a naval station near Cerro de Oro, a hamlet of Santiago Atitlán. The arrest was made by *marinos* (navy men) traveling in naval launches. It is not clear whether the commanders of the two military posts acted separately or in concert or in response to orders from above.

Just before making the arrest, a lieutenant from across the lake went about the town soliciting testimony from some of the many Pedranos who had been threatened or victimized by the commissioners. The lieutenant then went to the municipal headquarters. Mayor Jorge, accompanied by Chief Commissioner Jacinto, was away on a mission of some kind. But, as in all such cases, the vice-mayor was on duty, and he later recounted what happened that day. The lieutenant, who was working under orders from Ríos Montt to be very severe (in the opinion of the vice-mayor), demanded to talk to a certain commissioner, who happened to be seated with a companion in the municipal office. The two commissioners greeted the lieutenant cheerily: "How goes it, chief! What is your wish?" The officer whirled around and hissed at them not to move. He and his men then proceeded to round up the other commissioners, including Jacinto, returning from his trip. Under the ceiba tree shading the town square, the officer shouted at the men in chains that they were the real guerrillas who had been operating in San Pedro.

The seven captives were taken to the military base near Santiago Atitlán, where they remained ten days while confessions were extracted from them. On November 7, 1982, they were taken back to San Pedro for complaints to be presented. The prisoners appeared haggard and beaten. A thousand or more people assembled in the central square. About twenty heavily armed soldiers guarded a cleared space between the crowd and the municipal building. Over a loudspeaker set up for the occasion, a spokesman explained that the military was there to protect, not to threaten, people and that anyone seeing something wrong should tell the military authorities about it. The speaker added that civil patrols would soon be organized in San Pedro. The captives were held incommunicado in the local jail for four days, and then taken to Sololá.

The families of the arrested men, like the families of their earlier victims, sought desperately to locate captured relatives. In January 1983 we received a letter from one of Marta's younger sons, the only truly literate member of the family. He was working as a teacher in a remote hamlet of Uspantán, in El Quiché. After returning from a vacation in San Pedro, he wrote to describe the sad situation he had witnessed in Marta's household. His account can be paraphrased as follows:

My mother is sick and depressed because my brother Adolfo is now one of the seven prisoners. I wasn't there at the time of the arrest and don't know just what happened, but everyone turned against the commissioners, condemning them in many testimonials filled with slander and false accusation. A document denouncing the commissioners was taken to the military post at Santiago Atitlán, and the men were arrested that same day. After suffering for nearly a fortnight at that post, they were handed over to the mayor of San Pedro, but he did not want to try their case. They were then transferred to Sololá, but the judge there didn't settle anything. They were then shifted to the capital, but we don't know where. My mother grieves, not knowing whether Adolfo is dead or alive. She suffers from *bilis* [bile attack] and hovers near death. We were sad during Christmas and New Year's because a member of our family was missing. Adolfo's wife, my sister-in-law, is all undone. Together with my mother, she weeps day and night. Only God knows what's happening to Adolfo.

A month later Marta wrote to say that she had learned where the prisoners were kept in Guatemala City. They were in the custody of the Second Corps of National Police. Adolfo could be set free, she wrote, in exchange for $400, a sum utterly beyond impoverished Marta's means. She did not say who was the source of this information, but two months later, in April 1983, when we visited San Pedro, we were told that the source was Mario, the *güizache* with an unsavory reputation who had earlier gone with five others to the commander of the post in Santiago Atitlán to accuse Fernando of slander.

None of the seven former commissioners was released. In fact, in January 1983 they were joined in jail by an eighth former commissioner, who had been arrested on new evidence implicating him in murder. He was accused of stuffing sand into the sack used to sink the last man seized by the imprisoned commissioners. The town waited for the prisoners to be sentenced, worried that the culprits would return and again terrorize the town. But the people did not sit still. A four-man delegation traveled to Guatemala City to present a petition to President Ríos Montt, giving an extra copy of the document to the editors of the newspaper *Prensa Libre*.

On April 12, 1983, the newspaper ran a story on the contents of the document, listing the names of the eight former commissioners and their crimes: theft, kidnapping, extortion, blackmail, rape, abuse of power, and others. According to the newspaper, "about 8,000" Pedranos (an overgenerous estimate of the town's population) demanded trial without further delay and swift application of the death penalty. The petition, said the newspaper, also named and demanded the arrest of ten additional suspects "who are still going about freely as though they hadn't done a thing." The *Prensa Libre* article also carried a photograph and listed the names of the petition-bearers. One of those pictured, the leader of the four-man delegation, was a man named Pedro, who was to distinguish himself—and imperil his life—as an indefatigable foe of the criminal commissioners.

The eight prisoners continued to be transferred from one locality to another. From Guatemala City they were moved to Quezaltenango. By the time we visited San Pedro in April 1983, they had been moved again, this time to Huehuetenango. Months elapsed, and the prisoners still were not tried. In an effort to win freedom they resorted to a wily stratagem. Ríos Montt had offered amnesty to subversives who turned themselves in, and Mejía Victores, his successor, repeated the offer. On August 12, 1983, only days after Mejía Victores assumed power, the eight prisoners signed a petition addressed to the new president, claiming that they had been members of a guerrilla faction called "Ixim" and had been "100 percent subversive." They were responsible, the petition stated, for murder, blackmail, rape, and other criminal acts but were now determined to reform their ways and become loyal and productive citizens. Their request for amnesty was not granted.

After the arrest of seven commissioners, including their chief, in October 1982, one of the remaining commissioners, Salvador, took over unofficially as acting chief. His companions tried to have him named official chief of a fifteen-man slate of military commissioners they proposed. The Sololá military commander accepted their proposal, but the town objected vehemently to Salvador and his cohorts. At a meeting with the commander, veterans making up San Pedro's permanent force shouted down the commander's list and insisted that he endorse their own list of fifteen, with a chief other than Salvador. The commander backed down, accepting the town's new slate. The new chief military commissioner promptly sought to gain the community's confidence by making the rounds of all the churches in town to vow that he would defend his community.

With a trusted complement of commissioners in place, Pedranos at last consented, late in November, to organize a "voluntary" civil patrol system consisting of all able-bodied men between the ages of eighteen and fifty, a force of more than 1,000 divided into squads and platoons with rotating on-duty assignments. Before the change of commissioners, Pedranos had resisted pressure from the army to institute a civil patrol system. In San Pedro, as elsewhere, the civil patrol serves under the command of the chief commissioner, who takes his orders from the army command in Sololá. The new chief commissioner was replaced after about a year of service because of personal shortcomings: he had a weakness for women and drink. On October 5, 1983, he was succeeded by Lencho, a thirty-four-year-old Pedrano with an unimpeachable character, who was to sacrifice his life in the service of his community.

As 1983 drew to a close, five more former commissioners were arrested, four of them among the ten named in the April 12 newspaper article as collaborators still at large. They were detained in Sololá but were released after a fortnight. Another, more enduring year-end development was the dismissal of Jorge from the mayor's office by a colonel named Rébuli, who assumed command of Military Zone 14 on November 1, 1983.

Colonel Rébuli was asked to attend a meeting in San Pedro to hear complaints against Jorge, who was accused of being party to the plans and crimes of the former commissioners. It was pointed out, for instance, that before one abduction Jorge told the prospective victim that he was on the blacklist and would be killed. Realizing that the town was rebelling against the authority of a leader who worked against their interests, the commander told the mayor: "Jorge, the town doesn't want you any more. Resign!" Jorge did so.

Colonel Rébuli was well regarded in San Pedro not only because he had agreed to make Jorge step down but also because he had seen fit to send a one-hundred-pound sack of black beans and five sacks of corn to each of the widows of kidnapped Pedrano men. Unfortunately for San Pedro, Rébuli did not live long enough to authorize the appointment of Jorge's successor. On November 20, 1983, the colonel was killed in an ambush near Cerro de Oro on a side of the lake distant from San Pedro. To replace Jorge, the town had installed a mayor they could trust, but after one week of service he had to vacate his office to make room for the Pedrano selected by authorities in Sololá. With the untimely death of Colonel Rébuli, the conspiring supporters of the deposed mayor apparently could exert enough influence in Sololá to block the appointment of a person who would be their enemy. The mayor selected by Sololá was the man who had been vice-mayor under Jorge and who had assumed office at the same time (June 16, 1982). He became mayor on December 3, 1983. Most townsmen did not think he had collaborated with the evil former commissioners, although some citizens had reason to believe that he would be less than forceful in pressing the town's case against the criminals still walking the streets.

Colonel Rébuli was presumably killed by guerrilla forces. The ORPA guerrillas took credit for the action, claiming in a publicity release that the deed was in retaliation for the fierce counterinsurgency campaigns the colonel had launched in the departments of San Marcos and Quezaltenango before his appointment as commander of the Sololá military zone. Nevertheless, some Pedranos suspect that Jorge and his cronies had a hand in Rébuli's assassination.

The year 1984 passed without major incident, thanks to the determination and unimpeachable character of Lencho, the new chief commssioner. In sharp contrast to the imprisoned Jacinto, who had used his position to prey on his own people, Lencho was unswervingly responsive to the interests of his community, to his Protestant church (Pentecostés de América), and to his wife and three small children. He divided his time between work in the field and his official duties. Each day he mustered the men on civil patrol duty. Periodically he traveled to Sololá to report to a lieutenant named Rolando, his contact in military zone headquarters. Members of the old gang still at liberty tried to draw him into their orbit, to make him play their game. They tried unsuccessfully to extort three hundred dollars from him. Antagonized by his rectitude, they sought ways to undermine his standing with the army. "If they kill me, let them kill me," Lencho told his townspeople.

Since he was not paid for his service as chief commissioner, Lencho had trouble meeting the cost of traveling to Sololá by launch and bus. He had been orphaned at an early age, had inherited little land, and always had to work hard for a living. The permanent force, realizing that in Lencho the town at last had found a staunch defender, suggested that each member of the civil patrol contribute five cents a month to pay Lencho's transportation costs. Out of the fifty dollars a month thus raised, Lencho was given seven dollars each time he had to make an official trip. Salvador, piqued that he had been rejected as chief commissioner after Jacinto was arrested, informed the military intelligence unit in Sololá that Lencho was illegally taxing the personnel of the civil patrol. Lencho was summoned to Sololá for questioning. Although the military officers seemed to accept his explanation that the idea of a collection was not his but that of the permanent force, he resolved nevertheless to accept no more money for trips.

When Lencho was asked to turn in allegedly subversive Pedranos, he refused to cooperate without proof of culpability, pointing out that killing an innocent person went against the word of God. His protective policy, which won no favor with the military forces or their local collaborators, was demonstrated in December 1984 when soldiers arrived from Sololá to seize a certain Pedrano. The soldiers woke up Lencho late at night, ordering him to turn the man over to them, it being the responsibility of a town's chief military commissioner to approve an army arrest order. Lencho would not sanction the order, insisting that a hearing must be held the next day to consider charges and evidence. The inquiry that followed revealed a chain of events that began with Marta and her daughter-in-law, the women who had wept together during the 1982 year-end holidays when the whereabouts of Adolfo, their arrested son and husband, was unknown. The episode throws a shaft of light on the kinds of behind-the-scenes motives and maneuvers that can prompt "disappearances."

Marta knew from the start, of course, that her son Adolfo was a military commissioner. But for months she was apparently unaware that the commissioners were involved in the kidnappings. Her letters had expressed shock at the abduction in September 1980 of the baker Francisco and other abductions that followed. After mid-1981, however, she ceased writing. The tavern quarrel between Adolfo and his brother-in-law that resulted in the latter's death occurred about six weeks after Marta's last letter. In mid-1982, after a year of silence, she wrote again to say that she was deathly ill, but the letter made no mention of the continuing string of kidnappings or the murder scandal involving her son Adolfo.

For more than a year following the arrest of Adolfo and other commissioners, Adolfo's wife and two small children continued to live in their tiny cane-walled hut adjoining Marta's house. The two women shared their meals and their sorrows. But at the end of 1984, Adolfo's wife became interested in another man, who had courted her before she married Adolfo. Marta flew into a rage on discovering the lovers alone in a closed room. The younger woman left Marta's home and took up residence in her parents' compound. Marta, possibly encouraged by former associates of her imprisoned son, sought out a military officer temporarily in town to denounce the man who had stolen her daughter-in-law's affections. Marta claimed that he was a subversive. And that is why soldiers woke up Lencho one night in December and told him to order the capture of this supposedly subversive Pedrano.

The ensuing inquiry disclosed that the army was acting on derogatory information supplied by Marta. Called in to explain the basis for her accusation, Marta told the investigating officer that the man delivered food to guerrillas hiding in the hills and held guerrilla meetings in his house. When asked how she knew these things, she replied that she got the information from the man's seven-year-old daughter while she and the girl were washing clothes on the shore of the lake. The girl was summoned and swore that she had never said what Marta claimed she had said. It developed, moreover, that the two customarily did their washing at different locations on the lake. Lencho and others testified that the accused man was a good worker and a law-abiding citizen. With no proof that he consorted with guerrillas, the case against him was dropped.

Lencho's determination to protect the lives of innocent Pedranos did not please collaborators of the imprisoned commissioners, who, therefore, accused Lencho of supporting the guerrilla cause. Military authorities confronted Lencho with the fact that he was not turning in anyone from San Pedro. He stood his ground, asserting that the accusers lied and that no man should be condemned without a hearing.

While Lencho was earning the people's gratitude for courage under pressure, his elderly uncle Pedro was leading a struggle to prevent the eight prisoners from being set free. As indicated earlier, Pedro had led the four-man delegation that gave the newspaper a copy of the town's petition urging Ríos Montt to speed the trial of the arrested former commissioners and to effect the arrest of ten additional suspects named in the document. For a long time the prisoners were shunted from one city to another without trial. Finally on February 28, 1984, sixteen months after they had been arrested, their sentences were pronounced. Jacinto, who had been chief military commissioner, was sentenced to serve twelve years in prison; Adolfo, second-in-command, ten years; the six others, two to four years each. The convicted men were committed to the Cantel penal colony near Quezaltenango. They had served only a fraction of their time, however, when rumors began to reach San Pedro that they would soon be released. To forestall this unwanted development, Pedro, the indefatigable foe of the former commissioners, traveled repeatedly to Sololá, presenting evidence and submitting documents designed to persuade authorities to keep the culprits safely locked up.

Such was the situation through the end of 1984 and the beginning of 1985—Pedro fending off efforts to set the prisoners free, his nephew Lencho fending off attempts to capture alleged subversives—when a tragic blow rocked the town. Nephew and uncle were seized and brutally murdered, their corpses discovered at dawn on Wednesday, February 27, 1985.

The Tragic Blow

The impending calamity had cast its shadow on San Pedro one night a week earlier, when two strangers were seen walking about the town at 9:00 P.M. A Pedrano on civil patrol duty informed Lencho that an *alguacil* (errand man in the municipal service system) was showing the strangers the houses of military commissioners. When Lencho asked what the strangers were up to, the *alguacil* replied that they had been hired as boatmen by his uncle, the owner of a tavern and of several launches. Lencho found the two strangers at the boat owner's tavern. They were drinking with the proprietor and Jorge, the man who had been imposed and deposed as mayor of San Pedro. The strangers identified themselves as army agents and told Lencho that they were investigating a matter that did not concern him. A day or two later, heeding the advice of fellow commissioners, Lencho had a memorandum drawn up at town headquarters. It stated that if a commissioner disappeared the *alguacil* would be held responsible.

On Tuesday, February 26, 1985, Lencho went to plant corn on his brother-in-law's land. At home in the late afternoon he was visited by a neighbor who had just returned by boat from Panajachel. The visitor reported that Lencho's uncle Pedro had not come back on the afternoon launch. As Pedro was about to board the boat in Panajachel the day before, he had been suddenly summoned to appear in Sololá and had asked a passenger to tell his wife that he would be home the next day. But Pedro had not returned.

This news troubled Lencho. He went out to supervise the rotation of the civil patrol, urging the men to be particularly alert that night. Instead of eating his dinner, he decided to confer with one of his church brethren. That evening he did not attend church service. He was distraught, stayed up late, joined his wife in prayers, and eventually went to bed.

Around midnight Lencho's sister answered a knock on the door. The callers said that they were looking for Lencho. She assumed that they were civil patrollers with some routine problem that could wait and told them that her brother was not there. She knew that Lencho had worked hard in the field that day, and she did not want to disturb his sleep. The men left but soon came back and broke in forcibly. Lencho's wife rose, snapped on the lights, and saw four armed men in civilian clothes, their faces hidden by woolen *gorras* (stocking caps). "Fetch Lencho and make it fast," they demanded. She went to the other room and warned Lencho, "They want to grab and kill you." "Very well," replied Lencho. "Bring me my pants and shirt and jacket." "Hurry up. It's urgent," the men commanded. Lencho entered the lighted room and calmly addressed a man in the doorway whose *gorra* was pulled halfway up: "Buenos noches, mi teniente Rolando." The man jerked the *gorra* down over his face. The captors swiftly bound Lencho's arms and hustled him into the street. "Adiós, Mamá," were Lencho's last words.

Lencho's wife, joined by his sister and brother, tried to run after the men, but they spun around and ordered, "Stay back or be killed." The three doubled back and reached the main street in time to see a yellow pickup turn the corner and head up the road toward Santiago Atitlán. A lone civil patrolman on duty saw the vehicle coming; his companions were taking a coffee break. He signaled the pickup to stop, but it raced on.

The three relatives ran to the town center to report the abduction to the municipal guards and the on-duty commissioners. The church bells rang as they had never rung before, waking the town. By half past midnight a great crowd had formed to learn what had happened to Lencho. Women sobbed. Men shouted: "Make a list! Let's get them!" They first rushed to seize the *alguacil* and forced him to name his accomplices. He named his uncle, the boat owner; he named Salvador, Jorge, Mario, others. The elicited names only confirmed what the enraged citizens had long suspected. They did not need to draw up a list. In their collective mind they had already identified at least fifteen resident enemies, including the ten suspects listed in the petition Pedro and three companions had presented to the president and the press nearly two years earlier.

That night the mob captured as many of the fifteen as they could find. The boat owner and some others could not immediately be found. When they entered Salvador's house, his wife tried to hold them off with a machete. They knocked it from her hand and searched the premises. They found Salvador hiding in a clump of bushes, beat him soundly to make him confess and name coconspirators, and hauled him off to jail. They nearly killed another man when they pulled him out of his house. In their rage they destroyed suspects' property. Not finding Jorge in his house, they proceeded to wreck his television and smash his stereo set. Jorge, who was hiding elsewhere, turned himself in after the fury had abated.

By 1:30 A.M., a document had been drawn up in the town hall setting forth the facts and circumstances that would provide the basis for later legal proceedings. It stated that Lencho had been abducted at 12:01 A.M. on February 27. Referring to the memorandum drawn up a few days earlier, it implicated the *alguacil*, the two disguised military men he was escorting, the boat owner, and others. It accused the alleged conspirators of holding secret meetings at such-and-such a time and place, etc.

Before daybreak, Lencho's brother and several military commissioners who had served under Lencho left for Sololá to get help from army officials but reportedly found them unsympathetic. At dawn another Pedrano drove off toward Santiago Atitlán to get firewood. Three miles out of town at a place called Xequistel he came upon the bodies of Lencho and Pedro. Their throats had been cut, and they had been stabbed in the chest. Hanks of hair had been torn from their heads. Pedro's wrists and ankles were bound with nylon cord. Blood and skin were found on the trunk of a tree to which one of the victims had apparently been tied. When they heard the dismaying news, many Pedranos hurried to Xequistel to recover the bodies. The corpses were taken to Solalá for autopsy and returned to San Pedro for burial. That day more of the wanted fifteen were seized and jailed.

The next day, Thursday, the last of the fifteen were rounded up. Newspaper reporters arrived the same day to photograph the jailed suspects, take pictures of the thousands of mourners in the funeral procession, and hear Lencho's widow tell how her husband was kidnapped. Soldiers arrived to take the captured men to Solalá.

On the afternoon of the next day, Friday, the Solalá military commander, accompanied by three aides, went to San Pedro to preside at a general meeting he had called. Whether he wanted mainly to assure himself about the town's position or to reassure the assembly is uncertain. He found an enormous crowd awaiting him and was seemingly impressed by the Pedranos' unanimity in condemning the recently arrested fifteen.

A leading citizen opened the meeting with a prayer that made people cry. All the women who had lost husbands during the 1980–82 reign of terror were in the audience. Some of them spoke up. One widow said that she had noticed Jorge, Salvador, and other alleged conspirators convening at the boat owner's home and had overheard them plotting to kill the current commissioners. The people demanded that the fifteen captured men be tried and punished. They assured the commander that they sided with the army and not with the guerrillas. The commander promised to cooperate, asserting that the suspects would be duly tried.

On the following day, Saturday, the Pedranos themselves called a general meeting to consider forming a town defense committee, a proposal that was swiftly approved. Then and there committee officers were elected: chairman, vice-chairman, secretary, and treasurer. Papers were drawn up formalizing the committee and expressing the town's demand that the criminals be brought to book. The intent of the committee was to assemble testimony and produce documents for the courts, and to do so in a more forceful and official manner than the murdered Pedro had been able to do acting semicovertly as a private citizen without official backing. As a public entity, the town defense committee hoped to raise enough money to pay for legal and other costs. But when the committee's officers presented themselves to the governor of Solalá Department, their hopes were dashed. The committee was refused official authorization, without which it had no

right to exist or collect funds. Why the committee was quashed remains unclear. The explanation given by a Pedrano in the best position
to know is simple: "The governor is against us."

Pedro had complained that, despite efforts to work quietly, he had
been shadowed by confederates of the imprisoned men whenever he
traveled to Sololá. On his last trip to give authorities yet more evidence
and arguments, the day he was lured away from the Panajachel dock
with the message that he was awaited in Sololá, he had been driven off
in a yellow pickup. This was observed by the Pedrano who had told
Lencho that Pedro had failed to return on the boat as expected. The
same man had observed one of the alleged Pedrano conspirators sitting
in the yellow pickup, which presumably then made its way around the
lake to haul Lencho to the place where the two bodies were found the
next morning. In retrospect it was realized that the two military men
in civilian dress seen walking about San Pedro with the *alguacil* a few
days earlier were there to help lay the groundwork for the abductions
of Pedro and Lencho.

Informants offered reasons for Lencho's murder: he had been denounced to the army as a subversive for repeatedly failing to cooperate
in the capture of alleged subversives; the assassins knew that if he was
not killed along with Pedro he would work assiduously to avenge his
uncle's death and would carry on the slain man's battle to keep the
killers safely locked up. Lencho's wife had said that when she ran after
the kidnappers she saw and recognized four of the alleged Pedrano
conspirators leaving an alley. Informants believe that some of the suspects could not be found at home on the night of Lencho's abduction
because hours earlier they had already left for Xequistel, outside San
Pedro, to participate in the torture and killing.

The fifteen suspects taken to Sololá after Lencho was kidnapped
apparently suffered few restrictions; on the day after their arrest they
were reportedly seen disporting themselves on the Panajachel beach
below Sololá. In two weeks they were returned to San Pedro, accompanied by a contingent of eighty soldiers. The suspects were said to be
under house arrest and the soldiers to be in town to protect them from
harm. The soldiers were encamped on the outskirts of town and pro-
visioned by the army. The fifteen suspects seldom ventured out of their
homes.

The protected suspects, in all likelihood, were due to be released
before long without punishment. That indeed was the confident pre-

diction of the lawyer residing in Sololá who had been engaged to defend the fifteen Pedranos. He expressed the opinion that the violence in San Pedro was merely the settling of old scores by vindictive individuals in the bitterly divided town—a judgment that might well have applied to several of the men—and that the fifteen suspects were the objects of false accusations. But in June 1985, the unlikely occurred. After encamping in San Pedro for three months, the contingent of eighty soldiers was withdrawn, but the men they guarded were not set free. Instead they were once again sent to jail in Sololá. This probably would not have happened had a man named Arturo not entered the picture in May.

Arturo, a capable young Pedrano, was about to complete his law training at a university in Guatemala City. Apparently well versed in the country's legal code, he devoted himself vigorously to the task of bringing the suspects to book. His youth and lack of political clout placed him at a disadvantage in comparison to the experienced and well-connected Sololá lawyer who was defending the accused. We asked Pedranos why they did not hire an outside lawyer with more influence than Arturo and were told that that would require more money than they could raise (or were permitted to raise) and that, even if they had the money, no other lawyer would risk his life by taking on a case that challenged the military establishment.

When Arturo went to Sololá to look into the record, he discovered, to his and the town's surprise, that there was absolutely nothing pending with respect to the murder of Pedro and Lencho a few months earlier. The mayor of San Pedro, it seems, had failed in his duty to initiate *diligencias* (investigations). According to articles 318 and 319 of Guatemala's penal code, the mayor (who is also justice of the peace), is to begin the investigation and turn his findings over to a judge within three days of the crime. The mayor at the time of the double murder—who had been vice-mayor under Jorge until the latter was removed from office—was a friend of Jorge (though presumably not an accomplice). The mayor was also a son-in-law of the boat owner, another of the fifteen suspects. One can understand why the mayor would hesitate to initiate proceedings, but in these circumstances, as Arturo was quick to point out, it was incumbent on the mayor to call on a judge and explain his conflict of interest.

Despite the mayor's inaction, Arturo was able to start up the litigation process by arranging for a "reconstruction of the facts" at a meeting early in May 1985 attended by himself, the lawyer for the defendants, and the judge of the trial court in Sololá. Subsequently Arturo made numerous trips to Sololá, often accompanied by Lencho's twenty-six-year-old widow. The fifteen defendants were summoned from San Pedro to make declarations and, as already noted, were transferred to the Sololá jail in June. Acting through an intermediary, the Sololá lawyer reportedly offered Arturo a handsome sum of money if he would drop the case. Arturo refused, and for six months the suspects bided their time in jail while their attorney and Arturo kept filing briefs and petitions for and against them. On December 20, 1985, they were declared not guilty. Arturo immediately appealed the verdict, and for month after month the men remained in jail awaiting the decision of the appellate court in Antigua.

Meanwhile there were developments in the case of the eight former commissioners who had been captured in October 1982 and were serving time in the Cantel penitentiary. On June 25, 1985, six of them were set free on payment of money put up by their families. Before their release the town had drawn up a petition asking the authorities to prohibit any of the convicted men from setting foot in San Pedro. This request was never granted, either because the papers were stalled in the mayor's office or because the petition found no favor in Sololá. Of the six men released from Cantel, only two returned to San Pedro. One worked in the field by day, always accompanied by a relative, but stayed home evenings. The other kept to his house, fearful of attack by Pedranos whose sons or brothers had been kidnapped. Four of the freed men decided to live elsewhere: one in Santiago Atitlán, one in Quezaltenango, and two on the coast. Jacinto and Adolfo, who had been chief and assistant chief of commissioners, respectively, during the long *noche negra,* were serving longer sentences and were not released with the others.

That was the situation as recorded during a visit to San Pedro in March 1986. But by the time we made another visit in October 1986, the situation had changed considerably. Except for Jacinto, all the Pedranos imprisoned in Cantel or Sololá had been released. Adolfo, freed from Cantel, went to live in Guatemala City. Freed also were the many suspects who had been unceremoniously rounded up after word of Lencho's abduction aroused the town after midnight on February 27, 1985. Most of the freed men returned to San Pedro. Originally fifteen in number, the group had been reduced to twelve before the time of release. Three of the group, including José, the deposed mayor, had disappeared under mysterious circumstances in June 1985 when the fifteen suspects kept under house arrest were remanded to jail in Solola. The three were reportedly seized by military police and vanished without trace. Informants conjecture that they may no longer be alive.

One night a brood of penned-in piglets was set afire. The owner was a former commissioner back from prison, and neighbors speculated that the damage was an act of vengeance. Other than that minor incident, however, no serious harm has so far befallen any of the returned men held reponsible for having inflicted suffering on Pedrano families. The returned citizens venture into the streets only when necessary and only in the company of kinsmen. With good luck San Pedro may be spared yet another flare-up of the violence for which the military authorities, like their local collaborators, bear part of the blame.

The Army Connection

On the day the tortured bodies of Lencho and Pedro were found in Xequistel, townsmen notified the press as well as the army. On Friday, March 1, 1985, a detailed story, with pictures, on the double murder in San Pedro appeared in the *Prensa Libre* under a six-column streamer: "Commotion over Crimes." The account stated that, according to his widow, Lencho recognized one of his captors and said, "Good evening, my lieutenant." It also named the suspected *alguacil,* stating that he had confessed that he was one of the accomplices and that a lieutenant was another. The full name of the lieutenant had been given to the army, according to the article, but the newspaper did not print his name.

On March 2, the *Prensa Libre,* under a six-column heading, "Army Opens Investigation," quoted a colonel in charge of public relations for the nation's armed forces as saying that there was no army official in San Pedro but that, nevertheless, in view of the seriousness of the information appearing in the press, an investigation had been ordered to establish the truth of the claims. The colonel assured readers that the army would never retain in its ranks persons who acted illegally and that any officer accused of a crime, with evidence, would be turned over to the proper tribunal for judgment.

On March 3, under a six-column banner, "Calm Returns to San Pedro la Laguna," the *Prensa Libre* reported that the colonel in command of Military Zone 14 (Sololá) had spent a few hours in San Pedro talking with municipal officials and Lencho's widow and concluded that certain unnamed parties had coerced the widow to claim that an army lieutenant had been involved. According to the newspaper article, the commander said that the widow herself had disavowed the claim and that the stories of the army's participation in the crime were therefore totally discredited. He also said, according to the article, that the Pedranos informed him that they blamed the kidnapping and assassination of the commissioner and his uncle on a group of guerrillas known as Ixchil (Ixim) who previously were military commissioners. The commander assured the Pedranos, the paper reported, that the army would stay watchful to see that the forces of "subversive delinquency" did not continue to use the Pedranos as instruments for casting blame on the armed forces, whose only mission, he said, was to ensure "peace, tranquillity, and harmony."

The next day, another article appeared in the *Prensa Libre* under the headline "Army Affirms No Lieutenant Involved in San Pedro's Crimes." The story, based on a communiqué issued by the army's department of public relations, asserted that a subversive group self-styled Ixim had committed the crimes, that the perpetrators had been captured, and that they had induced Lencho's widow to make a false accusation.

The army's reconstruction of the events departs from the Pedranos' version. The story Lencho's widow tells is the same one she told reporters at the outset. She claimed from the first and she continues to claim that her husband recognized the lieutenant and greeted him by name. She does not recall ever being interviewed by the military zonal commander, as reported in the newspaper. According to knowledgeable sources, the lieutenant named by Lencho was quietly transferred from Sololá to a military prison in Guatemala City to await trial in a military court for kidnapping and murder. These same sources had persuasive evidence, they said, that the lieutenant had been paid seven hundred dollars to kill Lencho and his uncle and that they knew who had delivered the money.

The payment had allegedly been delivered by one of the five Pedranos who had recently been exposed as *confidenciales* (secret agents) working for army intelligence (G-2). The five were among the fifteen suspects rounded up after Lencho and Pedro were murdered. The other ten were virtually the same as the ten suspects described in the

April 12, 1983, newspaper article as "still going about freely as though they hadn't done a thing."

Two of the secret agents had also doubled as military commissioners during San Pedro's two-year *noche negra*. One was the man seen in the yellow pickup that drove Pedro away from the Panajachel dock. He was also one of the two commissioners who took a third commissioner for a fatal walk along the beach in San Pedro in August 1982. The other military commissioner who doubled as a secret agent was Salvador, who became acting chief after Commissioner Jacinto was arrested but whose bid to become formal chief was vigorously opposed by the community. The three other individuals revealed to be secret agents were the boat owner, the deposed mayor Jorge, and the *güizache* Mario.

It is interesting and ironic to recall that three of the secret agents—Salvador, Jorge, and Mario—had tried to silence Fernando, the shrillest of the whistle blowers, by accusing him of calumny at the hearing held by the commander of the army post at Santiago Atitlán only days before two of the other plaintiffs in that suit (Jacinto and Adolfo) were themselves arrested on October 28, 1982. The sixth plaintiff later turned out to be one of the first of the fifteen suspects captured after news of Lencho's abduction raced through the town. Thus all six of Fernando's accusers eventually found themselves in jail, while Fernando was free to get himself elected mayor of San Pedro in the November 3, 1985, elections.

The appointment of secret agents apparently was part of an extensive change in army strategy initiated during the Lucas García regime to counter the threat of insurgency. Previously based only in the capital and a few other cities, the army extended into the countryside to establish a center of strength, a zonal command, in each of the republic's twenty-two departments. The zonal command in turn infiltrated local communities such as San Pedro to create an espionage network. It remains unclear how the work of secret agents such as Salvador, Jorge, and Mario, was coordinated with that of the military commissioners to compile blacklists and stage abductions during the period when Jacinto was chief military commissioner.

The two army-connected groups were composed in the main of different kinds of people. Inspection of the characteristics of the eighteen former commissioners named in the April 1983 newspaper article—the eight prisoners who were awaiting trial and the ten others whose arrests were being sought—reveals that they tended to be rather impecunious, powerless, and undistinguished individuals. Most of them were laborers, fishermen, or petty traders. All were married with children; most were in their thirties. What they mainly sought was instant gratification. One informant, when asked why former commissioners had abused their offices, replied by making three digital gestures signifying money, liquor, and sex. Some of the men showed signs of corruptibility even before they became involved in extortion and violence. One commissioner, for instance, is said to have doctored the books when he was a municipal employee, paying workmen less than the amount he recorded and keeping the difference. In earlier days, when Jacinto was merely a recruiting agent, he would accept ten-dollar bribes not to recruit particular young Pedranos.

In contrast to the former commissioners, the secret agents were older men in their fifties and sixties, prominent in the community, ambitious, and fairly well-off. Three of them owned productive coffee land. Two owned commercial property—trucks for hauling goods long distances or launches for transporting passengers and cargo between San Pedro and the market town Santiago Atitlán. Two of the secret agents, with histories of extended service in the armed forces, had friends and connections in the military; one or two had political connections in high places.

The boat owner took advantage of his secret-agent status to negotiate profitable deals for himself. He accused a man in Tzununá, across the lake, of transporting guerrillas in a launch the man owned. The Pedrano flashed his army *carnet* (identification card) to frighten him. He then forced the man to sell the launch for a very low price, giving him only a small down payment and saying that he would pay the rest later. The Tzununá man lost more than one thousand dollars in the deal. He became despondent and reportedly drank himself to death. In a similar manner the unscrupulous boat owner is said to have acquired another launch for a low price from the administrator of a coffee plantation near San Pedro.

But what the secret agents mainly wanted, in contrast to the former commissioners, was political power. They sought to capture the two key posts, the mayor's office and that of chief military commissioner. For a while they were successful. Jorge was imposed as mayor and held onto his office for more than a year before the town persuaded the Sololá commander to remove him. Salvador, who had operated as a military commissioner overtly and as an intelligence officer covertly, was reputed to be the real leader of the commissioners, even while Jacinto, a less forceful person, was officially in charge. When Jacinto was taken prisoner, Salvador made an unsuccessful bid to be named chief commissioner.

Of the five secret agents, Mario, the *güizache* with an unsavory reputation, was undoubtedly the most noteworthy. According to our sources, it was he who had advised Marta that a four-hundred-dollar payment could ransom arrested Adolfo, and who later counseled the eight imprisoned former commissioners to apply for amnesty by claiming to be repentent Ixim guerrillas. He allegedly is the person who delivered seven hundred dollars to Lieutenant Rolando in payment for kidnapping Lencho, and he was one of the four men (all secret agents) whom Lencho's widow said she had seen leaving an alley while masked men were carrying off her husband.

It may seem strange that the army would punish operatives for deeds presumably committed in collaboration with army units, but it should be remembered that the army is a complex organization made up of separate suborganizations and subject to changing directives over time. One unit may punish people for actions ordered by a different, possibly clandestine, unit. The policy of a post commander may be reversed by the commander who succeeds him. But it is unlikely that the eight Pedranos sentenced by an army court were convicted of crimes committed jointly with army personnel. There was no need of that. Victimized Pedranos supplied enough evidence to convict the conspirators of crimes committed independently—rape, extortion, murder. In addition, the army wrung confessions out of the arrested men by methods of its own. One informant told us what he had learned on this score from former commissioners whom he visited in prison. During the ten days they were held at the Santiago Atitlán post following their capture on October 28, 1982, they were beaten with clubs. They were also put in a pit with water in it. The prisoners said that they thought this treatment was going to kill them.

We do not know whether any of the kidnapped Pedranos were taken to the same place or subjected to similar treatment, but we do know that the pit treatment was applied to suspected subversives in 1983. In the fall of that year an interview with a soldier stationed outside the army barracks in Santiago Atitlán was recorded on tape and printed verbatim in *Americas Watch Report* (January 1984) entitled, "Guate-

mala: A Nation of Prisoners." The soldier was asked how long captured persons generally remained in the camp. He replied, "Here,
about two months, and if they don't want to talk then they get put in
the hole with water."

"And how do they feel there in the hole?"

"Well, of course, they're going to feel terrible. Once you put them
in there, they can't take it, and they die."

"How many are in there now?"

"There are two in there. They've been in there for two days; we take
them out to tell us what they do, and if they don't say anything, we
stick them in again."

Divisiveness and Democracy

We must finally ask to what extent the trouble in San Pedro can be
ascribed to social cleavages within the community. The answer varies
with the category of offenders being considered. Jacinto, Adolfo, and
the rest of the venal former commissioners were mainly driven by
greed and the desire to settle personal scores. There is no need to seek
explanations in lines of cleavage dividing San Pedro society. They were
waging no interfaith warfare. Their group and the people they victimized included Catholics and Protestants in about the same proportion.
Their chief, Jacinto, was nominally Catholic; his close friend and
second-in-command was Protestant. The former commissioners were
not members of one political faction in battle against another; they
were not politically active as individuals.

The secret agents, in contrast to the former commissioners, were
politically ambitious. Now in his sixties, Mario, the most thoroughly
political of the several secret agents, has a history of continuous, often
acrimonious involvement in town politics dating back to the time local
political parties first sprang up under the democratic Arévalo-Arbenz
regime of 1945–54. Since 1968, Mario has been the leader of the local
branch of the ultrarightist National Liberation Movement (MLN),
which has been termed "the party of organized violence." This is the
party of Sandoval Alarcón, generally reputed to be the founder of Guatemala's Mano Blanca, the notorious paramilitary "death squad" organization. MLN leaders have counted on Mario to deliver votes during national and local elections. Mario in turn has counted on his
friendship with Sandoval to receive expert legal assistance to help him

in his role as *güizache,* win court cases in Sololá for his Pedrano clients—disputes over land titles and inheritances are common—and defend Mario himself whenever political opponents charge him with corrupt practices.

Over the course of years, political parties and coalitions have waxed, waned, and vied for power in San Pedro. By the mid-1970s, the political groups had sorted themselves into two opposing coalitions led by contending champions. The rival leaders were Mario on one side and civic-minded Antonio on the other. In 1974, Mario's slate lost, and Antonio served as mayor for a two-year term. In 1976, Mario's slate won, remaining in office four years. In 1980 a prosperous merchant ran for mayor. He had been a political ally of Antonio and, like him, known for his upright character and respect for the law. To run against the merchant, Mario's MLN party fielded a slate of candidates that included the unscrupulous boat owner and Salvador, the would-be chief of the military commissioners—men who, like Jorge and like Mario himself, were later revealed as secret agents for army intelligence. Mario's men, who labeled their platform "The Best Anti-Communist Program" (this was under the García Lucas regime), were defeated at the polls by the prosperous merchant, who began what was to be a four-year term but who was removed in June 1982 (no commissioner had yet been arrested) when Jorge was imposed as mayor.

If Mario and his association failed to win power overtly in 1980, they nevertheless were able to carry out at least part of their anti-Communist agenda by virtue of their covert army connections. Informants claim that by the time Mario was arrested, however, he had ceased being a protégé of Sandoval Alarcón because he had not been able to swing enough votes for the MLN.

It is interesting, if not surprising, to note that the alignment of political leadership prevailing before the onset of violence in San Pedro prefigured the antagonism between the exposed secret agents—the leaders in the group of fifteen suspects arrested after Lencho was kidnapped—and those who led the fight to have them arrested and punished: civic-minded Antonio, the prosperous merchant, the more respected of the town's two *güizaches,* and Fernando, one-time political ally of Ríos Montt.

It may be tempting to blame the outbreak of violence in San Pedro on social divisiveness and the settling of old scores, but the temptation

should be resisted. Religious competition and vigorous political in-
fighting were features of San Pedro life for decades before 1980 without producing violence. The same can be said for interpersonal an-
tagonisms. They arose in the past and were settled by means short of
murder. What disrupted the peace in San Pedro was not the presence
of differences and divisions but the army's recruitment of agents and
spies that had the effect of exploiting these cleavages.

Competition between parties is, after all, one of the hallmarks of
political democracy. Another hallmark is an informed electorate. By
this token San Pedro has become increasingly democratic. Compared
to the time during the Arévalo-Arbenz era (1945–54) when elections
for local office were introduced, Pedranos are now more literate and
informed about history and the world around them. The local school
system has been extended, and a good number of Pedranos have gone
on to acquire professional training in such fields as accounting, agron-
omy, and especially education. Two or three are physicians. Still another hallmark of democracy is freedom of expression. With experience and education, many Pedranos have learned to express their
differing opinions about justice, religion, and government.

Ever since the Arévalo-Arbenz era, San Pedro society has been moving in the direction of greater democracy, while the Guatemalan government has been moving in the opposite direction. Increasing diver-
gence between the two tendencies, the local and the national, can be
seen as a source of the affliction that befell San Pedro. Francisco the
baker spoke his mind about the abusive police and the militarization
of the lake area and was the first Pedrano to be "disappeared" by
"unknown parties" (*desconocides*)—two terms that have become common parlance in Guatemala, along with "criminal subversives" (*subversives delinquentes*). Lencho, the fearless chief commissioner, spoke
up in defense of civil liberties and fell victim to the violation of human
rights. It can be said that San Pedro has suffered punishment not for
the sin of displaying divisiveness but for the virtue of practicing
democracy.

CHAPTER 6

Story from a Peaceful Town: San Antonio Aguas Calientes

By Sheldon Annis

San Antonio Aguas Calientes is one of Guatemala's best-known and most accessible Indian towns. Less than fifteen minutes from Antigua and just another thirty-five minutes from Guatemala City, San Antonio is so thoroughly within the physical and psychological orbit of the capital that it is usually considered to be outside the zone of violence that has afflicted the highlands. Unlike places with names now synonymous with violence—Panzós, San Martín Jilotepeque, San Francisco Nentón, the Ixil Triangle—the name San Antonio Aguas Calientes still evokes peaceful images of tourist buses and backstrap looms. There, the only apparent struggle is an argument over the price of wall hangings and a rush to get back to the hotel in time. Yet, cut from Guatemalan cloth, the peaceful town too has its story.

Historical and Present-Day Setting

San Antonio was founded by the Conqueror of Guatemala, Pedro de Alvarado. When he built his capital at Santiago de los Caballeros (present-day Antigua), he also needed to develop agricultural lands that would provision his city. To do so, he established haciendas (ranches), which he gave to his lieutenants as rewards for service in the Conquest. San Antonio—initially called Milpa de Juan de Chávez after its initial owner—was one of five such towns settled in an uninhabited valley on the shores of a lake named Lago de Quinizilapa.

To provide workers for his new settlements, Alvarado populated the towns with captives and slaves who had been rounded up during the wars. Unlike other contemporary Indians in the Maya towns of Guatemala and Mexico, the people of the Quinizilapa Valley had no common pre-Hispanic roots. Not only were the initial settlers not necessarily Cakchiquel-speakers, but, in fact, many of the ancestors of San Antonio were not Indian at all but blacks brought from the Caribbean.

Taking into account frequent pandemics that leveled the population, one might suspect that a settlement so culturally diverse would, over 450 years, acculturate as ladinos. Yet that did not happen. Alvarado founded not just a town but a new class of beings. Socially and politically, Guatemala needed *indios:* the functional heirs of slavery (if not precisely the cultural-biological descendants of the Mayas), hardworking but passive people who would maintain themselves for hundreds of years in a permanent state of semiautonomous, unequal separation.

Over the long colonial and republican periods, the hybrid Indian village reliably played its role, supplying labor and producing the crops upon which successive Guatemalan export economies were based (sugar, indigo, cochineal, and, by the late nineteenth century, coffee). In return, the town prospered culturally and, by the relative standards of Guatemalan economy, financially.

Today Indians from other parts of the highlands think of San Antonio as "rich." Most people attribute this prosperity to the tourist economy, but, in fact, there is a better reason. While neighboring towns lost most of their communal lands during the coffee expansion of the late nineteenth and early twentieth centuries, San Antonio hung onto and may have even slightly expanded its land base. Reasonably abundant land in turn permitted cultivation of a broad range of commercial crops, particularly vegetables and coffee. Capitalizing its favorable location relative to Guatemala City with its wholesale urban markets and the Pacific Coast, San Antonio then became a bulking and distribution center for the marketing of midaltitude agricultural produce. Wealthier middlemen have been able to buy trucks. Constant trade and physical proximity to nearby cities have encouraged wage labor, creating a flexible regulatory mechanism for surpluses in the agricultural laboring force. With cash in the town, small-business enterprise—especially the sale of textiles to tourists—tended to flourish, in turn creating unusual entrepreneurial opportunities for Indian women.

By way of contrast, it is interesting to compare San Antonio to San Lorenzo el Cubo, scarcely five hundred meters down the road. The two towns were founded about the same time (in the 1520s) and with the same genetic stock (Indian slaves and blacks). Yet as the coffee boom of the late nineteenth and early twentieth centuries began, the prime lands of San Lorenzo were incorporated into export-oriented coffee fincas that helped form the fortunes of some of Guatemala's richest families; what was left was gradually taken over, by attrition, by the more aggressive farmers of San Antonio. San Lorenzo lost not only most of its land but also the productive basis for its earlier cultural stability. Today the town is ladino. It shows no remnants of its initial Indianness, unlike San Antonio, a stone's throw down the road, where women wear huipils and chatter in Cakchiquel.

San Antonio is also "rich" in its unusual array of human resources. More than a hundred years ago, José Navarro, a church chronicler, described glowingly the alert, animated demeanor of the citizens, the cleanliness, the *two* schools, the entrepreneurial spirit, and all the people's ability to speak Spanish "as if it were their native language." Even then the town was proposed as a model for less civilized, less progressive Indians.

Today San Antonio supports burgeoning Catholic, evangelical, and public schools. It supplies a relatively constant flow of students to the secondary school in Antigua, and even some to the university in Guatemala City. Newspapers and books are common in homes. Virtually all young people, most adult men, and even most women are both literate and bilingual. Compared to the "closed" communities that one encounters in Quiché, Huehuetenango, or Alta and Baja Verapaz, San Antonio is open and welcoming. The catechist, the missionary, the salesman, the anthropologist, the development technician, and the tourist have all been met here with warmth and curiosity.

Because of these characteristics—physical accessibility, a rich base of natural resources, widespread literacy, bilingualism, openness to outsiders, interest in new ideas—San Antonio has been a model town for "development"—almost as if the U.S. Peace Corps had wished it into existence. San Antonio farmers readily manage commercial crops. They understand fertilizers and pesticides. They cooperate with technicians to eradicate malaria, coffee rust, and malnutrition. The women take their birth-control pills, breast-feed, and have their children vaccinated. Farmers terrace their fields, join co-ops, borrow from the agricultural bank. They can be persuaded to raise rabbits for supplemental protein and install concrete slab covers over their latrines. When they are sick, they seek a doctor rather than the *ajitz'* (curer, shaman). They know how to hire lawyers and bribe police and government of-

ficials. When they have money, they send their children to school, buy
pickup trucks, reinvest in land, or start small businesses.

In a nutshell, they are Guatemala's "model Indians." If any Indians
are incorporated into the system—even moving up, benefiting from
it—it is the savvy, articulate, aggressive farmers, weavers, and merchants of San Antonio Aguas Calientes.

Elderly people in San Antonio recall hunting ducks and fishing in
the marshy bottomland that was once Lago de Quinizilapa in the early
years of this century. Before many decades had passed, however, the
much-reduced lake was mostly a health hazard. Yellow-fever epidem-
ics killed as many as one-third of the people. In 1927 the villagers
petitioned the government to drain the lake, diverting the natural
springs into a river. Two years later, the town decided to survey the
newly drained bottomland and divide it up into about 360 *cuartos*—
that is, one-fourth cuerda plots, each about 40 by 10 meters (about
1/16 acre). After much discussion, a "lottery" was set up through
which the plots were allocated to most farming families.

In the intervening half century, the population of San Antonio approximately tripled. Though the total land base probably did not decline, individual plots tended to become smaller and more intensively
farmed; and through inheritance and resale, land-ownership became
ever more skewed. Today, to maintain themselves in the traditional
agricultural economy, many of the poor must rent land from their
land-rich but labor-poor neighbors.

Most plots in what is called the "laguna" are now literally no larger
than medium-sized backyards in a U.S. suburb. Yet because there is
deep natural topsoil, as well as plenty of water, good drainage, an
international market for coffee, steady local demand for vegetables,
and easy access to urban markets, the plots are highly prized. With
both the economic and cultural health of the town so evidently dependent on land, the laguna has been an important element in the ability
of San Antonio farmers to consistently beat the averages of rural Guatemalan poverty.

A Town Intruder

Horacio Arroyave Pantiagua was a lawyer, a member of the Guate-
malan middle class. He owned houses in both Antigua and Guatemala
City. In the early 1970s, Arroyave developed an interest in the San
Antonio laguna, apparently when he was called upon to handle the

estate of Eugenio González, a ladino from nearby Ciudad Vieja. González had owned La Esperanza, a small farm of roughly 6 manzanas (42 cuerdas) in the San Antonio laguna.

Possibly González's heirs were eager to sell their father's farm, and possibly they received a fair price for it. But according to the people of San Antonio, Arroyave simply used his knowledge of the law and made himself the beneficiary of González's will. One way or another, it is certain that the lawyer, not the heirs, ended up with the estate.

Certainly, Arroyave was a man who recognized opportunity. One can easily imagine him driving into the volcanic valley and down the back roads through the rich, well-watered bottomland to his new farm. Looking around, he must have seen the land as underutilized, wasted on the dozens of Indians working their nontechnified microplots. Perhaps he looked admiringly to his nearby ladino (even some American) neighbors—modern exporters of coffee, Chinese snowpeas, garlic, macadamia nuts, exotic herbs, chrysanthemums, and long-stemmed roses. He doubtlessly knew that the National Development Finance Corporation (CORFINA) was encouraging nontraditional exports and that low-interest loans and even technical assistance were available for agroexport businesses. He must have seen his new estate with a vision that no San Antonio Indian could have had. And with pleasure he must have anticipated the prestige and convenience of weekends with his family in his new farmhouse, just forty-five minutes from his office in the capital.

In 1974, the farmers of San Antonio received their first indication that Horacio Arroyave was to be a different kind of neighbor from the late Eugenio González. Many San Antonio farmers worked on fincas near La Esperanza as day laborers. In exchange for their labor they received small plots of land or the right to harvest *tul* (marsh reeds) for making mats. Most worked in Finca Urías, near San Miguel Dueñas. For many years, they had reached San Miguel by walking along a road running through Arroyave's new finca, La Esperanza.

To their surprise, the lawyer closed the road. Incredulous at first, the articulate and self-confident farmers objected vociferously. Yet pressure as they might, Arroyave would not relent. Finally, confronted by loss of workers or poor relations with his new neighbor, the owner of the Urías farm finally resolved the problem by purchasing an adjoining plot of land and building a new access road parallel to the Arroyave farm.

The key to agriculture in the laguna had always been the small "river" (actually a well-regulated stream) that drained the marshland. Twice each year, at the beginning of the rainy and the dry seasons, the town would organize communal work projects to clean the stream, which ran the entire length of Arroyave's long, narrow farm. At its source, it drained directly from the reed-filled marsh, the only remnant of the former Lago de Quinizilapa.

In the year following the construction of the new road, Arroyave made a more provocative gesture: he refused to allow the communal work group access to his portion of the stream. This was serious, for if the stream was not cleaned regularly, in the dry season the water would not reach the higher, irrigated portions of the laguna, and in the rainy season a clogged channel would lead to flooding.

Alarmed, the town formed a committee to speak with Arroyave and then, failing to resolve the matter, went to the authorities in Antigua. Neither strategy worked. Despite escalating anger, louder protests, and two growing seasons of increasing damage to crops, the town was not granted access to clean the channel.

Instead, Arroyave responded by offering to buy people out. Having handled San Antonio land transfers in the past, he also began to scour the land title registry. As might be expected, he found plots unregistered or improperly recorded and boundaries and ownership hopelessly confused. Armed with this information, he confronted the Indians who came complaining.

"Look," he is said to have explained, "I am a lawyer; I know the law. And I know that you don't own the land that you think you own." Indians in San Antonio did not expect fairness from the law. To them, the lawyer appeared not only to know the law but to *be* the law. Arroyave acted on what he learned. For lands such as a prime cuerda of coffee belonging to Tereso Guachín, Arroyave simply registered the property under his own name and fenced it off, saying: "You didn't own it before. Now it belongs to me."

At other times, he forced formal sales. With his gun conspicuously visible during negotiations, he managed to act as though the Indians were somehow squatters. With agricultural production depressed because of the water flow that he had disrupted in this manner, Arroyave was able to purchase plots for 10 to 20 percent of their previous value.

As a professional in the law, Arroyave made sure that all acquisitions were properly titled. As his patchwork farm acquired new pieces, he would extend wires to mark off the new boundaries. According to the San Antonio farmers, he would intentionally make acquisitions three or four plots removed from his outer perimeter. Octopuslike, the wire would stretch from his old to his new boundary, scooping in the intervening plots, and then beginning pressure on a new farm family.

The farmers of San Antonio—the progressive, modern Guatemalan Indians who knew the system—did not feel like squatters. They were not Indians from some remote area where the ladino *finqueros* were the law. They were not *mozos* (serfs). They too had friends in government and access to the city.

So they did not just curse Arroyave and complain among themselves; they organized. They met with lawyers, they appealed to the authorities. They protested to anyone who would listen. And they were surprised when none of this seemed to make any difference.

With the hydrology of the laguna disrupted, water shortages regularly occurred at the higher elevations. In the lower ground, poor drainage led to mildew in the potatoes and worms in the carrots. Even the petate mat makers (mostly the elderly and the landless poor) were affected when the higher water levels cut off entrance to the laguna and prevented the harvesting of reeds, their raw material.

In 1978, Arroyave took a startling new action: he dammed the river. With cisterns and new embankments to regulate the water, he then built an artificial pond that he seeded with carp. This, of course, aggravated the flooding and further disrupted the water flow. But it solved the problem of ruining his neighbors' land while sustaining his own economic production.

The flooding had other effects—on health, for example. About that time I recall my own trip to the doctor in Antigua. He observed, "Must be malaria, typhoid, or hepatitis" (all water-related diseases— meanwhile I was unable to stand up, doubled over from the pain). "It's unhealthy to live up there any more." With immediate treatment, I soon recovered from what turned out to be typhoid, but I wonder what happened to my neighbors with less ready access to medical care.

As the problem worsened, some townspeople threatened the finca. In response, Arroyave called in police for protection. He hired armed guards when necessary and then purchased a wild bull to discourage trespassers.

Violence Overtakes the Town

At the outset of these events, the mayor of San Antonio was Marcelino Pérez, a well-to-do evangelical farmer who owned a pickup truck—

and land in the laguna. He was an older man, cautious and prudent by nature. Despite several years of intense personal effort, in the eyes of the town he was not very successful in leading the struggle against the incursions of Horacio Arroyave.

Carmelo López Santos, on the other hand, was a young, landless tailor. He was smart and ambitious. Sensing, perhaps, the impatience and anger growing in the town, he campaigned for mayor, promising to "do something" about the situation in the laguna. After he was elected, he took on not only Arroyave but problems such as housing reconstruction after the earthquake of 1976, competing demands to regulate local tourism, the need for municipal buildings, and the installation of additional potable water and electrical infrastructure.

During the following year, a core group mounted pressure on Carmelo to comply with his campaign promise. The mayor held endless *cabildos abiertos* (open town meetings) to discuss the problem. Virtually everyone owning land in the laguna participated, as well as dozens of people who were suspicious that the lawyer planned to expand beyond the laguna. Most of these were landholders; some were members of Carmelo's elected administration; others were simply angry townspeople. At one time or another, they discussed the matter with cooperative leaders, lawyers in Antigua, the *bufete popular* (university law student legal service), "friends" in political parties in Antigua, church leaders, the Peace Corps, and probably the Comité de Unidad Campesina (CUC), a radical peasants' political party that had not yet gone underground. In short, they talked to whoever would listen—all to no avail.

From there, events begin to move quickly.

First, an Indian woman "illegally" enters a fenced-off plot that she considers to be hers. Arroyave confronts her and orders her out. She responds angrily, threatening the lawyer with her machete and forcing him to retreat. She then cuts the wires encircling her land. Infuriated, Arroyave increases private police protection.

The Indian campesinos, for their part, seek and finally receive an audience with the governor of Sacatepéquez. He listens politely ("a matter of a few phone calls," he is said to have assured them). But nothing happens. Petitions are signed by everyone in town and collected for presentation to authorities in Guatemala City. Telegrams are wired to the ministers of agriculture and health requesting meetings, an investigation into the dispute, and intervention. Finally, on January

10, 1979, the Indians send a petition to the president of Guatemala, Gen. Romeo Lucas García. They urgently outline their complaints, and ask him to intervene and acknowledge their message within seventy-two hours.

No response to any of these requests is ever received.

On February 4, 1979, events come to a head. About five hundred townspeople are participating in a communal work project to clean and tend the cemetery. A report circulates that Arroyave has sent an engineer and a mason to begin construction of a giant gate that will mark the entrance to his farm. They have been seen taking measurements at a spot just outside the cemetery entrance, fully a quarter mile from the farthest extension of Arroyave's present boundary. It is also reported that he has purchased a plot on the volcanic ridges *above* the town. Everyone's worst suspicions seem confirmed: Arroyave will keep expanding until he eventually takes over the whole town. They will be kicked out or turned into *colonos,* permanent servants on their own land.

The work project turns into a tense and angry meeting. Carmelo speaks, bitterly denouncing Arroyave.

"What are we going to do?" he shouts. "We know how to fight with our own kind, with people like ourselves. But this guy knows all the tricks, he knows all the ropes."

The crowd is furious.

"Look, señores," shouts Carmelo, "are we going to put on our pants or not? How much longer can we stand here with our arms crossed?"

The crowd sets off to the farm to confront Arroyave. He is not there. Marching in, they knock out the retaining wall for the dam (rescuing the carp, which the women giddily carry back to town in their cloth tzuts). They cut down the offending barbed wire, restoring the boundaries according to their own version of who owns what. In all, they take back about half of the twenty-five manzanas to which the farm has grown.

Within days, Carmelo is notified that legal actions charging him with responsibility for damage to Arroyave's finca have been filed in Antigua. More ominously, unknown men, evidently *judiciales* (plain-clothes detectives), are seen in the vicinity of his home and office. In fear for his life, Carmelo moves to a different house each night. He also appoints a *ronda* (nightwatch) of town officials to patrol the town after dark and watch for intruders.

On February 12, about 1:00 A.M., a red pickup drives into town. It is spotted by the *ronda,* which assumes it to be a death-squad vehicle. In response to orders to halt, shots are fired from the pickup, which speeds off in the direction of Arroyave's finca.

The patrol notifies Carmelo, who runs to the plaza and tolls the church bell. Awakened, virtually everyone runs to the church trying to find out what has happened.

Angry denunciations are made of the perceived assassination attempt. Then, armed with machetes, stones, hoes, and several antique shotguns, an angry mob of several hundred people marches down to the finca to arrest the presumed assailants.

Inside the farmhouse are Horacio Arroyave Morales, son of the elder Horacio Arroyave Pantiagua; his sister, María Eugenia Arroyave de Virzi, on a visit from her home in the United States; and the farm administrator, José Raquel Castañeda. According to the family version, they are peacefully sleeping, unaware of the impending attack. According to the town version, someone is firing an automatic rifle from the house, allowing the elder Arroyave, and perhaps others with him, to escape out the back and seek help.

The villagers take cover and surround the house. Some set fire to outbuildings. Someone (reportedly Mardoqueo López, a leader of the group), sneaks up crablike on the house. With his machete he hacks viciously at the arm that is extended out the window firing the automatic rifle.

The arm belongs to the younger Horacio Arroyave. While he is disabled, the Indians rush the house and roughly haul out the three occupants. In the scuffle, the son receives a broken arm and at least three serious machete wounds, including two to his head and another that may permanently blind one eye.

The mob rolls and burns a Suzuki pickup, then the farmhouse, the remaining outbuildings, and houses belonging to workers.

"Avisas si quieres más!" ("Let us know if you want more!"), someone scrawls on the smoldering house.

Arroyave's son, daughter, and farm administrator are brought into town as prisoners. Because of the younger Arroyave's serious wounds, Carmelo orders him to be taken to the hospital in Antigua. The automatic rifle is confiscated, and the administrator and the daughter are charged with assault on the town and possession of firearms.

Recognizing the implications of what has transpired, Carmelo orders everyone to remain in the town square. Sensing a siege, the town waits. (Bruised and terrified in jail, María Eugenia Arroyave will later claim that she is subjected to repeated threats of immolation in the town square.)

About fifteen hundred people are present at dawn when the first two police cars arrive. Amazingly, the police are turned back with a shower of rocks and angry shouts of "Ellos tienen delitos aquí!" ("They've committed crimes here!").

Knowing that police will return, Carmelo sends about fifty men to the edge of town to dig trenches and build brush barricades across the road. At about 9:00 A.M., the police arrive in force: two buses carrying about sixty detectives commanded by the chief of the *pelotón modelo* (swat squad), Manuel de Jesús Valiente Tellez, and the Guatemalan chief of police, Col. Gonzalo Pérez Vásquez.

At the edge of town they arrest twenty-two persons. Some have been digging ditches and manning the barricades at the order of the mayor; others are merely bystanders or people passing to work.

When the police enter the plaza, they are accompanied by two Franciscan priests from Antigua, who plead for calm and order. What most frighten the crowd, however, are the unmarked cars with license plates taped over. The cars are filled with grim, watchful men in plainclothes, their faces covered with bandanas.

The police, well armed and in full riot gear, take charge. With tear gas and a bullhorn they soon disperse the milling crowd that is guarding the jail.

In what could well be an apocryphal, modern-day Tecún Umán story (the final battle of the Conquest, in which the conquistador Pedro de Alvarado slays and defiles the body of the Quiché warrior-chieftain Tecún Umán), Tellez himself, head of the secret police, is said to stride into the San Antonio mayor's office to liberate the two prisoners. There he publicly beats Carmelo. The prisoners—along with the automatic rifle that the town considers to be incriminating evidence—are whisked into police custody. No further charges are brought against the Arroyave family or, for that matter, the town. The "evidence" disappears.

The following day banner headlines appear in the Guatemalan press: "Indians Go Wild—Burn Farm—Attack Citizen." That is the gist of the press accounts that follow.

The town begins a desperate search for a lawyer who can fight for the release of the twenty-two people in police custody. The only one who will take the case is Aníbal Moreno, a young attorney in Antigua. The anguished families are sure that their relatives will never reappear.

In prison, the twenty-two are thoroughly interrogated. Some are said to be tortured. What is certain is that by the time they are released the police—or others who have interrogated them—have obtained highly detailed information about everyone remotely involved in the actions against Horacio Arroyave. And everyone, of course, believes that his or her name is on "the list."

At last the situation in San Antonio receives national attention. Police sources publicly ascribe the unfortunate events to a years-long attempt by the peasants to seize the land of the hapless *finquero*. The family stresses the legality of its ownership and blames the invasion on outside instigators who have manipulated the campesinos to embarrass the government.

I do not know to what extent outside groups, specifically guerrillas, actually were involved. Through their contacts with law students, and possibly through San Antonio's university students, the campesino leaders certainly had access to and consulted with university groups and labor organizations. Before the invasion of the farm, leaflets began to appear under doors and in the streets demanding that the government intercede to resolve the problem. Following the invasion, political wall grafitti ("Afuera Ladrón," "Arriba el CUC con el Pueblo," "64 Organizaciones con el Pueblo," "El Pueblo Unido Jamás Será Vencido") and leaflets denouncing the government for its inaction began appearing in the night.

With violence escalating throughout Guatemala—to which San Antonio is still generally considered to be relatively immune—the army starts patrolling more intensely and more suspiciously through the Department of Sacatepéquez. During a sweep for suspected insurgents, the upland hamlet Chimachoy, in an area dominated by Indian landowners from San Antonio, is bombed. The army then orders the population to leave. Most of the men have already fled; the remaining women and children arrive in San Antonio, where they set up a tiny refugee camp on the edge of town. In 1982 a woman described those times to me, her voice croaking in grotesque mimicry of a soldier's laughter as she told how he snipped off pieces of her son's ear, demanding to know the whereabouts of guerrillas.

The army begins to patrol San Antonio. One night in November, Mardoqueo López, the one who had led the attack on the farmhouse, eludes kidnappers in the night. Hearing their approach, he runs to the plaza and cleverly brings help by tolling the church bell. Temporarily safe, he flees. Later the army arrives in force and assembles everyone. An officer announces that Mardoqueo is a Communist and should be turned over to the authorities. He does not reappear.

Carmelo López completes his term as mayor. He is repeatedly warned that he is a marked man. His family and friends urge him to flee, but stubbornly he refuses. In an interview, he says: "Why are they looking for me now? They want to kill me. Well, if God says this is it, then what can we do? But I'm not guilty. I haven't done anything. As the legal authority, I feel caught from both sides."

On December 5, Carmelo is returning to San Antonio from the capital. He nervously watches a pickup that seems to be following the bus. In Antigua, he gets off and loses himself in the market. Then he boards another bus and resumes his trip home.

The pickup reappears, and a few kilometers outside town, the bus is pulled over. Armed men in civilian clothing enter. Without explaining who they are, they proceed down the aisle, demanding each passenger's papers. Carmelo blanches. They pocket his papers and order him off the bus. Though he has been advised to fight—that this will be his last chance—when confronted by the armed men, he is led off.

"Tell my wife they've got me!" he cries. And the bus is sent on its way.

After a fruitless report to authorities in Antigua, Carmelo's badly mutilated body appears three days later on Sunday, December 8. It has been thrown into coffee bushes just outside town. Clearly his torturers intend the corpse to be an object lesson.

The town views the remains of its former mayor. Upon seeing the mutilated corpse of his friend, Alcides López cries, "*Hermano mío,* what have they done to you?" Then, in what may be the town's final gesture of defiance, he foolishly shouts: "We will fix them in exactly the same way that they fixed you—*embrocado* [with mouth hanging down]."

Filoberto (Don Beto) Taj Taj, is a wealthy Indian landowner. An old political enemy of Carmelo, he is, according to members of the town, an *oreja* (informer) for Horacio Arroyave and is rumored to have played a role in the mayor's assassination.

And so now the pendulum of retribution begins to swing.

Three days after Carmelo's burial, Don Beto is working on his land in Calderas, on the slopes of Acatenango Volcano, several kilometers north of town. When advised that two campesinos are seeking work as laborers, he eagerly goes to speak with them. One pulls a pistol from his carrying pouch and shoots him dead.

Alcides López's wife, Nati, pleads with her husband to leave. The family has one financial asset, a cow, which Alcides carefully tends on his one-tenth cuerda in the laguna. He supports his wife and five daughters in part by making cheese.

"Sell the cow," plead Nati and their oldest daughter. "Flee."

"Why? I haven't done anything wrong, and I don't have any place else to go," he insists. "Besides, who will support the family?"

Alcides survives the first attempt on his life. Seeing strangers coming toward his house, he falls to the ground feigning drunkenness. They miss him.

He installs loose panels in the cornstalk walls of his house and survives the second attempt by crashing through the back wall on the run when the men come to his door.

But the third time he is not so lucky. A man comes to the front door, but others surround the house. Alcides throws a chair at the intruder, swings the machete that he always keeps at hand, and runs out the rear. Those who are waiting shoot him in the back as he runs by. Ignoring the screams of his wife and children, the men carefully inspect the corpse—this time riddling it with bullets before they drive away. Shortly thereafter, Nati sells the cow to pay for the funeral.

I knew Alcides well and suspect that he would be pleased that his neighbors now say that he was *muy valiente* (very courageous). But his wife and older daughters think differently. Nati must rise before dawn every day to take the bus to Guatemala City. She now sells vegetables in the terminal market and returns late at night. Their hopes for education dashed, the elder daughters must help support the younger girls and the grandchildren. The oldest is angry at her father, "an *indio*," she says bitterly, "who died struggling for a dried-up lake."

Pascual López was a poor single man who lived behind a store in the adjoining town Santa Catarina Barahona. His landlord, Don Mercedes ("Cheyo"), is said to have been involved with the CUC. When the killings started, Cheyo, unlike Carmelo or Alcides, took the threats to heart and fled. So when the hit squad arrived, they found only his renter. Whether through error, frustration, or guilt by association, they strangled and shot Pascual.

Pancho Zamora was Carmelo's first regidor (alderman), an adviser to the mayor. Don Pancho was caught and killed outside the town, up on the ridge where he farmed. That same night Don Cayetano, a cantina owner in nearby San Lorenzo el Cubo, was also killed. Don Cayetano had nothing to do with the events in San Antonio; the assassins were apparently just making better use of their time—two towns that night instead of one.

Manuel Zamora Pellecer was secretary in Carmelo's administration. When his tenure was up, he left town worriedly, to stay out of sight on his land in Parramos, away from the events unfolding in San Antonio. In 1981, his body was found there, machine-gunned in his house.

Miguel Gómez was a landless day laborer waiting to inherit a plot of land from his father. One night about 7:00 P.M., he was machine-gunned by the fountain at the foot of his street, two blocks from the center of town.

Two versions explain why Miguel Gómez was murdered. The first says that he was stealing coffee from Arroyave's temporarily abandoned farm. That discovered, his name was added to the list. The other says that he was involved in clandestine meetings and subversive leafleting late at night.

One year I traveled with Miguel Gómez and his wife, Camela, to the Catholic pilgrimage shrine Esquipulas—twelve of us crammed into a tiny hotel near the Honduran border after sitting four abreast on our bus seats for a day. It is hard to imagine the man I knew as either a thief or a "subversive." Unlike Alcides, Miguel Gómez was not a man of ideas. Unlike Carmelo, he was not a leader. He himself did not own land in the laguna. Yet for whatever reason, he was marked.

After Miguel's death, Camela took ill ("grief," according to her elderly neighbor) and died. Their two children—Maco, a clever, mischievous boy of about nine, and Soila, a girl of about five—were sent to live with relatives. (Somewhere, in a cardboard box, I have a cassette of that family—mostly giggling as the child Maco explores with delight the play and record buttons of my tape recorder. In the background Miguel and I can be heard talking and Camela fretting, "Don't break it; careful, don't break it," and then she and Miguel laughing at the replay of her voice.) I could not confirm to which relatives the two orphaned children were sent—only that it was not Miguel's older brother, for whom little Maco was named. The brother was kidnapped shortly after Miguel was machine-gunned, apparently for the same reason. His body was never discovered.

I remember Carmelo Guarán as a bit of a buffoon. His wife, Doña Soila, operated one of the first and best known tourist shops in town. Many visitors will recall Carmelo and Soila's house—the one with the framed letter from President Dwight D. Eisenhower.

Years ago, for an industrial exhibition, Soila wove the likeness of the president into a cloth *telarcito* (small cotton tapestry). It was mailed to the White House, which in turn sent a letter of thanks. For nearly twenty-five years, Carmelo Guarán discussed the letter and the accompanying photo of "Doña Soila and the *telarcito*" with the generations of tourists who came to their door.

Those who knew Carmelo Guarán doubt that he was deeply involved with Mayor Carmelo López's core group, much less with clandestine forces alleged to be on the periphery of the group.

Yet at about 10:00 A.M. one morning a pickup with long-haired men wearing hats pulled low over their faces pulled in front of the famous house. They lifted the struggling Carmelo Guarán, tossed him in the back of the truck "like a sack of corn," sat on the struggling man to keep him quiet, and calmly drove out of town. According to speculation, his kidnapping may have been related to his son Ofelio's kidnapping, which had taken place in the capital some years earlier.

Aníbal Moreno, the young lawyer who sought the release of the twenty-two persons detained by the swat squad, was said to be one of the best lawyers in Sacatepéquez. Certainly he was the *only* lawyer the Indians could find to take their case. (Three were released immediately after their arrest, and after six anguishing weeks the remaining nineteen were released.) The following year, Aníbal Moreno was kidnapped from his office in Antigua. His body was dumped near the entrance to the neighboring lake town San Miguel Dueñas.

Gonzalo Quiñones Paredes was mayor of a nearby city, Ciudad Vieja, but he was perhaps better known as the local correspondent for a popular national radio news program. As a fellow mayor, he had been a friend of Carmelo López for many years. And as a journalist, he had doggedly publicized the story of San Antonio for some time. He reported the land incursions by Arroyave and the details of the town's struggle to stop it. He reported the brutal death of his friend Carmelo López.

Why, people asked, did Gonzalo Quiñones so persistently broadcast the story of what had happened in San Antonio? Perhaps, speculated one listener, he had gone a little crazy—for he was also using the radio to find news about and denounce the kidnapping of his teenage son, who, despite his father's frantic search and appeals, never reappeared. Was it because the desperate father did not know when it was time to be quiet about his son? Or because he was a journalist who reported the wrong side? Or because he was the friend and associate of a marked man? Or simply because he was mayor of a town and an influential man? For whatever reasons, Gonzalo Quiñones too was pulled from his house and shot.

The killings in the wake of the events in San Antonio ended with the ouster of Lucas García by General Ríos Montt in March 1982. Arroyave, according to the town, lost his personal connections in the government.

Yet one final killing took place: last but not least, Horacio Arroyave. One day while he was sitting in his office in Guatemala City, seemingly safe and distant from the events that he had set in motion, a small motorcycle bearing two riders pulled up in front of his office. The two men entered, sprayed him with machine-gun bullets, dropped leaflets, and pulled off.

According to the San Antonio version, Arroyave's wife ran into the office and found the body. Like Camela Gómez, she too died shortly thereafter of *tristeza* and *cólera* (grief and anger). And shortly after that, it is said, the son who had been wounded at the finca. And then another son, an army officer.

Whether or not these secondary deaths actually happened, I do not know. But I think they must be symbolically true: that nearly everyone—and everything—that touched this chain of events died in the end, that there were no winners, only a widening circle of loss.

The Aftermath

In July 1985, I returned to San Antonio to try to reconstruct this story. Now that virtually all the actors are dead, what has happened to the farm? What happened to the land that the San Antonio Indians died to recover? What had happened to their anger and their willingness to fight back?

First, after nearly ten years of struggle, the Indians still lost their land. After the invasion of the farm, the army quickly upheld Arroyave's claims to ownership. And, as the lawyer indignantly pointed out to the press and others who would inquire, he did have legal title to every piece of land he occupied.

With the elder Arroyave's death the finca is now in the possession of another son—this one a doctor. The town seems to prefer the doctor to the lawyer. He is described as a decent man who wants to soothe and heal.

The house on the finca is still a gutted shell, "PGT" (Communist party) scrawled on one charred wall nearly overgrown by weeds. The carp pond is drained. The Nima Ya River channel once again is cleaned out by communal work projects from the town, and the water flows swiftly.

In 1986 the doctor rented the finca to an agronomist from Guatemala City. Apparently hoping to buy the finca himself, the agronomist cleaned up the land and began intensive production of vegetables and crops for export. Yet he had trouble finding workers, and was plagued by constant theft. He and the doctor quarreled over responsibility for losses, and, realizing that he would not be able to operate or eventually buy the finca, he left.

The doctor apparently is not quite certain what to do. According to locals, he has shown the finca to prospective buyers, but they shy away from the obvious problems with the town and unresolved disputes over title. Unable to farm the land himself or sell it to an outsider, the doctor has begun renting out small parcels to the San Antonio farmers.

So cows are once again grazing on small, wired-off microplots. Here is a tiny patch of carrots; there, a patch of coffee. Yet the farmers are renters rather than owners, and the doctor, healer or not, has not indicated a willingness to sell the land back to the town.

A friend who is a novelist read this account and commented: "It could not be fiction; there are too many deaths. The plot is too thin to support that many people dying." It is a story only in reality.

Certainly the main character, Horacio Arroyave, was a greedy, vicious man. I, for one, was quietly pleased to learn of his death, brutalized and demeaned in my own way by the events that he had set in motion. I was pleased, I suppose, by this final symmetry, by this last change on the lopsided scorecard.

Yet there is little comfort in saying that a man was victimized by his own greed, that there were no winners. There is no satisfaction in imagining that even those who murdered—those who pounded Carmelo's head with a hammer, those who shot Alcides in the back as he ran through the terrified screams of his children, those who sat on Carmelo Guarán as they rode through the town—that they too will probably die as they lived.

These events took place in the early 1980s. But the story has not ended, for a slower social dying replaced the killing. Certainly, those progressive, modern, educated, forward-looking Indians of San Antonio—those people both smart and foolish enough to believe that they too had rights—have been put in their place. They are, brutally, once again, the *indios* whom they were placed and bred at Lago de Quinizilapa to be. In a sense, they have been reintegrated into their historical role. Today religion thrives. Work continues in the field and at the loom. But there are no community organizations, no leaders, and no vocabulary of protest. The town once again produces, waits, and seemingly expects nothing.

In retrospect, it is extraordinary that in the year of the Panzós massacre and the burning at the Spanish embassy these Indians stood their ground and faced the Guatemalan police. Yet what is perhaps saddest is that they did not gain even a dignified story. The people I talked to have not mythified themselves or heroicized their resistance. To tell me what had happened, an old friend took me to a hillside far above the town. His seven-year-old son tagged along but was shooed away lest he casually tell his friends what his father had been talking about. Not only is his father afraid of retribution, but, more deeply, he is afraid to conjure up or articulate dangerous thoughts. In his precise recounting of the facts, he does not revel in the town's small symbolic victories but says only that he and his neighbors fell victim to temporary madness.

Perhaps that will change. Perhaps when the story is finally over, there will be a statue of Carmelo López in the town plaza, the Tecún Umán of San Antonio Aguas Calientes.

But for the time being there is only rawness, forgetting, a vicious, insidious state of calm.

CHAPTER 7

When Indians Take Power: Conflict and Consensus in San Juan Ostuncalco

By Roland H. Ebel

San Juan Ostuncalco is a community of more than 23,000 people in the western highlands of Guatemala about seven miles west of Quezaltenango, the nation's second-largest city. Situated in the center of the southeastern sector of the Mam-speaking population, the town has served as the historic market and transportation center for six smaller *municipios* (townships) within a fifteen-mile radius, namely, San Martín Sacatepéquez, Concepcíon Chiquirichapa, San Miguel Siguilá, San Mateo (a Quiché community), Palestina de los Altos (at one time an *aldea,* or canton, of Ostuncalco), and Cajolá. As such it early drew to itself a sizable ladino population, which today constitutes approximately 16.5 percent of the population. Concentrated predominantly in the urban center (*cabecera*), ladinos have historically dominated the economic and political life of the township, although the Indians have been dominant in the large Sunday market and have had a significant influence on the town's religious and social life.

The Indian majority maintained a civil-religious hierarchy of authorities in a modified form throughout the nineteenth century and until 1927 an independent town council alongside the ladino council. Stimulated by the liberal reforms of the 1870s, however, the process of "ladinoization" began relatively early, gradually eroding, although by no means obliterating, the more marked cultural distinctiveness of the Indian population—particularly the males. This erosion further reinforced the political, economic, and cultural dominance of the ladinos, which in turn stimulated a kind of "rear guard" cultural resistance movement among of the Indians, particularly in the protection of their religious customs and practices.

With the restoration of elected muncipal government in 1966, polarization between Católicos and Catequistas occurred. At first it appeared that a broad-based anticatechist, anti–Roman Catholic bloc made up of traditionalist Indians, evangelicals, and disaffected ladinos would be able to elect a predominantly Indian slate under the banner of the Partido Revolucionario (PR). Internal factionalism among the elders, exacerbated by charges of under-the-table payments to the leading elder and candidate for councilman, caused the bloc to split, thus creating a three-party race and perpetuating the ladino-catechist minority in power under the banner of the Partido Institucional Democrático (PID).

The imposition of competitive elections in predominantly Indian communities whose leadership recruitment practices had been traditionally built around cooptation, power sharing, and religious legitimation, created serious problems for those communities. Elections became a mechanism through which latent ethnic (Indians versus ladinos) rivalry was brought into the open. They also aggravated the natural factionalism in Guatemalan Indian communities. Most important, elections never had the capacity to confer the degree of legitimacy on local officeholders that an appointment based on community and religious service had previously been able to provide. In Ostuncalco the result was an intensification of political and religious conflict throughout the 1950s and 1960s.

The years between 1966 and 1968 marked an uneasy truce between San Juan Ostuncalco's traditional Indians and the catechists with their ladino allies. The PID party forces had taken the muncipality, while the PR party controlled the national government. Ladinos continued to dominate, there being only two Indian regidores (alderman) out of eleven on the municipal council.

Partisan political bickering began almost immediately after the elections of 1966. The council agreed to the traditional appropriation of money to celebrate the inauguration of President Méndez Montenegro, the successful PR national candidate, only after a prolonged debate and after the Conservative party (MLN) member of the council resigned his post, charging the mayor with misuse of funds.

The dispute over the saints' images also continued to simmer. Although the priest had succeeded in getting the images back into the church, the question whether the *cofradías* (religious brotherhoods) had the right to take them out to celebrate their fiestas was still in contention. The archbishop finally had to send a personal representative to town to settle the dispute. The agreement that was worked out called for a single procession for Señor Sepultado (Buried Lord), to be conducted under the ladinos that year and under the Indians the following year. After that the procession was to be directed by both Indians and ladinos. Most of the Indians accepted this compromise.

Overall the compromise produced a religious healing in the town. Católicos, catechists, and even evangelicals began to mingle freely and cooperate with each other on community projects. Ecumenism became so pronounced that Catholic priests and Protestant missionaries entertained each other at supper, and a Presbyterian elder was invited to pray at a farewell celebration for the priest. These developments allowed the town to take advantage of two political developments. The first was the election in 1968 of a PR-dominated town council, which aligned the town politically with the national administration. The second was the growing importance of a community development policy in President Méndez Montenegro's administration. Party connections at the departmental and national levels were used to gain access to national agencies and funding sources.

The twelve years between 1966 and 1978 saw the growing presence of national institutions in the life of the community. The National Electrification Institute (INDE), the Municipal Development Institute (INFOM), the National Committee for School Construction, and the National Program for Community Development financed rural schools, drainage and water projects, road and bridge repairs, a museum, and a monument to Jesús Castillo, the Ostuncalco-born composer of classical music for the marimba. These institutions not only provided new points of access to the national government by the municipal corporation itself but also actively encouraged the expression of demands by local groups.

The penetration of these national institutions into the political and governmental life of San Juan Ostuncalco resulted in greatly increased urban amenities. The community was no longer at the mercy of local revenues or the initiative of a particular mayor in securing help from a national ministry. National agencies now actively initiated projects and spent money in the community. There was also a growth of local

interest groups: municipal-betterment committees, the PTA, a municipal officials' union, a bus drivers' association, agricultural cooperatives, and church building committees. The economic activity of the
town increased. The many public works projects not only raised wages
but actually produced a shortage of labor in town. All these developments had the effect of politicizing the indigenous community. Betterment committees, church and cemetery committees, and the cooperatives were largely rural groups, organized by the Indians. Their success
and the organizational training provided by the National Community
Development Program and Protestant and Catholic missionaries enabled the Indians to see what could be accomplished by well-organized,
concerted effort. It was this, in part, which in 1976 led a group of
Indians to attempt to gain control of the town government.

The New Political Split

During the 1970s politicization of the Indians began all over Guatemala. It was stimulated by a number of factors. One was the rise of
the catechist movement and the modern religious and social ideas it
fostered. Closely related was the growing influence of liberation theology in the Roman Catholic church with its call for social organizing
and political revolution. Another factor was the indigenous linguistic
movement, designed to enhance the education of the Indian in his own
language and to promote bilingualism. Important too was the generally increased prosperity in many sectors of Guatemalan society, which
produced an expanded Indian entrepreneurial class. As a result of
these developments, by 1976 more and more young Indian men and
women were making the jump from the thatched hut to the university.
Cakchiquel Indians from Tecpán were employed as high school principals and as accountants with IBM; in Quetzaltenango, Quiché Indians were a growing force in business and the professions; and a young
Mam Indian from Ostuncalco was working on a native-language version of the Roman Catholic mass. Finally, Indian lands were being lost
to mining and plantation agriculture, resulting in the recruitment of
many Indians into the emerging guerrilla organizations. All these factors had a profoundly politicizing effect.

  In the western uplands a pan-Indian political movement called
Xel-hú emerged. Organized by young, well-educated Quiché Indians
from Quezaltenango to capture the town government there, it ex-

tended advice and assistance to other communities as well. Although Xel-hú failed to gain government posts in Quezaltenango in two attempts, it figured prominently in the election of the first Indian mayor in the modern history of San Juan Ostuncalco.

The sociopolitical trends described above served to put the Mam Indians in an ambiguous position. On the one hand they had become increasingly politicized by the organizations created to better their condition in life. At the same time, the growth of the catechist and evangelical movements, the weakening of the traditional religious brotherhoods by the events of 1967, and the dying off of the older generation of elders undermined the traditional community that had sheltered them and protected their culture. The ladinos of San Juan Ostuncalco, who had never clearly understood that their status rested on the willingness of the Indians to derive their identities and satisfaction from traditional culture or that it was the Indians' traditional culture that shielded the ladinos from the potential power of the numerically superior Indian townsmen, continued the historic practices and habits which downgraded and demeaned the Indians. The ladinos also did not realize that this situation was producing a younger generation of modern, secular Indians who would challenge them. One such Indian was Don Carlos.

Don Carlos, a Mam Indian, was born in the town center of San Juan Ostuncalco. He learned Spanish in the public school where he finished the first six years. Four years later he went to Guatemala City, where he worked in a factory and completed the seventh and eight grades at night. He was sought out by a language institute, the Proyecto Lingüístico Francisco Marroquín, to work on a Mam-Spanish dictionary. Resigning from the institute because of a dispute with his employer, he joined the national police, working for them until 1976, when he was approached by a group of Indians from San Juan Ostuncalco to run for mayor. They had formed a civic committee to back an "anti-discrimination" candidate in the upcoming elections. Don Carlos agreed to run, but when the electoral tribunal refused to inscribe the committee as a political party, it appeared that his political career had ended. A coalition of ladinos and Indians from the Christian Democratic Party (PDC), however, saw him as an Indian candidate with a chance to win locally in a presidential election year dominated at the national level by the PID and the MLN. An ethnically mixed party slate was selected with Don Carlos at the head, and for the first time in distant memory an overall majority of the candidates for municipal council was Indian.

The Christian Democrats' strategy worked. In an election that produced the largest voter turnout in two decades, the ladinos divided their votes among three candidates, while Indians of all persuasions— Católicos, Catequistas, and Evangélicos—combined to give Don Carlos a plurality of 573 votes. Don Carlos's strongest support came from the rural villages, where the Indian population was concentrated and where the betterment committees were well organized. Don Carlos, playing to the Indian sector, based his campaign on a promise to end discrimination in the running of the town hall and to guarantee every Ostuncalqueño equal treatment as far as legal disputes and fines were concerned. This helped get him elected, but also was to get him into trouble later.

One matter of concern to the Indian forces was a fair counting of the vote. To ensure this, Xel-hú provided Don Carlos's backers with well-trained poll watchers to scrutinize the voting. Special care was taken to ensure that none of the election workers became drunk, since one political ploy in San Juan is to try to incapacitate one's rivals. It is generally accepted that the Christian Democratic forces with their Xel-hú allies did an excellent job of ensuring that the election was not stolen.

Don Carlos's election came as a surprise. Never before had the Indians been able to overcome their personalistic and religious rivalries to organize a united political campaign. Even the Indian Protestant evangelicals, who, in their anti-Catholicism, usually voted for the more secular Partido Revolucionario, switched to the Christian Democrats and their indigenous candidate. The ladinos, who played their traditional game of running enough slates so that regardless of which party won they would control the town hall, made the mistake of assuming that the Indian electorate would divide along personalistic, religious, and ideological lines as in the past. This strategy only succeeded in splitting the ladino vote. Nevertheless, the ladinos quickly united their efforts to rid themselves of this Indian "usurper." In this effort they would eventually be successful and in the process unite much of the Indian community behind them.

The new mayor took office in July 1976 with a good deal of public support. As things turned out, however, three fundamental problems continually plagued his administration. The first was the unceasing hostility toward him of the ladinos, who had allies in the power structure in the departmental capital, Quezaltenango. Second, although Don Carlos won the election, he enjoyed none of the traditional bases of legitimacy in the Indian community—age, prior public service, or leadership in the Roman Catholic church or in the brotherhoods. Third, the very nature of his platform—equal treatment for all Ostuncalqueños regardless of race or ethnic origin—ran counter to the town's political culture, which is based on personalism, favoritism, and ethnic distinctions. As is true in all political systems, when culture and ideology are not congruent, culture invariably overwhelms ideology.

One of the new mayor's first acts was to fire the municipal secretary, who, he said, did not have his confidence. This made him an immediate hero among the Indians because the secretary, a ladino, was viewed as muy bravo and discriminatory in his dealings. As Don Carlos described it, an Indian with business to transact in the town hall might sit there all day while a ladino in a hat and tie would be told, "Pase adelante" ("Pass ahead"). The secretary along with several employees who had been fired for alleged economic reasons, appealed for assistance to the associations of the university students (AEOU) and the law students (Derecho de Occidente) in Quezaltenango. An alliance of these groups went so far as to appeal to the national directorate of the Christian Democratic party, arguing that, although the DCG called itself prolabor, one of its elected mayors was firing municipal employees. While it was not successful in saving the secretary's job, the coalition ultimately saved the jobs of other threatened municipal employees. This had the effect of isolating the mayor from a segment of the regional ladino elite—intellectuals, students, and trade unionists—who might have supported him in his fight against the local ladinos of San Juan Ostuncalco.

Other difficulties arose when Don Carlos, who served both as mayor and as justice of the peace, attempted to end discrimination in the handling of cases brought before him. On one occasion he ruled against a prominent ladino who was disputing a property line with an Indian. When the appeals court in Quezaltenango supported his ruling, the plaintiff became a leader of a faction opposing Don Carlos. In another case, with the concurrence of the town council, the mayor sold municipally owned wood to an Indian rather than to a ladino because he believed that the ladino had held a monopoly on the market for many years. This added another prominent ladino to the anti–Don Carlos faction.

Fuel was added to the fire when the National Committee for Reconstruction, the agency charged with rebuilding the country after the earthquake of 1976, offered municipal governments several lots of metal roofing at half price. The mayor wanted Ostuncalco to buy its share and make it available at cost to poor families in the rural areas. Learning that there were not enough funds in the treasury to make the purchase, he called a public meeting by beating the *tambores* in the rural villages and hamlets. At the meeting he offered to obtain the tin roofing once enough money had been collected from the people to buy it. When the money was raised, the sheets of tin were purchased by the mayor for 2.50 quetzales each and sold for 3.10 quetzales each to cover the cost of transporting them to town from the capital. For that he was later to be charged with *estafa* (fraud).

While these political problems were building up, the mayor was pushing ahead on a number of public works projects: water, drainage, a museum, and a bridge. Of particular importance was the initiation of three vocational training schools in the Indian cantons Pueblo Nuevo, Buena Vista, and Roble Grande. For most of these projects he had the support of the town council and the general public.

In April 1978 things came to a head. Don Carlos was forced to fire an Indian employee of the municipality for excessive drinking. The municipal employees, most of whom were ladinos, went out on strike and appealed once again to the university students for support. Although a substantial number of the students accepted the mayor's explanation of his decision, the bad press galvanized the leaders of the ladino opposition into action. Charges of every kind and description were hurled at him. He was accused of accepting bribes, threatening women with molestation, levying unjust fines, firing workers arbitrarily, stealing municipal property, failing to keep the plaza clean, and simply "abandoning the population." These charges were reduced to three when, in a formal legal proceeding (*antejuicio*), he was brought to court in Quezaltenango and forced, on May 16, to vacate the mayorship for thirty days.

This action polarized the town. The ladino opposition rejoiced to see their enemy on the ropes. A number of Indians, however, rallied to his cause. Not that they were that enamored of Don Carlos any longer, but they felt that if they lost this fight they would never regain power. Even Xel-hú was enlisted in the fight to save Don Carlos's job.

This flurry of support withered ten days later when the suspended mayor was accused of being the "intellectual author" of a vengeance murder of the young son of his alleged mistress. Although he was even-tually absolved of all responsibility for the crime, the taint of marital irregularity in a public official destroyed what remained of his support in the Indian community. As one Indian leader put it, "He brought shame upon us all."

Since none of the charges leveled against the suspended mayor could be proved in court, the law restored Don Carlos to his post on June 23. His return could not have been more ill-timed: he was immediately caught up in the aftermath of a national strike of municipal workers. During his campaign he had promised to work for increases in the salaries of the municipal employees of San Juan Ostuncalco. When, as a means of settling the national strike, the congress decreed a 50 per-cent increase in property taxes, the local employees' association be-lieved that the entire amount raised in town should go to them. Don Carlos, however, wanted to divide the total between the workers and the general budget. As a result, the local municipal employees' union went on strike, charging the mayor with undermining the national agreement. The dispute became very acrimonious. The president of the union claimed that the mayor had threatened him with the loss of his job, while the latter charged the labor leader with leading an illegal strike and instigating disorder in the town administration. The three-day strike was settled when the council, over the objections of the mayor, dedicated 95 percent of the aditional monies for salary in-creases. The hostility between the municipal workers and the mayor was cemented when he refused to pay three days' back wages for what he considered to be an illegal strike.

Almost immediately the ladino opposition renewed its campaign to remove Don Carlos. On September 8, 1978, a *memorial* accusing him of fraud, deceit, and robbing the communal forests was circulated throughout the town. Two weeks later the storeroom containing the records of the muncipal water project was broken into, and the papers were burned. Not surprisingly, the police found the broken padlock lying in the mayor's patio. On this occasion the mayor survived the attempt to embarrass him. The Indian-dominated council, in an ex-traordinary session, declared that the act was "against the town and not the town council, much less the mayor." The councilmen also de-clared that they suspected that the people involved were those who had formulated the *memorial* of September 8.

Don Carlos' victory was short-lived. Two months later the appeals court in Quezaltenango agreed once again to take up the charges against him. He was again suspended for thirty days, and an interim mayor was appointed from the council. Three days before the new year, having determined that the position of municipal mayor had been vacant for more than thirty days, the council named the interim mayor, Don Víctor, as the new regular mayor. Don Carlos's political career was at an end.

As far as the overall composition of the town council of San Juan Ostuncalco was concerned, the deposing of Don Carlos as mayor changed little. The new mayor was an Indian, and, of the eleven members of the reconstituted municipal corporation, six were Mam Indians, three were ladinos, and two were of Quiché Indian ancestry. Community reaction to the new state of affairs was mixed. The ladinos seemed to be satisfied: the new mayor, although Indian, was much more amenable to the traditional ladino interests and patterns of Indian-ladino relations. They believed that they had succeeded in ridding themselves of a corrupt and "pushy" Indian mayor without overturning the fundamental results of the 1976 election. They believed that they now had "their Indian" in office, or at least an Indian mayor whom they could control.

The Indians' reactions were ambivalent. On the one hand, there was a sense of relief that the worst of the bickering was over and that a mayor from within their own community was no longer in a position to embarrass them or their town. On the other hand, there was the feeling that power had once again eluded them. "There goes our industrial training school," said one Indian leader on hearing of the change. Another opined that the new mayor would not be able to handle the ladinos.

Don Carlos' political style worked against him. He went into office with a commitment to change. As a doer and a go-getter, he was out of step with his natural constituency. His unique, essentially non-Indian characteristics produced his unlikely victory in the first place and once in office led him to issue orders, directives, and commands. The traditional Indian decision-making style is one of consultation, of talking things over with community leaders until consensus is reached. In failing to employ this style in decision making, he undermined his acceptability to those who had elected him.

Don Carlos rode into office on a platform of fair treatment for everyone. Treating everyone fairly, however, meant stepping on some people's toes, both ladinos' and Indians'. Indian informants stated that, while they appreciated his attempts to control the special privileges customarily granted to ladinos in the town hall, they resented his heavy-handedness with them. Given the nature of the local political culture, it would have been better if Ostuncalco's first Indian mayor had been an older man, well versed in the traditions and consensus-building style characteristic of traditional Indian decision making.

San Juan Ostuncalco Under Pressure

When Don Víctor became the official successor to Don Carlos in December 1978, Ostuncalco's political life settled back into a semblance of a normal routine. Most everyone seemed satisfied. The Indians still had one of their own in the mayor's office, and one whose style was more acceptable to the ladinos. In fact, Don Víctor seemed determined to calm the agitation that had afflicted the town. Yet the increased political activity that had brought about the crisis in the first place continued apace. Civic betterment committees were now organized in almost every canton and barrio, and they were petitioning for additional school facilities, road repairs, and improved water systems. Likewise, all of the rural officials were better organized and prepared to lend support to the betterment committees in their jurisdictions. School principals, PTAs, and municipal employees were also better prepared to articulate their demands. In addition, various specialized committees for sports events, national and local festivals, beauty pageants, etc., were enhancing the town's organizational and political capacity.

The increase in local political organization and activity was brought about by a number of social and political trends, some of which have been previously noted. Foreign priests and their lay associates, heavily influenced by liberation theology, expanded their social and educational work in the rural cantons and neighboring townships. Similarly, the enormous growth of Protestantism meant that new congregations were being formed throughout the township. These groups were readily accessible to social and political mobilization on behalf of community improvement. Further, the growth and penetration of national administrative agencies created clientele groups with increased awareness of the urban services (water, roads, schools, and electric power) which they had previously thought would never be available to them. The opening up of national government administrative offices in Ostuncalco and the urban services they provided resulted in the development of a resident "middle class" that had not previously existed in the community. Many of these people became leaders of organizations seeking to gain benefits for their clientele from either the local or the national government. Finally, the increased level of political organization—particularly the municipal workers union and a number of cooperatives allowed to form during President Kjell Laugerud's administration (1974–78)—also had a politicizing effect.

The increased rhythm and tempo of demands on the town council led to longer and more extensive council meetings over a broader range of issues. It also resulted in the recruitment of a better-educated and technically more competent official staff, who had to prepare numerous reports for national agencies. The pace of business became so great that the municipal council asked the supreme court to establish a separate justice of the peace court in Ostuncalco to relieve the mayor of his judicial responsibilities.

Responding to pressure from constituents, town officials developed greater political sophistication. For the first time, local congressional deputies were used to lobby for policy changes that would benefit the community. Furthermore, a series of joint meetings was held with mayors of surrounding townships to formulate strategy for tightening up the law regarding certain forms of municipal tax evasion, a move that resulted in the establishment of an association of mayors, the Asociación de Alcaldes del Altiplano.

In April 1980, San Juan Ostuncalco enjoyed a peaceful, relatively low-key municipal election. Once again the Christian Democrats became the semiofficial party of the Indians. They selected as their candidate for mayor a young Mam Indian carpenter and farmer whose wife ran a *nixtamal* (corn-and-coffee-grinding business) in the urban center. They believed that, a leader of the new cooperative movement, he could use his contacts as well as his wife's customers, who were mostly Indian, to reinforce the appeal of the ticket to the town's Indian majority, as in 1976.

This time, however, the opposition was better prepared. The PID and MLN, which between them had received 40 percent of the valid votes cast in the previous election, formed a joint slate. As their candidate for mayor they chose Don Nestor, the ladino who had finished second in 1976. Picking a loser and a ladino to head their slate was a calculated risk, but behind it was a fairly well thought out strategy. It was generally believed that after the fiasco with Don Carlos the town was looking for the kind of proven leadership that the PID-MLN candidate could provide. A long-time civic activist, Don Nestor had been president of the artisans association, the local PTA, and the soccer football disciplinary committee. Thus he had ties with the local business community, educators and their supporters, and sports enthusiasts—most of whom were ladinos and likely to vote. It was assumed, therefore, that he would continue to appeal to the ladino electorate, which, although a distinct minority in the community at large, still constituted between 40 and 50 percent of the town's active voters.

A former town councilman, Don Nestor had worked closely with the civic improvement committees in the cantons where the Indians lived. He began assiduously to cultivate these contacts. He also served a large number of Indian customers in his shoe store. Hoping to run for office again, he had cultivated this clientele by extending more generous terms of credit. Don Nestor was helped, too, by the fact that the PID-MLN coalition made certain it balanced its slate with both Indians and ladinos, as well as with Protestant, traditional Catholic, and catechist candidates. It also made certain that a well-known candidate from each of the major villages of the township was on the slate. In short, Don Nestor was to consolidate the ladino vote in both the urban center and the rural zones and achieve sufficient Indian support to offset the appeal of the all-Indian ticket put forward by the DCG.

The third slate of candidates was fielded by the Partido Revolucionario, the party that had run a distant fourth in 1976. This slate was also ethnically balanced (it even included a woman), but its candidate for mayor was a middle-class lawyer who ran a very indifferent campaign. The ticket appealed almost exclusively to the small urban middle class and to young ladinos. It came in last.

The contest, in effect, was no contest. The PID-MLN coalition led by Don Nestor drew support from the broad spectrum of community groups, groups which were becoming increasingly differentiated, mobilized, and politically aware and which their candidate for mayor had astutely cultivated. In contrast, the Christian Democrats' Indian candidate had neither the money nor the experience to mount an effective campaign. He also made no attempt to secure the outside assistance that had produced Don Carlos's victory in 1976. As a local Indian from the artisan class, he did not have the contacts in the wider community that Don Carlos had been able to mobilize in the earlier election.

Don Nestor appears to have been one of the first of Ostuncalco's political leaders to become sufficiently aware of the changing political structure of the town to capitalize on it. How could the ladinos hope to win against an increasingly politically aware Indian population comprising some 84 percent of the community? By cultivating clientele groups, of course. Social differences had eroded the two ethnic power blocs to a greater extent than had been understood, and Don Nestor had the wisdom to exploit this. He won the election by about a three-to-two margin over his two opponents combined.

The new town council was seated in June 1980, and it immediately began working on the projects initiated by its predecessor: the new municipal hall, repairs to the public baths, the secondary school, the sports complex, and the reforestation project. Just as it appeared that a new era of progress was about to begin, the town began to experience the most sustained terror in its history.

On Saturday, September 13, 1980, the secretary of a university association centered in Quezaltenango (Centro Universitario de Occidente, CUNOC) was shot while attending a fiesta in San Juan Ostuncalco. The following day the Organización Revolucionaria del Pueblo en Armas (ORPA), a rural-based Marxist guerrilla movement made up primarily of Indians, came into town with a score of armed insurgents. They painted signs on the walls, brought the residents living in the town center into the municipal plaza for a forty-five minute "civic gathering" (*concentración cívica*) and killed a local policeman who attempted to resist. After the guerrillas left, army soldiers came in and beat up the son of the mayor, whom they accused of not having resisted the guerrillas with sufficient force.

For the next year and a half the townspeople were subject to anonymous threats from both left and right, bodies were found in the streets, buses were attacked and burned, and bombs were placed near the homes of prominent ladinos. One entire Indian family of eleven living in a remote part of the township was gunned down for allegedly having "fed strangers." The son of a former mayor was shot and killed while he was driving his car at night. Don Carlos, the former mayor who some believed had gone over to the guerrillas, disappeared and was never again seen in Ostuncalco. The regional military commander ordered the town council to beef up its police force with volunteeers, which it did, and also reinforced the windows and doors of the town hall. The local policemen petitioned the town council to be allowed to stay in their homes at night, and their petition was granted.

On December 30, after a number of bombs had exploded around town, the mayor, Don Nestor, submitted his resignation to the town council, citing as the reason the need for medical treatment for "high blood pressure." The council at first refused but on January 6, 1981, accepted his resignation. The council refused, however, to accept the resignations of some of its own number. The first alderman was named the new mayor.

The flight of the mayor and the retreat of the police gave the community a sense of great unease as the killings and threats continued. The town felt itself caught in the middle between the guerrillas, who were known to be operating in the hills just outside town, and the army, whose major garrison was just seven miles away in Quezaltenango. People did not want to talk about the troubles because they were unable to identify who was actually responsible for any given killing, the army or the guerrillas. Nevertheless, the military was suspected of massacring the Indian family mentioned above. Fear was rampant, for any reported "loose talk" could bring reprisals from an unknown enemy.

The difficulties of this period produced important changes in the community. Many of the most prominent foreigners in town were driven out. The two French-Canadian priests and their lay associates left the country, as did the American Presbyterian missionary. The Peace Corps volunteers were forced to leave, as was the Presbyterian nurse at the Mam Indian clinic, although, in her case, for internal organizational reasons. For the first time in decades the local priest was a Guatemalan, and the town's social services were almost entirely in the hands of nationals. Persons trying to precipitate change based on notions of modernization were replaced by persons much more amenable to working in harmony with the rhythms and culture of the community. The new priest, for example, was not perceived as being as dynamic as the Dutch and Canadian priests who had preceded him, but was viewed as being much more "democratic," that is, more willing to take a live-and-let-live attitude toward the various Catholic groups in town. As a result there was an almost total defusing of previous religious conflicts.

The troubles and pressures of 1980 and 1981 seemed to draw the townspeople together. They appear to have determined not to allow previous religious differences to divide the community, particularly since political violence was providing a cover for personal or group revenge taking. Catechists, traditional Catholics, and evangelicals, particularly in the absence of their overseas mentors, were attending each other's services, festivals, and funerals. Many old Catholic families were divided between Protestants and Catholics and accepted this division as natural.

In the area of municipal affairs, the town council, led by the new mayor—who was unscarred by the events of September and October 1980—pushed ahead with municipal projects without losing a step. Municipal improvement seemed to become something of a surrogate for the factional social and political activity that had only served to open up the community to the threat of reprisal or intervention from radicals of either the left or the right. Paradoxically, an era of trouble became something of an "era of good feelings."

Whatever criticism might be leveled against President Efraín Ríos Montt, the people in San Juan Ostuncalco credit him with bringing peace to the region. As a consequence, there was little objection to his decision on June 15, 1982, to replace the elected town council with a mayor appointed by the central government. After some negotiation between the local elites and the national authorities, the man finally appointed was a ladino who had owned and operated a local bus service. A man of energy and presence but with no previous political or governmental experience, Don Jorge was determined to carry out a politically neutral but govermentally active administration. Sensitive to the fact that he had not been elected by the community and that the work of the town hall was too much for a single person to handle, he asked Don Nestor, who had returned to town, to join him as vice-mayor. This was a particularly astute move. Not only did he bring an experienced and popular local politician into his administration, but, since Don Nestor's original term of office was not yet up, he graced his regime with an element of electoral legitimacy. At the same time he beefed up the administrative staff with a number of bright young men and women, both ladino and Indian.

Building on the agenda of municipal projects initiated by his predecessors and effectively utilizing national agencies and funding sources, the town government has taken on a decided "technocratic" character. Between June 1982 and December 1984, a total of 147,203 quetzales was spent on municipal projects ranging from an extension of the drainage system to the completion of the new town hall. The town government undertook efforts to spruce up the central plaza, and there appeared to be a kind of vibrancy and optimism in the community that had not been seen there for a number of years.

The Future

It is impossible to say with any certainty whether the current era of good feelings is a strictly temporary phenomenon produced by a combination of extreme pressure and a more centralized, nonpolitical administration of municipal affairs or whether it represents long-range cultural and political change. Furthermore, it is impossible to predict whether the peace will be maintained in the region. At the time of this writing (summer 1987) reports of guerrilla operations in the outlying districts still crop up, and at least one army incursion into the La Victoria canton of San Juan has been reported. Whatever the final answer to these questions may be, it is possible to identify the forces that are reducing the traditional factionalism and dissension.

After studying the politics of this highland Guatemalan community for twenty years, I have been driven to the conclusion that, because of its mixture of traditional and change-oriented groups, for political modernization to be successful not only the forces of change but also the forces of conservation are required. It is clear that the forces of change are now running quite powerfully in San Juan, but what about the forces of conservation? Will a form of political and ethnic chauvinism overtake the town once the threat of outside violence is perceived to have permanently subsided and the electoral process is once again allowed to fan the fires of factional competition?

Within the Indian community political legitimacy has always been based on religious activism and community service. These values are still very much in evidence in San Juan Ostuncalco. Now, however, the cooperative may be becoming a substitute for the *cofradía* and the betterment committees for the Indian elders. All of the candidates in the 1980 campaign indicated that in the next election, whenever held, success would be determined by a candidate's perceived capacity to manage municipal affairs, not his race or religion. Both the DCG and the PID-MLN candidates of 1980 (one an Indian, the other a ladino) predicted that the next campaign would be based on their records of community activism.

What about religion? Would the proliferation of churches simply dissolve the religious basis for political legitimacy? So far the answer seems to be no. A Protestant Indian was elected alcalde of Ostuncalco in November 1985, and he has been able to govern effectively. It appears that the growing religious pluralism in San Juan Ostuncalco continues to reduce the historic political tensions and factionalism in the town. Protestantism may even achieve the same status as Catholicism in providing religious legitimation for political leadership.

PART THREE
Indirect Violence

CHAPTER 8

Tourist Town amid the Violence: Panajachel

By Robert E. Hinshaw

Panajachel epitomizes the cultural diversity, charm, and beauty of Guatemala, "The Land of Eternal Spring." Lake Atitlán, a volcanic crater into which the Panajachel River flows, forming the delta on which the town is situated, lies fifty miles west of Guatemala City. Secondary volcanoes ring the lake and overlook the Pacific littoral on the south. Aldous Huxley, in the early 1930s, found Panajachel a "squalid, uninteresting place, with a large low-class Mestizo population and an abundance of dram shops." Regarding the lake, however, which "touches the limits of the permissibly picturesque, it is really too much of a good thing." The lake's breathtaking beauty is enhanced by the fourteen-centuries-old Indian communities along its shores. The cultural patterning of these communities was first described in scholarly fashion by the anthropologist Sol Tax, and in the intervening years scores of social scientists have deepened both Guatemalans' and foreigners' understanding of the pre- and post-Conquest history, cultural geography, demography, and ethnology of the region.

Apart from Guatemala City and the colonial capital of Antigua, Panajachel has been visited by more foreigners than any other community in Guatemala. By the 1970s, it had become a cosmopolitan melting pot of socioeconomic differences within the nation, as well as a haven for 85,000 foreign tourists each year from all corners of the Americas, Europe, and Asia—hardly the "squalid, uninteresting place" Huxley found it to be in the 1930s.

Yet despite its growing visibility and sophistication, Panajachel contrasts markedly with other communities in the Guatemalan highlands with respect to the direct impact of the civil war, which finally reached the highlands at the beginning of the 1980s. The ethereal quality of Panajachel has persisted through the violence, and the community has remained an island of comparative tranquillity. No Panajacheleño has been killed, abducted, or tortured, and there are no widows or orphans resulting from the war. To my knowledge no Panajacheleño has joined any of the guerrilla groups opposing the government. Several Panajacheleños have been involved in the war as military recruits, but, as far as is known, all of them enlisted voluntarily. Most of them had left Panajachel to join the army or to look for work elsewhere before the violence erupted. The bias of the great majority of Panajacheleños on the eve of the violence and still today is pro-Guatemalan government, pro–United States, and anti-Communist.

Because of Panajachel's anomalous position among highland communities, my focus is less on the current violence and more on its economic effects. All rural communities have been negatively affected economically by the war, but for Panajachel we have unusual longitudinal data which permit us to examine in detail the economic consequences of the violence.

Changes in Panajachel Through Time

Fifty years ago, Sol and Gertrude Tax commenced a study of the towns bordering Lake Atitlán. Of these, Panajachel was the first to become accessible by paved highway, and for that simple reason it was the first to attract tourists. But in 1941, when the Taxes ended six years of intensive documentation of Panajacheleños' income and expenditures, fully 95 percent of their income still derived from traditional agriculture. The handwriting was on the wall with respect to the potential impact of tourism, but that impact was yet to be felt by any of the Indian families of the mixed ladino-Indian population.

I commenced a restudy of Panajachel in 1964, by which time Panajacheleños' reliance on tourist-related income had climbed to 55 percent of the population, and by 1978—when fifteen Beloit College students joined me for a four-month stay in Panajachel to measure the impact of tourism—I estimated the reliance to have reached 75 percent. The population on Panajachel's one square mile of delta land had climbed from 800 in 1935, three-fourths of whom were Indian, to 6,000 in 1978, slightly more than half of whom were Indian. About

.540 Panajacheleños, representing fully half of the households, were employed in tourist-related services by 1978, their wages totaling $500,000, or one-tenth of the $5 million deposited in the community by foreign tourists that year. Panajachel-grown fruits and vegetables sold to hotels and tourist restaurants added to the Panajachel income derived from tourism, and if we include the construction industry in Panajachel and neighboring communities, which Panajacheleños dominate, it would be difficult to find a Panajachel household whose income in 1978 was not in part derived from tourism. Panajachel, therefore, had become the most tourism-dependent community in Guatemala, a dependency which brings both costs and benefits. We were able to examine costs and benefits at the zenith of tourism's growth in the 1970s on the eve of the violence which brought tourism virtually to a standstill. Finally, in the summer of 1984 I returned to determine how Panajacheleños had coped with the unexpected critical turn of events in the intervening half-dozen years.

Tourism in Guatemala had begun to wane by 1979, though it was still a good year for the country as a whole. Income from tourism that year totaled $200 million compared to $211 million from the sale of cotton and $495 million from the sale of coffee. By 1981, however, when Panajachel's largest hotel was bombed in a guerrilla raid from the lake, tourism came virtually to a halt. Also in 1981 a branch of the Bank of Guatemala in Panajachel was robbed. During the next year the municipal headquarters of both Panajachel and San Andrés, the neighboring *municipio* on the northeast, were held briefly by guerrillas, and the San Andrés municipal building was burned. Several soldiers were killed in the action at San Andrés, and as the guerrillas retreated northward out of Panajachel, they killed four residents of a village named Patanatic. In other regional incidents, two residents of San Jorge, the town bordering Panajachel on the west, disappeared and were assumed abducted and killed, and three similarly disappeared in 1982 from Santa Catarina on the east.

The hotel was rebuilt, and guerrilla attacks on tourist interests in Panajachel ceased, but even into 1984 tourism remained limited to Guatemalans and small numbers of Europeans. When I returned in June 1984, a national planning conference on tourism was in progress, and North American travel agents were being flown in by the national airline, Aviateca, to see for themselves that the areas of major tourist attraction were fully pacified. While North American tourists still were conspicuously absent, the mood in Panajachel was ebulliently optimistic, and tourist-oriented communities in the region were poised in anticipation of a much improved season in 1985. Apart from the fact that streets and hotels were empty of all but a few European tourists, Panajachel appeared just as it did during the height of tourism in 1978: hotels were open, restaurants and shops were open and fully stocked, and Panajacheleños, apart from a dozen young men and a few families who had left (for Guatemala City, the army, or the northern oil fields), were still there.

Employers have absorbed the losses these past several years as have their employees, obviously on the assumption that the depression was temporary, and, surprisingly, few Panajachel Indians have lost their jobs. Hours were cut back or wages otherwise reduced in many instances, and where more than one family member was employed, not uncommonly one was released. Remarkable sharing and self-help efforts by the community have enabled Panajacheleños to survive and even to absorb additional vendors of arts and crafts fleeing the violence in the north and west. The community rapidly developed a reputation as one of the safest places to be in Guatemala. The immigrant merchants also brought with them their contacts with foreign buyers, middlemen who had dominated the textile market in more remote *municipios* less frequented by tourists. As a result by 1984 even Panajachel vendors were catering largely to such middlemen, and a few of the wealthiest Panajachel merchants with capital reserves were well positioned to benefit from the violence: they purchased family heirlooms, such as old huipils (women's hand-woven blouses) from families throughout the highlands who were in need of money or who had been forced to abandon their homes and possessions. Some Panajachel homes are virtual museums, repositories of the cultural heritage of the region. The buyers are, for the most part, wealthy collectors from Europe and the United States. Huipils selling for $1,000 are not unheard of, but unfortunately this income is even less broadly shared by Panajacheleños than was the money spent by tourists before the violence.

The Economic Impact of Tourism

Let us turn now to a cost-benefit analysis of Panajachel's shift away from agriculture toward dependence on foreign tourism. Specifically, I want to report on the findings of my 1978 research and follow-up inquiries in 1984 on the cost of living in Panajachel, compared to that of neighboring communities. One of the questions addressed in 1978 was: Are the increases in wages keeping pace with the rising cost of living, reflected in food commodity prices in the weekly market? Since food purchases represented 70 percent of the average household expenditures in 1964, I have assumed that this continues to be the best single index of cost of living. Of course, there has been a steady inflation in most commodity prices throughout the region for many years, requiring me to control for that variable if I am to determine whether tourist competition for commodities has been an additional local factor in inflated prices.

I used the methods in the mid-1960s that Sol Tax had used in the 1930s to survey the Panajachel market: native data collectors, on several consecutive market days at the same time of year, asking the same questions. Paul Yamauchi, a member of the Beloit team in 1978, repeated the procedures, as did I again in 1984. We lack, however, reliable comparative information for neighboring markets. Only for 1978 do we have reliable comparisons with three markets in the area: one, San Andrés on the east, is considerably smaller than Panajachel; another, Sololá, the departmental capital on the west, is considerably larger; and San Lucas, across the lake, is of comparable size to Panajachel.

Yamauchi found negligible price differences among the markets in commodities common to towns in the region or imported into the towns. Fruits imported from the coast were cheaper in San Lucas, for example, because of its closer proximity to coastal supply routes. Prices in the markets were averaged for comparison with prices in Panajachel. Forty commodities were compared, attention being given to fifteen commodities which hotels and restaurants reported purchasing regularly to satisfy tourists' tastes. In determining the impact of tourist competition on inflated prices, I arbitrarily assumed that 1964 prices in Panajachel were the base line and that they were representative of prices in the entire region. Tourists in Panajachel even at that time were probably influencing prices, but with only seven hotels and four restaurants in 1964, compared with twenty hotels and forty-two restaurants-bars in 1978, any inflation owing to tourist competition for commodities would have been negligible in 1964. If we assume uniform prices in the region in 1964, then 1978 comparisons reveal an average price inflation of 190 percent for commodities outside Panajachel and 250 percent inflation for Panajachel commodities. Of the fifteen commodities most in demand by tourists, fourteen were priced significantly higher in Panajachel than in all of the other markets. We concluded that 75 percent of the inflation since 1964 was common to the whole region, while 25 percent of the Panajachel inflation was directly attributable to local tourism.

From Sol Tax's analysis (in his book *Penny Capitalism*) of the relative importance of different foods consumed by Panajacheleños, we judge that the foods most in demand by tourists also constitute approximately 75 percent of the average family's traditional diet. This assumes that Panajacheleños' diet has not changed, but data collected in 1978 and 1984 reveal shifts away from meat, fish, and dairy products; greater utilization of rice and potatoes; and less total fruit consumption than earlier. These shifts clearly reflect differences in commodity price inflation, and these differences have health and infant-growth implications, to be examined below.

Inflated cost of living is one side of the coin; the other is inflated income. The crucial question is, Has income inflation kept pace with cost-of-living inflation? In 1978 unskilled male wage earners were receiving up to $2.00 a day, most women and many of the men in the tourism labor force earning closer to $1.00 a day. The comparable figures and range in 1964 were $0.50-$1.00. While in 1978 larger numbers of skilled wage earners were earning up to two and even three times the unskilled wage of 1964, we judge that average wage income in Panajachel has little more than doubled over the fourteen-year period. When the increased income to Panajacheleños from sale of their produce at the inflated prices is factored in, Panajacheleños were earning from all sources considerably more than twice the community's income in 1964, but still short of the three-and-one-half times increase they would have needed to keep pace with the cost of living.

Only a very few of households have the marketable skills to command tourist income sufficient to keep pace with the rise in cost of living. Fortunately, half the households were not dependent on or were only minimally dependent on wage employment, using the community's shrinking agricultural land base to advantage in growing the products most in demand because of tourism. In between are roughly half the households, who have lost their land (except for house sites) and have become dependent on tourist employment at the minimum wage. These are the Panajacheleños who stood to suffer most from the demise of tourism and to whom we look for understanding of the adjustments in standard of living that have occurred.

This brings us to my latest visit to Panajachel. While my market surveys in June 1985 were not fully comparable to those in 1978 and 1964 (coming two months later in the year), there is no good reason to think that commodity prices changed during those two months, except that imported staples of corn, wheat, and beans were in perhaps somewhat shorter supply by early summer. Excluding these staples, vegetables (seventeen varieties) were down 5 percent over 1978 prices in Panajachel, fruits (eight varieties) were up 28 percent, and fish, meat, and eggs were up 40 percent. The explanation for such continued inflation in prices for fruits and meat, even in the absence of foreign tourists, lies in the increased use of Panajachel as a vacation site by Guatemalans. The recent decline in rural violence, coupled with government-imposed financial disincentives to vacation outside Guatemala, have resulted in the increased popularity of Panajachel to nationals; thus the continued competition for, especially, fruits, meat, and diary products in the Sunday market. Ironically, while domestic tourism results in continued cost-of-living inflation, it does not employ Panajacheleños nearly as fully in hotels, restaurants, and gift shops as does foreign tourism. Consequently, cost of living currently is running ahead of income more than ever before.

Dietary shifts, accordingly, have become even more pronounced this past year (1986), according to the physician who directs the local health center. There has been a noticeable upturn in infant illness, reflecting animal protein and fruit vitamin-mineral deficiencies. Panajacheleños would be more alarmed if it were not for the hope—encouraged by the local ladino elite and the government—that foreign tourists will be returning soon.

Unfortunately, with few exceptions, Panajacheleños do not understand how inexorably their destiny is linked to the ongoing turmoil in other Central American countries. North American tourists will probably continue to avoid Guatemala as long as war rages in El Salvador and Nicaragua, despite the anticipated calm in Guatemala over the next few years. The worst may be yet to come in terms of deteriorating health, and now that absence of violence is no longer a Panajachel monopoly, we might see a rapid upturn in out-migration if the North American tourists fail to return. It may well be that inadvertently I myself encouraged some out-migration, by sharing with friends what we learned from our analysis of the 1978 data: that only 10 percent of the $5 million spent by tourists at the height of tourism was returned to Panajachel workers in the form of wages, and that the cost of living was inflated locally about 25 percent higher than in the wider region. Panajacheleños have been aware of commodity inflation, of course, but have had no regular, public monitoring of prices in other markets, despite occasional intermarket visitations by virtually everyone. If their collective knowledge were effectively pooled, they would learn—and probably act on that knowledge—and bring Panajachel prices more into line by reducing the local demand. That this knowledge is not effectively pooled reflects the "impersonality" in social relations characteristic of Panajacheleños, so graphically described by Sol Tax forty years ago.

Most Panajacheleños probably believe not only that they are better off economically than their neighbors by virtue of tourism but also that their standard of living has improved over that of their parents and grandparents. From longitudinal information gathered since the 1930s, we know that they are not better off, and if this is the situation in Panajachel, it is reasonable to conclude that the standard of living has been deteriorating at least as rapidly, and probably more rapidly, in the highlands generally. Yet the western highlands have fared better economically than have regions of the country in the west and north, where in the late 1970s frustration first led to politicization of the Indians and then siding with guerrilla forces.

In 1978 I expected to find that tourism was reversing the negative regional and countrywide economic trends for at least the fortunate few in Panajachel, but, in fact, the data indicate that even Panajacheleños were worse off in 1978 than were their parents and grandparents. That they do not perceive this to be the case, and still harbor few reservations about living in Panajachel today, reflects the stimulus of life in the fast lane—or, rather, fast path (i.e., life oriented to tourism). Panajacheleños are more impressed with comparing their present income levels to those of neighboring communities than with comparing standards of living with those of earlier generations. The paradox is that Panajacheleños may not be faring much, if any, better than their neighbors who do not benefit from tourism. If this is the case and yet Panajacheleños perceive it otherwise, the reason may be that the economic benefits of tourism are more visible than its costs. Panajacheleños are less aware of the inflated cost of living than they are of the larger income they enjoy. But the same can be said of my coresidents in Boulder, Colorado. Boulderites know that they make more money on the average than the residents of outlying towns in the county, but they need an economist to tell them that equivalent housing costs 25 percent more in Boulder than elsewhere in the county.

It will be interesting to observe the choices Panajacheleños make over the next few years if, as I predict, tourism does not significantly improve and their understanding of their economic situation is finally clarified. Will they be able to act on this knowledge, when and if it comes, to better their life chances?

The Absence of Violence in Panajachel

Panajachel largely appears to have avoided the violence of the civil war. Directly or indirectly the community's dependence on tourism seems to provide an explanation for the community's good fortune in this regard. Over the past half century those Guatemalans who have purchased land for vacation homes in Panajachel; vacationed in the government-owned hotel, Casa Contenta; or driven out from Guatemala City to spend weekends on the beach and in the restaurants and bars have been among the wealthiest and most conservative of Guatemala's upper and middle classes. Many befriended and hired Panajacheleños, sometimes providing access to more remunerative employment elsewhere in the country. Panajacheleños early on chose to accommodate rather than to reject these national tourists and, accordingly, were disposed to assimilate many of their political biases.

Such conservative biases were reinforced by the foreigners, largely North American, who also began to frequent Panajachel fifty years ago. The first Protestant missionaries in the region were headquartered in Panajachel, and in the intervening years fully half of all Panajachel families have had some formal involvement in one or more of the several Protestant sects active in Panajachel. The missionaries were for the most part as politically conservative as the wealthy North Americans frequenting the hotels and purchasing or renting homes for more prolonged sojourns in Panajachel. The foreign tourists gradually became more diverse in age, life-style, economic status, and religious and political orientations. The sentiments of several hundred North American counterculture youths living for months at a time in Panajachel during the 1960s might have rubbed off on their Panajachel peers and friends if the civil strife had reached the community at that time. But by the late 1970s and early 1980s, the colony of hippies had become much smaller and was growing older and more conservative.

Panajacheleños have learned much about North America through association with its tourists. A number of friendships have resulted in visits to the United States by Panajacheleños and, in some instances, U.S. immigration and employment. North Americans are viewed as friendly, unprejudiced toward Indians and the poor, and, above all, prosperous. Panajacheleños like and admire North Americans more than the Europeans or the Guatemalan elite who frequent the community.

Panajachel's resident priest since the early 1950s is a Spaniard of means with basically conservative political views. He is well integrated in the social elite of Panajachel, accommodative toward tourists and upwardly mobile Panajacheleños exploiting the tourism opportunities, and pragmatic in his treatment of other religions. Professionals and representatives of national agencies (e.g., physicians and nurses, school-teachers, lawyers, extensionists) are similarly well positioned socially and often can use appointment or wealth to settle in this attractive community.

In short, exposure of Panajacheleños to non-Panajacheleños in their work, recreation, schooling, and worship has produced a political conservatism which goes beyond mere pragmatism. Few Panajachele-ños need to migrate to the coast for the seasonal employment upon which so many of Guatemala's Indian communities depend to tide them over the lean months each year. The *municipios* adjacent to Pa-najachel are among these latter communities, and so was Panajachel earlier in this century. Residents of most other lake communities, therefore, have more frequent contact with and knowledge of coastal plantations and the broad range of experiences that migrant laborers bring back from the plantations. ORPA, the guerrilla organization op-erating in the southern *municipios* of Guatemala, recruits more suc-cessfully in the plantation environment. It is not surprising that the lake *municipio* which has experienced the most violence and presum-ably has shown the most sympathy for the guerrillas' cause is Santiago Atitlán, across the lake from Panajachel and extending down to the coastal littoral, where plantations are much more easily and of neces-sity frequented. All the municipios bordering the lake on the south, including San Pedro la Laguna, have experienced more turmoil and violence than municipios like Panajachel bordering the lake on the north.

The *indirect* consequence of tourism has been to improve the economic opportunities for wage employment and to heighten family income in Panajachel to a point where no Panajacheleño need beg, emigrate, or seasonally work elsewhere. The *direct* consequence of tourism is a level of satisfaction with the status quo among Panajacheleños that is probably unmatched in the region. Panajacheleños have not been inclined to bite the domestic or the foreign hands that feed them. Given Panajachel's economic history, guerrillas did not focus much energy on recruiting support in the community. The image of Panajachel as a peaceful tourist center has been protected by both sides of the conflict to a surprising degree. The limited attacks by guerrillas in 1981 and 1982 seem to have been symbolic gestures, aimed more at demonstrating the left's ability to strike at will than at destroying Panajachel's image. When the hotel was bombed, very few tourists were staying there, and none were injured. The Guatemalan army has also contributed consciously to the maintenance of this image of tranquillity. Even the notorious and ubiquitous civil patrols are not visible in Panajachel; they operate only at night between ll:00 P.M. and 5:00 A.M., when tourists are asleep.

CHAPTER 9

Destruction of the Material Bases for Indian Culture: Economic Changes in Totonicapán

By Carol A. Smith

Many anthropologists who know Guatemala have argued that present state policies constitute a program of ethnocide, if not genocide. The truth of this assertion can be gauged by examining some of the changes that have taken place recently in San Miguel Totonicapán, where state policies have had an indirect but nonetheless powerful impact.

Totonicapán is a large township in the western highlands of Guatemala, whose present population is approximately sixty thousand, more than 95 percent Indian. It is an unusually prosperous and occupationally diversified community as Indian communities go in western Guatemala. Its wealth and capital reserves have helped it avoid the economic disasters of other Indian communities in the region. It has, in addition, escaped much of the violence that has enveloped Guatemala since 1981, during which time many Indian settlements have been essentially eliminated as communities. Given what has happened elsewhere, Totonicapán's experience of economic dislocation and stepped-up political repression may seem unworthy of extended treatment. But it is important to understand the pattern of changes taking place in Indian townships outside the major zones of counterinsurgency, for these changes suggest what the long-term consequences of the counterinsurgency campaign will be for Indian culture in all of Guatemala.

The counterinsurgency campaign was begun by Lucas García in 1981 and continued by Ríos Montt and Mejía Victores. In the process, Guatemala has suffered massive population displacements: some observers estimate that more than one million of Guatemala's seven and one-half million people were at least temporarily displaced between 1981 and 1983, mostly in the western highlands. In addition, two successive years of disastrously low food and export-crop harvests followed. One knowledgeable source estimated the 1983 food harvest to be 60 percent lower than normal. Finally, there have been extremely high rates of unemployment, especially in the rural areas, and generally very depressed market conditions throughout the country. I describe below some of the ramifications of these economic conditions on Guatemalan Indian culture, as seen through the economic and social transformations observed in San Miguel Totonicapán.

My base-line data on Totonicapán come from five years of field research on the regional economy of western Guatemala. Totonicapán was never the exclusive focus of my investigations, but it was the community in which I lived when I was doing fieldwork in Guatemala and where I made most of my Guatemalan friends. It is thus the place from which my personal interpretations of Guatemalan life are usually drawn. My information on the contemporary situation in Totonicapán comes from a brief revisit in September 1983 and an economic survey undertaken in one hamlet of Totonicapán in January 1984. Discussions I had with friends in Totonicapán, both during my visit and later by mail, provide a personal context for the information I report here.

The Special Character of Totonicapán

San Miguel Totonicapán is a very distinctive Indian community in western Guatemala, and I cannot claim that its social organization or cultural practices parallel those of other places. At the same time I do want to generalize from that community, for I believe that Totonicapán's reactions to the present economic crisis are, if anything, conservative with respect to the loss of Indian culture. I think that one can best understand Totonicapán's unusual characteristics and responses by situating it as a particular kind of place within the regional economy. In depicting the social features of Totonicapán for the period preceding the counterinsurgency program, I emphasize its economic position in western Guatemala and how that has made it both unique and yet representative of certain tendencies in Guatemalan Indian communities.

Three special features—one economic, one demographic, and one ethnic—define Totonicapán as a unique Indian community in western Guatemala. These features are related to each other and to the position of the community within the regional division of labor. First, Totonicapán's unusually diversified and capitalized local economy is necessary for a functioning regional economy lacking significant urban centers. The many large, booming marketplaces and long-distance traders of Totonicapán play important roles in carrying out the regional division of labor. And Totonicapán's artisans produce many items for domestic consumption that many former peasants, who are now part-time wage workers on plantations, can no longer produce for themselves. Totonicapán's key position in the regional economy explains its unusual local division of labor.

Second, Totonicapán has a number of peculiar demographic characteristics which are not unrelated to its economic profile. In particular, in Totonicapán, Indians tend to dominate in politics and in specialized occupations, whereas in other parts of Guatemala non-Indians or ladinos are dominant. One reason for this is that the dense populations in the Department of Totonicapán are primarily Indian. Even town centers, which are usually occupied by non-Indians in other parts of western Guatemala, are mostly Indian in Totonicapán. San Miguel is the largest municipality and the one housing the department capital. Because of its administrative status, San Miguel (population approximately six thousand) has a fairly substantial number of non-Indian residents, most of whom have some sort of government post to sustain them. But few ladinos live in the other municipalities of the department, no ladinos live outside the town center in San Miguel, and only a handful of ladinos own land. Most Totonicapán ladinos are restricted to occupations in government or professions—where they meet stiff Indian competition. The paucity and relative poverty of Totonicapán's ladinos, together with Totonicapán's elaborate division of labor, says more than anything else about the special character of Totonicapán. As a friend once put it, Totonicapán has a ladino economy—without the ladinos. In fact, this statement misleads (as I discuss more fully below), but it captures one aspect of both Guatemala and Totonicapán—that where Indians and ladinos are in direct competition, the differences between the two groups become accentuated.

A third distinctive feature of Totonicapán is the way in which Indian ethnicity is expressed. Totonicapán Indians seem "traditional" in certain respects and "transitional" in others. Many of the major Indian rebellions of the nineteenth century took place in the Department of Totonicapán and involved issues of ethnicity. Atanasio Tzul, a native of San Miguel Totonicapán, was hailed a Quiché "king" in 1820 during a rebellion that was interpreted by many people of the time as the first move in a major "race war." Virtually all native or Guatemalan accounts depict twentieth-century Totonicapán as a place of continued strong ethnic resiliency and resistance. Most Guatemalans recognize that it is not simply an accident of fate that there are few non-Indians in Totonicapán; rather, few non-Indians have settled in Totonicapán because it has presented a united and hostile front to non-Indians. Yet because Totonicapán Indians seem so Westernized and competent within the national Guatemalan context, a number of North American anthropologists consider Totonicapán Indians to be well into the transition to non-Indian ethnic identity.

I believe that one can properly interpret the meaning of ethnicity in Totonicapán only by making a careful distinction between the form and the content of ethnic identity. In comparison with other Indian communities, San Miguel has indeed lost many Indian cultural "traits," such as the cargo system, which in fact it lost long before most other communities. But since ethnicity has to do more with social ties than with innate traits, the existence (or number) of particular cultural traits does not measure its strength. The Indians of San Miguel base their Indian identity on a few general institutions, such as political organization. The symbols that define them change continuously over time in content but remain strictly defined as Indian in form. Thus when it comes to clarity of ethnic political stance, for example, there are few Indian townships as militantly Indian as San Miguel, even though the content of political behavior does not seem especially "Indian."

These particular economic, demographic, and ethnic features of Totonicapán made it appealing to me as a research site. But I was also attracted to Totonicapán by the historical image of the Totonicapán Indian "rebel" who assimilates just enough of Western ways to more effectively resist Western incorporation. I expected to find more "native pride" in Totonicapán than elsewhere in this country haunted by the image of the humble Indian. And, indeed, that is what I found from the beginning. After two weeks of struggling with Totonicapán Indians over the issue of housing (mine), I knew that I would never live as happily in another part of western Guatemala. I eventually moved in with a family dominated by women traders who lived in a hamlet bordering the town. They took pity on me when they heard of my housing plight and accepted my contradictory position of occasional employer and awkward daughter with the natural grace of proud people.

Totonicapán's "Traditional" Economy in Regional Context

Before 1980, Totonicapán's traders and artisans were supported by the Indian economy of western Guatemala, all of which had become highly market-dependent by at least 1950. Other Indian communities, while just as dependent as Totonicapán on the market for survival, had very different kinds of market specializations. People in poor communities obtained most of their cash by working several months of the year for wages on the lowland plantations. In some of these communities, especially those in Huehuetenango, northern El Quiché, and northern San Marcos, more than 50 percent of the adult male labor force migrated seasonally to the lowland plantations. People in wealthy communities, mostly in the Departments of Totonicapán and Quezaltenango, earned their incomes by producing and trading those items of domestic consumption no longer produced by most Indian households. Virtually no one from these communities migrated to the plantations for wage work, though many sold Indian commodities on the plantations during the harvest season. Specialization in food production for sale took place primarily in the Indian communities bordering Lake Atitlán or those in the Department of Chimaltenango or southern El Quiché. People in these communities had the most variable incomes, sometimes sending many people to the plantations and at other times relatively few.

Occupational information from the national censuses not only fails to reveal this occupational diversity in western Guatemala but partly conceals it. One of the reasons for the concealment is that most students of rural people in Guatemala assume that they are peasants and that peasants farm. Thus when Indian peasants of Guatemala tell people such as census takers that they are campesinos, it is assumed that they mean subsistence farmers. In fact, to most rural people of Guatemala, campesino signifies a particular status, not an occupation: the status of being rural, relatively powerless, and relatively poor, as well as a person who does *some* farming. How much farming is not revealed. In my fieldwork I often found Indians who considered themselves to be campesinos who obtained less than 10 percent of their food supply from their own farming efforts. Farming, moreover, amounted to less than 10 percent of their productive activities. These Indians simply did not consider their nonagricultural occupations to be *socially* significant.

Status is different in Totonicapán, where, because occupational specialization is advanced on an individual basis, many Totonicapán Indians will actually claim an occupation other than that of campesino. In particular, traders and artisans, who often hire field labor rather than performing it themselves, will tell investigators that they are tailors, weavers, carpenters, house builders (*albañiles*), merchants (*comerciantes*), or the like.

Because Totonicapeños report their specialized occupations whereas other Indians do not, examination of the national census materials reveals a falsely anomalous pattern (table 1). The 1973 census reports 57.2 percent of employed males in all of Guatemala to be engaged in agricultural work, in contrast to 71.5 percent in the western (Indian) region. This suggests that more people are agriculturally self-sufficient in the Indian parts of Guatemala than in the non-Indian parts. But in Totonicapán, the most Indian department in all of Guatemala, the national census reports only 34.1 percent of the male labor force engaged in agriculture. Yet Totonicapán only *appears* less dependent on local agricultural production than the typical Indian community—because its specializations are more clearly nonagricultural (whether or not local), more stable, and more successful at earning income than specializations developed elsewhere. In fact, all Indian communities are specialized and thus dependent on trade within the regional division of labor.

Other investigators in Guatemala have observed the unusual occupational profile of Totonicapán revealed by the censuses. But most of them have attributed it to Totonicapán's poverty in land—and with some reason. The rural population density of San Miguel Totonicapán in 1973 was 135 people per square kilometer, more than twice the regional average of 65 people per square kilometer. And the amount of arable land available to the average Totonicapán family in 1977 was only about 10 cuerdas (slightly more than an acre). The average family in much poorer communities had access to more than ten times the amount of land. But for lack of market access, a family in the poorer

Table 1. General Occupational Distribution of Employed Males
(National Census, 1973)

| | Percent of All Employed Males | | |
| | | Western | |
Occupation	Guatemala	Region	Totonicapán
Agriculture	57.2	71.5	34.1
Manufacturing/			
construction	17.9	14.7	37.5
Commerce	7.4	5.8	23.2
Services	15.3	6.9	4.1
Other	2.2	1.1	1.1

community produced little more food for itself than the Totonicapán family produced. Totonicapán farmers have high crop yields because of their nonfarm sources of wealth. They can hire labor to prepare the land (by hand), turning over the rich soil to a depth of more than two feet, planting the corn closely, and intercropping with pine trees (firewood), fruit trees, and wheat. And they can also afford to use considerable amounts of chemical fertilizers. I emphasize this to make two points. First, Totonicapán incomes, even from farming, depend heavily on general (regional) marketing conditions. Second, the economic health of a Guatemalan community depends as much on its place in (and the condition of) the regional marketing system as on access to certain factors of production, such as land. In other words, the entire regional economy is so closely interdependent and tied to a complex division of labor that no part of the region can suffer severe hardship without affecting the economies of other places.

Table 2, based on my occupational statistics, shows how general is the degree of nonfarm specialization in all of western Guatemala. The table is set up to contrast my data, based on a survey of three thousand rural Indian households in different parts of western Guatemala (between 1976 and 1978) with that reported by the 1973 national census (cf. table 1). It is also set up to contrast the occupational structure of core townships situated mainly in the Departments of Totonicapán and Quezaltenango and peripheral townships situated mainly in the northwestern periphery of the highlands. It shows that the degree of dependence on nonagricultural sources of income is high in both core and peripheral communities of western Guatemala.

Core townships have slightly higher levels of dependency on manu-

Table 2. General Occupational Distribution of Males, Aged Fourteen to
Eighty, by Zone for Western Guatemala
(Smith Survey, 1977–78)*

Occupation	Western Highlands (4,160 workers)	Percent of Workers Peripheral Communities (1,556 workers)	Core Communities (1,341 workers)
Agriculture	32.5	37.9	18.5
Manufacture†	41.1	35.6	53.8
Construction	8.9	12.3	5.7
Commerce	16.8	14.1	20.8
Other‡	0.7	0.1	1.2

* See text.
†In this grouping I combine what some persons would consider service work with "manufacture" since there is little to distinguish the two kinds of work in rural areas.
‡This category covers mainly those people who find employment through the government as teachers, policemen, and the like.

facturing and commerce than those peripheral townships. But one would expect much more dependency given the great differences in wealth between the two zones. To explain the wealth differences, it is important to depict more carefully the kind of specialization outside agriculture that exists. In much of western Guatemala, rural Indian households supplement incomes earned from farming and seasonal work on plantations with petty trade and the sale of simple crafts produced by the family. But in the more highly specialized townships, such as Totonicapán, artisanal production has become a full-time occupation that requires both a capital outlay and occasional use of nonfamily labor. In other words, Totonicapán households do not simply supplement farm income with the production and sale of handicrafts; they run large, complex artisanal firms.

Table 3 gives some sense of the capital-intensive pattern by showing a more detailed occupational breakdown for the township of Totonicapán, distinguishing between those who are self-employed and those who are employed by others, and by delineating the main artisanal branches. Most of the goods produced and sold by Totonicapán specialists are oriented toward an ethnic or Indian market. Weavers, for example, produce the skirt cloth and huipils worn by native women throughout the western highlands. Potters and leatherworkers also make goods consumed mainly by Indians. Tailors and carpenters produce goods that might appear to have a more general market, but most

Table 3. Primary Occupations, Rural Totonicapán, Male Heads of
Households
(N = 7,125)
(Smith Survey, 1977)

Occupation	Percent	Average Age
Agriculture (24.4%)		
Self-employed	10.4	56.8
Wage labor	14.0	32.0
Artisanal production (41.8%)		
Self-employed	27.4	43.5
956 weavers		
813 carpenters		
354 tailors		
75 potters		
66 leather workers		
59 other		
Wage labor	14.4	25.3
Simple crafts	4.8	44.4
Construction	5.1	28.3
Commerce	23.9	42.5
Other	0.4	34.6

of these items are also purchased by Indians. The non-Indians of Guatemala like to distinguish themselves from Indians by purchasing industrial goods produced by foreign (usually U.S.) firms rather than
artisanal goods produced by local Indians. The feeling is reciprocated.
Most wealthy Indians prefer finer, more diverse artisanal goods to foreign industrial products.

The results of my survey may seem surprising at first consideration,
given the common assumption that rural peasants, such as Guatemalan Indians, live from the land. But on second consideration it is not
so surprising. Guatemalan Indians own too little land on a per capita
basis to depend solely on agriculture for subsistence. Some households, of course, can maintain an agricultural orientation by supple-
menting farm work with seasonal work on lowland plantations. But
even more households find that inadequate and must find work outside agriculture altogether. Indians in the Department of Totonicapán
began nonfarm specialization early on, possibly even before the vast
reorientation of the Indian economy with the development of export
agriculture (coffee) in the late nineteenth century. Because of its head
start and its good location near the commercial network that grew up

to feed the plantation economy, Totonicapán is more successful in its nonfarm specialization than most other Indian communities. It is important to recognize, however, that Totonicapán's wealth and economic autonomy are possible because most rural Indians in the western highlands are incorporated into a market economy. The incomes that most Indians earn from the sale of food or from plantation work are spent in large part on goods produced or purveyed by Totonicapán specialists.

What is significant about my findings on occupations in Indian communities of western Guatemala is that they portray a regional economy with much less peasant self-sufficiency (in all parts of the region) than that depicted in the traditional accounts, but one that is more autonomous relative to the national or plantation economy of Guatemala than that suggested by more recent accounts. On the basis of these findings it can be argued that a well developed *Indian* market economy in western Guatemala provides the material basis for Indian cultural autonomy and Indian political resistance to the state. This argument is obviously important to the present political crisis; if the hold that the Indians have had over the domestic market economy is broken by present military control and "development" efforts, the material basis for Indian culture and autonomy may well be eradicated.

Two Cases Studies from 1984

Most of what I want to say about the economic changes that are taking place in Totonicapán rests on the results of my survey in 1984 of occupations in Chipol, an Indian hamlet near the town center of San Miguel Totonicapán. Chipol is relatively prosperous, noted for its high-quality weavers. Data from this hamlet suggest that artisanal enterprises, the mainstay of Totonicapán prosperity and political autonomy, are unlikely to survive the present restructuring of western Guatemala's economy. To depict the effect of this change on people's lives, something the data themselves do not convey, I begin with a brief description of the economic changes that are taking place in two particular Totonicapán families living there. What we see from these accounts is a pattern of temporary adjustment, illustrative of the broad range of adjustments possible in an artisanal economy which allows it to survive periods of depressed market conditions. Yet the extraordinary flexibility of this economy, evidenced in both the cases and the data, should not blind us to its fragility and vulnerability to market conditions. With this in mind we need to consider how long the adjustments I describe can last.

My first case is Emilio (a pseudonym), the young man who undertook the survey of Chipol. Emilio, who had been a student in Totonicapán's secondary school, had carried out similar surveys for me in 1976–78 during school vacations. Upon graduation from secondary school in 1980, Emilio became a rural teacher in a small Indian community in Alta Verapaz. Because access to the village in which Emilio taught was difficult, his working conditions poor, and his salary lower than that paid to most other professionals ($175 a month), few non-Indians competed with Emilio for the job. But Emilio was quite pleased with his position, for its prestige as well as its pay. Even though he had heavy travel and living expenses (he maintained a household for his wife and two children in Totonicapán), he earned nearly as much as his father, a weaver who, by Totonicapán standards, was wealthy. Emilio worked at the school for two years, came to know the local people well, and observed nothing unusual about the village. But after Easter break in 1982, during which time he visited his family in Totonicapán, Emilio returned to his post to find that the village had disappeared. Not a single individual of a community of about two hundred individuals remained; the school itself, along with most other buildings, had been burned. Emilio was told by people in a neighboring community that the military had come through and had killed thirty-five people thought to be subversives (including women and children) and burned the buildings and crops. All of the survivors had fled. Authorities in the departmental capital told Emilio that the village had been destroyed by guerrillas and suggested that he apply for a new teaching position. Emilio applied for three years, but was not appointed anywhere. Nor was he likely to be appointed in the foreseeable future, inasmuch as few Indian teachers are being hired in the resettlement zones of the devastated north.

Emilio was forced to find some other way to support his family. His father no longer hired weavers, because conditions in the weaving industry at the time had nearly bankrupted him. He could not even employ Emilio, who had worked for his father as a weaver for many years. Emilio's younger brothers had quit school and like many other Totonicapán youths had entered the market on the "fair circuit," selling cotton candy, Totonicapán apples, and popcorn. Emilio joined them.

When I visited Emilio in 1983, he was earning about ten dollars a week—in a good week. Some weeks he made no money at all. His wife tried to help out by selling powdered milk (CARE milk that was distributed to poor Indians, who then sold it to non-Indians) in the town of Totonicapán. Occupied with two small children, however, she had little luck in this or several other small-business ventures. With the money I paid him for doing the survey, Emilio bought several blenders and set up a permanent refreshment stand in the city of Quezaltenango. About half of the population of Quezaltenango is non-Indian and thus less seriously affected by the economic disasters of the highland countryside, though business overall is very poor. Today Emilio earns about fifteen dollars a week from his business. With this salary he must support a family of four that has no farmland. The family eats plain tamales (meatless and sauceless) and wild greens at almost every meal, adding beans several times a week in place of the meat that they once ate. Emilio's wife has not bought new clothing for several years, though the woven goods for her native costume are very cheap. She is dressing her oldest daughter in non-Indian clothing (she says it is cheaper), though she expects that she will continue to wear traditional clothing herself. The situation Emilio finds himself in today is much worse than anything he has experienced before; still, he considers himself relatively fortunate. Many of the young men he grew up with in Chipol have had to leave their families to seek work outside the community.

The other account is that of Juan, the first friend I made in Totonicapán, who was once a weaver. In the late 1970s he had switched to selling woven goods (mainly skirt cloth obtained from local weavers) in the large rural marketplaces of Totonicapán and El Quiché. He visited five marketplaces a week and spent his two days off obtaining supplies and working on his quarter acre of land. Juan had eight children and was proud of having sent all of them, even the girls, to school. In 1978 Juan's four youngest children, (two boys and two girls) were in secondary school. Three others helped their father in the clothing business. They had their own market stalls but not their own capital, so they turned the day's proceeds over to their father. The oldest son, having recently married, had set up his own selling business, assisted by capital from his father and the labor of his wife. He sold a less traditional form of clothing than that sold by his father, sweaters knitted by locals on small Japanese knitting machines. He and his wife lived in separate quarters in his father's house but assisted the family in domestic chores. All of these arrangements were quite typical in Chipol.

In 1983 the oldest son left for Guatemala City, where he sold sweaters; his wife and three children continued to live with Juan. Juan's second son worked for a baker in the town of Totonicapán. He earned only room and board, though presumably he also learned a skill. The two older daughters had married upon leaving school. María had married a well-educated young man from a very wealthy weaving family who had worked for several years for the ministry of education in bilingual education. In 1983 her husband was in exile in Costa Rica, having received a death threat. María and her two young children had moved in with her father, Juan. She had not moved in with her husband's family, which is the expected pattern, because she did not feel welcome. She explained to me that her husband's family was having a very difficult time because of the deterioration of the weaving business. The other married daughter, Manuela, had finished school but had not found a teaching job, nor had her husband. They, too, lived with Juan, together with their two small children.

In my occupational census, all of the adult members of this household claimed to be working as clothing merchants. In fact, they only helped Juan, and thus a business that supported nine people in 1978 (four of them small children) now supported eighteen people. And the business was faring badly. In the late 1970s, Juan had averaged a profit of $75 to $100 a week. But in 1983 he claimed to be making only about $25 a week. He no longer sold in the rural or Indian marketplaces of the area because business volume there was so low that he did not even meet travel expenses. He said, moreover, that it was dangerous to travel widely, especially in the Department of El Quiché, where before he had regularly attended two markets. Juan sold mainly in the town marketplaces of Totonicapán and Quezaltenango, which served non-Indians as well as Indians. And, significantly, like many other traders from Totonicapán, he had dropped his line of native woven cloth. Now he sold sweaters worn by Indians and non-Indians alike. He had purchased a sweater knitting machine in 1980, and his wife and two older daughters produced about half of the goods he sold.

All the women in Juan's family continued to wear "traditional" native clothing, but they had bought little new in the last several years and were accepting certain changes in the traditional "costume." Factory-made towels or sweaters were acceptable substitutes for hand-woven shawls; embroidered factory cloth was an acceptable substitute for the hand-woven huipil; and a skirt cloth completely devoid of design, though still hand-woven, was replacing the colorfully designed cloth of the past. With each substitution the traditional weavers of Totonicapán lost work. Juan and his family understood that this happened and that it hurt everyone's business in Totonicapán. But they were constrained by their own economic problems to make the changes.

Juan himself suggested that Totonicapán's highly developed weaving art was in danger of disappearing under the present conditions. He compared the simplicity of designs of the present with those of his childhood, which he argued was the consequence of poverty. He also observed that "native" clothing was disappearing altogether from certain parts of the country, such as the towns and the plantation area (as well as the Department of El Quiché), and that it might never recover. Many people in those parts of the country, he noted, were afraid to identify themselves as Indians. He did not expect native clothing to disappear from Totonicapán any time soon, but he pointed to increasing numbers of local Indian children wearing factory-made clothing.

Let us now consider the impact of the changed material circumstances illustrated by these two accounts on the occupational profile of Chipol, many of whose workers were weavers. Within this context let me note that the weavers of Totonicapán supply the skirt cloth (*cortes*) worn by approximately three-fourths of the Indian women of the region. They produce both general "Indian" designs, recognized as originating from Totonicapán, and "local" designs, tailored to the traditional styles once hand-loomed by the wearers. Totonicapán weavers also supplied huipils to a large number of Indian townships in the region, as well as other forms of native dress, some in "standard" Totonicapán styles and some in "local" styles. Weavers in several municipalities of Totonicapán took over much of the clothing production in the early part of this century when Indians from other parts of the region began working for wages on the lowland plantations. As Totonicapán weavers commercialized this domestic art, they introduced considerable variety and elaboration. Despite commercialization, the "native" cloth of Guatemala remains an important and authentic symbol of Indian ethnic identity. The elaboration of ethnic goods, moreover, has become a means by which many Indian communities sustain themselves economically and thus retain a certain degree of autonomy from the dominant, industrial culture emanating from the cities. In this respect, weaving symbolizes the economic *and* political autonomy of Indian communities.

The occupational changes in Chipol to be described were reported by Emilio, who, as noted above, is a native of the hamlet, and they are reasonably accurate except in one important respect. All of the men in Totonicapán are now registered by the military civil patrol system, whose operation in Totonicapán I describe below. Men who leave the community permanently are not registered, which makes them "illegal aliens" in their own community. Knowing this, I told Emilio not to press for information about people he knew to be missing. Emilio estimated that nearly half the young men between the ages of fourteen and twenty-five were "missing" from his count, for they were working or seeking work outside the community.

Table 4 contrasts the primary occupations of males between the ages of fourteen and eighty in Chipol in 1980 and 1984 (a sample of 301 individuals). We found that a large number of unemployed males (7.3 percent) had left the community between 1980 and 1984 to seek work elsewhere. Most of those individuals were reported to be either in the southern plantation area or in Guatemala City, trying to make a living in petty trade. An additional 12 individuals left the community for the military in this period, all having been forcibly drafted. When these individuals are added to the officially reported "unemployed" rate of 5 percent, we see a general loss of local employment of more than 15 percent; if we add in the "missing" young men, the figure is more like 25 percent. The nature of nonlocal employment is also different from before. Whereas most individuals who were not employed locally in 1980 were either students or teachers, very few people were so occupied in 1984. Of the 18 individuals who were employed as rural teachers in 1980, only 6 maintained their positions in 1984. I should note that all 6 individuals who were "unemployed" in 1980 were young men between jobs, whereas half of the 18 unemployed men in 1984 were married men with children. This is a very significant change in the employment picture of Totonicapán, where labor had always been somewhat scarce relative to demand.

Since this was a rapid qualitative survey, it is difficult to determine the rate of underemployment. But there is no question that underemployment existed. Apart from the fact that virtually all of the people I talked to complained of it (and Emilio continuously commented on it in his notes on different households), we see from these statistics a

Table 4. Occupational Distribution of Males, Aged Fourteen to Eighty, Chipol, Totonicapán, 1980 and 1984
(N = 301)
(Smith Survey, 1980 and 1984)

| | Percent | |
	1980	1984
Agriculture		
Self-employed	4.0	4.7
Wage	11.3	12.0
Plantation	1.3	5.3
	16.6	22.0
Artisanry		
Self-employed	34.7	20.0
Apprentice	6.7	2.0
Wage	11.3	11.3
	52.7	33.3
Simple crafts	3.3	4.7
	3.3	4.7
Construction		
Self-employed	3.3	—
Wage	2.0	5.3
	5.3	5.3
Commerce		
Self-employed	14.7	15.5
Wage	2.7	7.3
	17.4	22.8
Other (nonlocal employment)		
Teachers	6.0	2.0
Military	—	4.0
Urban factory	2.0	3.3
Unemployed	—	7.3
	8.0	16.6
Wage labor		
Non-agricultural	18.0	31.3
Total	29.3	48.7

jump in the number of people engaged in local agricultural occupations, even though the amount of land put into cultivation had not increased. We see an even larger jump in the number of men seeking work as plantation laborers, even though demand for plantation labor had been extremely low in the 1983–84 season. More significant still was the large increase of men employed in petty commerce. This occurred in a period when everyone in the community was complaining about the lack of business.

The most significant change in the occupational profile of Chipol was the drop in people engaged in artisanal production. All artisans complained that demand for their products was lower than they had ever experienced. Some artisans were hanging on, even though they were making less than half the income from this kind of work that they had made in 1980. They explained that they were hanging on for lack of viable alternatives. But weavers, most of whom produced cloth for Indian women's costumes, did not have that option because they were making no income at all. A few weavers were switching into the production of "utility cloth," bought by non-Indian as well as Indian consumers. But a large number of weavers had changed occupations, most moving into petty trade. No new apprentices had been taken on in any of the trades; in fact, all of the apprentices of 1984 had been apprentices in 1980. Some of them had been working as such for more than five years, something that rarely occurred in the late 1970s. Furthermore, no "workers" had become "independent proprietors" between 1980 and 1984, and, as the figures attest, nearly half of the artisanal firms of 1980 had gone out of business by 1984. Many of the remaining businesses were, in the words of their owners, "eating their capital"—waiting and hoping for better times.

In addition to checking on occupational changes in Chipol, Emilio queried people there about price and wage changes between 1980 and 1984. Table 5 shows the results, contrasting wage ranges for the main types of workers in Chipol in 1980 with those of 1984, as well as the changed prices of major food staples.

The overall pattern is one of wages dropping precipitously, sometimes to half the earlier level, at the same time that prices show significant increases. Wages fell most dramatically for artisanal workers, especially weavers, but they also fell for agricultural laborers. House building, which was a booming industry in Totonicapán in the late 1970s, had fallen off sharply. The few people who were able to find work as builders (*albañiles*) were now being paid one-third the amount paid in 1980.

The plantation wage figures require explanation. A minimum wage of 3.25 quetzales a day had been established on the plantations in 1980 after a long, severe, and very bloody strike. Before the strike,

Table 5. Wages and Prices, Chipol, Totonicapán, 1980–84

Wages and Prices	1980	1984
Wages (quetzales per day)*		
Fieldwork	3.00	1.50–2.50
artisanal work	3.00	1.50–2.00
construction work	3.00	2.00
plantation work	3.25	2.00
artisan	5.00–6.00	1.50–2.50
builder	6.00	2.50–3.00
Prices (cents per lb)		
Lowland corn	8–9	14–15
Highland corn	10–11	16–18
Beans	25–30	35–40
Firewood (quetzales per load)	8–10	12–14
Coffee	25–30	40–45
Cooking oil (bottle)	90–100	125–130
Sugar	13–14	20–22
Tomatoes	10–15	25–30

* One quetzal was worth $1 U.S. until devaluation in 1983.

average daily wages on plantations were approximately 2 quetzales. Plantation owners responded to the strike by hiring as many people as possible at piece rates, even though that rate had also risen as a result of the strike. Plantation owners preferred the piece rate, however, because it was more manipulable and required less investment in the worker. Thus during the coffee harvest season of 1983–84 they hired far more workers than usual at the piece rate because of the large number of people looking for work. The workers were unable to make more than 2 quetzales a day for a full day of work owing to overpicking. In this way plantation owners were able to pay less than the minimum wage. Nonetheless, a larger percentage of Totonicapán workers were seeking employment on plantations than ever before for lack of alternatives.

Prices rose while wages dropped, but not as much as one might have expected given that Guatemala was suffering severe food and firewood shortages in late 1983. Firewood shortages were extremely severe in the fall of 1983 because of the tactics used by the Guatemalan army in its counterinsurgency campaigns, which included burning trees and crops in large sectors of the western highlands. Many people complained that there was no corn or firewood to be obtained at any price. Nevertheless, food prices had not reached historic highs. The price of corn in Totonicapán after the 1976 earthquake, for example, was higher than prices reported in 1984; at one point in 1976 local corn reached about 25 cents per pound. I surmise, on the basis of what friends told me, that profit margins were being significantly cut on all marketed items in 1983 and 1984. Guatemala's market in staple foods and in items of Indian consumption is extremely competitive since Indians, who do not have the political means of acquiring commercial monopolies that ladinos do, are the main merchants involved in their distribution. Large numbers of unemployed and underemployed people were entering the market as petty traders, the market always having been the last-resort employer for rural Indians. Large urban merchants and some trade specialists, such as certain clothing salesmen of Totonicapán who had the capital to carry large and diverse arrays of goods, held protected positions in the market and thus made decent livings from sales in the 1970s. But it appears that in 1984 even these protected markets were being undermined by competition, the price rises reported there indicating extreme shortages of basic goods rather than any pattern of hoarding or gouging.

I do not include here price figures for woven goods because of the difficulty in determining a comparable unit: each woven item has individual elements that give it value. But I did find mostly simple (and thus cheap) woven goods in the marketplaces at extremely low prices. Many of the weavers I talked to in 1983 told me that they were selling cloth at cost in order to recover the cost of materials they had sunk into production. Even at historically low prices for woven goods, the demand was lower than the weavers had ever experienced.

The consequence of the price-and-wage scissors in Totonicapán was thus a major restructuring of the local economy. Perhaps the most significant figure in Table 4 is the percentage of people working for others rather than for themselves. In 1980, 29 percent of the men of Chipol worked for wages, whereas in 1984 nearly 50 percent worked for wages. This change is all the more significant given the transformation in the conditions of wage work. In the 1970s most wage workers in Totonicapán were young men who were working at an artisanal specialty to obtain the skill and capital needed to set up their own businesses, which most young men did upon marriage. Under these conditions, Totonicapán did not have a permanent "proletariat." It had an artisanal economy in which people changed positions in artisanal firms as they matured and learned the ropes of the business. The wage workers in 1984, by contrast, were older men working in enterprises from which there was little hope of escape: farm work, construction, urban sales (note the large percentage increase of wage workers in commerce), and urban factories. Seen in this light, the major restructuring of the Totonicapán economy was the reduction of many independent producers into permanent wage workers.

When I asked people in Totonicapán what they would do if market conditions remained as bad as they were for another few years, most of them simply threw up their hands. I pressed friends for serious responses. Emilio, like several other close friends, said that he would leave Guatemala if he could find a way out. Many young men said that they would look for work in Guatemala City—they knew Totonicapeños who had small artisanal sweatshops there. Other young men who had been draft dodgers for years said that they might join the military—"let the military catch them," as they put it. Older men were more uncertain. Juan, for example, knew that he could not support eighteen people forever on his dwinding business. But he had no idea what he could do about it. He expected all of his sons eventually to leave the community, one way or another. But he also expected that they would leave their wives and children behind, in the traditional pattern. Though reluctant, he was ready to allow one unmarried daughter to work as a domestic in Guatemala City if she could find a job. Juan surmised sadly that several years from now his hamlet would consist only of old men like himself, women, and children. Juan was assuming that the civil patrol system—which prevents the spatial mobility that has always helped Totonicapeños survive hard times—would not continue in operation.

The Long-Term Economic and Political Consequences of the Counterinsurgency Program

The counterinsurgency program put into effect by Lucas García and expanded by Ríos Montt entered a second phase under Mejía Victores. The first phase saw the physical destruction of what was presumed to have been the support base for the few thousand guerrillas operating in western Guatemala—that is, the destruction of hundreds of rural Indian communities thought to harbor and supply the guerrillas. I have described above the economic impact of this program on an Indian community that was relatively unaffected by the physical destruction associated with the army's counterinsurgency program.

The second phase of the program, which is still under way, involves fewer killings and less physical destruction, although these too continue on a smaller scale. But its long-term consequences may be even more destructive of the independent forms of Indian economy that I described above. The key elements to the second phase of the program are: (1) military control of the movements and social relations of all rural Indian males through the civil patrol system; (2) the development of "strategic hamlets" in the devastated zones, which concentrate dispersed populations into centers controlled by the military; (3) military control over the distribution of many basic foods and a considerable portion of labor in the regional economy; (4) creation of a dependence on goods and services produced by the "modern industrial" sector rather than the artisanal sector through the promotion of a particular program of export-oriented (rather than domestically oriented) economic "development;" and (5) an attempt to "incorporate" Indians into a program of Guatemalan national unity by blaming Indian economic backwardness on Indian culture.

The program that had most affected Totonicapán in 1983 was the civil patrol system, which has been imposed universally on rural areas. As it operated in 1983, Totonicapán's civil patrol system was one of the least onerous in western Guatemala. Nonetheless, it had direct economic and social ramifications. The other programs mentioned above will have a powerful but more indirect effect on the entire western region by further reducing Indian economic autonomy. We can guess what the likely long-term consequences of these programs will be on Indian political and community life in Guatemala by considering what has already happened in places like Totonicapán.

Let us examine the impact of the civil patrol system on Totonicapán through the experiences of the two families described earlier. Emilio, who had found work near Totonicapán, had no difficulty meeting his civil patrol duties, though he lost four to six days' earning power every month. When his civil patrol group had to "practice" on Sundays, he lost that day of work, on which he obtained about half his weekly receipts. But Emilio's family of origin was in a much more difficult situation. Two of his brothers, working on the fair circuit, were not registered for the patrol system and thus could visit their family in

Totonicapán only at great risk. They told Emilio that they had to travel in groups on an established circuit (making competition all the stiffer), because they could get into serious trouble with civil patrols in other communities if they were found alone. Because military sweeps continued in many areas, large parts of the fair circuit were out of bounds.

Emilio had estimated that nearly half the young men in his community were in situations similar to those of his brothers. It is common for young men in Totonicapán to work outside the community for a few years before they marry. Through such experiences as "sojourners" elsewhere, in fact, Totonicapán traders develop the contacts that allow them to compete successfully with traders from other places. Under present circumstances, however, many young men may never return. As they lose contact with home, they are likely to marry and settle down elsewhere, changing both community *and* ethnic identity. Young men or women domestics who marry outside the community are the only Totonicapeños who have changed ethnic identity in the past. Some young men were on the civil patrol lists and thus liable to persecution or worse, if they went home. Others managed to visit home on occasion, but many did not. Thus what had once been a trickle of people lost to the community was likely to become a torrent. At least that seemed likely to Emilio.

Juan, who had joined the military as a youth and achieved the rank of sergeant, had been appointed local militia commander for his hamlet. His job in 1983 was to keep tabs on all males in his community above the age of fourteen, organize them into civil patrol groups, and see that they obtained training for their patrol duties. In late 1983, all the men of Chipol had to train once a week in the town center, where they mainly learned how to march. And they had to patrol their hamlet in local teams for twenty-four hours every fifteen days. Because their hamlet was populous, they could divide into enough patrol teams to make that possible, whereas in smaller communities patrol duties fell more often. These men could not leave their communities for extended periods unless they found and paid a replacement to undertake their patrol duties, and replacements were very difficult to find. This created considerable hardship for those who earned a living by traveling or working elsewhere. It had already become impossible for itinerant peddlers who sold goods house to house in remote areas to keep up their routes because it was simply too dangerous to travel off the major roads.

Juan, a generous and kind-hearted man, found himself in a difficult position as militia commander. It was widely rumored that his son-in-law was a subversive, so Juan felt that he had to cooperate with the authorities. He thought that he could also help his neighbors and, indeed, was instrumental in persuading the authorities to hold military practice sessions on weekdays rather than Sundays—Sunday is the major market day in all of Guatemala, and many merchants would be ruined if they were to lose that day of sales. For a while Juan was able to give "passes" to local merchants who had to travel on practice or patrol days. But the pass system was tightened up in late 1983, and Juan felt increasingly constrained as the "middleman" in the system. When the program was first instituted, Juan did not register many young men from the community who were working (or seeking work) elsewhere. While this made it possible for them to find work, it also made it both difficult and dangerous for them to visit their families. And once the registration system was drawn up, Juan felt unable to help others who wanted to leave the community to seek work else-where. As economic circumstances continued to deteriorate, some of these men simply vanished. Their absence from civil patrol duty had to be reported to the authorities. Since Juan kept the list of names, he was the responsible person. When I talked to him in late 1983, he was not sure what he would do about the situation. He was hoping that the system would end as "peace" became general.

I asked Juan what he thought would happen if the civil patrol system became permanent. At first Juan argued that such a thing could not happen, for it would "kill" the community. I pointed out that the civil patrol system was now in place throughout the entire rural area of western Guatemala and that Indians who had put up resistance had literally been killed. This was not news to people in Totonicapán, many of whom, like Juan, had once had close contact with people in the devastated zones. Juan's face, composed and cheery until then, became very grave. He rose and closed the shutters of the room we were sitting in, something he had never done before. "At that point," he said, "we will either have to leave Guatemala or join the guerrillas."

The system has not ended, even though the level of violence is much lower than before. At present (1987) the civil patrol system incorporates nearly one million men in Guatemala—which is to say virtually all men in rural communities. Letters tell me that Juan is still the local commander of the civil patrols in his hamlet. They also report that most people avoid him. There have been no general "town meetings" in the hamlet for two years because of the high level of distrust and suspicion. This hamlet had been one of the most political and unified hamlets in a township known for its political activity and unity.

Letters also report that economic circumstances in Totonicapán are continuing to deteriorate. Emilio writes that he now has four competitors for his small refreshment stand where he had none a year ago, and his weekly receipts are now half of what they were. Prices also remain high while wages stay low, even though the 1984 harvest was much better than that of 1983. In consequence, more young men have left Totonicapán permanently, some to take positions in towns for room and board alone. Others have simply disappeared. According to Emilio, the situation in the weaving industry is much as it was when he carried out the survey, some older weavers trying to hang on while younger men look for other kinds of work. Though Totonicapán women continue to wear traditional dress, increasing numbers of their young daughters do not. Emilio says there is no demand for native cloth in the towns and plantation area and suggests that most people who have moved to those places are trying to hide their Indian ethnic identity. Elsewhere, though older women continue to wear native dress, they cannot afford to buy anything new. Clothing styles continue to simplify even in the most "traditional" areas. I have no more specific information than this: Emilio does not want to do another survey of his hamlet because people are too suspicious now, even of a native son.

Reading between the lines, I get a picture of political disunity brought on by economic desperation and terror. Totonicapán Indians have been nearly as terrorized by the state-sponsored violence in the highlands as communities that have felt the violence more directly. One result is that Totonicapán Indians are much more willing today than ever before to redefine themselves in ways that will mean cultural loss. Traditional forms of organization, self-help, and protest are no longer considered possible. The people of Chipol distrust more than strangers: they distrust and avoid discussions with each other. What was once a source of support, the community, is now a trap, a place of confinement and restriction. Many people want to give up and leave. Almost every letter I now receive from friends in Totonicapán

broaches the subject of exile. They do so with reluctance, because Totonicapán is still home, but it is a home that may not allow its members to survive.

Conclusion

Indian women's clothing has long been an important symbol of native
ethnic identity, almost as powerful as the use of native languages. Guatemalan Indians maintained that symbol even when they were so
caught up in the plantation-market economy that they could no longer
weave their own clothing. They were able to do so by buying traditional designs produced primarily by Totonicapán specialists. If the
weaving art dies out in Totonicapán, it will mean more than hardship
for a large group of artisans. It will also destroy one of the material
bases of Indian ethnic identity. But Indian culture can survive the
death of weaving. What it cannot survive is the death of autonomous
communities. The present material basis for autonomous Indian communities is Indian control over domestic trade and the production of
many Indian consumption goods. If this too is eliminated by the new
"development and control" strategies planned by the state for the
western region, there will no longer be a material basis for autonomous Indian communities. In this respect, then, consideration of the
case of Totonicapán helps reinforce the depiction of present-day ethnocide. Because of the violence, death, and destruction that have taken
place elsewhere, Totonicapán's indigenous economy—the material basis for its ethnic strength—is also near death.

Ethnic struggle has taken a violent form many times in Guatemala,
beginning with the initial conquest in the sixteenth century. Indians
survived the first conquest—in which foreign diseases killed 90 percent of them in some regions and a foreign culture attacked most of
their social patterns and beliefs—by creating strong, ethnically distinct communities. They survived the chaos of the early independence
period, which saw the Guatemalan state try to destroy the legal and
property basis of independent Indian communities, by widespread and
coordinated revolts. They survived the plantation economy of the late
nineteenth century, which took a great deal of labor and much of the
land base from Indian communities, by creating local specializations
and a dynamic market economy over which they held control. On
these grounds, then, there is some hope that Indian culture will find

some other reserve of resistance to the present attack on its existence. But Indian culture did not survive the great Matanza in El Salvador in 1932, and the parallels of that holocaust to the present situation in Guatemala are hard to ignore.

My romantic image of Totonicapán Indian rebels has changed over the years as I have observed firsthand the brutality with which Indians are treated in Guatemala. But even now, as I perceive the social tragedy that Indian cultural resistance has become for many Indian people, my admiration for their culture remains. We will all be impoverished should they lose the present struggle.

PART FOUR

Refugees of Violence

CHAPTER 10

Struggle for Survival in the Mountains: Hunger and Other Privations Inflicted on Internal Refugees from the Central Highlands

By Ricardo Falla

The following account, originally prepared for the United Nations special rapporteur to Guatemala in July 1983, shows that the Guatemalan government has systematically used hunger, malnutrition, illness, and lack of clothing and housing as political and military instruments in its struggle against the revolutionary movement. This activity is in clear violation of human rights as set forth in United Nations documents. As the reader will discover, the information on which the account is based comes from Indians from the central Guatemalan highlands who have been persecuted by the army. It provides, therefore, crucial testimony independent of that provided by external refugees, such as those who have crossed into Mexico, or by former refugees inside Guatemala who have come under army control.

The Political and Military Context

In late 1981 the army began its first large-scale operations against the guerrillas in Chimaltenango and southern Quiché. These operations were designed to "remove the water in which the fish [the guerrillas] swim." The army launched an almost indiscriminate attack on the civilian population, many villages of which had been supporting the guerrillas. To escape the army, the civilians left the villages and began living in the hills, in the high forests, and, where possible, in the mountains.

At the end of the Lucas García regime and the beginning of the Ríos Montt government (1982), there was a sharp increase in massacres of civilians in villages that the army thought had guerrilla sympathies. As a result, the number of civilian refugees heading for the mountains grew rapidly, reaching a peak in July and August 1982. To the army, the civilians who took flight to the hills were, by definition, guerrilla accomplices. As a result, when army units came across deserted homesteads and farms, they burned them down, after stealing what they could use, such as tape recorders and radios, and killed domestic animals to feed the soldiers. Animals that were not eaten on the spot or taken back to the barracks were also slaughtered.

There are many instances of civilians and even whole village groups who did not flee, believing that they had committed no crimes and that taking to the hills would be seen as an admission of guilt. Some of these people were massacred by soldiers as they tried to extract information on the whereabouts of the guerrillas or other villagers who had fled.

Survivors who were too far away to consider crossing the frontier began a struggle for survival in the inhospitable mountains. It was difficult to take refuge from the heavy rains which in some areas last all day and night during Guatemala's "winter" (rainy season). In their hurry to escape, many had been able to carry away only a few clothes and some tortillas. They soon ran out of the latter and had to begin eating roots, particularly in those areas where they were unable to return to their homes by night to recover a little corn. They could not cook by day because smoke from the fires would give away their position to the army, so they cooked by night and suffered the cold by day.

Some areas in which the army suspected that civilians were hiding were bombed. People moving in a group were sometimes able to break the army's siege, escaping from the pincer movements. But the situation became increasingly unsustainable as hunger, cold, malnutrition, exhaustion, and illness overcame the groups. In general, those migrants who were closest to the highways and the cities and who could not find safe hideouts because of the absence of vegetation or hills, could hold out only for two or three months before making their way to the cities. There they could disappear without trace into the shantytowns. Others could not outlast the army's siege and had to surrender after taking heavy losses.

There are inhospitable areas in the mountains which continued to harbor refugees long after 1982. The army's siege of these areas was particularly tight and the refugees, suffering from hunger, illness, and the elements, found it difficult to get food, medicine, clothing, or sheeting for rainproof shelters. The army tried to tempt the refugees out, speaking to them from helicopters with loudspeakers and dropping leaflets or blankets. But many refused to come out for fear of being massacred or tortured. The army tortured to extract information about others in hiding. The testimonies that follow are from refugees in three central highland regions where the army has violated and continues to violate human rights. The account comes from direct witnesses of the terrible struggle for survival going on in these mountain refuges.

Patzún: An Account from Chimaltenango

Our informants tell the story of three hundred people who fled from the army between May and July 1982. We have three main sources. The first is an account by a local inhabitant who witnessed the events as they happened and later wrote them by hand on two sheets of paper. The second source is a tape-recorded interview with a Patzún villager. The third source is a report by a Cakchiquel Indian informant who talked with the villagers involved and taped the interview referred to above. We do not mention the villages by their true names to avoid possible reprisals, for some of them are now inhabited again.

Patzún, the township in which the events to be described took place, is a picturesque place formerly visited by tourists. From its highland setting west of Guatemala City a blue lake and volcanoes are clearly visible. The population is made up almost entirely of Indians who speak the Cakchiquel Maya language. The Patzún women wear Indian blouses (huipils) decorated with bright red flowers. The beauty and the mountain isolation of the community make it an unlikely place for the violent events that unfolded there.

There was international denunciation of massacres that took place in Chipiacul, Patzún, on April 26, 1982. According to Amnesty International, twenty people were burned alive in a massacre carried out by the army. In a letter to Amnesty dated September 15, 1982, Thomas Enders, then in charge of Latin-American affairs for the U. S. Department of State, said that the massacre had probably been committed by guerrillas, since most of the victims were supposedly members of the local civil patrol. This claim is disputed by our sources, which support the findings of Amnesty International. Our sources say: "They [soldiers] arrived in Chipiacul to massacre the people; they killed 22 peasants and burned them. The men who went there were over 75 [in number]. And the next day they returned and said, 'Here is the work of the *guerrios* [Guerrillas]', but they were the killers."

We shall call the village of our account Amá, one of the many villages that make up rural Patzún. Before these events took place, Amá had a population (all Indian) of 1,010. The army went to the area five times in 1982 before Amá's inhabitants fled to the hills. It is evident that the army was trying to trap the guerrillas who had support in the region.

The first army incursion took place on January 1982, when about thirty *judiciales* (secret police) entered the village by night and kidnapped the deputy mayor and his ten-year-old daughter. They were accused of harboring guerrillas. A female guerrilla was also arrested. After this incident the villagers set up lookout posts on the main approaches, and when the army appeared, most fled to the hills, returning only after the soldiers had left. The second army incursion on January 22, 1982, involved one hundred soldiers, who burned houses, beds, mattresses, and blankets and killed a thirty-year-old man. The third army incursion, on February 8, 1982, consisted of about one hundred soldiers, who surrounded the village so that no one could escape. They rounded up twenty men and killed one of them. The others, together with women and children, were beaten. In the afternoon they took two youngsters with them. One managed to escape from the soldiers; the other was killed near the road to Patzún. Soldiers of the fourth army incursion, on April 25, 1982, found that the entire population had left, unlike the previous incursions, when some had stayed behind. In anger the army moved on to other villages, among them Chipiacul, where it massacred twenty-two Indian peasants. Chipiacul's residents had not fled beforehand as had those from Amá. The fifth army incursion, on May 2, 1982, took place in one of Amá's neighboring villages. The soldiers rounded up the whole population; the women were taken to the Evangelical church, where many were raped. Ten peasants were killed in their homes. The soldiers gave other peasants grenades, instructing them to use them against the guerrillas.

On May 3, 1982, the inhabitants of Amá decided to leave the village for good to take up a nomadic life in the mountains. Some, however, were able to take refuge in neighboring villages. One of the inhabitants involved in the migration recounts what happened: "We left, I remember, on May 3, Holy Cross Day. Everyone was satisfied, happy, because that day there was going to be a holy mass. But it didn't take place because of the enemies. So it didn't take place, and instead of having a moment of happiness all the people fled to the mountain to escape the enemy."

The next day, May 4, the army arrived again at the neighboring village. The villagers still had the grenades. The army accused them of not collaborating and asked who had trained them. They responded, "The villagers from Amá." The soldiers took eleven peasants from the village and marched them to Amá, killing two of them on the way. The remaining nine had to show the soldiers the houses of the Amá villagers who were "organized." But when they arrived, the whole village was empty. In fury, the soldiers killed the remaining nine guides and buried them in the village center.

That same day the soldiers burned sixteen houses in Amá, along with large quantities of maize, beans, and wheat. They burned clothes, blankets, and everything else in the houses that would burn. Evidently they wanted to prevent the return of the villagers (a policy which the army later changed) and to cut off their food supplies so that they could not return by night to take maize back up the mountain. The Cakchiquel linguist records: "At the beginning of May they began fleeing and taking refuge definitively in the mountains surrounding the villages. The population survived in the mountains eating roots, leaves, river crabs, some animals they managed to hunt down, and wild fruit. They were able to live about three months on the mountain, exposed to the elements."

On May 9, 1982, the army realized where the villagers were hiding. The soldiers returned to Amá and burned another twenty houses. They also killed a thirty-five-year-old man who had not taken proper precautions. They killed about seventy-five chickens and all the dogs. In this way they destroyed all the food supplies. Then the soldiers ate their lunch in the village school. As night fell, the army began to bombard the mountains from Amá village. This is the account of one villager: "On Monday, May 9, we were in a place far away from our village. And they found out where we were. They shot at us with grenades and grenade launchers, and they shot at us with guns, but no casualties. All of us people were there. We were more than 300 girls, boys, youngsters, and young women and wives."

By day the soldiers unsuccessfully searched for the villagers. This was clearly a civilian population, although it had some protection by armed cadres of the revolutionary organization. Civilians were being persecuted and bombed. For a month people from neighboring communities, at great risk, offered help: "Those communities, when they knew that the Amá people had fled, asked everyone for support to send food, and for about a month while we were in the mountains they collaborated with us." But the other villages also suffered repression. For example, in Cablah, a neighboring village, the army killed about twenty-two men: "After we had been in the mountain for about a week, the repression fell on Cablah. The Cablah people did not flee, but, eh, none of them left. What the enemy did was get all those people. That first time it arrived, it killed 22 or 24 men. When they realized that Cablah was dead (that is, the village would be annihilated), many of their people had to flee, but there weren't many left. They fell into enemy hands."

On June 23, 1982, frustrated by lack of success, the army prepared to bombard the mountain from an unexpected direction. It positioned two tanks, one at Godínez and the other at Agua Escondida (two villages in the Department of Sololá on the road that connects the plateau with the southern coast). The tanks were about seven miles from Huitz Mountain. They were to fire again by night, the time when the refugee population rested and could not move easily. If the refugees used lights to find their way along the tortuous mountain trails, they would present easy targets:

Well, all those communities [such as Agua Escondida], they all collaborated with our people since we were in the mountain. They had heard that the Amá comrades had fled, and they knew where we were. A messenger arrived telling us that the enemy was going to bombard the mountain. A new plan was drawn up with the people. We had to leave that place to go to another behind the mountain or behind the hill. We left at about five in the afternoon, climbing the mountain with all the people, children, old ones, women, everything, eh, carrying on our shoulders, taking blankets, clothes. There were approximately 300 people. In the afternoon as we were climbing up the mountain or the hill, getting to the top of the hill, I was going last, as the rear guard, then we heard, eh, we heard like a bomb, like one of those fiesta bombs, which came from the sky. So I told the people to throw themselves down on the ground, because it was something the enemies were throwing at us. In a few minutes that bomb fell below where the people were. The people advanced more quickly to turn the corner round the hill, and we had to walk about half the night to be able to advance, so as not to fall into the hands of the enemy.

In other words, with support from other villagers in the form of advance warning, the three hundred people were able to hide on the other side of Huitz Mountain to escape nighttime shelling. The army bombed the hill from 6:00 P.M. that evening until 4:00 A.M. the next morning.

The villagers remained in their new hideout for about three days. The soldiers continued searching but did not climb to the summit of the hill. On June 25 they caught a man who lived in a hut on Huitz Mountain and took him to Chimaltenango, where he was tortured and, after a week, released. Out of anger the soldiers continued their destruction of Amá, this time turning to the central symbols of the community, those of the church: "But because of the fury of not finding the people they took the bell of our people's church, they took the instruments [violins and guitars used in the mass], the peoples' beds, tables, chairs. They took all that to Patzún."

Hunger forced the villagers to leave their hideout and go back to Huitz Mountain, where it appears they had left some provisions. The children first suffered the effects of lack of food and began crying. This forced the adults to move quickly so that the cries would not alert the army to their whereabouts: "On the third day we had to leave that place because we had no food left. All the people suffered, were hungry. Mainly the children were asking for food. They could not stand that hunger. We had to return. But by bad luck when we were returning that afternoon a downpour came, and we had to come out to find the way back to where we had been before."

The rain also hampered the army, which at that moment was coming out of the village with the stolen furniture. The convoy of army vehicles got stuck in the mud outside the village. With total disregard, the soldiers used the load and foodstuffs taken from the village to throw into the mud to make a solid surface for the wheels to grip: "All the beds which were in that house beside the road were all stuck under the convoy to get it out. All the coffee and the beans in the houses were brought out and thrown under the wheels to get the convoy out. Next day we realized that all this had happened, because the young combatants decided to go into the village to find out what the enemies had done."

The source makes a clear distinction between the "people" and the "combatants" (guerrillas), which indicates that those who were fleeing were civilians ("the people") and that the army was fighting not only the guerrillas but also the civilians. The combatants (guerrillas) sometimes stayed with the civilians and at other times left them to explore the terrain. For example, when the bombing of Huitz Mountain began, some combatants left the civilians, and others stayed with them: "Over there in Huitz a group of armed combatants, who did not want to leave with the people, stayed behind."

On July 17, 1982, there was a confrontation between the army and the combatants in Amá village itself. For some weeks the army had eased the siege and stopped coming into the area, so the combatants and a group of peasants who had organized themselves into a kind of militia known as the FIL (Local Irregular Forces) became confident enough to take shelter in one of the houses on the outskirts of the village. They had been there a few days when, on the morning of the seventeenth, the army surrounded the village, including that house. In the resulting clash, eleven revolutionaries and thirty-five or more soldiers died. It is important to note how our source distinguishes between the combatants and the FIL members: "At that moment [after the revolutionaries had neutralized an army machine-gun emplacement] the comrades [compañeros] were given the chance to leave, because there were about 18 combatants, and when they left, the army took out about four of the combatants and some of the comrades from the community, of the FIL's, eh. They fell too; the total of comrades, combatants, and FIL who fell was about 11." The source calls both the combatants who were not from the community and the FIL members from the community "comrades." The FIL members fell halfway between the categories of civilians and combatants. In Amá the FIL was virtually unarmed except for some grenades. The confrontation taxed the army, which had to call in two helicopters to deliver more munitions and carry away the wounded. The dead were removed by the convoy. In all about thirty-five were killed.

From that moment onwards the army increased its persecution of the civilian population. The helicopters searched the mountain without finding anything. Then, on July 21, the army reached a hamlet of Amá village whose inhabitants had not yet fled: "There were about 40 people, men, women, and children, at the hamlet. They got four men and tied their hands behind their backs and took them to a shed full of corn cobs. They burned it, and pushed them into the fire. The four men died there. Then they found a young man from Achí. They got him and killed him near Achí village." It appears that the four men were burned as a reprisal for the help the army assumed that the hamlet had been giving the refugees, presumably by sending food. The army acted in fury, making no attempt to distinguish between civilians, combatants, and the FIL.

The next day the soldiers continued destroying all possible sources of food, together with instruments for food preparation, fertilizers, and clothing: "And the next day they got to Amá and took away a corn grinder motor, all the furniture, wardrobes, horses, cows, goats, maize, fertilizers, and so on." The grinding mill, used to make the corn dough for tortillas, is driven by a small gasoline or diesel engine. In the villages it is usually owned by one family and is used to meet the needs of thirty or forty neighboring families.

Finally, within a few days, the army found the refugees in a deep gorge on the mountain. The people were able to escape and scramble away in disorderly fashion, but they had to leave all their cooking utensils and provisions out in the open. Before, they had moved as a single group, but now they dispersed. They hid as they could in the mountains while the army opened fire in haphazard fashion. It was the culmination of three months of hardship. The community lost all sense of itself. Later the population escaped toward the coast in atomized bands, taking refuge in the capital, departmental cities, or other distant towns where relatives had been living for some years.

It is worth quoting one of the sources on other reasons why the community left the mountains: a kind of desperation and a disillusion with the combatant comrades (i.e., the guerrillas) who had left for the mountains with them: "I too had to leave, because there was no other way. Because all that we had suffered in those three or four months in the mountains was hard on our people. And at that time all our people, eh, became desperate because the combatant comrades never . . . eh, they told the people that they were the vanguard but they were always going in the rear guard." In other words, the guerrillas were unable to rise to the occasion, because they were insufficiently armed, because they too became demoralized, or because little by little the civilians began taking the initiative and the "vanguard" role. It is important to emphasize that there was no use for the guerrillas to use terror against the civilians to maintain control, but they did fail to provide leadership in the extreme circumstances of the time.

We note too that, unlike other communities, Amá did not surrender to the army. Rather, it lost itself inside the country once it had lost the will to resist in the mountains. The refugees who took to the mountains probably numbered more than 300 persons; the informant estimated the figure as high as 600. It is probable that the number fluctuated. The average number of guerrillas—their numbers also fluctuated—was 25. The local forces (FIL) totaled another 25 or so men. Twenty-five civilians from Amá were murdered by the army. In the two neighboring villages whose residents did not flee to the mountains, about 150 people were killed.

Rabinal, Baja Verapaz

In September 1982 a group of Rabinal villagers fled from repression. In April 1983 they were still on the run. Our information comes from two letters, dated September 25, 1982, and April 15, 1983, written by an Indian woman who carried out religious work in the area. In September 1982 she reported the anguished state of many of the villagers, some of whose relatives had been massacred by the army. She mentioned the massacre of Agua Fría village, which took place on September 13, 1982: "This week in the villages where I work, the army, mixed in with civil patrols, massacred an entire village which is called Agua Fría, near Los Pajales on the limit of Baja Verapaz and Uspantán [Department of El Quiché]. They didn't leave one survivor. They were all covered with gasoline and burned alive, children, women, and men." Some villagers, like those of Amá, in Patzún, escaped death by fleeing to the north or into the mountains: "There is a village which has had army repression six times now, and they are under the rocks, in the scrub, giving birth to children in the jungle itself, without sanitation or clothes to look after the little children who are wrapped in old rags and go two, three days or more without eating."

Once again the situation involved not only hunger, malnutrition, and lack of medical attention but also army bombings. With experience, the people became accustomed to the bombing, which, therefore, no longer caused either the terror or the deaths the army wished. Those who became leaders, such as the woman who wrote the letters, provided encouragement and training in civil defense. The army explained these atrocities as psychological domination and imprisonment by guerrillas, but the woman's testimony tells a different story. She was living among the refugees in the mountains: "Little by little, after bombings by helicopters, tanks, and light aircraft, people are getting to know those devices. At first they asked, 'What is that?' When they were told about them and how one should take defensive action, they became calmer and looked for holes in which to put their children. And so we have been saving our lives in each army attack."

Besides the bombings to terrorize and kill the civilians, the army also took away food supplies. Here the army operated in keeping with the season, cutting down the maize plants of the milpa: "The hardest is when they see the army lead away their animals and they are left with nothing. And now that the milpa is ripe, they have arrived to cut it down. We villagers are condemned to die, not of bullets but of hunger."

It was not enough, however, to cut production, because international opinion was aware of the hunger of these poor people and sent money through representatives. So it was necessary to cut potential supplies from the municipal markets. That could be done by laying siege to the mountain refugees or by controlling purchases at the open markets: "All the municipal centers are super-guarded and nobody can go shopping in the markets. If someone tries, he doesn't come back. That happened to a little old man of 80 last week. He went to buy tomatoes, sugar, chiles. He didn't return." The letter writer does not say explicitly that the old man was murdered, although she suggests it. The fact is that he did not return. And the result was that the community could not feed itself. The army would say that it had liberated thirty or forty people who gave themselves up at a military base, but to carry out that "liberation" it forced the population into unbearable hunger, intimidation, and persecution through bombings.

In the second letter, of April 1983, the woman reported how the army laid siege to a civilian group for a week. She wrote: "In the barren hills of Baja Verapaz, the army ambushed the Rabinal villages from March 6 to 11, 1983. The poor people were hidden in the slopes under rocks. After four days they could not take the hunger. The children began to faint, so the parents decided to take their children out and find something to eat. Two men, three women, and two girls were massacred by criminal bullets, and three girls were wounded; the two women of the men who fell are now widowed." In other words, first the army laid siege (an ambush, because the terrain is barren) to the population; next, the civilians took their children out of the burrows to look for food; and, third, the army opened fire. It was like a wild-boar hunt, the animal being trapped in its cave and the hunter waiting for it outside. And then the army would claim to be liberating the civilians from the guerrillas.

The woman continued the letter, recounting that after this massacre of seven dead and five wounded, all noncombatants, one of the wounded women approached her when she was passing through her village and showed her her wound. It is a good example of the lack of first aid and medical attention. Here is her chilling testimony:

A woman with bullet wounds—she seemed to me to be the woman of the Gospel behind Jesus. I had nothing to give her and I went on to another village. Next day, four hours' walk away, my great fright! I see her and she takes off her clothing to show the wound. Tremendous misfortune! My impotence! I have no medicine; there is not even salt to wash her with salt water. My stomach is turning, my heart, to be in the midst of so much misery. Then I met her a third time and she said: "Look at my breasts. I was so scared by the bullets that my milk has gone, and now I have nothing to give my four month old daughter." She is not a demanding woman; she says it with hope that she may get something, but no! So I had to give her a few cents to buy sugar if she got the chance, to give sugared water to the girl. That is the kind of misery here. There are not four or five people, but hundreds. It cannot be resolved with a few cents.

We do not have statistics on infant mortality in these circumstances, only the general description of health conditions among children, women, and old people, who seem to form the bulk of the civilian population: "Health conditions are frightening. Rickets are most intense among the children. The children ooze pus from their infections. The old people's knees are shapeless, so swollen are they from rheumatism. Pale women with children stuck to their milkless breasts because of so much malnutrition. This is what you find in all the villages."

In this situation, it can be asked, How was it possible for the civilians to have the resistance to continue as mountain refugees, at least from September to April? Evidently the answer is that the alternative was possible death, as had happened to others, at the hands of the army. But apart from this the letter writer mentions two factors that helped to maintain morale: religious faith and communitarian living:

How do people sustain their morale? They constantly organize celebration of the word of God, and that is their only consolation. That's true, the life they lead is incredible. Everything is shared. Like the life of the first Christians. Nobody keeps corn or whatever apart. Everything is administered by those responsible in the community. And by "squads" which go out looking for herbs for everyone. Others go to prepare the land for sowing. Others serve as lookouts lest the army come.

This shows that these refugee communities reached a level of organization which kept them united so that they did not break up and, evidently, so that they did not become demoralized and surrender to the army. The organizing that occurs, as we have seen, is both religious and economic, and it appears to consist of giving general direction to the community. The leaders can be either religious or economic, and they can overlap.

When our witness says that they "organize celebrations," that implies the existence of organizers besides herself, and when she tells of administering possessions, that implies that certain members of the community were responsible for distribution. She mentions "squads," groups who were given collection and production tasks. Perhaps they were called squads because they also had self-defense roles, such as keeping a lookout for the army. Or perhaps, since community life took place in the midst of war—although the letter makes no mention of it as in Patzún—the squads may have had a relationship with guerrilla camps. It is clear that, despite the use of the word "squads," this was a civilian population.

We see that the communitarian life was based on collective work and that this work was carried out because of the need to produce food. This was a key element for sustaining morale. The letter was written in April. That is the key month, in which the soil must be prepared for sowing. Although the army violates the inalienable rights of the community, pushing it into hunger, nakedness, illness, and death, the people still nurture the hope of being able to sow and to produce and in some way to defend their production or hide it in distant places.

The letter ends with this testimonial: "As you can see, only I understand my writing. My arm hurts from so much work, I would like to write more, but cannot. My fingers are numb from the cold. And my intestines are rumbling from hunger."

Cobán and San Cristóbal Alta Verapaz

Involved in the events to be described are several villages whose people were on the run from the army for at least a year (April 1982 to April 1983). Our information comes from two letters, dated September 28, 1982, and April 15, 1983, from two different women. The writer of the second letter is the woman who also wrote about Baja Verapaz.

The refugees took to the mountains because of the repression. Some of the civilian camps in the mountains were made up of the survivors of army massacres at Cobán and San Cristóbal villages, which occurred soon after Ríos Montt took power in 1982: "The past two weeks [July and August 1982] I went with the comrades to some villages. In others they are camped out in the jungle far from where they used to live. They are the ones who left their homes because of the repression, survivors who fled because of a massacre, a bombing. They are all at a camp, but in different subdivisions." Information on this massacre has been available for some time. We have the testimony of a church spokesman, according to whom the army bombed Las Pacayas, a village in San Cristóbal, killing men, women, and children. The "military" operation continued up to March 27, 1982. According to the same testimony, on March 24 the army burned all the houses of a village in the township of Cobán but did not kill anyone because the civilians fled in time. In the following days the army continued burning houses in the neighboring villages of Cobán. The soldiers destroyed everything they found—clothes, foodstores, and animals.

The massacres in the area continued. There are reliable testimonies, such as that of Marlise Simmons (New York Times, September 15, 1982), who went to Las Pacayas and interviewed people from there and from San Cristóbal. According to her, on June 17, 1982, soldiers dressed as civilians entered the village before sunrise and killed sixty men, women, and children, shooting wildly into the houses. About three hundred survivors went down to San Cristóbal looking for refuge, determined not to sleep any more in Las Pacayas.

The report of the Justice and Peace Committee to the United Nations Human Rights Commission states that on June 14, 1982, after a helicopter machine-gun attack on another village of San Cristóbal township, men in camouflaged green uniforms and civilian clothes surrounded the village. Many of the villagers escaped to the mountains, but the army killed 96 people, mainly children with their mothers who were unable to run. The army version is that the guerrillas were responsible for the massacre. The army says that in Las Pacayas the killers wore civilian clothes. Men interviewed in the presence of an officer at the new 150-strong strategic village Las Pacayas said that the killers were "the subversives." Nevertheless, Simmons, after a careful reconstruction of events through interviews with army officers, health workers, leaders of a nearby town—presumably San Cristóbal—

and with survivors, concluded that those who attacked at dawn were soldiers from the Cobán military base. We do not know how the army argues its case for the bombing of Las Pacayas in March 1982 and the helicopter machine gunning of another village on June 14: the guerrillas do not have aircraft or helicopters.

Returning to the letters, we find many details and an account that coincides with the published versions cited above. There are references to the survivors of those villages, indicating that not all their inhabitants fled to the mountains. Some died in the massacres and the bombings, but, as Simmons indicates, others fled to the municipal center from which they were taken back to their original village, now under military control. There they lived in tents, as in Las Pacayas.

The people who fled to the mountains formed civilian camps, different and separate from the guerrilla camps. We have seen this clear distinction in Patzún. Here it was more marked because, for the sake of their security, the guerrillas prevented most of the civilians from knowing their whereabouts. Each civilian camp contained 100 to 200 families grouped into camps. One letter describes these camps: "The first time I went to one of these places I was struck by the situation at one camp where we rested and had 'corn water.' There were 15 families. There was no place for me to sit, because the floor was covered with people. In almost all the corners there were sick people, children and adults. The camp was both kitchen and dormitory. It was the size of a classroom." The scarcity of goods was similar to that described in Baja Verapaz. Nevertheless, in this letter, written in September 1982, we find that the shortage of grain supplies was not as serious in July and August as it became later: "In those places there was still some corn and beans, and salt could be obtained from the village. But now. . . ."

The later shortages were caused in part by the natural depletion of existing stocks, and also by the army's stricter control of markets, shops, and municipal centers. The tactics of repression had changed. There were fewer massacres and bombings, simply because the population had dispersed. The army set up a system of controlled villages and changed its image to attract those who had fled, offering "beans" rather than "bullets." At the same time it made life impossible for the mountain refugees. They were persecuted, besieged (food was cut off, and so on) to get them to surrender to an army which was now showing a kindlier face in the controlled areas. The letter tells how this system worked in September: "But now nothing can be obtained because there is much checking by the army. They search the women's baskets, and when they find more than three pounds of one item, they suspect she is buying for the guerrillas and confiscate her things."

The money which the fugitives had taken with them to the mountains as a possible lifeline was also running short. But even money was of little use because of the army checkpoints: "In those places there is still a little bit of money. Those who were able to hide it away saved it. But most people have none now." Among the refugees were rich peasants, perhaps a minority, but repression had made everyone equal: "And they'd say to me: 'We had milpa, animals, and 3–4 cows. And now we don't have anything. Not even clothes. In the kitchen they broke the pots and they destroyed the sheeting walls of the house. And you can see this, all the sheeting has holes made by the bayonets!'"

The army surveillance made it difficult to use the little money that was left, and this caused great hardship because the worst scarcities were necessities that were not produced in the area, such as salt and sugar: "There are communities where they eat twice a day, with a ration of 2 or 3 tortillas. On my last trip there were communities that had run out of salt and it was worse with sugar. In some places they used sugar cane juice instead of sugar, but the canes are not cultivated in all places. And the salt, where are we going to get it from?"

Even the commonest medicines were scarce. As soon as they were purchased, they were used up: "That month everything was scarce. You couldn't even find aspirin. I felt bad when I heard the children's bad coughs. I said they should take a hot drink made of orange leaves and sugar, but they told me, 'We have no sugar.' And to get the leaves they would have to walk for an hour."

By September, as in Baja Verapaz, the milpa was being destroyed. Other persecutions of the civilians are mentioned: "Three weeks ago the soldiers went to a village north of Cobán. They burned 200 cuerdas [about 31 acres] of milpa and the camp of a community. Nobody died, because our people know how to carry out their emergency plan. There is now no maize in that place where there are 200 families." It is not clear whether the loss of maize was due to the burning of the milpa or also to the burning of the camp, the ranches, and the food stores.

Cooking was part of the collective work: "In many places there are collective kitchens, where tortillas are made and distributed to the squads. Where beans can be found they are cooked too. But where they can't then there is nothing." The collective kitchens distributed food to the squads, which appear to have been the same type of unit as the camps. The camp mentioned above was at one and the same time kitchen and dormitory for fifteen families. Collectivization strengthens social control and helps prevent the community from breaking up or squads from surrendering to the army in a moment of collective depression. According to one of the letters, each camp was led and coordinated by a small group, with its own head: "Each camp has its local head, and its head for daily life: supply, medical services, production, culture, etc."

As far as can be understood, there was one overall head, with leaders for different daily activities. We may suppose that the head of production, for example, was in charge of organizing the work of the squads in the fields, sowing, cleaning, looking for herbs, etc., while the supply leader took charge of controlling and distributing goods.

As in Baja Verapaz, we are told of the good atmosphere and fraternity prevailing in the camp, despite the scarcities:

In this place where I have been you sense a feeling of tranquillity. Everyone is friendly with one another. All that there is to fear is the arrival of the army, which to date has reached only the periphery of the place. Our people are very committed to ending the war. They have not lost hope. What is nice is that all live in communities and have a collective life. It is like the first Christian communities, everything is distributed according to necessity.

Other reasons are given why the community does not surrender to the army: "They do not surrender because they fear that they would have to collaborate with the army and cause the deaths of those who did not surrender; also because of what might be done to them should they surrender. The people hold out because the Indians have always held out under extreme conditions. Furthermore, they think that their economic condition is sustainable."

The last reason was also a factor in Baja Verapaz: the economic situation could be maintained, although it was difficult. The other reasons are new. The first two reasons for holding out imply fear of the army and aversion to the idea of becoming collaborators in harming or even killing their comrades from the camp. That is why life is fraternal and deeply tranquil in the camp, because surrendering to the army would be a betrayal. It can be inferred that some, though not all, of those who surrender make statements in which they describe the civilian camps as concentration camps where they have been held by force. But I say "some" because others may have succumbed out of hunger and simple weakness, not out of treachery. This weakness may also have caused them to collaborate with the army and make statements favorable to its point of view. The third reason for holding out is perhaps especially important: the Indians, particularly in that area, where wages were low, had a long tradition of resistance to outside authorities.

Conclusions

These accounts are important for what they tell us about internal refugees who did not surrender to the army. The sources give us their point of view, a view which is different from that of those under Guatemalan government control or of the external refugees in Mexico.

I have reviewed accounts from three areas of central Guatemala, basing them on reports of witnesses who participated in the events described. I have sought not to add further data to this list of human rights violations but to illustrate with different examples a system of violation of human rights, a system in which hunger, malnutrition, illness, lack of clothes, and exposure to the elements are privations imposed on the civilian population by the army as a mechanism of control.

The army used many arguments to defend this system of human rights violations, which it called "guns and beans:"

1. Many people support the guerrillas without being combatants; this is a crime for which they can be shot.

2. If this civilian population were to be fed, clothed, and cured, it would pass on part of the food, clothes, and medicines to the guerrillas or, at least, would continue supporting the guerrillas.

3. It is necessary to separate the population from the guerrillas; this separation is described as "removing the water in which the fish swim."

4. The population is imprisoned by the guerrillas; it must be liberated, and even if it suffers in the process, this is for its own good.

5. Any social cost is small in comparison to the harm which the installation of a regime along Nicaraguan lines would bring.

All these arguments by the army presupposed that the guerrillas had a broad base of popular support. The process by which the army seeks to control this supposed civilian basis of guerrilla support has two phases:

Phase 1: Intense Repression ("Guns")

First, civilian populations in rural units (villages, hamlets, and so on) are massacred totally, in part, or selectively, provoking terror among the survivors, who then flee. The exodus can be temporary or permanent. Communities which are to a greater or lesser extent allied to the army surrender at this stage.

Second, the houses, the food supplies, the cooking instruments, and the clothes of those who have fled are destroyed, the army then maintaining that the act of escaping is an admission of guilt. If the community has fled only temporarily, the army continues to destroy its possessions and food sources. This produces a larger exodus.

Third, the community is placed under siege, prevented from producing food, bombed, and persecuted. The siege can be temporary or permanent. Both the siege and the attacks on food production are designed to cause hunger, malnutrition, illness, and death so that the refugees will surrender to the army. The persecution is designed to terrorize and demoralize the population.

Fourth, where the army is successful, the results are hunger, malnutrition, illnesss, and exposure to the elements.

Throughout this phase, the army also joins in a battle to the death against the combatant units, seeking to discover and destroy their camps.

Phase 2: Benevolent Assistance ("Beans")

First, the army feeds, cures, and cares for those who surrender. It shows them a certain benevolence, particularly if there are evangelicals within the community.

Second, the army selectively eliminates those who are most closely identified with the guerrillas, choosing its own time and place to carry out the executions. The first to surrender—those most visible in the public eye—must not see any hint of the first phase of repression. The army, nevertheless, seeks to eliminate infiltrators; the objective is population control.

This two-phase process is a one-way street. The second phase cannot work without the first, although the first may work without the
second. To make the population want to eat the army's "beans," it
must first use its "guns" to destroy other sources of food. But the guns
can be used without the beans. The objective of the system is to separate the civilian population from the guerrillas so that the latter cannot
take power. At times the army regresses to phase 1 when in phase 2 it
loses control of the population. This loss of control can come about in
many ways, as when the army loses control over food supplies. Although nationally the government wants to be seen as in phase 2, different regions may be out of step. Massacres still occurred (the first
step of the first phase) after tens of thousands of refugees were still in
the last step of phase 1. This does not necessarily mean that any of
them entered phase 2.

Something of the character of the guerrillas' relationship with the
civilian population has been shown in the three accounts. This relationship had the following features:

1. There was a link between the civilians and the guerrillas. The
civilians, who at times may have defended themselves with stones or
other crude weapons, were not combatants. Between the two in some
parts of the country were the FIL, who at times might be absorbed by
the combatants and at other times merged back into the civilians.

2. The leaders maintained social control over the civilians to maintain self-defense and to avoid the dangers of surrender—which could
lead to massacre. This was a two-edged policy. On the one hand, it
was necessary to be hard on infiltrators or others who "advised" people to surrender but who later claimed that they had been imprisoned
and terrorized by the guerrillas. On the other hand, it is clear that the
guerrillas needed to allow their supporters free exercise of choice.
Sometimes the temptation to produce a mirror image of the army's
two-phase policy to control the civilians became too great for the
guerrillas to resist.

3. Collective work in the mountain camps was organized to stimu-
late production and provide objectively based hope of survival, and
improvement of the refugees' situation. This was aimed at frustrating
the army's first phase.

4. Equality and fraternity were encouraged through egalitarian dis-

tribution of scarce resources. This increased the community's cohesion and reduced the risk of treachery.

5. Religious celebrations were encouraged in some places, not as an escape from collective work but as a "space" in which to recover hope and happiness.

6. At camp meetings army propaganda was neutralized as survivors recounted their experiences of suffering and death at the army's hands.

CHAPTER 11

Mayas Aiding Mayas: Guatemalan Refugees in Chiapas, Mexico

By Duncan M. Earle

As the political situation in the western highlands of Guatemala began to deteriorate in the late 1970s, it became increasingly difficult for
anthropologists like me to work with the rural Mayas. There was always the danger of personal harm, but the more serious threat was to
one's Guatemalan friends and professional contacts. I had worked
with an international aid and relief agency for two years after the 1976
earthquake and had gotten to know local indigenous leaders, many of
whom were involved in private or church-administered development
agencies and programs and who were the first to begin to be "disappeared" by the agents of the local military base. Later, one of these
leaders, whom I shall call Juan, who had been a good friend during
the postearthquake reconstruction effort, feared that his family might
be attacked by the military agents. He had been community leader
through the auspices of the Catholic church, and his wife worked in
the local credit union, giving health promotion classes to rural Maya
women. When the military turned to more overt tactics, attacking
whole villages in the area, Juan and his family wisely fled the region.
The international agencies, the Catholic priests, the archaeologists,
and the Peace Corps volunteers also left. With the news that a close
anthropological colleague was on a government "hit list," I realized
that it was time for me to leave as well.

It was personally painful to have to abandon one's friends, and the
culture and language of one's first fieldwork, especially without any
certainty that those remaining on the lands of their ancestors would
survive the growing wave of government-instigated violence. Further,

it proved difficult to discuss my field area without being either vague or incriminating, and the last thing I wished to do was create circumstances where even more people would be "disappeared" the way it is done in Guatemala. So I returned to the United States to begin again, to retool, to study another Maya language, and to return to the field, this time to Chiapas, Mexico, another stronghold of the Mayas. It was with mixed feelings that I set out to reside in a Tzotzil-speaking colony: excitement about a new and unexplored area mixed with the heavy heart of an exiled anthropologist.

I took up residence with a leader and founder of the first indigenous land collective, or *ejido*, in the region who, with a dozen other Tzotzil-speaking Chamulas, had founded Nuevo San Juan Chamula in 1964 on the southern edge of the Lacandón jungle, not far, as it happens, from the Guatemala border. In my first seven months of fieldwork in 1979, I remember often gazing off toward the Cuchumatán Mountain range, wondering what was afoot back there, as I struggled to be accepted in the comparatively aloof Chamula community. Work went well. I was able to get a good sense of the history of the *ejido* and charted the evolution of agricultural strategies that the colonists employed to utilize the tropical rain forest without destroying it. I came to appreciate how these Mayas, similar in many ways to the people I had known before in Guatemala, were in fact carrying out a self-development program without outsiders and creating the kind of community that development agencies dream of but rarely cause to appear. Fleeing dismal economic conditions in the crowded and infertile Chiapas Highlands, many had come to care for and responsibly manage their rain-forest environment in a way that compared favorably with the cattle ranchers and the monocrop-oriented ladinos. It was a kind of a rough-hewn, no-frills paradise, and one of considerable therapeutic value for this displaced anthropologist.

By the conclusion of my first fieldwork in the Chiapas colony, I had developed some attachment to its two dozen families. Such a small community is hard to hide in, and everyone, even the rivals of my host family, let me know that I was welcome to return at any time. Early in 1983 I again took up residence in Chiapas to assist in a research effort focused on the Chamula colonization process throughout the state of Chiapas and soon found myself on a familiar road heading out of Comitán for the remote corner of the township of Las Margaritas, where the Tzotzil colonies are situated. I was well aware that thousands of refugees were fleeing the violence in Guatemala by crossing the border into Chiapas, but I was unprepared for what I was to find in Nuevo San Juan.

Maya Refugees Among the Chamula Colonists

Crossing the river on the new hammock-style footbridge, I could see behind me in the neighboring ladino collective a large cluster of palm-thatch huts tucked into a corner of a pasture. In front of me lay the Chamula colony, still basically the same as I remembered it, except that each 40-by-80-meter house plot now held two or three new houses, of palm-thatch and pole construction. As I reached the gate at the far side of the bridge, I saw a familiar young face in the company of several unfamiliar faces. Because Chamulas in this region rarely interact informally with people outside their community, it struck me as very odd until I realized that they were Guatemalans. The community of nineteen collective members had taken in eighty-four Chuj- and Kanjobal-speaking Maya families from across the nearby border. Three-fourths of the community's members were now Guatemalan Mayas.

The great majority of the refugees are from one community, Nueva Concepción, an "agrarian distribution" which had been obtained through the Arbenz government's land-reform program in the early 1950s and which received confirmed land titles from the National Institute of Agrarian Transformation (INTA) in 1972. It was formerly part of the Ixquisís farm adjacent to the Yulchén hamlet, all in the township of San Mateo Ixtatán. According to the community leader, one of his relatives originally solicited half of the farm's 36 caballerías (more than 1,600 hectares, or about 4,320 acres), since most of the farm had not been in use. The owner, Chiliano Maximiliano Palacios, intervened, paying off a lawyer, with the result that the community ended up with only 3 caballerías (approximately 360 acres). "We took what we could get," said the community leader.

Soon after they had settled in, the farm was sold to Felipe Villatorro, of Huehuetenango, who began to develop his new property much more aggressively, using the adjacent community as a source of paid labor. He cleared much of his land and brought in additional cattle (the previous owner had maintained only about forty head). The wages earned from part-time work on the farm provided the community of Nueva Concepción with much-needed cash to improve their own parcel. In the 1970s, they began to plant coffee, in addition to raising sugar cane. They also began to raise cardamom, a very valuable aromatic spice requiring even more rigorous environmental conditions than coffee, but a cash crop that by weight fetches a higher price. In remote areas such as this, with transport being a major expense, cardamom became a most cost-effective product.

In May 1982, the Mayas began hearing reports of killings in the Ixcán region on the east from people fleeing that area who passed through their community. They were not overly concerned, according to the community leader, because in radio broadcasts from Barrillas it was claimed that the trouble in Ixcán was due to nonpayment by peasants for land acquired with the help of foreign priests. According to the radio accounts, these priests had gotten the land from the government, but outstanding debts remained which the peasants were supposed to pay, and that was why they were being driven out. Since the community of Nueva Concepción had its papers in order, the people were not concerned. But as more news of army killings came to them and more groups of survivors passed through their area with accounts of sudden military attacks, they became increasingly alarmed. One party, in April, told how the army had rounded up women and children, put them in a church and burned it down. Then came news of the massacres in Finca San Francisco and Yalambojoch, in the township of Nentón, not far to the west. So, on July 24, all but three families packed up what they could carry and fled. Those who stayed included some who were too weak to travel and one man who refused to leave. It took them only about three days to get to Mexico, since they knew well where they were going. They have had no news from those who stayed on and presume them to be dead.

The people from Nueva Concepción did not come to Mexico totally unfamiliar with the region. In fact, people from this Guatemalan community helped the first Chamulas clear the settlement site that is now their temporary home, and when they crossed the border, they immediately sought out their friends of twenty years before. Another resident refugee in the collective had been living near Ixcantzaán, a farm in San Mateo Ixtatán. He had been born, however, on another Chamula farm in Mexico, San Pedro Viejo, for his mother was from the Mexican side. He had moved to Guatemala and cultivated 500 cuerdas (about 59 acres) that he had solicited from the government. "I am back where I began," he lamented, "but the souls left behind are dust," referring to his lost family and friends who had been burned in a military sweep. Clearly, the border serves to demarcate a political and climatic division, as well as a linguistic frontier between Maya groups, but it has not served in recent times as an impermeable barrier between adjacent groups. In addition, the refugees are close enough to their original lands to pick out familiar topography in the distant horizon. They derive solace from being able to look back across the border to Guatemala, just as I did while I lived in the Chamula colony.

Refugee Living Conditions

Unlike the adjacent ladino collectives, the Chamula colonists had not shunted the refugees off to a separate camp settlement but had assigned two to four refugee families to each collective member, following a pattern initiated years earlier to cope with seasonal workers who came from their highland home communities. During the height of the coffee harvest season (November to January), the colonists had always exploited their kin and fictive kin networks back in their hamlets or neighborhoods of origin to recruit temporary workers, in a manner similar to the way thousands of highland Chamulas are recruited by plantation foremen and the local Chamula elite to harvest coffee on the coastal piedmont of southern Chiapas. When colonists construct new homes, they are careful to maintain their previous homes as residences for temporary workers. Not only did this provide needed additional hands in the coffee groves, but also it provided additional means of establishing or maintaining social contacts. Because of this, working for Chamula colonists is generally viewed as preferable to coastal work, even though wages are frequently lower. Chamula *ejido* members usually worked alongside their workers, quizzing them about the latest events back in "Cold Country."

This pattern of *bankilal-itzinal* ("older brother–younger brother") kinlike work relationship, which also exists between nonkin Indians in Chamula, has been adapted for the Maya refugees from Guatemala. Each collective head of household is responsible for one group of families and renews their temporary work cards with the Mexican immigration authorities, as well as providing them a plot to settle on and the use of three to five acres of land to plant for their own food needs. In turn these refugees owe primary allegiance to their sponsoring colonists. As one refugee explained: "Before we look for a job somewhere, we ask permission from the colonists on whose land we now live. For maybe he has a job for us, and this is the one we have to think of first."

There are remarkably few complaints on either side about the arrangement. The refugees are paid the same wages as any temporary workers, and labor alongside their Chamula patrons. My Chamula colonist friends respect their Guatemalan guests because they are hard and efficient workers in the coffee fields, consistently outdoing their highland Chamula counterparts. In addition, while temporary workers from Chiapas must be fed by their hosts, the refugees plant their own corn and prepare it themselves, taking a major burden off the women of the colony. Clearly, then, taking in the refugees is not purely a humanitarian act. For these labor-short colonists, the Guatemalan refugees are a benefit, and the colonists have been able to take advantage of their presence to improve their own economy. It has not been at the expense of the refugees, however, who live more stable, healthy, and well-fed lives than the great majority of the Guatemalan refugees in Chiapas and enjoy the benefits of the Chamula community as well. In addition to land-use rights and employment, benefits include a school for their children, access to the Mexican medical personnel who visit the collective, and a community that cares for them and interacts with them as equals, as Mayas.

There were many signs that confirmed this last, somewhat less measurable benefit. One was the amount of language sharing. In less than two years many of the refugees and colonists had come to share their respective Maya languages, Tzotzil and Kanjobal. They shared church services, too, Catholic with Catholic, Protestant with Protestant. They also shared their knowledge. For example, I witnessed one young colonist teaching two refugees how to play a hymn on a guitar. The lesson was in Spanish, but the hymn was in Tzotzil, as are many of the Chamula religious songs. I also noted that when the government-appointed schoolteacher for the colony school was delinquent in his duties the *ejido* leaders had him unceremoniously removed and quickly replaced him with a refugee who had abandoned his educational training in Guatemala only two weeks short of receiving his teacher's title. This bright Kanjobal's first teaching job was with Chamula colony children, and his performance was praised by parents and children alike. These were among the many signs of true community integration. The refugees' only complaint was about their housing, for, while it was recognized as the best the colony could provide at low cost and short notice, they were painfully aware that their palm-thatch houses could be visually identified as recently constructed. Said one refugee: "If the [Guatemalan] army comes in here, they will still know which ones we are by the houses. That the colonists can't hide." Nevertheless, with a river and another *ejido* separating them from the border, and with the Chamula community surrounding them, they were far safer than many refugees in border settlements.

The attitude of the Chamula colony leader is, I believe, typical of this sense of community integration. While there have been a few problems of adjustment between hosts and guests, he views the refugees with fundamentally sympathetic eyes. He admitted that there had been some trouble at the start, owing to the influence of alcohol, which had made people say "bad things." But the community came to an agreement to ban alcohol consumption, knowing that the trauma of having lost so much might tempt their guests to drink. There was also one refugee who fancied the wife of his Chamula sponsor, but he was reprimanded and publicly embarrassed, and appears to have changed his ways. Despite these conflicts, the point the leader made a number of times was that the situation could have been the other way around. That is, it is easy for the Chamula colonists to imagine what it would be like to have to flee Mexico and rely on other Mayas for their well-being in an alien country. The colonists are aware that their treatment of the refugees should reflect how they themselves would like to be treated in similar circumstances. As in a number of other Maya colonies in the region, there was a genuine sense of identification with the Guatemalan Mayas in their current suffering. In varying degrees this was also the attitude of the non-Indian peasant population in that part of Chiapas.

A striking example of this sense of identification is the Tojolabal Maya community of Río Azul, a good day's walk farther along the Chiapas-Guatemala border of the Nuevo San Juan colony. A community of 29 male heads of household, they received more than 400 Guatemalan families from at least five Kanjobal communities from June through September 1982. As of March 1983, when I visited the colony, the camp census figures revealed a resident refugee population of 1,846 individuals. Most of the refugees, like camp leader Antonio Juan, had left Guatemala because of massacres in nearby towns like Xoxlac, where 95 people were said to have been killed, including children, on June 24 and 25, 1982. In describing the massacres, the leader became visibly upset, especially when he noted, "Children, two years, four years old, they just grabbed them and tore them in two." When the army came close to his own settlement, three community representatives went ahead, carrying with them their identification papers, while a fourth villager went behind, out of sight. When the last man saw the army kill the first three and burn their papers, he returned swiftly and told the others. They left for the border immediately, descending to the tropical colony of Río Azul, Chiapas, within a few days.

Malnourished, ill, and traumatized when they arrived, they lost between five and six hundred people in the first months, mostly children, owing in large part to medical complications related to malaria, which spread rapidly because of the weakened condition of the people, who were unaccustomed to the heat of the tropical rain forest. They were taken in and given food, shelter, and a place to plant, at clear risk to the health of the colony. Since they were less than a kilometer from the border, the risk of problems with the Guatemalan army was another reality the community members faced bravely. From 1981 on, the Guatemalan army has made numerous incursions into Mexico side of the border to attack refugees (more than sixty incursions between 1982 and 1984 have been documented by human rights groups). None have resulted in confrontations with the Mexican army, which has a presence in the region.

In October 1982, for example, about two hundred Guatemalan soldiers crossed the border and entered Mexico according to the community leaders (their accounts conformed in detail with those offered by the refugees). The soldiers were Kaibiles, or "Special Forces" troops commonly employed in assaults on indigenous communities. They came down to the edge of the small river that separates the settlement from the jungle with the intention of crossing the hanging, hammock-style footbridge. The Tojolabal colonists went to the opposite bank unarmed to confront the Guatemalans. Striken with panic, the Kanjobals prepared to flee for their lives again.

One of the community leaders, I was told, shouted across the river, asking the soldiers what they were doing inside the Republic of Mexico. The soldiers, brandishing their guns, shouted back that they were coming to kill the "shit" guerrillas. The leader answered back that there were no guerrillas in their community, only "poor peasants, like ourselves." He added that the soldiers had no right to be in Mexico, that the president would hear about it, and that they would have a war on their hands if they tried to enter the community. After some discussion the soldiers left. It was the general consensus of both Maya groups that this brave act by the Tojolabals saved the lives of the Kanjobal refugees.

The frequent and unchallenged military incursions into these remote border regions were intended, no doubt, to have a chilling effect on relations between Mexicans and refugees. The government accusations that refugees were guerrillas, a fact never substantiated by any evidence or confirmed by any inquiry, were broadcast over Guatemalan radio stations received by the border communities. Many colonists asked me what I thought of the radio announcements inviting the refugees back under Ríos Montt's general amnesty, announcements stating that anyone refusing to return under the amnesty must have something to hide and, therefore, must be a guerrilla. This created added anxiety for many Mexicans, and they frequently commented on the danger that harboring refugees represented for them. At times, especially in some of the non-Indian communities, serious conflicts arose, often owing to concerns about refugees using scarce community resources or spreading diseases, but also because of fear of the Guatemalan military. Even the non-Indian rain-forest colonies of the Las Margaritas region, while not allowing the Guatemalans to reside in their villages, nevertheless showed remarkable sensitivity about the plight of the refugees.

The now "ladinoized" or hispanicized Tojolabal Maya inhabitants at Santa Elena would not allow the one thousand refugees in their charge to share their house compound area but nevertheless cared for them, providing campgrounds, jobs, clothing, sponsorship before the immigration authorities, and, more fundamentally, a sympathetic community. From surveys I made of fifteen refugee communities and camps, plus interviews with numerous refugee relief workers and refugees in Mexican hospitals, it is clear that the closer the host community was in ethnic and socioeconomic background to the incoming refugees, the greater was the integration of the new population into the community. While other factors influenced host-guest relationships, this was the most striking contrast between the treatment of refugees in the Las Margaritas and La Independencia colony region of Chiapas and their treatment farther east in the Lacandón region.

Refugees in the Lacandón Jungle

The region east of the Chamula colonies has received international attention, for it is in this Lacantún River–Marqués de Comillas border region that the largest refugee camps were formed, some of them almost overnight. Further, these were among the camps forcibly relocated in 1984, most notably the Ixcán, Chajul, and Puerto Rico camps. When I visited the Chajul camp in March 1983, it had more than five thousand refugee inhabitants, divided into barrios, or internal subdivisions, that reflected their home communities. The other camps were equally large. Their perilous condition was heightened by the fact that the camps were completely inaccessible by road, making the logistics of feeding them a nightmare. Most supplies had to be brought in by shallow-bottomed boat, a three-day trip (in good weather) from Boca Lacantún, where the last jungle road into the area ended. Most of the camps were based in Mexican collectives or private landholdings that maintained airstrips, but only light single-engine planes could land on them, so they could not serve as a means of providing an adequate supply of food. The Catholic church established health posts that provided the only medical attention and used airplanes to carry out the extremely ill. They were flown to the hospital in Comitán, which set up a special section for children, or to the Catholic hospital in Altamirano, Chiapas, which also set apart a special area for refugee children.

The bad condition of the Lacantún River camps derived to an important degree from the difficulty of getting food in, although that was not the only factor. Refugees consistently cited figures showing that the amount of food they received was less than half what would be considered the minimum necessary. Some reported as little as four pounds of corn meal per person for a two-week period, while one pound a day is only half of what is typically eaten by adults on a corn-based diet. Health workers in the hospitals, including the director of the public hospital in Comitán, reiterated the concern for sufficient and consistent food supplies, stating again and again that the most serious health problem for refugees was lack of food. One seven-year-old boy arrived in the hospital at Comitán weighing 7 kilograms (about 15.4 pounds); another boy, three years old, weighed 3 kilograms (about 6.6 pounds).

While everyone agreed that food deliveries had been inadequate, it was never entirely clear how much this was due to the inefficiency of the Mexican Committee to Help the Refugees (COMAR), the government agency charged with funneling aid from the United Nations High Commission on Refugees (UNHCR), and how much of it was an intentional policy of COMAR to make Mexico particularly unattractive to future refugees, as was suggested in the Mexican press. High-level refugee policy statements by the ministry of the exterior and the ministry of the interior often seemed contradictory and may have led to mixed signals being passed on to COMAR (which is affiliated with both ministries) about treatment of the refugees. Corruption may also have played a role, according to one UNHCR employee.

Whatever the cause or causes, many people were unable to get enough food to maintain good health. In addition to food problems, many of the the people in the camps had arrived in Mexico in a bad state of health, some having hidden in the mountains for months and having eaten little or nothing during the journey to the border. This is confirmed by the fact that the highest rate of adult and infant deaths was always registered during the first weeks after the arrival of a new group of refugees. This period was particularly stressful because of the changes in climate and the psychological distress caused by dislocation. Combined with the trauma of having witnessed the deaths of family members and friends—either in an initial attack or during the subsequent flight—these stresses added up to powerfully debilitating psychological problems that contributed to poor overall health. As one refugee put it, "Ah, yes, many of us came to Mexico only to die."

The conditions described above—the lack of food and medical attention, the prevalence of illness owing to malnourishment, the shock of dislocation, and emotional trauma—are only the most obvious problems the refugees encountered. They frequently commented on the fact that Mexican landowners who in Chajul, Puerto Rico, and Ixcán were ladinos, that is, were not Indians (and frequently were not even from Chiapas), would not let the refugees plant maize fields. The only work available was house building by the men. They complained bitterly about not being able to work. Further, the refugees were forced to live crowded together, in contrast to the more dispersed household layouts in Guatemala, and this tended to pass illness from one family to another. While the camps were well organized, each section representing some home community (Chajul had refugees from Kaibil Balam, San Antonio Seja, Rosario Canijá, Santo Ical, Santa María Seja, San Antonio Chiquito, Santo Tomás Ixcán, and San

Juan Ixcán, among others), they were severely restricted by the conditions of their arrangement with the host people. This unsatisfactory relationship was reinforced by COMAR and immigration officials, who frequently prohibited people from leaving the camp to seek work elsewhere or engaging in work activities without the approval of the host community.

The unstable relationship between the Maya refugees in these large camps and Mexican nationals often led to exploitation of the refugees. In the Puerto Rico camp the de facto landowner took advantage of the refugee labor to have jungle areas cleared, ostensibly giving the refugees permission to plant corn and then, with his sons, staging a simulated military attack to scare off the refugees to put cattle on the cleared land. While this man had no legal claim to the land he occupied, his collaboration with immigration officials provided him with the backing he needed to carry out these and other abuses, using the fear of military incursions to his advantage.

After their terrible experiences in Guatemala, the treatment the refugees received in these remote areas only compounded their difficult condition. Bunched into large, crowded camps, with little or no contact with the outside world, and under the unchecked authority of officials trained in immigration law enforcement who viewed them as subversives and troublemakers, life for many refugees was barely worth living. A note passed secretly to a member of an American television crew visiting the Ixcán camp is characteristic of the frustration experienced by the Lacandón region "megacamp" refugees. I quote it in full:

Mr. Newsmen: Accept our cordial greetings and welcome to this camp. Mr. Newsmen, we inform you, that during our refugee experience, we have been mistreated by the authorities, by the military group, by Immigration, and by the employees of COMAR. They have robbed our animals, they have raped our women, they have treated us like guerrillas, and they have threatened our lives. Now they no longer allow us to communicate or go to any other places. Mr. International Newspeople, we want to know if this is so because of international, superior orders. If so, fine, we will accept it, but we feel like enslaved people. We left Guatemala, mistreated, we got to Mexico to be mistreated, and where do we turn? If they do not want us poor people, better they should just take away our lives. We remain very grateful [to you]. Goodbye. Ixcán, October 17, 1983.

The Mexican authorities were concerned about the problems caused by these huge camps and were worried about the possibility of armed confrontation with Guatemalan soldiers who were emboldened to

cross the line by the proximity of the refugees and the lack of immediate Mexican response. But they were unwilling to allow the refugees
to disperse themselves among the Chiapas population for fear they
might be an economic burden and a political liability. Children of non-
citizens born in Mexico have the constitutional right to Mexican citi-
zenship, and the parents can obtain legal rights through their "Mexican" children. There was palpable concern that the people of Chiapas
would resent the attention and aid given to the refugees, since historically the area had been neglected by the federal government. Any aid
in the form of land would be especially controversial, with Chiapas
already in the throes of land-reform conflicts.

Chiapas is rich in resources, but its people, especially the approximately 40 percent of the population who are of Maya descent, are
extremely poor. The state produces more coffee than any other state
of the republic, but its coffee pickers are among the lowest-paid in
Mexico, and unemployment and underemployment plague the labor
force. Land-tenure problems exacerbate peasant poverty in some regions, while cattle, timber, and plantation export crops make a minority of farmers wealthy. Chiapas, rich in proven oil deposits and
hydroelectric power and bordering on troubled Central America, is
seen by the Mexican government as a potential trouble spot which the
government has in the past expended little to develop. During my
sixteen-month stay in the state, the newspapers frequently reported
peasant land conflicts, and these often led to political strife between
land-poor Indians and state authorities. Further, there were undoubtedly official fears of adverse political impact on the state from
presumed radicalized Guatemalans, although I saw no evidence that
guerrillas or other political groups resided among the refugees. The
official view from Mexico City was understandably tempered by a
sense of insecurity relative to its closest Central American neighbor.
The political slogan Todo en Chiapas Es México ("All That Is Chiapas
Is Mexico") reveals this insecurity, and the fact that the slogan appeared before the thousands of Guatemalan peasants poured across
the border demonstrates that this insecurity is not just a reaction to
recent problems in Guatemala. The arrival of 100,000 or more refugees has no doubt heightened their sense of anxiety.

The widespread belief among Mexican officials that the refugees
were supporters of Guatemalan rebel forces and that their presence in
the state would radicalize a local peasantry already disgruntled about

socioeconomic inequities was not borne out by my own inquiries. Most people I talked with knew of guerrillas only as a term used by the army and had never actually seen any. As one man said, "We don't have the studies, the knowledge for those things; we only know the hoe, the machete, how to work the land." But because there was very little social inquiry into who the refugees were and the exact circumstances under which they had fled, incorrect assumptions frequently guided official actions. This is not to say that the refugees lacked sympathy for many of the issues the rebels support, especially issues of community empowerment and organization. But such sentiments could contribute to Chiapas culture, not threaten it.

To allow these people to integrate themselves into the Chiapas population, as they were doing in other regions, represented for the authorities a perceived loss of control over them and their activities. Some feared that fair treatment would encourage more Guatemalans to come to Mexico. "We don't want to create a Shangri-La," is the way one COMAR official phrased it. I was never able to find evidence that favorable or unfavorable treatment in Mexico affected the flow of refugees from Guatemala. The facts available on the time and places of repression inside Guatemala suggest that violence was the single most important factor influencing out-migration. Few refugees returned to Guatemala because of ill-treatment in Mexico. In fact, the attitude of one eloquent refugee reflects, I believe, the position of most Guatemalan refugees toward repatriation. The refugee, who had survived a massacre at Xalbal on January 4, 1983, and had witnessed another at Cuarto Pueblo in March of the previous year, in which his father and many other members of his family were killed, stated:

With tourniquets they killed the children, of two years, of nine months, of six months. They killed and burned them all. That is why we don't believe in their politics anymore. Like the case of my father. Would they respect his card [showing membership in a progovernment party]? Well, what they did was put a machete in here (pointing to his chest) and they cut open his heart, and they left him all burned up. This is the pain we shall never forget. We want to return to our towns but not until we see there are going to be changes. Now if they [the Guatemalan government] say there is a change, better we should stay right here. Better to die here with a bullet and not die in that way, like my father did

This attitude, echoed in the note from the Ixcán camp, was held by many other refugees I talked to, including those in Nuevo San Juan.

The Future of the Chiapas Refugees

It is tragically ironic that the areas of extensive, official Mexican attention and effort became the places of the worst refugee suffering, and
this at the very time a workable model for coping with the refugees
was being developed by the Mayas themselves at little or no cost to
the government or international agencies. The situation is reminiscent
of the contrast between the Maya colonists' practice of growing coffee
and the state-funded cattle ranching. The former costs the state nothing more than land titling and surveying of empty jungle. The colonists
engage in a form of horticulture that is appropriate to the tropical
ecosystem and does not degrade it. The cattle ranchers require considerable initial capital outlay and management, and their productive
practices are inappropriate to the ecosystem, eventually destroying the
fragile rain-forest ecology. Like the rain forest, the refugees are fragile
and need responses appropriate to their condition; otherwise, they too
suffer irrevocable damage.

Most of the large Lacandón camps are gone now. Most of the large
ones were forcibly moved in the months following an attack by the
Guatemalan army on the large Chupadero camp, in the Comalapa
area of Chiapas, in April 1984. A few refugees have remained in the
Chajul camp, and some are still across the river from the remains of
the Puerto Rico camp, which was burned along with its medical clinic
and food stores by the Mexican authorities to "encourage" the refugees to accept relocation. Most refugees have been placed in new
camps in Campeche and Quintana Roo, though a few have found refuge in church-sponsored Chiapas camps. It is believed that some went
farther into the jungle on their own, despite the fact that the heavy
rains had begun. The move to Campeche was costly, inefficient, and
vigorously opposed by many of the refugees, who feared that the move
would seal their fate as permanent refugees and that the relocation
areas would present even worse conditions.

By contrast, dispersed refugee populations like those in the western
jungle have retreated farther from the border and have again been
taken in by other colonists. The Río Azul refugees slipped away before
they could be "officially" moved and took up residence in a number of
recently formed Mexican colonies in the north. Almost none of the
some 16,000 refugees in the Margaritas jungle area where the Cha-

mula and other Tzotzil and Tzeltal Maya colonists live have left the region. They are now far enough from the border to be safe from incursions against them by the Guatemalan army. Without coercion and at very little cost the people of the region solved their "refugee problem," and it did not require embarking on another lengthy and traumatic journey into an even more foreign land.

The situation of the Margaritas region is not unique. Historically there has been close contact between Guatemalans and Chiapas Mexicans. In the area around the southern coastal mountain range near Motocintla it has been noted that poor people of both countries along the border view the land on the other side as an extension of known and familiar territory. In this region, as well as in areas of central Chiapas such as Pujiltic and in the coastal area around Tapachula, Guatemalans have been received by their Chiapan neighbors.

There are many reports of refugees being protected from official detection, especially in the Tapachula region. For many years Guatemalans have crossed into this area as seasonal workers on the coffee plantations there. From 1981 on, large numbers of Guatemalans who crossed the border legally as temporary workers did not return to their violence-torn home communities. Unfortunately, because of their status as temporary workers, few such Guatemalans are recognized as political refugees, and those caught without proper documentation are routinely deported by the immigration authorities. Nevertheless, out of sympathy for the plight of the refugees, many Mexicans have helped them stay hidden from official view. In 1984, the Catholic church reported more than 50,000 Guatemalan refugees residing in this area, mostly Maya peasants. Without formal recognition as refugees, they must rely solely on the generosity of their hosts for survival.

By 1985, 18,000 refugees had been moved out of the state of Chiapas and transferred to camps in Campeche and Quintana Roo. As of early 1987, no more than 23,000, or half of the 46,000 officially recognized refugees in Chiapas, have been relocated. In addition, since the election of Vinicio Cerezo as president of Guatemala in 1985, an estimated 3,000 to 7,000 refugees have returned to Guatemala voluntarily (this figure includes refugees from throughout Mexico, where it is estimated that at least 300,000 Guatemalan refugees are currently residing). It is generally believed that no more forced relocation will be carried out until repatriation negotiations are thoroughly explored with the Cerezo government. Currently, most refugees are unwilling to return without guarantees of their security and rights to their original lands.

The remaining refugees either stayed in Chiapas or moved independently to other regions in the north. Clearly, therefore, despite efforts to relocate the Guatemalan Mayas to regions far from Chiapas, most will remain there until they feel that it is safe to return to their homeland. Chiapas has become their home away from home, and in many respects it is a good one. The people of Chiapas are generally to be commended for their kindness, generosity, and heroism in receiving them, especially given the impoverished conditions of the state.

This inherent Chiapan sympathy may explain in part the desire to move the Guatemalan refugees to other states of Mexico, where they would be under more direct government control. In my view this would be unfortunate and unnecessary. A better alternative has been put forth by the Maya colonists with whom I lived and worked, a model that could well be applied to the refugee population in general. The chief concerns expressed by refugees are safety, employment, community cohesion, and proximity to Guatemala, the last to facilitate their eventual return. Recalling the traumatic experiences associated with forced removal, the refugees emphasize the need for stability and continuity. Being received by people of their own culture and socioeconomic orientation provides them with a stable, structured community, work opportunities, and a sense of security. It spares them abject dependency without creating autonomous immigrant settlements that might be viewed as competing with Mexican peasants for land. This process could be aided by the national government, particularly in areas where there are labor shortages (which include much of the border region), as a form of community-level development. Rather than alienating the local population by trying to remove their valued guests and creating antagonistic relations with the refugees themselves, this approach would do much to assure the loyalty of Chiapans and the respect of the Guatemalans for Mexico.

No one knows the Mayas of Guatemala as well as the Mayas of Chiapas, Mexico. Their response to the refugees is an example of their ability to fashion an arrangement of mutual benefit and one that could also benefit Mexico. Working Guatemalans feed themselves rather than being dependent on costly and difficult-to-manage food-distribution programs. Their labor becomes a resource for the region, one that helps the general economy of the state. While this might seem to be a political liability, I do not believe that it is. Mayas fleeing Guatemala do not wish to be involved in armed struggles or political organizations seeking to overthrow the government of their hosts. Their loyalties lie with their patron hosts, the Maya colonists, who are firmly with the Mexican government, since it was the government that awarded them their lands.

The Chiapas Mayas of the rain forest recognized the refugees as a resource rather than a danger. Most Guatemalan peasant refugees are enterprising farmers, and they quickly organized themselves into rural cooperatives. Many had been quite successful at agricultural and commercial activities in Guatemala. Studies of the violence in the Indian areas of Guatemala suggest that Indians who had been successful in development programs were principal targets of the government's counterinsurgency program. Chased out of their own country, in Mexico these refugees continue to be productive, possessing valuable skills and talents that can contribute to their host country. But for their productive value to be actualized, the Mexican government must be willing to follow the lead of their own Mayas and trust them enough to give them the opportunities they need to continue this development experiment in Chiapas. Just as the arrangement has been beneficial for both host and guest in the Nuevo San Juan colony, so it could be for Mexico in general. What is needed is attention to the wisdom of those most capable of understanding the refugees, the Chiapas Mayas who share the refugees' view of the world.

CHAPTER 12

Conclusions: What Can We Know About the Harvest of Violence?

By Richard N. Adams

The chapters in this book were written to help explain what has been happening to the over three million Mayas of Guatemala since 1976. Except for Sheldon Annis, a geographer, and Roland Ebel, a political scientist, all the authors are anthropologists. All have spent some years directly studying the peoples about whom they write. Understanding what has occurred in Guatemala is not easy because the knowledge and experience of tens of thousands have been lost with their deaths. Events in Guatemala have reached the world through a curtain of misrepresentation and obfuscation imposed by the Guatemalan government and military and, sad to state, also through the Reagan administration's desire to support anyone they think is fighting "Marxism-Leninism." The support of the United States would be unimportant were it not for its influence on the media and, therefore, on the information that reaches the American people. At the same time that media coverage was memorializing the Jewish Holocaust, the Guatemalan government was indulging in a slaughter of Indians "in our backyard," and many Guatemalans and Americans denied it.

Anthropological Reporting

Professional ethnographers and social anthropologists have been working in Guatemala for well over half a century. While their number includes Guatemalan, Mexican, German, French, British, and other researchers, by far the greatest number have come from the United States. Modern Guatemalan ethnography emerged half a century ago with the work of Oliver La Farge, Douglas Byers, and Ruth Bunzel. While anthropologists differ in political philosophies, they share a generally coherent picture of the nature of Guatemalan Indian society within the social, political, and economic history of Guatemala. Until the 1950s research focused heavily on rather traditional ethnography. In the 1960s the work of various students of Guatemalan society and history swung interest toward the place of the Indian population in the ongoing dynamics of the Guatemalan nation.

Anthropologists, however, have not been in the forefront in the study of violence, terror, and war. Traditional anthropology directs scholars to spend many months and, if possible, years with a small population before its lifeways can be rendered clearly in the cultural idiom and language of the anthropologist. When in the late 1970s events of the kind recounted herein were increasing, anthropologists had no ready response. Communities that had hospitably received scholars were now the scenes of bloodly assassinations. Refugees began to appear, and word trickled out about close friends now dead or disappeared—not merely occasional deaths, but exterminations of whole families and communities. People well known to the anthropologists, people who they knew had little reason to become involved, were killed or "disappeared"—or so it was reported—because they were allegedly "guerrillas," "Communists," or "Marxist-Leninists." When they sought further information, the events were denied and travel was threatened, and Indians who had been close to the missing were afraid to discuss the matter.

Reporters can dash off at a moment's notice, but scholars have responsibilities to their regular jobs, they are usually without extensive funds, and research requires preparation. It has taken time for them to get back to the areas in which they worked, to obtain sound data, and to prepare findings that warrant readers' confidence. Anthropological inquiry depends on all sorts of methods and access to information, and all of it has to be weighed and judged for both veracity and coherence. Since one can rarely "prove" the quality of specific field reporting, readers' credulity depends on confidence in the work of the anthropologist. Indeed, the reputation not only of the individual scholar but of all professional peers is at stake with every report.

Much other work on this subject is under way. Perhaps the first results of intensive anthropological work were Ricardo Falla's study of the massacre of the community of San Francisco in Huehuetenango and the interview survey of observers and survivors by Shelton H. Davis and Julie Hodson. Latin-American scholars such as Gabriel Aguilera Peralta, Jorge Romero Imery, Ricardo Gallindo Gallardo, and Guillermo Monzón Paz analyzed the results of terrorism from daily news reports; the last three named were killed for their efforts. In chapter 1 of this book Davis cites reports from the Guatemalan judiciary on the number of orphans that the killings have produced and the Americas Watch Committee and the Human Rights Commission reports. And a Guatemalan sociologist, Arturo Arias, has published a fragment of his extensive study of the evolution of Indian involvement in the guerrilla activity.

The authors of the chapters of this book were free to describe what they felt to be important in the region or community of their concern. In general the reports concern different communities or regions. The papers provide the most profound examination available to date about the events and the conditions from which they stemmed. Why, however, should the general reader have any more confidence in these reports than in the seldom verifiable reports and speculations of daily newspaper or TV newscasts?

These chapters warrant high confidence for a number of reasons. All the papers concerning towns and villages cover reasonably long historic spans. The chapters on the refugees obviously relate a shorter run of events. Tracing complexly interwoven events not only permits an appreciation of the sequences—who did what to whom and when—but also provides specific locations in time and space, so that we know that we are reading of real people dealing with historical realities. There is another, more important reason for historical accounts, however. Events can have meaning only in terms of their context. Knowledge of history provides a broader context and permits more profound understanding. Knowledge of the history surrounding events makes it more difficult for us to impose our own imaginary histories. What does a running Indian mean? In chapter 4, Stoll recounts how Protestant missionaries in Nebaj corrrected the army's failure to understand how to interpret a running Indian. For the army, they were guerrilla "Communists" trying to escape, whereas the recent history of the region made it clear that most were simply terrified peasants trying to survive. There is no reason to expect that non-Indians will ever really understand how Guatemalan Indians perceive their problems, but an understanding of the context of the events that they confront brings us much farther along the way.

Second, the anthropologists' major source of information comes from extensive interviews. If one accepts that a long acquaintance allows both better judgment of an informant's veracity and a greater likelihood of confidence, then these reports offer a quality of data that is simply not available in any other way. These are not reports in which a microphone was shoved into an Indian's face by a reporter in a hurry. Rather, the information was gathered in a context in which the reliability and relevance of what the informants revealed could be evaluated and interpreted. That is one reason why it takes longer to get the information.

Third, the authors have revisited their sites and can judge for themselves the physical consequences of the events that have filtered out to the rest of the world. You will find here no simplistic stereotypes that all is disaster or that things have not changed at all. Burned or disappeared villages, however, speak for themselves, and the environment of new "model villages" will be visible unless visits are forbidden or prohibitively dangerous. Annis, Carmack, Davis, Ebel, Hinshaw, Manz, and Paul were able to compare before and after and thereby obtain and carefully evaluate reports on the intervening years. These kinds of data are hard to fake.

For those familiar with Central America and Guatemala, these chapters speak for themselves. For others, however, it may help to spend a little time seeing them in context. These tragic processes grew out of events; the seeds were already present, and these accounts describe how they were cultivated into a mortal harvest. In the remainder of this chapter I look first at the way the events described in these cases are the substance of Guatemalan society and history. They are not unusual or exceptional; rather, they illustrate processes fundamental in the area. Second, I look at the consequences of the events over the longer term.

Putting the Accounts in Context

Guatemala is part of the political economy of Western capitalism and lies in the sphere of influence, or hegemony, of the United States. Within this sphere, Guatemalan Indians have maintained distinctive lifeways, products of an evolution of indigenous cultures resulting from interactions with the non-Indian populations that lived off them. While Indians have rebelled from time to time, their principal concern has been to survive in a natural environment consistently degraded by political and economic forces far beyond their control. They have not tried to take over the Guatemalan state. Until the revolution of 1944, their principal mode of coping with adversity varied from consolidating for community defense to fragmenting into dispersed social units. They survived on agricultural subsistence and handicraft production for their own use, complemented by wage labor or salable produce to obtain cash necessary for indispensable industrial products such as the machete and the hoe, basic medicines, cotton thread and dyes for their cloth, and cash for taxes and support of the rituals of their religion. The ladinos' interest was to ensure that the Indians remained available for wage labor. In the nineteenth and the first half of the twentieth centuries labor was scarce, and various kinds of forced labor persisted until the revolution of 1944. Indian population growth, however, has increased the supply of plantation labor in recent years.

Sheldon Annis's description of the events in San Antonio Aguas Calientes and, in comparison, San Lorenzo Cubo (chapter 6), is a microcosm of four centuries of Indian experience in Guatemala. It illustrates (1) the inherent competition for basic resources by the native population and the ladinos, (2) the growth of Indian population beyond the resource base available, (3) the fact that Indian rights merit little consideration under national law, (4) the advantages that ladinos reap from favorable connections at higher political levels, and (5) the willingness of the ladinos to exterminate Indians and, by extension, others who fail to accept the preceding assumptions. The processes that are currently eating away at San Antonio have long since left San Lorenzo Cubo without land and, as Annis indicates, have shorn it of its Indian character. Indians throughout the western highlands of Guatemala are confronting the same problems of growing numbers of people with too little land remaining for them; the accounts of El Quiché and Totonicapán are further examples.

The economic relations reflected here affect not only the Indians but also the ladino rural population. The ladinos also have confronted increasing dependency on access to cash, a loss of subsistence or small-scale enterprises to large-scale export agriculture, and an increased population. These have resulted in increasing "proletarianization" (dependence on wage labor), coupled with a very slow growth of possible employment. This in turn is creating a continuing, and surely structural, state of under- and unemployment. Smith's material on Totonicapán (see chapter 9, table 4) provides a stark example that in no way exaggerates the nature of the problem in the country at large. It may be added that, beyond all this, the economic crisis faced by Guatemala in the 1970s and 1980s is not unique but is shared by all other Central American countries. High external debts are draining surpluses away from internal investment, changing international prices for the agricultural commodities that provide most of the national income, and (in common with El Salvador, Honduras, and Nicaragua) uncertain political conditions constantly encourage a drain of capital and profits.

Guatemalan Indians have long specialized in regional and local products, many of which supply internal regional trade. Some products, such as weaving and pottery, have moved into the national market and a growing international market. Totonicapán has always been a major production area, and Smith's analysis cuts directly to the heart of the problems faced in that process. Panajachel, directly dependent on both national and international tourist traffic, also has been directly affected. While the terrorism and fire fights of the revolution have affected Panajachel much less severely than some neighboring towns—for example, Santiago Atitlán—troops are stationed there, attacks have occurred, and tourists have stayed away.

Through all of this, however, Indian regional trade has continued, if at a seriously reduced level, and, except where communities such as those in El Quiché and Huehuetenango have been eradicated, artisan production has continued as one of the few ways to bring in cash from the outside. An important product of San Antonio Aguas Calientes has been the extremely high quality hand weavings, the sale of which has long been important to its economy. While Smith correctly emphasizes the differing dependence on local manufacture and agriculture, the two activities are closely related both socially and economically.

The events in San Antonio Aguas Calientes provide textbook examples of the classic relation between the ladinos and the Indians. In chapter 6, Annis describes the gradual expropriation of Indian land in which the ladinos resort to legal and illegal means. In doing so, the ladinos can generally bring to bear their contacts in the centers of power—the ladino national and provincial government officials and the national police—whenever things become difficult. This process leaves the Indians with few alternatives. They can try to obtain legal redress through the usually ladino-dominated judicial and administrative authorities. Failing in this, they then can accept their losses, be driven from their lands, and become progressively more proletarianized, or they can take matters into their own hands and try to force the ladinos to desist.

Annis has pointed out (in correspondence) that a popular assumption shared by many non-Indians is that the Indians, as an ethnic category, are "culturally retarded" and constitute a backward-looking drag on development. While it is true that some isolated regions may lack knowledge of what is scientifically available for development, this view is simply wrong with respect to many of the peoples described in this volume. They are, in fact, most interested in their own development and have long since begun using fertilizers, improved agricultural practices, and contraceptive pills; supported literacy; and adopted a host of other aspects of "modernization." These activities have not, however, changed the ladinos' generally prejudicial view of the Indians as at best "quaint" and at worst dangerously "primitive."

The latter attitude has inevitably brought excesses by the ladinos, who almost always draw on administrative authorities for support. Before World War II it was common for ladinos to take the law into their own hands. During the revolutionary era of 1944 to 1954 this kind of illegal process was severely challenged by the government. Subsequently, however, right-wing death squads such as the "Mano Blanca" ("White Hand") began to reassert this kind of paragovernmental action, and in the late 1970s evidence grew that the government was sponsoring such groups. The recrudescence in both San Antonio and El Quiché of killer squads had been a familiar expression of ladino power since the 1950s. For ladinos its appearance in the context of the threat of the *guerrillería* gave it de facto legitimacy. For Indians it raised already familiar abuses to a level unknown in living memory.

Indian revolts in this region have often brought quick and massive retribution. Thomas Anderson has described how, in 1932, the Salvadoran government responded to a revolt of Indians and other peasants with a *matanza* ("slaughter") in which it is estimated that between twenty and thirty thousand Indians were killed. In the 1940s a minor revolt by Indians in the Guatemalan town of Patzicía was answered with a slaughter of local Indians. It is not really possible to date a "beginning" of the killings described in this book; in a sense it began in 1492. More immediately it began with the ladino guerrillas of the 1960s who, with the crushing of that effort, moved to the northwest border area. The Ixcán events depicted here show that the genocidal era was under way by 1976. International attention came with the

Panzós massacre in the Alta Verapaz in 1978, and the destruction of entire villages apparently began about 1982. In the same year the farmers of San Antonio rose up against Hector Arroyave Paniagua, and the killing of Indians began in that town. A year later the events related by Paul and Demarest in San Pedro la Laguna (chapter 5) began to unfold, and the community mass killings described by Carmack began in El Quiché.

There were other dimensions to Indian-ladino relations. A number of the studies illustrate the "vertical" relations—personal familiarity, economic interactions, patron-client alliances—that bind individual Indians in the communities into cooperative networks with ladinos at various levels. The account of San Pedro la Laguna details how such relations are crucial for the operation of the larger society. They are present everywhere, often prevailing over the competitive issues that are usually sources of conflict. Totonicapán saw much less Indian-ladino hostility, and Ebel asserts that in San Juan Ostuncalco the combined pressure of the guerrillas and the army brought some political harmony among the ethnic groups. Quezaltenango, the provincial capital only seven miles from Ostuncalco, was the seat of the commercially most successful Indians in Guatemala. Ladinos had long recognized Indian abilities and capacities and well knew that they were not ignorant peasants. Ebel's account of the political election processes (chapter 7) provides us with tantalizing glimpses of an ethnic accommodation that needs extended study.

These vertical relations and larger networks were not merely sources of integration but also channels for divisive factors that linked Indian communities with factions elsewhere in the national society and the world at large. The chief sources of contention were expressed in religious and political idioms: the issues of Protestantism and Catholicism, as related by Stoll; the so-called Christo-pagan (hybrid Indian and Catholic religious practices) or traditional *cofradía* ("brotherhood") Catholics and the reformist priest-directed catechist and Catholic Action, described in the chapters on El Quiché and San Juan Ostuncalco, which were extremely active throughout the western highlands; and Communist or Marxist-Leninist ideology which arrived in the 1920s, was instrumental in the revolt in El Salvador in 1932, was the rationale for the CIA's participation in the "liberation" of Guatemala in 1954, and currently provides one component of the ideology of some of the guerrilla bands.

These sacred and secular, "religious" and "political" idioms are closely similar in an important way: all are expressions of dogma whose sponsors demanded behavioral conformity. The democratic elective process was another of these asserted dogmas, but following the crushing of the revolution in 1954, it was stifled as an operative device for politicization and participation. Carmack describes how the efforts of Spanish priests to promote Catholic Action were coupled with the establishment of cooperatives and support from the U.S.-sponsored Alliance for Progress. Catholic Action of El Quiché was closely allied with the Christian Democrat political party and the National Federation of Campesinos. These progressive steps in the hamlet La Estancia elicited strong opposition from local and regional ladinos, who branded them "Communist."

The interweaving, intermixturing, and combining of political and religious functions and ideologies had become standard under the revolutionary governments of Arévalo and Arbenz and not only served as the source of labels for local actors and policies in subsequent years but has become ingrained in international discourse. While the vocabulary of "democracy" and "communism" carries familiar ideological baggage in the United States and Western Europe, in Guatemala the terms become instruments of manipulation and repression. They do not readily penetrate as new elements or criteria of ideological identity. While there are Guatemalans, mainly ladinos but also now some Indians, who identify themselves as "capitalists" or "Communists," such ideological identity is generally secondary to identity defined in terms of nationality (e.g., Guatemalan), ethnicity (Indian or *natural*), national ancestry (e.g., German), place of birth (e.g., Ostuncalco), and sometimes religion (Católico or Evangélico).

The retention of Indian identity is strong. This is clear from the descriptions of San Antonio Aguas Calientes, Totonicapán, San Pedro la Laguna, San Juan Ostuncalco, and El Quiché. Even in the new community of Ixcán, Manz reported identification of being an *antiguo*. Indian society is undergoing countless formal cultural changes—changes in costume, shifts to bilingualism and even monolingualism, frequent commercial interaction, proletarianization, economic and entrepreneural success, changes to reform Catholicism or Protestantism. These changes, however, do not in themselves destroy Indian identity as long as that identity is reinforced by the separate and discriminatory identification of ladinos as ladinos. In the new Ixcán community "La Esperanza" (chapter 3), the awareness of being Indian has been enhanced by the fierceness of the suffering.

For an Indian to lose Indian identity—to become a ladino—two things must happen. The Indian must, for whatever reason, find it undesirable to be an Indian, and the ladinos with whom the Indian associates must also desire or at least accept it. While some Indians may feel that there are advantages to becoming ladino (for example those of El Salvador in the 1930s, discussed below), there is rarely any complementary reason leading ladinos to accept them. Thus mestizos in Guatemala and other Latin American countries are still often referred to as indios irrespective of the traits and desires of the individuals.

It has sometimes been thought that gaining wealth or, at the other extreme, being subjected to grinding poverty leads to a loss of Indian identity. In fact, many formal "Indian" traits require some level of income. We have known for years that the income gained by seasonal labor in the coffee harvests and more recently the cotton harvests has helped maintain Indian communities. Smith recounts how the Indians of Totonicapán enhance their Indian identity through economic success. What can be expected, however, is that the Indian identity of Totonicapenses who have migrated to Houston, Texas, will gradually change in response to the manner of discrimination that is more common in Houston. Deep poverty can lead to the gradual loss of Indian material traits but does not allow ready learning of a new language or acceptance into ladino society.

The genocidal policies of the Guatemalan government have viciously exacerbated the discriminatory characteristics of the ladino-Indian relationship. Discrimination, however, was not a standing government policy, nor was it limited to the government. Carmack's account of the sequence and crescendo of violence meted out to the Indians of El Quiché and those described by Manz in the Ixcán are the logical extension of a pattern or relationship that had long existed, a latent distrust and antipathy that could be awakened when ladinos felt seriously enough threatened. The interesting thing about this response is that it extends to anyone who is identified as being associated with the Indians. In El Quiché it was carried over to the priests of whatever nationality and to anthropologists who happened to be North Americans.

In chapter 1, Davis refers to the "culture of fear" that emerged in the Indian population as a result of the government's genocidal policies. It is not possible yet to evaluate how this may change the patterning of Indian life. In neighboring El Salvador, before the 1932 massacre the Indian population wore dress similar to that worn in many

Guatemalan Indian communties. That experience, however, was interpreted by many to indicate that wearing Indian dress was dangerous.
The result was that it was largely given up and is a rarity today. It is
clear that events such as those that have transpired in the past decade
will have a permanent impact. Today Indian refugees in Mexico, Los
Angeles, Houston, and Miami are differentially evaluating the virtues
of continuing their Indian culture, and many, like the Salvadoran Indians of half a century ago, are deciding that Indian dress does not
help survival. For the moment we do not know what is happening in
this respect in the Guatemalan highlands.

The roots of this "fear," however, reach far beyond the bloody
events that triggered it, and it has been intentionally cultivated by
army policy. It was a planned effort that grew out of the fact that the
ladinos themselves feared the Indians. Fear has always been an intrin-
sic part of the psychodynamics of the ladino-Indian relationship. Its
historic genesis lies in the Conquest, it has been reborn in every subsequent generation, and it has periodically been fired up into bloody
events.

These roots lie in the fact that a conquest that fails to exterminate
or assimilate the conquered inevitably leaves a population of divided
identities. The Spaniards arrived in Mesoamerica under the assumption that the peoples of the region had already been granted to them
by the papal bull of Pope Alexander VI. Resistance was naturally seen
as being not merely the reluctance to be conquered but also a rebellion
against the crown's preordained hegemony. In the centuries that followed the Indians' defeat, the autonomy of native kingdoms remained
strong in ethnic memories and was acted out in the Dance of the Conquest and the Dance of the Moors and the Christians.

The survival of native cultural elements was inevitable because destruction was not the goal of the Conquest; the Spaniards needed the
natives' labor. However, they recognized and feared the possibility of
native revolt. Their concern was not unique to them. It replicated the
long-standing fear of peasant rebellions among European rulers. In the
"New World," however, the subordinated Indian laborers also re-
tained their pre-Conquest cultural memory. Control was based on
physical conquest, and its continuation required periodic physical re-
inforcement. Thus the emerging ladino population feared the Indians
as a potentially rebellious people who had to be periodically reminded
of their conquered status; and the periodic reminders have, quite naturally, reinforced a fear already long present in the minds of the Indians.

If the psychodynamics of genocide are not new, the elements of capitalist and socialist ideologies that have been added to that substratum are new. In the colonial era English Protestantism was seen as the incarnation of the devil; today it is the Marxist-Leninism of the Eastern Bloc and Cuba. The security of the Spanish crown required that the region be orderly enough to pay him his due; today the United States is concerned that security not be threatened. Hence, while the U.S. government refused direct military aid to Guatemala because of the human rights abuses, it did not prohibit private shipments and, in fact, rejoiced that the Guatemalan army had succeeded in stemming, if not eliminating, a rebellion seen to be generated by the archdevil, Marxism-Leninism.

Trying to Understand the Consequences

Events incorporating the Indians into the Guatemalan revolution have followed on each other with the rigid determinism of a Greek tragedy. Although the Indians were bystanders in the rebellion and guerrilla war that focused in the northeastern and southern parts of the country in the 1960s, the guerrilla reorganizations in the 1970s recognized that involving the Indians was probably essential to success. Since the guerrillas were principally ladino, their initial attitude toward the Indians displayed the same lack of understanding that has characterized the relationship for centuries. Indeed, relations between the guerrillas and the Indians have not been uniform and consistent. The initial Indian reaction has generally been to see the guerrillas as merely another ladino imposition, another source of ladino-inspired fear. Soon, however, the guerrillas began taking pains to try to educate the Indians, to convince them that the cause of the rebellion was also their cause. In this they were unquestionably successful. Nevertheless, the process has not been simple. In many parts of the country there was a real genera tion or mobilization of Indian concern and commitment to action.

The guerrilla author Mario Payeras reports that EGP guerrillas had been in Ixcán since 1972. Army reprisals were under way soon thereafter but remained selective in the early years. The first schoolteacher slain was killed in January of the next year. The development of the Comité de Unidad Campesina (CUC) began in 1974, and Carmack describes how its members went into action after the earthquake of 1976. The general approach of the guerrillas was to try to demonstrate to the Indian population the advantage of cooperating and giving allegiance to the revolutionary effort. Given the increasing threat from the army, this pressure forced Indian communities to try to appear loyal to both "states." The guerrillas also had to defend themselves and were ready to kill Indians who were thought to be sympathetic to the army. Irrespective of what the individual Indian's sympathies may have been, life consisted in finding ways to cope with, please, and fend off two states in conflict.

While revolution is a natural occurrence, it does not occur without considerable effort. A wellspring of frustration is just as likely to lead to irrational thrashing as to a carefully planned strategy of displacing the state. Before the 1970s, Indian actions—revolts and rebellions—were localized and usually directed against local ladino interests. The last major such occurrence was the Patzicía massacre of the 1940s, which evidently started with some killings of ladinos by Indians and ended with a slaughter of the Indians. The Panzós slaughter of 1979 was similarly a local (but evidently not militant) Indian action that was met with a bloody response. The events of the 1970s marked a new departure in Indian-ladino relations. The Indians' participation posed a new kind of threat to the ladino population. Until that time the revolution had had no ethnic connotation. It was far from clear in the late 1970s just what the nature of the Indians' role was. As reported in some of the chapters here, however, many Indians found fewer and fewer alternatives. Their problem became one of survival. Traditional survival was, obviously, to continue the agrarian and commercial practices that they already knew. But as some of their fellows began working with the guerrillas, and as the army began striking at what it saw to be an increasingly Indian threat, the choices were narrowed.

The full extent of the Indian participation in the efforts of the guerrillas will never be known, since few of the participants will ever be able to present their case. The figure of 260,000 for adherents in 1981, cited by Manz, could be low; a long-term resident in the highlands estimated that there where 500,000 participants by early 1982. The actual number who carried arms is surely much lower: Davis places it at about 3,500 at the height of the movement. Two things, however, seem certain. First, the conservative interests blamed every undesirable event on the guerrillas and extended that association to anyone whom they found threatening. Indians, who were inherently threatening anyway, now became specific targets. The conservatives were, therefore, able to justify killing anyone who was seen as threatening. It was not necessary to demonstrate overt association with guerrillas; it was enough to brand Indians as revolutionaries. Hence efforts to gain the Indians' allegiance, if seriously considered at all, were not pursued.

Second, whatever may have been the degree of the Indians' sympathy or participation in 1981 and 1982, a stunning failure in the guerrillas' strategy left the swelling population of guerrilla sympathizers without arms. If more of them had been armed, the outcome could have been different—surely much more bloody that it was, but possibly also victorious for the guerrilla side. By the early 1980s the army increasingly saw the Indians as the "water in which the fish [the guerrillas] swim." With its long-standing fear of the Indians and the ladinos' stereotype of them as its only guide, it meted out retribution to all Indians in the vicinity, as it had in El Salvador and Patzicía.

The government's response intensified with the success of the guerrillas. It relied on various devices, some of which are recounted in these chapters. Police, usually the judicial police dressed as civilians, menaced Indians whom ladinos regarded as threatening, as in San Antonio Aguas Calientes. Most threating to the ladinos and the government were activities aimed at organizing the Indians, particularly local government leaders, schoolteachers, and labor-union participants. Manz says that the first community leader murdered in Ixcán was the schoolteacher killed in January, 1976. The flights from the Ixcán began as early as 1979, and the depopulation was complete by 1982. The army and the hit squads assassinated local officials and teachers across the highlands, as related here in the chapters on El Quiché, San Antonio Aguas Calientes, San Juan Ostuncalco, San Pedro la Laguna, and "La Esperanza."

When the army began draining the water that supported the fish is not entirely clear. Manz indicates that the guerrilla forces grew and expanded over much of the northwestern and central highlands during the second half of the 1970s. Manz and Stoll cite 1982 as the first appearance of the army's strategy of destroying entire communities and the beginning of the mass flights. Not only were the Indians regarded as expendable, but the government believed that it was necessary to remove them from the scene. Part of the strategy was to cut down the trees for ten meters on each side of the main roads to make ambushes impossible, a strategy that is still (1987) being used around the new model towns. It was, in a sense, an ecological argument: if the environment is destroyed, the species cannot survive.

The success of the army's effort, glimpses of which are recorded in this book, is now history. The EGP lost its Indian base of support in the central highlands and the Indians themselves (1) were killed, (2) were often forced to kill other Indians, (3) became internal refugees, as described by Falla (chapter 10), (4) fled the country (many to Mexico, where some were fortunate enough to be taken in by local communities, as described by Earle in chapter 11), (5) died in flight, or (6) were captured or returned voluntarily to submit to living under army controls or to try to take up their lives again in the remains of their communities.

The military strategy was not merely to eradicate the present threats but also to make repetition as difficult as possible. With this in mind, the government set up "poles of development," in which "model towns" were established, peopled by refugees and controlled by the army. The production of basic foods and Indian labor used on roads or in the production of export crops were also controlled by the army. The army also established civil patrols, which brought some quiet to the countryside but also caused extraordinary economic dislocations, as in Santa Eulalia, Ixcán, and Totonicapán.

In towns that were not directly affected by guerrilla activity and attendant dislocation, the government neverthless intervened directly, as in San Juan Ostuncalco and in San Pedro la Laguna. In some towns, such as San Pedro, the intervention was regarded as a blessing because it put at least a temporary end to local chaos, corruption, and killing. In San Juan it evidently provided a basis for a workable reorganization of the local government.

This book can do no more than summarize a decade of disaster. Many of the consequences are not yet evident. We have no adequate accounting of the individuals, populations, and communities that have disappeared. Work with the refugees in Mexico is only gradually yielding a history of particular cases. Earle's account of the Chiapas Indians' response to the needs of the refugees is heartwarming, but he also makes it clear that most Guatemalans who fled had far less than a benign reception. To the Mexican government the wave of refugees was anything but welcome; it is to their credit, irrespective of abuses that occurred in the process, that they kept the border open to the refugees. Research is under way in some of the Mexican refugee camps, but it is not readily available and is not extensive. There is even less systematic work on the problem in Guatemala. Falla's chapter on the internal refugees throws considerable light on why many ultimately found it preferable either to flee the county or to turn themselves in to the army. Research among the refugees in the United States is weak to date, and few reports have appeared.

In terms of the revelations in the foregoing chapters, two important questions arise. The first is the immediate question: What remains upon which people can rebuild their lives? The second question concerns the longer term: What pattern for future lives will evolve from this struggle for survival?

The immediate effects have been extremely varied. Some regions—such as the Ixil, the central Quiché Department, neighboring Chimaltenango and Alta Verapaz, and many parts of Huehuetenango—have suffered overwhelming disasters. They have been described in the chapters by Stoll, Carmack, and Manz. In areas that were not subjected to the scorched-earth campaign, such as San Antonio Aguas Calientes and San Pedro la Laguna, individuals were searched out to be assassinated, as described here by Annis and by Paul and Demarest. Other regions, such as Ostuncalco, Panajachel and neighboring Totonicapán, described here by Ebel, Hinshaw, and Smith, were less directly affected by violence but felt the consequences through networks of acquaintance, familiarity, and kinship and through economic relations. Having visited in Panajachel often during this era, I know that fear was a constant companion and that the tourist business on which many local people depended was in constant depression.

More widespread and profound economic damage of the kind described for Totonicapán has affected much of the western highlands. The doubtless permanent damage to small commodity production, especially the regionally characteristic handicrafts such as weaving, has yet to be evaluated. In the establishment of new villages and in forced repopulation of old ones, Indians from different places speaking different languages were brought together. In the refugee camps in Mexico and the United States, learning different languages is often necessary for survival. Manz argues that this mixing has been part of army strategy in that it has made the emergence of internal organization much more difficult. Whether carried out by guile or simply through ignorance of the significance of local communities, it is the same technique of conquest that the Spaniards used over much of the New World in the sixteenth century. The colonial policy of establishing *reducciones* and *congregaciones* (bringing together dispersed populations) was for precisely the same purpose and helped achieve the conquerors' goals of dividing local communities. The colonial policy of forced labor of Indians, a practice that had finally been put aside after the 1944 revolution, was reinstituted by the army in the Ixcán and in roadwork elsewhere. The civil patrols, requiring the time of every able-bodied male, have gone unpaid.

The internal organization of communities has suffered seriously. The destroyed cooperatives and other organizational efforts will need several years to recover. As long as the army is in direct control, any progressive organization will be inhibited and probably clandestine. Communities have reacted with both a show of unity and fragmentation. San Antonio Aguas Calientes and San Juan Ostuncalco did the first; San Pedro la Laguna was split over the problems. Local disputes and conflicts are used, as always, to provide leverage points for external interests. In Ixcán the *antiguos* are few, and given the intentional linguistic and cultural mixing of the new populations, it will take years to achieve social cohesion.

All this means that we have to take a long view. Manz's report from Ixcán concludes by arguing that, in spite of all the repression and destruction, there survive many members of a generation that knew of the development of the local community as a "grass-roots movement." It is, of course, impossible to evaluate at this time how widespread is this recognition and memory, but her account is encouraging. Immediately following the CIA-backed repression of the reforms of the revolutionary decade of 1944–54, I directed a study of persons jailed by the Castillo Armas government and concluded that, while revolutionary activities had left little ideological imprint, there had been an important "sociological awakening," an awareness of hitherto unimagined possibilities of social opportunity. The repression in 1954 was relatively brief. In contrast, the era from 1975 to 1985 was a decade of disaster. A strenuous effort was made to destroy any confidence in new social or political opportunities. Manz's Maya informant reflects not only a continuity of Indian identity but one now much more closely related to political understanding. The "model towns" of the Ixil Triangle and elsewhere, it can be assumed, will gradually find their own organization, their own kind of unity. People do pick up their lives and go on, families will re-form around survivors, and eventually the conscious fear will be repressed to some degree so that the society can function.

It is unpredictable at the moment just how the guerrilla activity will continue. One might assume that, were it to stop, the community role of the army would be reduced in some measure. But at present reading it seems clear that the army intends to keep its presence felt indefinitely. It remains the single strongest corporate element in the nation, and the reestablishment of civil government is not resulting in a retreat to the barracks. For now, it appears that, while some guerrillas may cease their activities, not all are prepared to do so. Their presence provides the military with all the reasons it needs for continued repressive actions.

If the relatively mild repression following the 1954 conservative victory brought in its train the revolutionary activity of the 1960s and 1970s, one cannot ignore what may be harvested from this decade of violence. What will be the future thoughts of the thousands of children, whose numbers will doubtless exceed 100,000 before the present era ends, growing up with the knowledge that their fathers or families were unreasonably killed by the army? What of the growing channels of information about different ways of doing things that are now coming in from refugees in Los Angeles, Houston, and Miami? And, finally, what is the political future of a population that first learned about democratic participation in the revolutionary decade of 1944–54, only to have it snatched away by a CIA-backed coup, and to have been brought by frustration into active revolt, only to have it result in the slaughter of 1975–85?

Appendix

Chronology of Local and National Events Described in This Book

1944	Guatemalan revolution ousts the dictator Jorge Ubico Castañeda
1954	President Arbenz deposed; "liberation" by Castillo Armas and the CIA
1963	Army coup consolidates military control of the government; Gen. Enrique Peralta Azurdia heads the regime
1966	Julio César Méndes Montenegro, a civilian, elected president
Ca. 1968	Colonel Arana defeats the guerrillas in the eastern zone
1970	Gen. Carlos Arana Osorio elected president
	La Esperanza cooperative initiated in the Ixcán
1972	Rise of Ejército Guatemalteco de los Pobres (EGP), centering in northern Quiché
1974	Election of Christian Democrat Ríos Montt stolen by the army; Gen. Kjell Laugerud García becomes president
1975	EGP guerrillas execute plantation owner Luis Arenas
1976	Rosa Aguayo, teacher of "La Esperanza" cooperative, murdered
	Earthquake kills more than 25,000 persons
	Father Woods, director of Ixcán Grande cooperative, dies in plane crash.
1978	Election of Gen. Romeo Lucas García
	Horacio Arroyave Paniagua dams river in San Antonio Aguas Calientes
	Panzós massacre
	Don Carlos removed as mayor of San Juan Ostuncalco
1979	Fall of Anastasio Somoza in Nicaragua
	Death-squad killings begin in San Antonio Aguas Calientes
	Organization of the People in Arms (ORPA) guerrilla group begins public operations in the western highlands
1980	Occupation of Spanish embassy
	San Pedro la Laguna visited by ORPA guerrillas; reign of terror begins in the community shortly thereafter
	Avelino Zapeta, mayor of Santa Cruz del Quiché, assassinated
	La Estancia hamlet attacked by army; its inhabitants leave
1981	Hotel in Panajachel bombed by guerrillas
	Major army counterinsurgency operations in Chimaltenango and Quiché, according to Falla

Massacre in Chupol, Chichicastenango
Civil patrols organized in Santa Cruz del Quiché
1982   Army destroys La Esperanza cooperative in the Ixcán
Ríos Montt takes power through military coup
Selective violence in San Juan Ostuncalco ends with appointment of mayor
    by Ríos Montt government
Horacio Arroyave killed in Guatemala City
Pastor Nicolás Toma begins collaboration with army in Cotzal
Massacres in Patzún, Baja Verapaz, and Alta Verapaz described by Falla
Schoolteacher Emilio, of Totonicapán, returns to Alta Verapaz to find his
    village "disappeared"
Indian refugees settle in a Chamula colony of Chiapas, Mexico
Evangelicals celebrate 100 years of missionary labors in Guatemala
Army begins scorched-earth campaign in Huehuetenango
352 men, women, and children massacred in Finca San Francisco
1983   Militarization of Santa Cruz Quiché *aldeas* completed
"La Esperanza" (Ixcán) resettled under army supervision
Ríos Montt deposed; Gen. Mejía Victores takes command
1984   Guatemalan refugees forcibly removed from Chiapas to Campeche and
    Quintana Roo, Mexico
Nearly half of Totonicapán artisans go out of business
1985   Chief military commissioner and his uncle murdered in San Pedro la Laguna
Christian Democrat Vinicio Cerezo wins presidential elections
1986–87 President Cerezo addresses United Nations Assembly
Selective "disappearances" and killings continue throughout Guatemala, as
    do armed encounters between the army and guerrillas; a trickle of Indian
    refugees return to Guatemala from Mexico and elsewhere

Authors' Notes on Sources

(Publication data for works listed in the Selected Bibliography are omitted from these notes.)

Editor's Preface, Robert M. Carmack

The strategic importance of Guatemala relative to the other Central American countries is discussed in many recent books. Important examples are Thomas Anderson, *Politics in Central America;* Robert Leiken, ed., *Central America: Anatomy of Conflict;* Tom Berry and Deb Preusch, *The Central American Fact Book;* Howard Wiarda, ed., *Rift and Revolution: The Central American Imbrolio;* and Steve Ropp and James Morris, eds., *Central America: Crisis and Adaptation.* Two of the best regional histories are Ralph Woodward, *Central America;* and Walter LaFeber, *Inevitable Revolutions.* For developments in Guatemala since 1954, including the emergence of revolutionary opposition to the government, see Richard Adams, *Crucifixion by Power;* George Black, *Garrison Guatemala;* Jim Handy, *Gift of the Devil: A History of Guatemala;* Michael McClintock, *The American Connection, Volume Two: State Terror and Popular Resistance in Guatemala;* and the special issue of *Cultural Survival Quarterly* entitled "Death and Disorder in Guatemala," Spring 1983.

The number of political deaths in Guatemala during the past thirty years has been subject to dispute. In 1986 the Commission on Human Rights of the Organization of American States estimated that 40,000 persons had disappeared and another 100,000 had been assassinated during the preceding fifteen years. An estimate of deaths since 1978 by the Juvenile Division of the Guatemala Supreme Court, based on the number of orphans created by the violence, suggests that 50,000 to 70,000 persons were killed. Other scholarly and journalistic surveys of deaths resulting from the violence generally corroborate these estimates.

As for U.S. policy toward Central American governments, it is true that the Carter administration stressed human rights. Nevertheless, as both LaFeber (*Inevitable Revolutions*) and McClintock (*The American Connection, Volume Two*) show through careful review of the available documents, the overall strategy and policy remained the same. Similarly, the Kissinger Bipartisan Commission Report on Central America (1984) makes reference to economic and political factors as partial causes of the Guatemalan crisis, but the report's overall thrust and even more clearly that of the Reagan administration follow the traditional line.

A particularly lucid expression of the widely held scholarly view of the Guatemalan crisis is Lars Schoultz, "Guatemala: Social Change and Political Conflict," in Martin Diskin, ed., *Trouble in Our Backyard*. Schoultz's study was commissioned by the U.S. State Department, which chose to ignore his findings. The significance that U.S. policy toward Guatemala will have for the rest of the region, the United States itself, and the world community is explored in scholarly fashion in Richard Feinberg, ed., *Central America: International Dimensions of the Crisis*, and the other, more general works cited above.

The two studies cited in the Preface as representative of the general scholarly view—Shelton H. Davis and Julie Hodson, *Witnesses to Political Violence in Guatemala*; and Jim Handy, *Gift of the Devil: A History of Guatemala*—show that most of the recent violence in Guatemala was perpetrated by the Guatemalan government and its associates. Many other reputable works that reach the same conclusion could be cited. The persistence of deep social problems and extensive violence despite the election of a new civilian government is documented in Allan Nairn and Jean-Marie Simon, "Bureaucracy of Death: Guatemala's Civilian Government Faces the Enemy Within" (*New Republic*, June 30, 1986), and the Guatemala News in Brief reports published each month by the Americas Watch Committee.

The most thorough documentation of official U.S. attitudes toward the violence in Guatemala can be found in the works of McClintock (*The American Connection, Volume Two*), and George Black (*Garrison Guatemala*). A particularly convincing critique of those attitudes is Shelton H. Davis, "State Violence and Agrarian Crisis in Guatemala," in Diskin, ed., *Trouble in Our Backyard*. A more intimate look at the U.S. government's thinking about the Guatemalan crisis is provided by Richard Graham, the senior political officer in the American embassy in Guatemala during the crucial years 1981 to 1985. His testimony before the U.S. Immigration and Naturalization Service in August 1985 is recorded in 285 pages of answers to questions about recent events in that country. While it does not reflect the official position of the State Department, it provides unique insight into how that agency obtains its information and the political interpretations it places on events.

It must be remembered, of course, that there are powerful forces within the U.S. political system that impede a more effective Central American policy by our government, even when the facts are known and the need for change is recognized. Some of these are insightfully discussed by Laurence Whitehead in "Explaining Washington's Central American Policies" (*Journal of Latin American Studies* 15). It is likely that only strong public pressure can push the U.S. government onto a different track.

The Guatemalan army's strategy of classifying Indian communities as red, pink, yellow, or green—and then applying the proper dose of counterinsurgent violence and terror—was explained publicly on many occasions by army officers. It is described and analyzed by George Black in *Garrison Guatemala* and by McClintock in *The American Connection, Volume Two*.

Chapter 1: *Introduction*, Shelton H. Davis

The Inter-American Commission on Human Rights, a specialized agency of the Organization of American States in Washington, published country reports entitled *Report on the Situation of Human Rights in the Republic of Guatemala* in 1981, 1983, and 1985. Reports by nongovernment organizations on the human rights situation in Guatemala include Amnesty International, *Guatemala: A Government Programme of Political Murder;* and *Guatemala: Massive Extrajudicial Executions in Rural Areas Under the Government of General Efraín Ríos Montt;* and Americas Watch Committee, *Human Rights in Guatemala: No Neutrals Allowed; Creating a Desolation and Calling It Peace;* and *Guatemala: A Nation of Prisoners*.

Changes that took place in the Guatemalan agrarian structure before the violence are described in Thomas Melville and Marjorie Melville, *Guatemala: The Politics of Land Ownership;* Carlos Figueroa Ibarra, *El proletariado rural en el agro guatemalteco* (Guatemala: Editorial Universitaria, 1980); and Shelton H. Davis, "State Violence and Agrarian Crisis in Guatemala: The Roots of the Indian-Peasant Rebellion," in Martin Diskin, ed., *Trouble in Our Backyard: Central America and the United States in the Eighties.*

For discussions of the Catholic Action movement and its influence on local Indian communities, see Douglas Brintnall, *Revolt of the Dead: The Modernization of a Mayan Community in the Highlands of Guatemala* (New York: Gordon and Breach, 1979); Ricardo Falla, *Quiché rebelde* (Guatemala: Editorial Universitaria, 1978); and Kay B. Warren, *The Symbolism of Subordination: Indian Identity in a Guatemalan Town.* A general overview of the Roman Catholic church in contemporary Guatemala and other Central American countries is contained in Phillip Berryman, *The Religious Roots of Rebellion: Christians in Central American Revolutions.*

The Oxfam America study referred to in the text is Shelton H. Davis and Julie Hodson, *Witnesses to Political Violence in Guatemala: The Suppression of a Rural Development Movement.* Other studies of the social effects of the political violence and the military's counterinsurgency program include Programa de Ayuda para los Vecinos del Altiplano [PAVA], *Final Report on Guatemalan Displaced Persons Needs Survey Covering Huehuetenango, El Quiché, Western Petén, and Playa Grande;* and Chris Krueger and Kjell Enge, *Security and Development Conditions in the Guatemalan Highlands.* On the civil patrol system see Americas Watch Committee, *Civil Patrols in Guatemala.*

For background on the return to civilian rule in Guatemala and the election and early performance of the Cerezo government, see Piero Gleijeses, "Guatemala: The Struggle for Democracy," *Latin American Series* (Cork, Ireland: Department of Modern History, University College Cork, January 1986); and Richard Millet, "Guatemala's Painful Progress" (*Current History* 85 [1986]).

Chapter 2: *The Story of Santa Cruz Quiché*, Robert M. Carmack

The *Popol Vuh*, the so-called bible of the Quichés, was originally written in Latin characters in Santa Cruz Quiché by native lords around the middle of the sixteenth century. Later, knowledge of the work was lost to the Western world until the Franciscan priest Francisco Ximénez, laboring in the neighboring community of Chichicastenango, obtained from the Indians a manuscript version written in the Quiché language. He transcribed the text and translated it into Spanish, and all subsequent versions derive from Ximénez's copies. The three main English translations of the *Popol Vuh* are Delia Goetz and Sylvanus G. Morley, trans., *Popol Vuh: The Sacred Book of the Ancient Quiché Maya;* Munro Edmonson, *The Book of Counsel: The Popol Vuh of the Quiché Maya of Guatemala;* and Dennis Tedlock, trans., *Popol Vuh: The Definitive Edition of the Mayan Book of the Dawn of Life and the Glories of Gods and Kings.*

The description of social life in Santa Cruz Quiché around 1970 is largely based on my field observations and those of my students. Some of this information is presented in greater detail in my book *The Quiché Mayas of Utatlán: The Evolution of a Highland Guatemala Kingdom.* Ruth Bunzel, *Chichicastenango* (New York: J. J. Augustin Publisher, 1952), is an additional English-language source that can be consulted for an understanding of social conditions in the area in the years before 1970. Conditions in Guatemala as a whole, and specifically the context for the Conservative and Moderate (Christian Democratic) political parties mentioned in the text, are outlined in Richard N. Adams, *Crucifixion by Power: Essays on Guatemalan National Social Structure, 1944–1966;* George Black, *Garrison Guatemala;* and Jim Handy, *Gift of the Devil: A History of Guatemala.*

I regret that I did not acquire any written examples of Alcalde Zapeta's thinking. It would be an invaluable text from an Indian strategically placed at a critical time in Guatemala's history. But then I had no way of knowing what his tragic fate was to be. I am left with a photocopy of a single document that he signed, newspaper clippings of his death, my own notes of conversations with him, and vivid memories. Someday I shall return to Santa Cruz and find out more about this man, who symbolizes for me the profound contradictions that still afflict Guatemalan society.

I interviewed José Efraín in November 1982, during one of his trips to the United States from exile in Nicaragua. He also gave testimony to the Washington Office on Latin America (WOLA) on October 21, 1982, and before the Permanent Peoples Tribunal held at Madrid, Spain, in January 1983. I cross-checked information that he gave me for internal consistency and compared it with data obtained from my earlier interviews with Indians from La Estancia. His account is consistent and credible. Additional testimony from La Estancia Indians can be found in *Indian Guatemala: Path to Liberation,* a volume published by the Ecumenical Program for Interamerican Communication and Action (EPICA); in the Spanish publications of the Guatemalan Church in Exile (in particular the December 1982 special edition); and from testimony of Indians from La Estancia living in the United States taken by the Immigration and Naturalization Service in 1985. José Efraín is the source on the identity of Alcalde Zapeta's assassins and the reaction of his family. José Efraín claims that there were spies in Santa Cruz who collaborated with the death squads and who reported directly to the local ladino congressman mentioned in the text. For this reason José Efraín believes that the congressman was the main instigator of Alcade Zapeta's execution. I have not yet been able to corroborate this conclusion with more direct testimony.

Much of the reconstruction of the war fought between the Guatemalan army and the guerrillas in the environs of Santa Cruz Quiché derives from Guatemalan, Mexican, and U.S. newspaper accounts that appeared from 1980 to 1982. Convenient but incomplete summaries of these accounts can be found in Amnesty International, *Guatemala: A Government Program of Political Murder;* and Shelton H. Davis and Julie Hodson, *Witnesses to Political Violence in Guatemala: The Suppression of a Rural Development Movement.* Some newspaper accounts quote statements by Guatemalan military officials that are surprisingly candid about the terror the army was "forced" to inflict on the civilian population. The estimated deaths caused by the army and its paramilitary forces in Santa Cruz must remain tentative until it again becomes possible to reside in the community and reconstruct events of the past few years. A study of the area commissioned by the U.S. Agency for International Development in Guatemala, Programa de Ayuda para los Vecinos del Altiplano [PAVA], *Final Report on Guatemalan Displaced Persons Needs Survey Covering Huehuetenango, El Quiché, Western Petén, and Playa Grande,* leaves out Santa Cruz Quiché (though it notes devastating destruction of the surrounding Indian communities, including Chichicastenango). The report estimates that about 53 percent of the population of the Department of El Quiché has been displaced or has been in serious economic straits.

The guerrilla side of the war at Santa Cruz is reconstructed from my interviews with José Efraín and testimony from various guerrilla participants (such testimonies appear in newspaper and magazine articles, publications by the Guatemalan Church in Exile, etc.). An especially useful source is a collection of articles in English from the journal *Compañero,* the official publication of the Guerrilla Army of the Poor (EGP). We still know little about the Guatemalan guerrillas as a whole, and less about those operating in the Santa Cruz Quiché area. In fact, we may never know much about them, and for the present the political climate in Guatemala is not amenable to seeking information on the topic.

My reconstruction of the nature of military control imposed on the Santa Cruz population after 1982 is based on interviews with military officials and residents conducted by reporters and professional social scientists. Especially important are the reports by two members of our original research team, Beatriz Manz and Duncan Earle. During those years many reporters from leading U.S. and Mexican magazines and newspapers visited Santa Cruz, where they had surprisingly candid interviews with army officials. Thus, for example, a report from the *New York Times* provides the basis for the description of the "beauty contest" associated with the Day of the Indian celebration at the site of the old Quiché ruins. The dramatic account of the "executions" carried out by members of the civil patrol at Cruz Che comes from eyewitnesses whose testimony was published by the Guatemalan Church in Exile. The rather pessimistic but realistic quotation summarizing recent social conditions in Santa Cruz comes from the Americas Watch report *Guatemala: A Nation of Prisoners.*

The folk story in which the Quiché hero Tecum is associated with the modern-day guerrillas was recorded by Duncan Earle from an Indian residing near Santa Cruz Quiché. The analogy between the Guatemalan army and the *Popol Vuh*'s infraworld (Xibalba) was drawn by Rigoberta Menchú in an EPICA publication, *Indian Guatemala: Path to Liberation* (Washington, D.C.: EPICA Task Force, 1984). The larger perspective of this remarkable Indian woman relative to the recent political violence in Guatemala is presented in *I, Rigoberta Menchú: An Indian Woman in Guatemala* (1984). The suggestion that Quiché culture would someday again inspire the Indians of Guatemala was made in my *Quiché Mayas of Utatlán.*

Chapter 3: *The Transformation of La Esperanza, an Ixcán Village,* Beatriz Manz

As the text makes clear, the description of La Esperanza and its recent tragic history is based primarily on my observations and interviews with officials and inhabitants associated with the colony. A more formal and general treatment of the same area can be found in my monograph on the Guatemalan refugees, *Refugees of a Hidden War: The Aftermath of the Counterinsurgency War in Guatemala.*

Cooperatives in the La Esperanza area have been sponsored by the U.S. AID Mission in Guatemala, and are described in that agency's *Final Report: Northern Transversal Strip, Land Resettlement Project* (Project No. 520-0233). The cooperative projects can be compared with the Guatemalan army's settlement program by consulting such army publications as *Polos de desarrollo y servicio: Filosofía desarrollista* (1984); "Polos de desarrollo" (*Revista Cultural del Ejército,* 1985); and "Pensamiento y Cultura" (*Revista Cultural del Ejército,* 1985).

Information on the violence in La Esperanza and surrounding communities is found in Mario Payeras, *Days of the Jungle,* trans. George Black; and Payeras, "La estrategia antiguerrillera del ejército guatemalteco, 1974–84" (manuscript). In 1981 the Mexican weekly *Por Esto* devoted eight issues to the guerrillas in Guatemala, in which are described military events taking place in fourteen communities, including La Esperanza, of the Ixcán area. The report by Programa de Ayuda para los Vecinos del Altiplano (PAVA) of the U.S. AID Mission in Guatemala (Project No. 520-84-04) presents the general results of the violence in the area. Another report, prepared by Philip A. Dennis, Gary S. Elbow, and Peter L. Heller, *Final Report: Playa Grande Land Colonization Project, Guatemala,* provides ample testimony to the violence unleashed on communities like La Esperanza by the Guatemalan army.

Statements in the text regarding to the emergence of pan-Indian unity in the face of army repression were taken from Gabriel Ixmatá, "Con nuestra propia voz" (*Polémica,* 1983); Rigoberta Menchú, "Me llamo Rigoberta Menchú y así me nació la conciencia" (1983); and an undated manuscript, "La primera gran confrontación: El movimiento campesino indígena del Altiplano guatemalteco."

Chapter 4: *Evangelicals, Guerrillas, and the Army*, David Stoll

Unlike most of the contributions to this book, this chapter is not the result of long-term anthropological fieldwork. Instead, it is based on three short visits to the Ixil area between November 1982 and January 1983, as the Guatemalan army regained control and the shooting abated. During my week in Nebaj and an additional night in Cotzal, I was able to talk with dozens of refugees, townspeople, government personnel, and missionaries. What most surprised me was the willingness of refugees to detail human rights violations by the army, even though they were now under that institution's control and blamed the guerrillas for bringing on their misfortunes.

The 1936 novel in which a Russian Bolshevik leads a Maya Indian uprising appeared serially in *Revelation* magazine of Philadelphia from April through October of that year. It was written by William Cameron Townsend, the founder of the Wycliffe Bible Translators/Summer Institute of Linguistics. As for recent evangelical growth in Guatemala, the most comprehensive source is Clifton L. Holland, ed., *World Christianity: Central America and the Caribbean* (Monrovia, Calif.: World Vision, 1981).

The portrait of Gospel Outreach is based on conversations with the church's elders in Guatemala City and cassette tapes and fund-raising literature obtained from its headquarters in Eureka, California. The group's role in Ríos Montt's government is based mainly on information collected while I was living in the country from November 1982 to March 1983, as well as during a subsequent visit in August 1985. Valuable insights are provided by Gospel Outreach's biography of Ríos Montt, by Joseph Anfuso and David Sczepanski, originally entitled *He Gives, He Takes Away* and later reissued as *Servant or Dictator?*

On the origins of the guerrilla movement in the Ixil area, my main printed sources are from the Guatemalan Church in Exile, organized by some of the Catholic clergy who were forced to leave the country in 1980. The most helpful of these were a ten-page undated typescript entitled "Sebastian Guzmán: Principal de principales;" the special December 1982 number of *Iglesia guatemalteca en el exilio;* and the September–October 1984 number of the same periodical. Despite its ill-founded optimism, *Days of the Jungle*, the memoir by EGP leader Mario Payeras, published in English by Monthly Review Press, provides a valuable account of how that group's ladino founders recruited Ixil Indians into their movement. The observations of the Summer Institute translators in Nebaj are quoted from three of their memoranda that circulated in Guatemala during the period.

The most comprehensive report on the Finca San Francisco massacre is Ricardo Falla, *Masacre de la finca San Francisco, Huehuetenango, Guatemala*, published in 1983 by the International Work Group for Indigenous Affairs. The fate of Patricio Ortiz Maldonado is based on press reports, particularly the report in the *New York Times* of September 11, 1983, and my own interviews.

Chapter 5: *The Operation of a Local Death Squad in San Pedro la Laguna*,
Benjamin D. Paul and William J. Demarest

There are no published sources on the violence in San Pedro other than the series of articles that appeared in the national press. Full and explicit use of these newspaper accounts has been made in the text, and special care has been taken to balance these sources when they are contradictory.

The pertinent source for our chapter clearly are our field interviews with victims and many other Pedranos, as well as our own knowledge of the town's earlier history. We earlier published some of this information as "Mayan Migrants in Guatemala City," in J. Loucky and M. Hurwicz, eds., *Mayan Studies: The Midwestern Highlands of Gua-*

temala (Los Angeles: UCLA Press, 1981); and "Citizen Participation Overplanned: The Case of a Health Project in the Guatemalan Community of San Pedro la Laguna" (*Social Science and Medicine* 19 [1984]).

Other publications by Paul that provide cultural background to the events in San Pedro are "Life in a Guatemalan Indian Village" (*Cultural Patterns*, 1950); "Changing Marriage Patterns in a Highland Guatemalan Community" (*Southwestern Journal of Anthropology* 19 [1963]); and "San Pedro la Laguna" (*Los Pueblos del Lago Atitlán*, 1968).

Chapter 6: *Story from a Peaceful Town*, Sheldon Annis

I lived in San Antonio during one year in which this story began to unfold (1977–78) and lived nearby or in Guatemala City between 1976 and mid-1980. Since then I have regularly visited the town and have maintained close contact with many persons directly or indirectly involved in these events. In August 1985, I spent several days conducting systematic interviews in San Antonio to piece together the story described here. Further documentation was obtained from accounts that appeared in the Guatemalan press and from interviews taped and transcribed by Elissa Miller in 1979–80. Additional historical documentation on San Antonio—including materials on these contemporary events—was generously made available from the archives of the Centro para Investigaciones Regionales de Mesoamérica (CIRMA), in Antigua.

The surviving members of the Arroyave family were not interviewed; however, the family's version of the story was published in relative detail in interviews that appeared in the Guatemalan press. In addition, to obtain nonlocal interpretations of the events, I consulted with several middle-class Guatemalans who knew the family or were familiar with the circumstances.

A detailed account of contemporary San Antonio society is found in my forthcoming book, *God and Production in a Guatemalan Town* (Austin: University of Texas Press). The early history of the area is reconstructed in Christopher Lutz, *Historia sociodemográfica de Santiago de los Caballeros, Guatemala, 1541–1773* (Antigua and South Woodstock, Vt.: CIRMA, 1983).

Chapter 7: *When Indians Take Power*, Roland H. Ebel

Data for this study of San Juan Ostuncalco have been secured from interviews with informants in that community and in Quezaltenango, as well as from historical documents housed in the municipal archives of San Juan, the *Libro de actas* of the municipal council, fiscal records stored in the municipal treasury, and electoral records held by the Electoral Tribunal in Quezaltenango and Guatemala City.

More in-depth, formal treatment of San Juan Ostuncalco and its political system can be found in articles I have published over a period of twenty-five years. Of special importance are my "Political Change in Guatemalan Indian Communities" (*Journal of Inter-American Studies* 6 [1964]); "Land and Politics in Rural Guatemala: A Study of a Highland Aricultural Community" (with Oscar Horst), in John P. Augelli, ed., *The Community in Revolutionary Latin America* (Center of Latin American Studies, University of Kansas, 1964); *The Process of Political Modernization in Three Guatemalan Indian Communities* (New Orleans: Middle American Research Institute, Tulane University, 1969); "Political Modernization and Community Decision-making Process in Guatemala: The Case of Ostuncalco" (*Annals of the Southeast Conference on Latin American Studies* 1 [1970]); and a slightly longer version of the chapter published here in *Annals of the Southeast Conference on Latin American Studies* 16 (1985).

Guatemalan Indian community politics are the subject of two important publications from the 1950s: Richard N. Adams, ed., *Political Changes in Guatemalan Indian Communities: A Symposium* (New Orleans: Middle American Research Institute, 21 [1957]); and K. H. Silvert, *A Study in Government: Guatemala, Part I, National and Local Government Since 1944* (New Orleans: Middle American Research Institute, 21 [1954]). From the same period is B. F. Camara's important comparative piece on Middle America, "Religious and Political Organizations," in Sol Tax, ed., *Heritage of Conquest* (Glencoe, Ill.: Viking Fund Seminar on Middle American Ethnology [1952]).

Information on the most recent elections in San Juan was provided to me by David Scotchmer, doctoral candidate in anthropology at SUNY Albany.

Chapter 8: *Tourist Town amid the Violence,* Robert E. Hinshaw

The economic and demographic data utilized in this chapter derive from published accounts of field research by Sol Tax (1935–41), my own research (1963–65 and 1969–70), and research by Beloit College students whom I supervised in 1978. My findings on my return to Guatemala in 1984 have not been previously published.

The principal publication of Sol Tax is *Penny Capitalism: A Guatemalan Indian Economy* (Washington, D.C.: Smithsonian Institution, Institute of Social Anthropology, 16 [1953]). *Penny Capitalism* gives a comprehensive description and analysis of income and expenditures of the Indian population of Panajachel in 1937. My study of Panajachel's economy was published in *Panajachel: A Guatemalan Town in Thirty-Year Perspective.* The Beloit College Field School data utilized are summarized in an article by Paul Yamauchi, "Guatemalan Tourism and the Efficacy of Wage Employment in Panajachel" (*Annals of Tourism Research* 11 [1984]). Information on the economic impact of tourism beyond Panajachel was obtained from the 1979 *Annual Report* of the Guatemalan Tourism Institute (1980).

Income from tourists visiting Panajachel during 1978 was estimated for the year on the basis of detailed counting of tourists during the months of the field school and several hundred interviews with tourists. By comparison of the numbers of hotel and nonhotel tourists during those few months, access to hotel records for the previous months of the year permitted extrapolation of numbers of nonhotel visitors for those months as well. The average length of stay of Panajachel's 85,000 foreign tourists that year was two days and nights, and average expenditures were determined for tourists in several categories. In this way the total expenditures of slightly more than $5 million were determined.

The reference to Panajachel by Aldous Huxley is found in *Beyond the Mexique Bay* (1934).

Chapter 9: *Destruction of the Material Bases for Indian Culture,* Carol A. Smith

The author carried out the occupational and wage surveys in Totonicapán in 1984. I was assisted by an elderly field assistant, who carried out a simple house-to-house census on current employment in his own hamlet, one of forty-eight traditional *cantones* of Totonicapán. Because this hamlet was one of the communities I sampled in a 1977 occupational survey of Totonicapán, I could compare its present condition with that of the past. My assistant also obtained current information on wages and prices. In the occupational census he obtained past (1980) occupations, as recalled by the informants, as well as present (1984) occupations, and these are the figures reported here. I compared the 1980 data with my 1977 data on the hamlet, however, to check the accuracy of the retrospective information. I found very little difference between my 1977 and 1980 occupational profiles and assume on this basis that the information for 1980, collected in 1984, was reasonably accurate. The 1980 price and wage data reported here are those remembered by informants in 1984 and reported to my assistant. I had previously collected price and wage data in Totonicapán in 1979 and 1980, and the figures from that period are similar to those reported here. The data recalled by informants are used because they are fuller than the 1980 figures.

In addition to the above-mentioned surveys, I resided in Totonicapán for five years while carrying out fieldwork on the regional economy intermittently between 1969 and 1979. For further information on weaving in Totonicapán see my article "Does a Commodity Economy Enrich the Few While Ruining the Masses?" (*Journal of Peasant Studies* 11 [1984]). Further information on the place of Totonicapán in the regional economy is found in "How Marketing Systems Affect Economic Opportunity in Agrarian Societies," in R. Halperin and J. Dow, eds., *Peasant Livelihood* (1977); and "Local History in Global Context: Social and Economic Transitions in Western Guatemala" (*Comparative Studies in Society and History* 26 [1984]).

Information on general economic conditions in Guatemala at the time of my survey (1984) is based on information on the death and destruction provided in several reports by Amnesty International (1981, 1983, 1984, 1985), Americas Watch (1982, 1984, 1985), and Cultural Survival (1983, 1984, 1985). Amnesty International reports that in April 1982, before the heaviest army sweeps were undertaken during the Ríos Montt regime, the Guatemalan Bishops Conference estimated that more than one million Guatemalans, one-seventh of Guatemala's total population (mostly in the western highlands, where the Maya Indian population is concentrated), were displaced. No one has been able to determine exactly what proportion of these people were killed as opposed to those displaced within or to countries outside Guatemala, though almost everyone recognizes that the actual loss of life was very high—at least 50,000 since the beginning of the counterinsurgency campaigns. The official Guatemalan censuses report a 22.9 percent loss of population between 1973 and 1981, and much counterinsurgency activity in these municipalities only began in 1981.

Beatriz Manz, in a report given to the Advisory Panel on Guatemala of the American Anthropological Association in 1983, described hundreds of thousands of people seeking work in the plantation area, which she had visited in the fall of that year. In addition, the Guatemalan Social Security Agency (IGSS) reported to Manz a decline of 32.5 percent of workers affiliated with that institution (up to 60 percent reduction in the western highlands in the fall of 1982), while the Colegio de Economistas of Guatemala reported an unemployment rate of 36 percent. Chris Krueger and Carol Smith heard similar reports about employment conditions throughout the western highlands in the fall of 1983.

More recent reports clarify what is being planned to institutionalize military control of the highland economy. An especially useful perspective on the second phase is provided by a book recently produced by the Guatemalan army, *Polos de desarrollo: Filosofía desarrollista* (1984), in which an entire development strategy is outlined. The consequences of this strategy are described by Chris Krueger and Kjell Enge in their 1985 report to the Washington Office on Latin America and by Michael Richards in "Cosmopolitan World View and Counterinsurgency in Guatemala" (*Anthropological Quarterly* 3 [1986]). Both of these sources also give information on the organization of the civil patrol system.

Chapter 10: The Struggle for Survival in the Mountains, Ricardo Falla

The question of credibility is crucial in accounts like the one in this chapter. How is it possible that a human institution, even an army, as in this case, can commit such horrible massacres? In 1983, I described such a massacre in *La masacre de la finca San Francisco, Huehuetenango, Guatemala (17 de julio de 1983)*. In that study special attention is given to the cognitive state of those massacred. That state changed from not believing that such a thing could befall them to the overwhelming realization that it was about to befall them.

The San Francisco massacre was easy to document because refugees from it became accessible to outsiders. But in struggles for survival in the mountains such as those dealt with here, the victims are not accessible to the outside world. That fact diminishes the credibility of accounts such as the one presented here, but the internal consistency of the testimonies cited gives them the irresistible force of truth. It becomes clear that the army's stategy was basically the same, whether in Finca San Francisco, Patzún, Rabinal, Alta Verapaz, or other Indian areas (my original article demonstrates this also for the Ixil and Ixcán areas).

The massacre at Chipiacul on April 26, 1982, is documented in Amnesty International, *Testimony on Guatemala;* and in the *Dallas Morning News,* May 16, 1982. The massacre at Agua Fría, Rabinal, on September 13, 1982, is reported by the Pro-Justice and Peace Committee to the United Nations Human Rights Commission (1983). The bombing of Las Pacayas, San Cristóbal Verapaz, in March 1982 is reported by Reggie Norton in "The Military Coup in Guatemala" (Washington Office on Latin America, 1982); and by Marlise Simmons in the *New York Times,* September 15, 1982. The Pro-Justice and Peace Committee mentions the machine-gun firing on Pambach from a helicopter on June 14, 1982.

The counterinsurgency methods described in this chapter are similar to those applied by the Allies in Malaya and Vietnam, as described by Robert Thompson, *Defeating Communist Insurgency* (London: Chatto and Windus, 1974). The similarities in such methods in Central America and Vietnam are explicitly drawn by Richard Allan White, *The Morass: United States Intervention in Central America.*

Chapter 11: *Mayas Aiding Mayas,* Duncan M. Earle

Historical and cultural backgrounds of peoples residing in the Chiapas-Guatemala border area are found in three volumes compiled by Mario Humberto Ruz, *Los legítimos hombres: Aproximación antropológica al grupo tojolabal* (1981, 1982, 1983). The collective *ejido* that accepted the Guatemalan refugees into its community is described in detail in my doctoral dissertation, "Cultural Logic and Ecology in Community Development: Failure and Success Cases Among Highland Maya" (SUNY Albany, 1985).

The most comprehensive account of the Guatemalan refugees is Beatriz Manz, *Refugees of a Hidden War: The Aftermath of the Counterinsurgency War in Guatemala* (Albany: SUNY Press, in press). The same author provides a summary of the refugee camps along the Chiapas border in "The Forest Camps in Eastern Chiapas" (*Cultural Survival Quarterly,* 1984). Two other published sources on the Guatemalan refugees in Mexico are Americas Watch, *Guatemalan Refugees in Mexico, 1980–1984;* and Sergio Aguayo, "El exodo centroamericano," *Foro 2000,* 1985.

Guatemalan refugees are studied along with other Central American refugees in Edelberto Torres-Rivas, *Report on the Conditions of the Central American Refugees and Migrants* (Washington D.C.: Center for Immigration Policy and Refugee Assistance, Georgetown University, 1985). How the Guatemalan refugees compare in numbers on a worldwide scale can be learned from U.S. Committee for Refugees, *World Refugee Survey* (Washington, D.C., 1984).

Chapter 12: *Conclusions,* Richard N. Adams

There is a very large body of literature on the Guatemalan Indian population. But as starters for the especially serious reader, Robert Wauchope, ed., *Handbook of Middle*

American Indians (Austin: University of Texas Press, 1969), vols. 6, 7, provides a good general introduction. The economic blockage the Indians confront is well described in Margarita Melville and Thomas Melville, *Guatemala: The Politics of Land Ownership.* Concerning attitudes between the ethnic groups see John Gillin, *The Culture of Security in San Carlos* (New Orleans: Middle American Research Institute, 16 [1947]); Melvin Tumin, *Caste in a Peasant Society* (Princeton, N.J.: Princeton University Press, 1947); and Kay B. Warren, *The Symbolism of Subordination: Indian Identity in a Guatemalan Town.* The colonial situation is summarized in Severo Martínez Palaez, *La patria del criollo: Ensayo de interpretatión de la realidad colonial guatemalteca* (Guatemala: Editorial Universitaria, 1970).

The revolutionary situation in contemporary Guatemala is well described in George Black, Norma Chinchilla, and Milton Jamail, *Garrison Guatemala.* On the Salvadorean massacre of Indians in 1932, see Thomas P. Anderson, *Matanza: El Salvador Communist Revolt of 1932* (Lincoln: University of Nebraska Press, 1971).

The principal works describing the Indian revolution and state violence are Shelton H. Davis and Julie Hodson, *Witnesses to Political Violence in Guatemala: The Suppression of a Rural Development Movement;* Ricardo Falla, *Voices of the Survivors: The Massacre at Finca San Francisco, Guatemala;* Elizabeth Burgos, *I, Rigoberta Menchú: An Indian Woman in Guatemala;* Víctor Montejo, *Testimony: Death of a Guatemalan Village;* Mario Payeras, *Days of the Jungle;* Gabriel Aguilera Peralta, "The Massacre at Panzós and Capitalist Development in Guatemala" (*Monthly Review* 31 [1979]); Arturo Arias, "Historia del movimiento indígena en Guatemala, 1970–82," in Daniel Camacho and Rafael Menjívar, eds., *Movimientos populares en Centro América, 1970–1980* (San Jose, Costa Rica: EDUCA, Centroamérica, 1985); "The Indian Peoples and the Guatemalan Revolution" (*Compañero* 5 [English section 1985]). Concerning the level of violence in general, see Gabriel Aguilera Peralta and Romero Imery, *Dialéctica del terror en Guatemala* (San Jose, Costa Rica: EDUCA, Centroamérica, 1981).

Selected Bibliography

Sources on the Guatemalan crisis are extensive, and no attempt is made here to include them all. The works listed below were selected primarily because they contain references either to Indians or to recent political developments in Guatemala. Many important Spanish sources have been omitted. Additional references appear in the Authors' Notes on Sources.

News Services

Central America [Latin-American weekly report]. London.

Central America Newspak [biweekly news and resource update]. Central America Resource Center. Austin, Texas.

Central American Report. Guatemala: Infopress Centroamericana.

Guatemala News in Brief. New York: Americas Watch Committee.

Guatemala Watch. Guatemala: Foundation for the Development of Guatemala.

Information on Guatemala. Washington, D.C.: Enfoprensa USA.

Latin America Regional Report [Mexico and Central America and Latin America weekly report]. London: Latin American Newsletters.

Mesoamerica. San Jose, Costa Rica: Institute for Central American Studies.

Mexico and Central America. Oakland, Calif.: Information Services on Latin America.

Report on the Americas. Berkeley, Calif.: North American Congress on Latin America [NACLA].

Report on Guatemala. Washington D.C.: National Network in Solidarity with the People of Guatemala [NISGUA].

Reports

American Association for the International Commission of Jurists, New York.
  Guatemala: A New Beginning. 1987.
American Friends Service Committee, Philadelphia.
  Pekenham N. *Guatemala, 1983*. 1983.
Americas Watch Committee, New York.
  Human Rights in Guatemala: No Neutrals Allowed. 1982.
  Creating a Desolation and Calling It Peace. 1983.

Guatemala: A Nation of Prisoners. 1984.
Guatemalan Refugees in Mexico, 1980–1984. 1984.
Civil Patrols in Guatemala. 1986.
Human Rights in Guatemala During President Cerezo's First Year. 1986.
Amnesty International, London.
   Guatemala: A Government Program of Political Murder. 1981.
   Testimony on Guatemala. 1982.
   Guatemala: Massive Extrajudicial Executions in Rural Areas Under the Government of General Efraín Ríos Montt. 1983.
   Disappearances in Guatemala Under the Government of General Oscar Humerto Mejía Victores. 1985.
Annual Review of Anthropology, Stanford University, Stanford, Calif.
   Smith, C. A., and J. Boyer. *Central America Since 1979: Part 1.* 1987.
Canadian Inter-Church Fact-finding Mission to Guatemala and Mexico, Toronto.
   Why Don't They Hear Us? 1983.
Center for Strategic and International Studies, Georgetown University, Washington, D.C.
   Sereseres C. Latin American Insurgencies: The Highland War in Guatemala. 1985.
Concerned Guatemala Scholars, Brooklyn, N.Y.
   Guatemala: Dare to Struggle, Dare to Win. 1981.
Field Foundation, New York.
   Lernoux, P. *Fear and Hope: Toward Political Democracy in Central America.* 1984.
General Assembly of the Presbyterian Church, U.S.A., New York.
   Adventure and Hope: Christians and the Crisis in Central America. 1983.
Guatemalan Church in Exile, Managua, Nicaragua.
   Guatemala, "A New Way of Life:" The Development Poles. 1984.
   Development: The New Face of War. 1986.
Guatemalan Patriotic Unity Committee [URNG], San Francisco, Calif.
   Guatemala: The People Unite. 1982.
Guatemala Scholars Network, Houston, Texas.
   Response to the Report by the National Bipartisan Commission on Central America. 1984.
   Reports from the Network. 1987.
Guatemala's Guerrilla Army of the Poor [EGP], San Francisco.
   Compañero. Vol. 1. 1982.
   Compañero. Vol. 2. N.d.
Infopress Centroamericana, Guatemala City.
   Guatemala, 1986: The Year of Promises. 1987.
Institute for Policy Studies, Washington, D.C.
   Arnson, C.; D. Miller; and R. Seeman. *Background Information on Guatemala, the Armed Forces, and U.S. Military Assistance.* 1981.
   Arnson, C., and F. Montealegre. *Background Information on Guatemala, Human Rights and U.S. Military Assistance.* 1983.
Inter-American Commission on Human Rights, Washington, D.C.
   Report on the Situation of Human Rights in the Republic of Guatemala. 1981, 1983, 1985.
Inter-American Committee on Agricultural Development, Washington, D.C.
   Land Tenure and Socioeconomic Development of the Agricultural Sector: Guatemala. 1975.
Inter-American Foundation, Washington, D.C.
   Annis, S.; S. Cox; and B. Sogge. *Findings of Guatemalan Reassessment Team: Memorandum.* 1984.

International Work Group for Indigenous Affairs, Copenhagen.
   The Massacre at Panzós. 1978.
LASA Forum, Latin American Studies Association.
   Concerning the Kissinger Commission Report. 1984.
National Bipartisan Commission on Central America, Washington, D.C.
   The Kissinger Report: Guatemala. 1984.
National Lawyers Guild, New York.
   Guatemala: Repression and Resistance. 1980.
Oxfam America, Boston.
   Davis, Shelton H., and J. Hodson. *Witness to Political Violence in Guatemala.* 1982.
Permanent People's Tribunal, San Francisco, Calif.
   Guatemala: Tyranny on Trial. 1984.
Rand Corporation, Santa Monica, Calif.
   Ronfeldt, D. *Geopolitics, Security, and U.S. Strategy in the Caribbean Basin.* 1983.
   Gonzalez, E.; B. M. Jenkins; D. Ronfeldt; and C. Sereseres. *U.S. Policy for Central America: A Briefing.* 1984.
Resource Center, Albuquerque, N.Mex.
   Guatemala: The Politics of Counterinsurgency. 1986.
School of Advanced International Studies, Johns Hopkins University, Baltimore, Md.
   Sereseres, C. *The Guatemalan Legacy: Radical Challengers and Military Politics.* 1983.
   Report on Guatemala. 1985.
Spokesman, Nottingham, England.
   Holland, S., M.P., and D. Anderson, M.P. *Kissinger's Kingdom? A Counter-Report on Central America.* 1984.
Survival International, London.
   Nelson, C. W., and K. I. Taylor. *Witness to Genocide: The Present Situation of Indians in Guatemala.* 1983.
U.S. Agency for International Development, Guatemala.
   Land and Labor in Guatemala. 1982.
   Programa de Ayuda para los Vecinos del Altiplano [PAVA]. *Final Report on Guatemalan Displaced Persons Needs Survey Covering Huehuetenango, El Quiché, Western Petén, and Playa Grande.* 1984.
U.S. State Department, Washington, D.C.
   Country Report on Human Rights Practices, 1977–86.
Washington Office on Latin America, Washington, D.C.
   Quan, J. *Guatemalan Agriculture.* 1981.
   Krueger, C., and K. Enge. *Security and Development Conditions in the Guatemalan Highlands.* 1985.
   Booth, J. A. *The 1985 Guatemalan Elections: Will the Military Relinquish Power?* 1985.
   Krueger, C. *The Guatemalan Highlands: Democratic Transition or the Continuation of War.* 1987.

Articles in Periodicals

Albizurez, A. "Struggles and Experiences of the Guatemalan Trade Union Movement." *Latin American Perspectives* 7 (1980): 145–59.
Aguilera Peralta, G. "The Massacre at Panzós and Capitalist Development in Guatemala." *Monthly Review* 31 (1979): 13–23.
———. "Terror and Violence as Weapons of Counterinsurgency in Guatemala." *Latin American Perspectives* 5 (1980): 91–113.

———. "The Process of Militarization of the Guatemalan State." *Latin American Research Unit Studies* 5 (September 1982).

Berryman, P. "One Year of Cerezo 'Civilianization." *Update Central America,* 1987.

Black, George. "Under the Gun." *NACLA Report on the Americas* 19 (1985): 10–23.

Boloyra, E. A. "Reactionary Despotism in Central America." *Journal of Latin American Studies* 15 (1983): 295–319.

Bonpane, B. "The Church and Revolutionary Struggle in Central America." *Latin American Perspectives* 7 (1989): 178–89.

Booth, J. A. "A Guatemalan Nightmare: Levels of Political Violence, 1966–1972." *Journal of Interamerican Studies and World Affairs* 22 (1980): 195–225.

Bossen, L. "Plantations and Labor Force Discrimination in Guatemala." *Current Anthropology* 23 (1982): 263–68.

Brockett, C. D. "Malnutrition, Public Policy, and Agrarian Change in Guatemala." *Journal of Inter-American Studies and World Affairs* 26 (1984): 477–97.

———. "The Right to Food and United States Policy in Guatemala." *Human Rights Quarterly,* 1984, 366–80.

Chace, J. "Deeper into the Mire." *New York Review,* 1984, 40–48.

Chinchilla, N. "Class Struggle in Central America: Background and Overview." *Latin American Perspectives* 7 (1980): 2–23.

———. "Guatemala: A Different Revolution." *Cultural Survival Quarterly* 7 (1983): 36–37.

———. "Guatemala: What Difference Does a Civilian Make?" *Center for the Study of the Americas,* 1986.

Davis, Shelton H. "The Social Roots of Political Violence in Guatemala." *Cultural Survival Quarterly* (1983): 4–11.

———. "The Social Consequences of 'Development' Aid in Guatemala." *Cultural Survival Quarterly* 7 (1983): 32–35.

Delgado, Enrique. "The Impact of the Economic Crisis in Central America and in Guatemala." *Latin American and Caribbean Center, Occasional Papers Series,* 12 (1985): 1–47.

Delli Sante, A. "Crisis in Guatemala: Repression, Refugees, and Responsibilities." *Our Socialism* 1 (1983).

Dennis, P. A.; G. S. Elbow; and P. L. Heller. "Development Under Fire: The Playa Grande Colonization Project in Guatemala." *Central America Writer's Bulletin* 7 (1986): 1–33.

Diener, P. "The Tears of St. Anthony: Ritual and Revolution in Eastern Guatemala." *Latin American Perspectives* 5 (1978): 92–119.

Dinges, J. "Why We Are in Guatemala." *Inquiry,* November 1982.

Driever, Steven L. "Insurgency in Guatemala." *Focus,* 1985.

Gleijeses, P. "Guatemala: The Struggle for Democracy." *Latin American Series,* 1986.

———. "The Guatemalan Silence." *New Republic,* June 10, 1985, 20–23.

Goldman, F. "The Girls of Guatemala." *Esquire,* 1981.

———. "Guatemalan Death Masque." *Harper's* 272 (1986): 56–63.

Handy, J. "Resurgent Democracy and the Guatemalan Military." *Journal of Latin American Studies* 18 (1986): 383–408.

James, R. "Guatemala: The March Coup and the Civil War." *Canadian Forum,* August 1982.

Johnson, V. "The Agony of Guatemala." *Sign* 60 (1981).

Kinzer, S. "Walking the Tighrope in Guatemala." *New York Times Magazine,* November 9, 1986, 32–38.

LeoGrande, W. M. "Through the Looking Glass: The Report of the National Bipartisan Commission on Central America." *World Policy Journal* 1 (1984): 251–84.

Lovell, W. George. "From Conquest to Counter-Insurgency." *Cultural Survival Quarterly* 9 (1985): 46–49.

Maloney, T. "The Social Impact of the Franja Transversal del Norte Program in North Central Guatemala." *Natural Resource Sociology Research Lab* 13 (1982): 412–32.

Martin, D. "Changing Masks: Four Decades of Military Rule in Guatemala." *Sojourners*, 1983.

Melville, T. R. "The Catholic Church in Guatemala, 1944–1982." *Cultural Survival Quarterly* 7 (1983): 23–27.

Millet, Richard. "Guatemala: Progress and Paralysis." *Current History*, March 1985.

———. "Guatemala's Painful Progress." *Current History*, December 1986.

Nairn, Allan. "The Guns of Guatemala: The Merciless Mission of Ríos Montt's Army." *New Republic* 14 (1983).

———. "Endgame." *NACLA Report on the Americas*, 19 (1984): 19–55.

———, and Jean-Marie Simon. "Bureaucracy of Death: Guatemala's Civilian Government Faces the Enemy Within." *New Republic*, June 30, 1986, 13–17.

Paige, Jeffrey M. "Social Theory and Peasant Revolution in Vietnam and Guatemala." *Theory and Society* 12 (1983): 699–737.

Payeras, M. "The Guatemalan Army and U.S. Policy in Central America." *Monthly Review* 37 (1986): 14–20.

Peckenham, Nancy. "Land Settlement in the Petén." *Latin American Perspectives* 7 (1980): 169–77.

Perera, Victor. "Can Guatemala Change?" *New York Review of Books*, August 14, 1986, 39–43.

Petras, J. F., and M. H. Morely. "Anti-Communism in Guatemala: Washington's Alliance with Generals and Death Squads." *Socialist Register*, 1984, 261–277.

Power, J. "Guatemala: Stirrings of Change." *World Today* 42 (1986): 31–36.

Premo, D. L. "Political Assassination in Guatemala: A Case of Institutionalized Terror." *Journal of Inter-American Studies and World Affairs* 23 (1981): 429–56.

Richards, M. "Cosmopolitan World View and Counterinsurgency in Guatemala." *Anthropological Quarterly* 3 (1986): 90–107.

Riding, A. "Guatemala: State of Siege." *New York Times Magazine*, August 24, 1980.

Rubenberg, C. A. "Israel and Guatemala: Arms, Advice and Counterinsurgency." *Middle East Report* 140 (1986): 16–44.

Simons, Marlise. "Guatemala: The Coming Danger." *Foreign Policy* 43 (1981): 93–103.

Smith, C. A. "Beyond Dependency Theory: National and Regional Patterns of Underdevelopment in Guatemala." *American Ethnologist* 5 (1978): 574–617.

———. "Local History in Global Context: Social and Economic Transitions in Western Guatemala." *Comparative Studies in Society and History* 26 (1984): 193–228.

Stoll, David. "Guatemala: The New Jerusalem of the Americas?" *Cultural Survival Quarterly* 7 (1983): 28–31.

Torres Rivas, E. "Guatemala—Crisis and Political Violence." *NACLA Report on the Americas* 14 (1980): 16–27.

Wasserstrom, R. "Revolution in Guatemala: Peasants and Politics Under the Arbenz Government." *Comparative Studies in Society and History* 17 (1975): 443–78.

Weeks, John. "An Interpretation of the Central American Crisis." *Latin American Research Review* 21 (1986): 31–54.

Woodward, R. L., Jr. "The Rise and Decline of Liberalism in Central America: Historical Perspectives on the Contemporary Crisis." *Journal of Interamerican Studies and World Affairs* 26 (1984): 291–312.

Books and Articles in Books

Adams, Richard N. *Crucifixion by Power: Essays on Guatemalan National Social Structure, 1944–1966.* Austin: University of Texas Press, 1970.

Anderson, Thomas P. *Politics in Central America: Guatemala, El Salvador, Honduras, and Nicaragua.* New York: Praeger, 1983.

Barry, Tom. *Roots of Rebellion: Land and Hunger in Central America.* Albuquerque, N.Mex.: Resource Center, 1987.

————, and Deb Preusch. *The Central America Fact Book.* New York: Grove Press, 1986.

Berryman, Phillip. *The Religious Roots of Rebellion: Christians in Central American Revolutions.* New York: Orbis Books, 1984.

Black, George, with Milton Jamail and Norma Stoltz Chinchilla. *Garrison Guatemala.* New York: Monthly Review Press, 1984.

Bowen, Gordon L. "Guatemala: The Origins and Development of State Terrorism." In D. E. Schulz and D. H. Graham, eds. *Revolution and Counterrevolution in Central America and the Caribbean.* Boulder, Colo.: Westview Press, 1984.

Calvert, P. *Guatemala: A Nation in Turmoil.* Boulder, Colo.: Westview Press, 1985.

Castellanos Cambranes, Julio. "Origins of the Crisis of the Established Order in Guatemala." In S. C. Ropp and J. A. Morris, eds. *Central America: Crisis and Adaptation.* Albuquerque: University of New Mexico Press, 1984.

Coleman, Kenneth M., and George C. Herring. *The Central American Crisis: Sources of Conflict and the Failure of U.S. Policy.* Wilmington, Del.: Scholarly Resources, 1985.

Davis, Shelton H. "State Violence and Agrarian Crisis in Guatemala: The Roots of the Indian Peasant Rebellion." In Martin Diskin, ed. *Trouble in Our Backyard: Central America and the United States in the Eighties.* New York: Pantheon Books, 1983.

————, and Julie Hodson. *Witnesses to Political Violence in Guatemala: The Suppression of a Rural Development Movement.* Boston: Oxfam America, 1982.

Dixon, Marlene, and Susanne Jonas. *Revolution and Intervention in Central America.* San Francisco: Synthesis Publications, 1983.

Early, John. *The Demographic Structure and Evolution of a Peasant Society: The Guatemalan Population.* Boca Raton: Florida Atlantic University Press, 1982.

Feinberg, Richard E., ed. *Central America: International Dimensions of the Crisis.* New York: Holmes & Meier Publishers, 1982.

Fletcher, Lehman B., et al. *Guatemala's Economic Development: The Role of Agriculture.* Ames: Iowa State University Press, 1970.

Fried, Jonathan; Marvin E. Gettleman; Deborah T. Levenson; and Nancy Peckenham, eds. *Guatemala in Rebellion: Unfinished History.* New York: Grove Press, 1983.

Galeano, Eduardo. *Guatemala: Occupied Country.* New York: Monthly Review Press, 1969.

Gleijeses, Piero. "Perspectives of a Regime Transformation in Guatemala." In W. Grabendorff, H. Krumwiede, and J. Todt, eds. *Political Change in Central America: Internal and External Dimensions.* Boulder, Colo.: Westview Press, 1984.

Grabendorff, Wolf; Heinrich-W. Krumwiede; and Jorg Todt, eds. *Political Change in Central America: Internal and External Dimensions.* Boulder, Colo.: Westview Press, 1984.

Handy, Jim. *Gift of the Devil: A History of Guatemala.* Boston: South End Press, 1984.

Hawkins, John. *Inverse Images: The Meaning of Culture, Ethnicity, and Family in Postcolonial Guatemala.* Albuquerque: University of New Mexico Press, 1984.

Helms, Mary. *Middle America: A Culture History of Heartland and Frontier.* Englewood Cliffs, N.J.: Prentice-Hall, 1975.

Immerman, Richard H. *The CIA in Guatemala: The Foreign Policy of Intervention.* Austin: University of Texas Press, 1982.

Jonas, Susanne. "Guatemala: Land of Eternal Struggle." In R. G. Chilcote and J. C. Edelstein, eds. *Latin America: The Struggle with Dependency and Beyond.* New York: Schenkman/John Wiley, 1974.

———, and David Tobis, eds. *Guatemala.* Berkeley, Calif.: North American Congress on Latin America, 1974.

Jones, Chester Lloyd. *Guatemala, Past and Present.* Minneapolis: University of Minnesota Press, 1940.

Kinzer, Stephen, and Stephen Schlesinger. *Bitter Fruit: The Untold Story of the American Coup in Guatemala.* Garden City, N.Y.: Doubleday & Co., 1981.

LaFeber, Walter. *Inevitable Revolutions: The United States in Central America.* New York: W. W. Norton & Co., 1983.

Leiken, Robert S. *Central America: Anatomy of Conflict.* New York: Pergamon Press, 1984.

McClintock, Michael. *The American Connection, Volume Two: State Terror and Popular Resistance in Guatemala.* London: Zed Books, 1985.

Melville, Thomas, and Marjorie Melville. *Guatemala: The Politics of Land Ownership.* New York: Free Press, 1971.

———. "Oppression by Any Other Name: Power in Search of Legitimacy in Guatemala." In J. Nash, J. Corradi, and H. Spalding, Jr., eds. *Ideology and Social Change in Latin America.* New York: Gordon and Breach, 1977.

Nuccio, Richard A. *What's Wrong, Who's Right in Central America? A Citizen's Guide.* New York: Facts on File Publications, 1986.

Painter, James. *Guatemala: False Hope, False Freedom.* London: Latin America Bureau, 1987.

Payeras, Mario. *Days of the Jungle: The Testimony of a Guatemalan Guerrillero, 1972–1976.* Translated by George Black. New York: Monthly Review Press, 1983.

Pearce, Jenny. *Under the Eagle: U.S. Intervention in Central America and the Caribbean.* London: Latin American Bureau, 1981.

Pearson, Neal H. "Guatemala: The Peasant Union Movement." In H. Landsberger, ed. *Latin American Peasant Movements.* Ithaca, N.Y.: Cornell University Press, 1969

Perera, Victor. *Rites: A Guatemalan Boyhood.* New York: Harcourt Brace Jovanovich, 1986.

Plant, Roger. *Guatemala: Unnatural Disaster.* London: Latin American Bureau, 1978.

Schoultz, Lars. "Guatemala: Social Change and Personal Conflict." In Martin M Diskin, ed. *Trouble in Our Backyard: Central America and the United States in the Eighties.* New York: Pantheon Books, 1983.

Smith, Carol A. "Causes and Consequences of Central-Place Types in Western Guatemala." In *Regional Analysis.* Vol. 1. New York: Academic Press, 1976.

———. "Labor and International Capital in the Making of a Peripheral Social Formation: Economic Transformations in Guatemala, 1850–1980." In C. Bergquist, ed. *Labor in the Capitalist World Economy.* New York: Sage, 1984.

Stanford Central America Action Network. *Revolution in Central America.* Boulder, Colo.: Westview Press, 1983.

Torres-Rivas, Edelberto. "Problems of Democracy and Counterrevolution in Guatemala." In Wolf Grabendorff, Heinrich-W. Krumwiede, and Jorg Todt, eds. *Political Change in Central America: Internal and External Dimensions.* Boulder, Colo.: Westview Press, 1984.

Trudeau, Robert, and Lars Schoultz. "Guatemala." In M. J. Blachman, W. M. LeoGrande, and K. E. Sharpe, eds. *Confronting Revolution: Security Through Diplomacy in Central America.* New York: Pantheon Books, 1986.

Weaver, Jerry L. "Guatemala: The Politics of a Frustrated Revolution." In H. J. Wiarda and H. F. Kline, eds. *Latin American Politics and Development*. Boulder, Colo.: Westview Press, 1985.

Weeks, John. *The Economies of Central America*. New York: Holmes & Meier, 1985.

West, Robert C., and John P. Augelli. *Middle America: Its Lands and Peoples*. Englewood Cliffs, N.J.: Prentice-Hall, 1966.

White, Richard Alan. *The Morass: United States Intervention in Central America*. New York: Harper & Row, 1984.

Wiarda, Howard J., ed. *Rift and Revolution: The Central American Embroglio*. Washington, D.C.: American Enterprise Institute for Public Policy Research, 1984.

Williams, Robert G. *Export Agriculture and the Crisis in Central America*. Chapel Hill: University of North Carolina Press, 1986.

Wolf, Eric. *Sons of the Shaking Earth*. Chicago: University of Chicago Press, 1959.

Woodward, Ralph Lee, Jr. *Central America: A Nation Divided*. New York: Oxford University Press, 1976.

Zinser, Adolfo Aguilar. "Mexico and the Guatemalan Crisis." In R. Fagan and O. Pellicer, eds. *The Future of Central America: Policy Choices for the U.S. and Mexico*. Stanford, Calif.: Stanford University Press, 1983.

Sources on the Indians—Books and Articles

Adams, Richard N. *Political Changes in Guatemalan Indian Communities: A Symposium*. Middle American Research Institute, Vol. 24. New Orleans: Tulane University, 1974.

Annis, Sheldon. *God and Production in a Guatemalan Town*. Austin: University of Texas Press, 1987.

Anthony, Angela B. "The Minority That Is a Majority: Guatemala's Indians." In S. Jonas and D. Tobis, eds. *Guatemala*. Berkeley, Calif.: North American Congress on Latin America, 1974.

Bossen, Laurel. *The Redivision of Labor: Women and Economic Choice in Four Guatemalan Communities*. Albany: SUNY Press, 1984.

Burgos-Debray, Elisabeth, ed. *I, Rigoberta Menchú: An Indian Woman in Guatemala*. London: Verso Editions, 1984.

Carmack, Robert M. *The Quiché Mayas of Utatlán: The Evolution of a Highland Guatemala Kingdom*. Norman: University of Oklahoma Press, 1981.

———. "Indians and the Guatemalan Revolution." *Cultural Survival Quarterly*, 1983.

Clay, Jason, ed. *Death and Disorder in Guatemala*. Cambridge, Mass.: Cultural Survival, 1983.

Colby, Benjamin N., and Lore M. Colby. *The Daykeeper: The Life and Discourse of an Ixil Diviner*. Cambridge. Mass.: Harvard University Press, 1981.

Conde, Daniel. "Guatemalan Refugees in Mexico." *Cultural Survival Quarterly*, 1983.

Cook, Garrett W. "Quichean Folk Theology and Southern Maya Supernaturalism." In G. Gossen, ed. *Symbol and Meaning Beyond the Closed Community*. Albany, N.Y.: Institute for Mesoamerican Studies, 1986.

Davis, Wade. "Observations from Guatemala." *Cultural Survival Quarterly*, 1983.

Earle, Duncan M. "The Metaphor of the Day in Quiche-Maya Daily Life." In G. Gossen, ed. *Symbols Beyond the Closed Community: Essays on Mesoamerican Thought*. Albany, N.Y.: Institute for Mesoamerican Studies, 1986.

Edmonson, Munro S., trans. *The Book of Counsel: The Popol Vuh of the Quiche Maya of Guatemala*. New Orleans: Tulane University Press, 1971.

Falla, Ricardo. *Voices of the Survivors: The Massacre at Finca San Francisco, Guatemala*. Cambridge, Mass.: Cultural Survival and Anthropology Resource Center, 1983.

Frank, Luisa, and Philip Wheaton. *Indian Guatemala, Path to Liberation: The Role of Christians in the Indian Process.* Washington, D.C.: EPICA Task Force, 1984.

García, Christian. Guatemalan Refugees in Chiapas." *Cultural Survival Quarterly,* 1983.

Goetz, Delia, and Sylvanus G. Morley, trans. *Popol Vuh: The Sacred Book of the Ancient Quiché Maya.* From the Spanish translation by Adrián Recinos. Norman: University of Oklahoma Press, 1950.

Guatemala! The Terrible Repression and Its Roots in the U.S. National Security State. New York: Four Arrows, 1981.

Guatemala! The Horror and the Hope. York, Pa.: Four Arrows, 1982.

Hinshaw, Robert. *Panajachel: A Guatemalan Town in Thirty-Year Perspective.* Pittsburgh, Pa.: University of Pittsburgh Press, 1975.

Kendall, Carl; John Hawkins, and Laurel Bossen, eds. *Heritage of Conquest: Thirty Years Later.* Albuquerque: University of New Mexico Press, 1983.

Lovell, W. George. "Surviving Conquest: The Guatemalan Indian in Historical Perspective. *Latin American Research Review,* in press.

Manz, Beatriz. *Refugees of a Hidden War: The Aftermath of the Counterinsurgency War in Guatemala.* Albany, N.Y.: SUNY Press, in press.

Montejo, Victor. *Testimony: Death of a Guatemalan Village.* Willimantic, Conn.: Curbstone Press, 1987.

Nash, Manning, ed. *Social Anthropology.* In Robert Wauchope, ed. *Handbook of Middle American Indians.* Vol. 6. Austin: University of Texas Press, 1967.

Pop Caal, Antonio. "The Situation of Indian Peoples in Guatemala." *Akwesasne Notes* 7 (1975).

Scotchmer, David G. "Convergence of the Gods: Comparing Traditional Maya and Christian Maya Cosmologies." In G. Gossen, ed. *Symbol and Meaning Beyond the Closed Community.* Albany, N.Y.: Institute for Mesoamerican Studies, 1986.

Sexton, James, trans. and ed. *Son of Tecún Umán: A Maya Indian Tells His Life Story.* Tucson: University of Arizona Press, 1981.

———. *Campesino: The Diary of a Guatemalan Indian.* Tucson: University of Arizona Press, 1985.

Shaw, Mary, ed. *According to Our Ancestors: Folklore Texts from Guatemala and Honduras.* Guatemala: Summer Institute of Linguistics, 1971.

Smith, Carol A. *Indian Class and Class Consciousness in Prerevolutionary Guatemala.* Working Paper 162, Latin American Program. Washington, D.C.: Wilson Center, 1984.

———. "Culture and Community: The Language of Class in Guatemala." *The Year Left* 2 (1987).

Smith, Waldemar, R. "Beyond the Plural Society: Economics and Ethnicity in Middle American Towns." *Ethnology* 14 (1975).

———. *The Fiesta System and Economic Change.* New York: Columbia University Press, 1977.

Stephen, David, and Philip Wearne. *Central America's Indians.* London: Minority Rights Group, 1984.

Tarn, Nathaniel, and Martin Prechtel. "Constant Inconstancy: The Feminine Principle in Atiteco Mythology." In G. Gossen, ed. *Symbol and Meaning: Beyond the Closed Community.* Albany, N.Y.: Institute for Mesoamerican Studies, 1986.

Tax, Sol, et al. *Heritage of Conquest: The Ethnology of Middle America.* Glencoe, N.Y.: Free Press, 1952.

Tedlock, Barbara. *Time and the Highland Maya.* Albuquerque: University of New Mexico Press, 1982.

———. "On a Mountain Road in the Dark: Encounters with the Quiché-Maya Culture

Hero." In G. Gossen, ed. *Symbol and Meaning: Beyond the Closed Community.* Albany, N.Y.: Institute for Mesoamerican Studies, 1986.

Tedlock, Dennis, trans. *Popol Vuh: The Definitive Edition of the Mayan Book of the Dawn of Life and the Glories of Gods and Kings.* New York: Simon and Schuster, 1985.

————. "Creation in the Popol Vuh: A Hermeneutical Approach." In G. Gossen, ed. *Symbol and Meaning: Beyond the Closed Community.* Albany, N.Y.: Institute for Mesoamerican Studies, 1986.

Vogt, Evon Z., ed. *Ethnology, Part One.* In Robert Wauchope, ed. *Handbook of Middle American Indians.* Vol. 7. Austin: University of Texas Press, 1969.

Warren, Kay B. *The Symbolism of Subordination: Indian Identity in a Guatemalan Town.* Austin: University of Texas Press, 1978.

Guatemala—Unpublished Materials

Casaverde, R. Juvenal. "Jacaltec Social and Political Structure." Ph.D. dissertation, University of Rochester, 1976.

Cook, Garrett W. "Supernaturalism, Cosmos, and Cosmogony in Quichean Expresive Culture." Ph.D. dissertation, SUNY Albany, 1981.

Dow, Leslie. "Ethnicity and Modernity in the Central Highlands of Guatemala." P.h.D. dissertation, University of Michigan, 1981.

Goldin, Liliana R. "Organizing the World Through the Market: A Symbolic Analysis of Markets and Exchange in the Western Highlands of Guatemala." Ph.D. dissertation, SUNY Albany, 1985.

Hurwicz, Margo-Lea. "Values in the Context of Sociocultural Change: A Case from Western Highland Guatemala." Ph.D. dissertation, University of California at Los Angeles, 1982.

Koizumi, Junji. "Symbol and Context: A Study of Self and Action in a Guatemalan Culture." Ph.D. dissertation, Stanford University, 1981.

Lutz, Sally S. "Guatemala: Conquest and Reconquest, 1524–1985." Manuscript. Darmouth College, 1985.

Pansini, Joseph J. "'El Pilar': A Plantation Microcosm of Guatemalan Ethnicity." Ph.D. dissertation, University of Rochester, 1977.

Riklin, Scott. "Guatemala: The Revolution Approaches." Manuscript. Rye, N.Y., 1980.

Schmid, Lester. "The Role of Migratory Labor in the Economic Development of Guatemala." Ph.D. dissertation, University of Winsconsin, 1967.

Trudeau, R. H. "Democracy in Guatemala: Present Status, Future Prospects." Paper delivered at meeting of Latin American Studies Association, Boston, 1986.

Veblen, Thomas. "The Ecological, Cultural, and Historical Bases of Forest Preservation in Totonicapán, Guatemala." Ph.D. dissertation, University of California, Berkeley, 1975.

Watanabe, John. "We Who Are Here: The Cultural Conventions of Ethnic Identity in a Guatemalan Indian Village, 1937–1980." Ph.D. dissertation, Harvard University, 1984.

The Contributors and Their Chapters

Adams, Richard N. Richard Adams (chapter 12) received the Ph.D. in anthropology from Yale University in 1951 and has since been on the faculty of Michigan State University and the University of Texas, Austin. He is currently Rapaport Centennial Professor of Liberal Arts and Director of the Institute of Latin American Studies in the University of Texas, Austin. He has served as Research Ethnologist for the Smithsonian Institution, Scientist for the World Health Organization; Project Adviser for the Ford Foundation; Fellow at the Center for Advanced Studies in the Behavioral Sciences; and Visiting Professor and Researcher in the University of California, Berkeley; the Federal University of Rio de Janeiro; the Universidad Iberoamericana, Mexico; the Universidad de São Paulo, Brazil; the Australian National University, Canberra; and the Colegio de Michoacán, Mexico.

Adams has served as consultant for many public and private agencies (e.g., the Peace Corps, Education and World Affairs, the Ford Foundation, U.S. AID, and the World Bank) and has received research grants from the Social Science Research Council, the Ford Foundation, the Guggenheim Fellowship, the U.S. State Department, the U.S. Department of Transportation, and others. He has provided expert testimony before a subcommittee of the U.S. Senate Committee on Foreign Affairs. He is an internationally recognized authority on systems of power and is one of anthropology's foremost students of Latin America. He has been honored as President of the American Anthropological Association, Fellow and Chairman of a section of the American Association for the Advancement of Science, President of the Society for Applied Anthropology, and President of the Latin American Studies Association. The results of his research have been published in eleven books, four other volumes of which he is editor, and about one hundred articles in scientific journals.

Adams has carried out field research in most of the Latin-American countries, his country of special focus being Guatemala. He was continuously resident in Guatemala from 1950 to 1956 and has subsequently lived there part of every year up to the present, except for the period 1980 to 1983. Thus his knowledge of Guatemalan society is based on many years of direct contact as well as intensive field investigations. His books and articles on Guatemala cover a wide variety of topics, including an Indian community study, a survey of ladino culture, a comparative study of political change in several Indian communities, and his best-known work, a comprehensive analysis of changes in Guatemalan national society, *Crucifixion by Power: Essays on Guatemalan National Social Structure, 1944–1966.* He continues to investigate and publish on Guatemala, and is currently preparing a work on Indians and politics in Central America.

Annis, Sheldon. Sheldon Annis (chapter 6) earned the M.A. in social sciences and urban studies and the Ph.D. (1985) in geography from the University of Chicago. While he was at Chicago, he was also trained in anthropology under the direction of Sol Tax, and much of his research has been of an applied-anthropology nature. Between 1976 and 1980 he lived in Guatemala, evaluated development projects for U.S. AID, the OAS, the

World Bank, the UN, Project Hope, and other organizations. In that capacity he worked on development projects in primary health care, family planning, rural development, nutrition, potable-water services, bilingualism, and tourism. From 1981 to 1985 he was program officer and then senior research officer for the Inter-American Foundation. He supervised and evaluated research on grass-roots development projects in many Latin-American countries and edited the journal *Grassroots Development*. Currently he is a visiting lecturer at Princeton University, and a fellow at the Overseas Development Council, where he is writing a book on the relationship between grass-roots organizations and the public sector based on fieldwork in eastern Costa Rica, Mexico City, northeastern Brazil, and Cass County, Indiana.

Annis lectures frequently at major universities and government agencies in the United States and has delivered many papers on geographic and international topics at scientific conferences. He is the author of nine journal articles and editor of a book, *Direct to the Poor: A Reader in Grassroots Development* (1987). A book based on his doctoral research was published by the University of Texas Press in 1987. Entitled *God and Production in a Guatemalan Town*, the book provides the most closely argued case to date on the relationship between economic activity and religious belief in Guatemala. Annis's chapter in this book concerns the same town described in that book, San Antonio Aguas Calientes, and is based on the research that went into its making. He lived for almost five years in Guatemala, a year of that time in San Antonio (1977–78). He made additional brief visits to the town in 1982, 1984, and 1985. In writing his chapter, Annis also benefited from interviews carried out by a colleague, Elissa Miller, who by chance was living in the community when the major events described in the chapter took place, and from interviews that appeared in Guatemalan newspapers.

The story of San Antonio demonstrates how pervasive the violence has been in Guatemala. As a model community with respect to economic growth and development, San Antonio would be expected to escape the violence from either left or right. As Annis shows, however, even local injustices can lead to savage violence when the whole country is in revolutionary upheaval. Larger, external forces blow local problems tragically out of proportion, and many die for causes they neither espouse nor understand. Annis tells us that a novelist friend of his found the plot of the story "too thin to support that many people dying." That is true only if the plot is confined to local issues; if they are placed in the context of Guatemala's centuries of racism and inequality, brutal counter-insurgency, and the imposition of East-West geopolitics it becomes thick enough.

Annis wishes to thank Christopher Lutz, Director of the Centro para Investigaciones Regionales de Mesoamerica (CIRMA); Elissa Miller; and Ron Weber for their collaboration in preparing his account. Above all, he wishes to express his gratitude to the people of San Antonio who told the story despite the pain and the fear its telling evoked.

Carmack, Robert M. Robert M. Carmack (chapter 2) received the Ph.D. in social anthropology from the University of California, Los Angeles, in 1964. He has been on the faculty of Arizona State University and the University of California, San Diego, and is currently a member of the faculty of the State University of New York, Albany. He also taught at the University of San Carlos in Guatemala and was a Research Associate of the National Autonomous University of Mexico. His specialization is political anthropology, with emphasis on relations between power and authority structures. He served for several years as Director of the Institute for Mesoamerican Studies and was appointed to the American Anthropological Association panel on the Guatemalan crisis. His research has been primarly in Guatemala among the Quiché Mayas, but he has also carried out fieldwork in Chiapas, Mexico, and Costa Rica. Funding for his field research has come from numerous granting agencies including the National Science Foundation, the National Endowment for the Humanities, the Ford Foundation, the Social Science

Research Council, the Wenner Gren Foundation, and the National Geographic Society. He also served as consultant on two occasions for the American embassy in Guatemala, first in a program to adapt radio-diffused agricultural information to highland Indians and second in a program to aid earthquake victims in the highlands. He has published seven books and thirty scientific articles on his research findings. He also has served as editor of four volumes, a function that he again performs for the present volume.

Carmack's fieldwork in Guatemala has been carried out over the past twenty-three years, during which time he has spent more than forty-six months in residence there. He has surveyed extensively in the Quiché area and has conducted community studies in Momostenango and Santa Cruz del Quiché. He also carried out historical studies in the National Archives of Guatemala, as well as those in Spain and other important repositories. The results of his archival studies are published in *The Quichean Civilization* (1973), while the fieldwork in Santa Cruz del Quiché is summarized in *The Quiché Mayas of Utatlán* (1981). Translations of several important native chronicles written in the Quiché language during the sixteenth century, discovered by Carmack in Totonicapán in 1973, are being published in Mexico by the Center for Maya Studies.

The story of Santa Cruz described here by Carmack is typical of the stories of many large, relatively prosperous Indian communities in the Quiché, Chimaltenango, and Baja Verapaz departments. These Indians from Quiché "heartlands" have been deeply involved in the social and economic reforms that have swept through rural Guatemala during the past forty years or so. As well-organized communities in control of some productive resources, their resident Indian populations might be seen as "middle peasants" who, according to Eric Wolf (*Peasant Wars of the Twentieth Century*, 1969), can become the dynamite that may cause a country to explode into revolution. Indeed, that came very close to happening in Guatemala, precisely because communities such as Santa Cruz moved toward the insurgency camp. Just how that took place and why it was drastically cut short is illustrated in the Santa Cruz story recounted by Carmack.

Davis, Shelton H. Shelton H. Davis received the Ph.D. in social anthropology from Harvard University in 1970; he also studied at the London School of Economics and Political Science. He has taught anthropology at MIT and Harvard and was Executive Director of the Anthropology Resource Center, in Boston and Washington, D.C. He is internationally known for his defense of the rights of native peoples around the world. Besides writing numerous monographs and articles on the subject, he has testified before U.S. congressional committees, UN human rights agencies, and the Inter-American Commission on Human Rights of the OAS.

Davis has conducted research in Brazil as well as in Guatemala. His Guatemalan fieldwork was carried out in the northwestern region of the highlands, where he spent a total of twenty-four months in the years 1967 through 1969, 1973, and 1985. In the 1980s he began investigating the situation of Kanjobal Maya Indians from Guatemala now living in the United States, particularly in Indiantown, Florida, and Los Angeles, California. His doctoral dissertation is widely hailed as a seminal case study of Guatemalan native land tenure. His summary of political violence in rural Guatemala (*Witnesses to Political Violence in Guatemala*, 1982) has become a standard source, and his timely summary of the causes of Indian participation in Guatemala's revolutionary conflict (see M. Diskin, ed., *Trouble in Our Backyard*) is one of our most insightful essays on that topic. The reader will find a similar clarification of the roots of Guatemalan violence in Davis's introductory chapter to this book.

Earle, Duncan M. Duncan Earle (chapter 11) received the Ph.D. in anthropology from the State University of New York, Albany, in 1984, and has taught at Dartmouth College, Hanover, New Hampshire, and the University of Maryland, Baltimore. He is now a member of the Department of Anthropology of Vanderbilt University, Nashville, Tennessee. He is a cultural ecologist whose specialized interest is the role of culture in human adaptation to different social and environmental conditions. He has lent his professional expertise to several important applied projects among the Maya Indians of Guatemala and Mexico, such as earthquake reconstruction among the Quichés, health programs among the Tzotzils, and developing crafts among Guatemalan Indian refugees in Mexico. He has published a number of articles on his research in scientific journals and is currently revising for publication his important doctoral dissertation on how one colony of highland Chiapas Mayas was able to adapt successfully to a lowland setting.

Earle has extensive field experience in both Guatemala and Mexico. He spent about twenty-four months doing fieldwork in Guatemala, mostly in the Quiché area, and another twenty-four months in Chiapas, Mexico. In addition, he worked for a year in Guatemala aiding victims of the 1976 earthquake as a consultant for the Save the Children Alliance. He has lived for several months along the Chiapas-Guatemala border, where he was able to interview Guatemalan refugees and observe their problems firsthand. His knowledge of both the Tzotzil and the Quiché Maya languages has proved invaluable in providing a true picture of why those refugees fled to Mexico and how they have fared there. His extensive research on a Mexican collective community near the border that took in Guatemalan refugees gave him the unique opportunity to compare the official treatment of refugees by the Mexican government with their informal treatment by peasants already living in the area.

Americas Watch estimated in 1984 that about 150,000 Guatemalan Indians had fled into Mexico as a result of the counterinsurgency violence. Approximately 50,000 of them moved into the camps, mostly along the northern border of Chiapas; another 50,000 lived outside the camps in Chiapas, especially around Tapachula, and the other 50,000 were scattered throughout the rest of Mexico. Earle describes the condition of refugees living in the Chiapas camps and some of those living outside the camps near the border. He makes it clear that, contrary to propaganda being circulated in Guatemala and the United States, the vast majority of refugees are neither guerrilla spies nor laborers in search of work but victims of violence fleeing for their survival. They are a great embarrassment to the Guatemalan government, living witnesses to the calculated program of terror against its native peoples. They are a burden on the Mexican government, already struggling to maintain order and justice in that volatile border state. And they are a thorn in the side of a U.S. government that has supported the military regimes in Guatemala that are responsible for creating these refugees and that cannot be officially charged with legitimate human rights complaints lest the whole U.S. policy toward Guatemala be shown to be morally bankrupt. As Earle dramatically recounts, only the poor Chiapas peasants, particularly the Mayas among them, seemed to understand the refugees' plight and find a way to treat them humanely. We have much to learn from this home-grown example of accommodation between poor Maya peoples.

Ebel, Roland H. Roland Ebel (chapter 7) received the Ph. D. in political science from Michigan State University and is currently on the faculty of Tulane University, New Orleans, Louisiana. He is a recognized authority on Central American politics, counting among his publications a seminal article on the topic in a recent book summarizing political developments in that area (*Rift and Revolution: The Central American Imbroglio*, ed. H. Wiarda) and an appendix to the National Bipartisan Commission report on Central America. His primary interest has been in political modernization, especially in Latin America. Much of his research has focused on the municipal level of government, as in his chapter in this book.

Ebel is an unusual political scientist in that he has carried out extensive field investigations. In connection with his research on San Juan Ostuncalco, he has visited Guatemala six times over the past twenty-three years, living a total of twenty-two months in the community. His strong ethnographic interest, along with his concern for the cultural factors that affect politics, gives his work an anthropological orientation. That orientation is particularly clear in his major book on Guatemalan politics, *Political Moderniza-tion in Three Guatemalan Indian Communities* (1969), in which he compares Ostuncalco with two other communities in the same region. That book may be the single most comprehensive political study of a Central American rural community to date, and also is one of the most detailed historical accounts of local-level politics available.

San Juan Ostuncalco, like the Totonicapán and Panajachel communities described elsewhere in this book, has been touched by the recent political violence in a relatively limited way. The fact that the community has a large resident ladino population and a significant urban Indian sector seems to provide a social explanation for the limited violence in San Juan. When the town was on the verge of sinking into political chaos and local conflicts got caught up in the revolutionary whirlwind, educated mediating Indians and ladinos were available to help stabilize the situation.

Falla, Ricardo. Ricardo Falla (chapter 10) is a Guatemalan Jesuit priest who has a Ph.D. in anthropology from the University of Texas, Austin. He has taught anthropology in the Catholic University in Guatemala and has lectured on numerous occasions at universities and conferences in the United States. His pastoral duties have primarily been among the Guatemalan poor, Indian and ladino, rural and urban. He is an internationally respected social anthropologist whose theoretical interests center on the question of religious conversion and social change. Many students of Guatemalan society, including myself, consider him to be Guatemala's foremost anthropologist. His best-known book is an analysis of the conversion of traditional Quiché Indians to reformed Catholicism (Catholic Action), for which he received Guatemala's highest literary prize, the Quetzal de Oro. That book is complemented by an important study of popular religion among the ladinos of the south coast, published in El Salvador.

Falla spent thirteen years off and on (1966–79) doing fieldwork in Guatemala, primarily among the Indian and ladino peasants. From 1982 to 1985 he studied the violence in Guatemala and its effects on refugee populations now living in Mexico. As a result of the latter studies he has provided our most thorough documentation of an Indian massacre by the Guatemalan army (the San Francisco massacre, first reported in the *New York Times* in July 1982) and a powerful document accusing the Guatemalan government of genocide before the Permanent People's Tribunal in Madrid, Spain (1983). Reliable information on the violence perpetrated by security forces in isolated Indian communities is exceedingly difficult to obtain, for obvious reasons. Falla has made an invaluable contribution with his painstaking interviews and piecing together of evidence to reconstruct the gruesome reality of some of Guatemala's recent history. Chapter 10 was originally prepared in 1983 for the special rapporteur of the United Nations Commission on Human Rights, Viscount Colville of Culcross. Falla brilliantly weaves the fragments of information into a cohesive and all-too-credible account of what happened to internal Indian refugees in the central highlands.

It is often overlooked that many communities of the central highlands were as devastated by Guatemalan counterinsurgency actions as those of the western highlands. This is particularly true in Chimaltenango, Baja Verapaz, and Alta Verapaz departments, where hundreds of peasant Indians were killed in the violence, and tens of thousands escaped into the surrounding countryside to become internal refugees. Because of the closeness of these departments to the capital, extraordinary control of information was maintained by the Guatemalan government to prevent the full scope of the violence from becoming known. By describing the fate of three refugee groups trying to survive in the mountains, Falla reveals for all to see the terrible tragedy that took place there. The minute details and rough narrative style of the eyewitness accounts quoted by Falla lend an authenticity to this chapter that will be hard to deny.

Hinshaw, Robert E. Robert E. Hinshaw (chapter 8) received the Ph.D. in anthropology from the University of Chicago, where he was under the tutelage of Sol Tax, the dean of anthropological studies in Guatemala. He has taught at the University of Kansas, Illinois State University, Beloit College, the University of Colorado at Denver, and San Carlos University, in Guatemala. He also served as President of Wilmington College (Ohio) and is currently Executive Director of the Associated Colleges of Central Kansas.

Hinshaw's primary professional interest is in applied anthropology. Projects he has undertaken include developing the social sciences in Central American universities (for U.S. AID), ascertaining possible anthropological input to the study of population change (for a UN population conference), providing assistance to earthquake victims in Guatemala (for the American Friends Service Committee), and developing therapy for victims of lung disease (in Colorado). He has received numerous grants from research foundations to carry out his applied and basic research interests, including the National Institutes of Health, the National Science Foundation, the Ford Foundation, the National Endowment for the Humanities, and the Wenner Gren Foundation. Guatemala has been the site of most of his research, but he has also conducted anthropological studies in the United States. He has published the results of his work in six major articles in scientific journals and an important book documenting economic change in the community of Panajachel.

Hinshaw carried out research in Guatemala on eight different occasions during the last thirteen years, his most recent trip taking place in 1986. He has surveyed most of the Indian communities surrounding Lake Atitlán, but his concentrated fieldwork has been in Panajachel, the famous tourist town. The original base-line study in Panajachel was carried out over eighteen months of residence there in 1963–65, later updated with follow-up studies of four months in 1978 and another month in 1985. Building on the initial studies of Tax in Panajachel in the late 1930s and early 1940s, Hinshaw is able to detail changes in that community over a fifty-year period. This makes Panajachel probably the most intensively studied Indian community in Guatemala, which fact, along with its international popularity as a tourist center, heightens our interest in the impact Guatemala's crisis has had on it.

Panajachel's profound commercialization, oriented to the tourist industry, helped immunize it from the worst of the violence that afflicted other highland communities. We are reminded of the Totonicapán community as described for us by Smith (chapter 9), where an Indian population oriented to trading in woven goods also escaped much of the physical violence. In both communities the Indians took on many ladino ways, including a conservative political outlook, and this made them unattractive for either military repression or guerrilla recruitment. But both communities suffered severe economic depression as a direct result of Guatemala's raging conflict. As Hinshaw's account teaches us, among Guatemala's Indians the conflict has yielded no winners or losers, good or bad guys, just victims.

Manz, Beatriz. Beatriz Manz (chapter 3), born in Chile, studied anthropology in the United States, receiving the Ph.D. from the State University of New York at Buffalo in 1977. Since then she has taught anthropology at Wayne State University, in Detroit, and Tufts University, in Medford, Massachussets. She currently teaches at Wellseley College, in Wellseley, Massachusetts. She is also Research Associate at Harvard University's Center for International Affairs. In 1984–85 she occupied the prestigious position of Peace Fellow in Radcliffe's Mary Ingraham Bunting Institute. She also served on the Latin American Studies Association Human Rights Task Force. Her anthropological specialty is stratification systems, particularly as these have emerged in Latin America as a result of the spread of world capitalism. Her current work is on Guatemalan refugees living in Mexico, for which she is the recipient of a Ford Foundation grant.

Manz has carried out field research in Guatemala since 1973, having traveled there on numerous occasions and spent a total of more than seventeen months there. Most of her work has been in the western highlands, particularly the Quiché area, but she has also studied on the Pacific Coast. Recently, her fieldwork shifted to the Guatemalan refugees in Mexico, whom she visited on several occasions between 1982 and 1986. She has reported her findings in both scientific and popular forums. Since 1981 she has regularly presented papers on Guatemala at the annual meetings of the American Anthropological Association and the Latin American Studies Association. Her publications include articles in several issues of Cultural Survival and a textbook on cultural anthropology. She provided expert testimony on the Guatemalan crisis in 1985 for the Committee on Foreign Affairs of the U.S. House of Representatives, and she is one of the authors of the 1984 Americas Watch report on Guatemala (*Guatemala: A Nation of Prisoners*). Her refugee research has resulted in a book, *Refugees of a Hidden War: The Aftermath of the Counterinsurgency War in Guatemala*, to be published by the State University of New York Press. Her views on the crisis have also appeared in the *New York Times*, the *Boston Globe*, and the *National Catholic Reporter*.

The Ixcán area described by Manz in many ways symbolizes the overall tragedy of recent violence in Guatemala. This marginal jungle area, far from the centers of Guatemalan power and population, became the showplace for the United States-backed military governments of the post-1954 era. Colonization and cooperative programs in the Ixcán were sponsored by private enterprise, the Roman Catholic church, the Guatemalan government, and U.S. AID. They were to be an acceptable substitute for the politically suspect agrarian reforms undertaken by the Arbenz government and would bring relief to the land-hungry peasants of the highlands. Given the magnitude of the land needs of Guatemala's millions of peasants and the relatively limited productive capacity of most of the Ixcán area, the idea that the Ixcán could save the peasants was foolish. Nevertheless, as Manz's account makes clear, the colonies became remarkably successful for the people involved and took on enormous symbolic importance for the masses of Guatemalan poor. In Manz's vivid account we see that the colonies' very success, in fact, spelled their doom, especially after one of the guerrilla organizations (the EGP) chose the area as its base of operations.

Manz wishes to recognize the funding she received from the Ford Foundation to conduct the research upon which her chapter is based.

Paul, Benjamin D., and Demarest, William J. Benjamin Paul (chapter 5) received the Ph.D. in social anthropology from the University of Chicago; and William Demarest, from Stanford University. Paul is one of the leading medical anthropologists of the United States. He has been on the faculty of Harvard and Yale universities, was Chairman of the Department of Anthropology at Stanford University, and spent a year as Fellow at the Center for Advanced Study in the Behavioral Sciences. He is now Professor Emeritus of the Department of Anthropology in Stanford University. He has also served on numerous panels and councils of leading U.S. research institutes, including the Social Science Research Council, the American Public Health Association, the National Research Council, the National Insitutes of Health, the National Science Foundation, the Ford Foundation, and the American Association for the Advancement of Science. He is the author of twenty seven-major articles for scientific journals and editor of a seminal anthology of case studies relative to public health (*Health, Culture, and Community,* 1955). Demarest has collaborated with Paul on articles in two previous publications.

Paul initiated field studies in San Pedro la Laguna with his wife, Lois Paul (now deceased), in 1940, and has returned to the community for follow-up research many times (1956, 1962, 1964, 1965, 1968, 1969, 1973, 1974, 1975, 1976, 1978, 1979, 1983, 1985, 1986). His numerous months of residence in San Pedro over the years give his work a time perspective and degree of detail probably unequaled by any other U.S. social scientist who has conducted research in Guatemala.

Demarest has spent about twenty-eight months in Guatemala, most of the time in San Pedro la Laguna. His most recent trip was in 1985, when he and Paul updated their findings on the impact of violence on the community. Readers of Paul and Demarest's account will recognize the years of dedicated fieldwork that went into its making. Only by such long-term, in-depth research could the intricate details of the San Pedro violence be synthesized into a cohesive story. The authors' concern for accuracy of fact and cautious interpretation are by all standards exemplary.

The events that have recently taken place in San Pedro la Laguna illustrate an insidious form of counterinsurgency violence: selective abductions and kidnappings by "unknowns"—actually paramilitary or national police and collaborating local terrorists. This more indirect form of repression has been characteristic of acculturated communities caught up in the mainstream of national life and lying outside the territories controlled or partly controlled by the guerrillas, such as Guatemala City and its environs, the Lake Atitlán area, the Pacific Coast, and Totonicapán. While more direct forms of military repression (sweeps, massacres, scorched-earth tactics—see chapters 2 and 3) have been stopped or dramatically curtailed in most areas, this indirect repressive violence, typified by San Pedro's experience, continues to the present day. The total number of deaths resulting from such actions may even rival the deaths caused by the massacres and more direct means of counterinsurgency action.

Paul's recent travels to Guatemala were supported by Stanford's Center for Latin American Studies and by Stanford's Emeriti Faculty Development Program (sponsored by the Ford Foundation); the latter program also supported Demarest's travel costs.

Smith, Carol A. Carol A. Smith (chapter 9) received the Ph.D. in anthropology from Stanford University in 1972 and is now a faculty member at Duke University, Durham, North Carolina. Besides Guatemala she has carried out fieldwork in Ecuador, Mexico, and Nicaragua. She has received numerous grants to conduct her research, including awards from the Social Sciences Research Council, the National Science Foundation, and the National Academy of Sciences. She has also served as panel and council member for some of the most important funding and research institutes of the United States: the National Institutes of Health, the National Science Foundation, the Society for Economic Anthropology, and others. One of the leading economic anthropologists in the United States, Smith has focused much of her research and writing on regional market systems. Her extensive publication list includes two edited volumes on regional analysis of economic and social systems and more than thirty articles for important scientific journals.

During the past eighteen years Smith has devoted fifty-two months to fieldwork in Guatemala, almost all of it in the western highlands. She was able to update her findings with brief visits to the highlands in 1983, 1985, and 1986, obtaining valuable information on the impact of the violence on the region she had formerly studied in depth. She has published ten articles based on her research in Guatemala, two of which place the western highlands in a broader world context. It is not an exaggeration to say that her writings have had a major impact on the thinking of social scientists about the Guatemalan situation.

San Miguel Totonicapán, the community described by Smith, is one of the most commercially oriented of all the Indian communities in the western highlands. It was also one of the Indian communities least afflicted with violence during the worst of the crisis in Guatemala (1978–83). In other publications Smith has expressed the view that Totonicapán escaped much of the repression because its autonomous and commercial development was not threatening to the state or attractive to the counterinsurgents. Be that as it may, in her account here she demonstrates through a careful analysis of her data the devastating economic effect the violence has had on Totonicapán. Similar economic problems accompanied the crisis in other communities that avoided much of the physical terror befalling most of Indian Guatemala (Panajachel is another example—see chapter 8).

Smith's account should be carefully contemplated by those who believe that military action and economic development are compatible in Central America. It suggests that the economic costs of militarizing political problems can be very great indeed.

The author wishes to express her gratitude to Chris Krueger for the key role she played in the preparation of her chapter. Krueger helped organize anthropological research on western Guatemala in 1983 for the purpose of documenting the impact of violence on the western highlands, and she accompanied Smith on her 1983, 1985 and 1986 visits, during which they traveled to Indian communities in five different departments of the highlands. Smith also expresses gratitude to her Totonicapán friends, who, she says, came through with information and assistance, even at personal cost, "as they always have."

Stoll, David. David Stoll (chapter 4) earned the master's degree in anthropology from Stanford University and is working on his doctoral degree there. From 1975 to 1977 he traveled through Colombia, Peru, and Ecuador, researching the controversies over the Summer Institute of Linguistics, an evangelical mission working in several hundred indigenous languages of Latin America. His work on the Summer Institute has been published by *Survival International,* the *International Work Group for Indigenous Affairs,* and *Cultural Survival.* It includes a detailed history of the group, *Fishers of Men or Founders of Empire?;* an essay in *América Indígena* criticizing left-wing conspiracy theories about evangelical missions; and an article in *Missiology* analyzing the Summer Institute's approach from a methodological point of view. Recently his research has focused on the larger social and political significance of Protestantism in Latin America, with special attention to evangelical growth, confrontations between fundamentalism and liberation theology, and the situation of evangelicals in the Sandinista revolution of Nicaragua.

Stoll's chapter in this book is based on a four-month stay in Guatemala from November 1982 to March 1983, during the Ríos Montt period, followed by a return visit in August 1985. His contribution focuses on the Ixil Triangle, the area probably most devastated by guerrilla insurgency and army counterinsurgency. Thousands of Ixil Indians were killed during the fighting, mainly by the army, and tens of thousands more escaped into the mountains. Outside the main town centers of Nebaj, Chajul, and Cotzal, every public building and human dwelling was burned to the ground. Ixil Indians joined the guerrilla movement in large numbers, and they apparently continue to make up an important part of the EGP forces.

As the Guatemalan army recaptured the Ixil area late in 1982, Stoll reached the garrison town of Nebaj on three occasions. He was able to interview intensively on the role of evangelicals in the shifting fortunes of the war, as well as on responsibility for the massive human rights violations taking place. Since the Ixil area and its evangelicals figured prominently in the Ríos Montt administration's "beans and bullets" pacification program, Stoll's penetrating treatment allows us to get beneath the propaganda war on this subject. It will be difficult to see the Ixil evangelicals either as heroes or as villains; they turn out to be victims and survivors of a bloodbath like much of the rest of Guatemalan society. The impact of militarization and violence on the Ixils has been so disastrous that some observers doubt their future as a people. While Stoll does not attempt to summarize all the tragic events that have taken place in the Ixil Triangle, his penetrating account of what happened to the evangelicals there leaves no doubt about the wider story that unfolded in that small, faraway area.

Index